COMPLETE GUIDE
to COMPACT DISC (CD)
PLAYER
TROUBLESHOOTING
and REPAIR

OTHER BOOKS BY JOHN D. LENK

- (160359) COMPLETE GUIDE TO MODERN VCR TROUBLESHOOTING AND REPAIR (1985)
- (160813) COMPLETE GUIDE TO LASER/VIDEODISC PLAYER TROUBLESHOOTING AND REPAIR (1985)
- (160820) COMPLETE GUIDE TO VIDEOCASSETTE RECORDER OPERATION AND SERVICING (1983)
- (392473) A HOBBYIST'S GUIDE TO COMPUTER EXPERIMENTATION (1985)
- (372391) HANDBOOK OF ADVANCED TROUBLESHOOTING (1983)
- (377317) HANDBOOK OF DATA COMMUNICATIONS (1984)
- (380519) HANDBOOK OF MICROCOMPUTER BASED INSTRUMENTATION AND CONTROLS (1984)
- (381666) HANDBOOK OF SIMPLIFIED COMMERCIAL AND INDUSTRIAL WIRING DESIGN (1984)

To order, write: Steven T. Landis
Book Distribution Center
Route 59 at Brook Hill Drive
West Nyack, New York 10995
or call: (201)767-5049 through 5053

COMPLETE GUIDE to COMPACT DISC (CD) PLAYER TROUBLESHOOTING and REPAIR

JOHN D. LENK

Consulting Technical Writer

Prentice-Hall, Inc., Englewood Cliffs, New Jersey 07632

Library of Congress Cataloging-in-Publication Data

LENK, JOHN D.
  Complete guide to compact disc (CD) player troubleshooting and repair.

  Includes index.
  1. Compact disc players—Maintenance and repair. I. Title.
  TK7881.75.L46 1986   621.389'33   85-17035
  ISBN 0-13-159955-0

Editorial/production supervision and
  interior design: **Kathryn Pavelec**
Cover design: **Photo Plus Art**
Manufacturing buyer: **Rhett Conklin**

© 1986 by **Prentice-Hall, Inc.**, Englewood Cliffs, New Jersey 07632

All rights reserved. No part of this book may be reproduced, in any form or by any means, without permission in writing from the publisher.

Printed in the United States of America

10 9 8 7 6 5 4 3 2 1

ISBN 0-13-159955-0 01

PRENTICE-HALL INTERNATIONAL (UK) LIMITED, *London*
PRENTICE-HALL OF AUSTRALIA PTY. LIMITED, *Sydney*
PRENTICE-HALL CANADA INC., *Toronto*
PRENTICE-HALL HISPANOAMERICANA, S.A., *Mexico*
PRENTICE-HALL OF INDIA PRIVATE LIMITED, *New Delhi*
PRENTICE-HALL OF JAPAN, INC., *Tokyo*
PRENTICE-HALL OF SOUTHEAST ASIA PTE. LTD., *Singapore*
EDITORA PRENTICE-HALL DO BRASIL, LTDA., *Rio de Janeiro*
WHITEHALL BOOKS LIMITED, *Wellington, New Zealand*

To Irene,
Karen, Tom, Brandon, Justin, Michael, Cathie,
Pat and Gene Moffett,
and Glenn Moffett of Action TV, Pomona, California,
and to our very special little Lambie.

CONTENTS

Preface xi

Chapter 1 Introduction to Compact Disc (CD) Players 1

- 1-1 The CD Player 2
- 1-2 Compact Discs versus LP Records 3
- 1-3 Compact Disc Structure 9
- 1-4 Optical Pickup Systems 13
- 1-5 Signal Processing 17
- 1-6 Digital Sound Reproduction Basics 19
- 1-7 Constant Linear Velocity 20
- 1-8 The Advantages of Digital Recordings 21
- 1-9 Typical Features of a CD Player 21

Chapter 2 Encoding, Decoding, and Optical Readout 26

- 2-1 Encoding the Compact Disc 26
- 2-2 Channel Modulation (Cutting the Master) 31
- 2-3 Decoding the Compact Disc 37
- 2-4 Optical Pickup or Readout 42

viii Contents

Chapter 3 User Controls, Operating Procedures, and Installation 52

3-1 Leakage Current Tests 52
3-2 Transit or Shipping Screw 55
3-3 External Connections 56
3-4 General Operating and Installation Notes 57
3-5 Typical Top-load Operating Controls and Indicators 60
3-6 Typical Front-load Operation (Without Programming) 65
3-7 Typical Front-load Operation (With Programming) 67
3-8 Typical Remote-Control Operation 69

Chapter 4 Test Equipment, Tools, and Routine Maintenance 72

4-1 Safety Precautions in CD Player Service 72
4-2 Test Equipment for CD Player Service 81
4-3 Tools for CD Player Service 82
4-4 Periodic Maintenance for CD Players 83

Chapter 5 Typical CD Player Circuits 87

5-1 Typical Top-load and Drawer-type Front-load Circuits 88
5-2 Power Supply for Top-load Circuits 90
5-3 Laser Control Circuits for Top-load 93
5-4 Optical System Photodiodes, Error Signals, and HF Signals for Top-load 94
5-5 Focus Servo for Top-load 99
5-6 Turntable Motor Amplifier for Top-load 102
5-7 Radial Servo for Top-load 104
5-8 Signal-processing Circuits for Top-load 118
5-9 Typical Front-load Circuits 131

Chapter 6 Mechanical Operation, Adjustment, and Replacement 162

6-1 Vertical Front-load Mechanical Section 163
6-2 Horizontal Front-load Mechanical Section (Single-load Motor) 180
6-3 Horizontal Front-load Mechanical Section (Two Motors) 195

Chapter 7 Troubleshooting and Adjustment 200

7-1 The Basic Troubleshooting Functions 201
7-2 The Troubleshooting Approach 203
7-3 Electrical Adjustment Procedures for Early-model Players 204
7-4 Introduction to Early-model CD Player Troubleshooting 214
7-5 Door or Tray Does Not Open or Close Properly 217
7-6 Laser-Diode Problems 219
7-7 Pickup Does Not Move to Inner Limit When Power is Applied 220
7-8 Pickup Does Not Change Speed During Search 221
7-9 Pickup Does Not Focus Properly 221
7-10 Pickup Does Not Track Properly 224
7-11 Disc Motor (Turntable) Does Not Rotate Properly 226
7-12 Signal-processing Circuit Problems 229
7-13 Audio Circuit Problems 231
7-14 Programming and Operating Problems 232
7-15 Electrical Adjustment Procedures for Late-model Players 232
7-16 Introduction to Late-model CD Player Troubleshooting 241
7-17 Tray Does Not Open or Close Properly (Late-model) 242
7-18 Laser-Diode Problems (Late-model) 243
7-19 Pickup Does Not Move to Inner Limit When Power is Applied; Disc Directory Does Not Read Properly (Late-model) 244

7-20 Pickup Does Not Focus Properly (Late-model) 246
7-21 Pickup Does Not Track Properly (Late-model) 248
7-22 Disc Motor (Turntable) Does Not Rotate Properly (Late-model) 250
7-23 Signal-processing Circuit Problems (Late-model) 252
7-24 Audio Circuit Problems (Late-model) 254
7-25 Programming and Operating Problems (Late-model) 254

Index 255

PREFACE

The main purpose of this book is to provide a simplified, practical system of troubleshooting and repair for the many types of compact disc (CD) players. It is virtually impossible in one book to cover detailed troubleshooting and repair for all CD players. Similarly, it is impractical to attempt such comprehensive coverage, since rapid technological advances soon make such a book's detail obsolete.

To overcome this problem, this book concentrates on a basic approach to CD player service, an approach that can be applied to any CD player (both those now in use and those to be manufactured in the future). The approach here is based on the techniques found in the author's best-selling *Handbook of Practical Solid-State Troubleshooting, Handbook of Advanced Troubleshooting, Complete Guide to Videocassette Recorder Operation and Servicing, Complete Guide to Laser/Videodisc Player Troubleshooting and Repair,* and *Complete Guide to Modern VCR Troubleshooting and Repair.*

Chapter 1 is devoted to the basics of CD players, including their relationship to stereo systems. With the basics established, the chapter then describes the technical characteristics for the various models of CD players now in use.

Chapter 2 describes the encoding and decoding processes involved for compact discs. The chapter also describes the basic principles of optical readout used in all CD players. An understanding of these processes and principles is most helpful, even for the very practical technician whose main concern is with efficient troubleshooting.

Chapter 3 describes user controls, operating procedures, and installation of typical CD player models. Although CD players are not difficult to install or operate, the basic procedures are quite different from those of a typical LP player, or phonograph, found in conventional stereo systems.

Chapter 4 describes the test equipment and tools needed for CD player service. The chapter also discusses routine maintenance for CD players and the care of compact discs. Special emphasis is placed on safety (including laser safety), and the relationship of features found in present-day test equipment to specific problems in CD player testing and service.

Chapter 5 describes the theory of operation for a cross-section of CD player circuits. By studying the circuits found in Chapter 5, you should have no difficulty understanding the schematic and block diagrams of similar CD players. Circuit descriptions are supplemented with partial schematic and block diagrams that show such important areas as signal flow paths, input/output, adjustment controls, test points, and power-source connections (the areas most important for service).

Chapter 6 describes operation for the mechanical sections of typical CD players. Although all types of players are covered, the chapter concentrates on mechanical operation for the most popular player models. The chapter also describes adjustment and replacement procedures for the mechanical sections of typical players, as recommended by their manufacturers. By studying this information, you should have no problem understanding the mechanical operation of similar CD players. This understanding is essential for logical troubleshooting and repair, particularly since most CD player faults are the result of failure (or tampering) with the mechanical section.

Chapter 7 describes troubleshooting and service notes for a cross-section of CD players, both early-model and late-model units. Electrical adjustments for both types of players are also included in this chapter. To show what typical adjustments involve, the chapter describes complete electrical procedures for sample CD players, as recommended by their manufacturers (to complement the mechanical adjustments described in Chapter 6). Using these examples, you should be able to relate the procedures to a similar set of adjustment points on most CD players. Where it is not obvious, the chapter also describes the purpose of the procedure. The waveforms measured at various points during adjustments are also included. By studying these waveforms, you should be able to identify typical signals found in most players, even though the signals may appear at different points for your particular unit.

With adjustments well established, the chapter then describes *circuit-by-circuit troubleshooting* for both early- and late-model CD players. This circuit-by-circuit approach is based on *failure or trouble symptoms,* and represents the combined experience and knowledge of many CD-player service specialists and managers.

Many professionals have contributed their talents and knowledge to the preparation of this book. The author gratefully acknowledges that the tremendous effort to make this book such a comprehensive work is impossible for one person, and he wishes to thank all who have contributed directly and indirectly. The author wishes to give special thanks to the following: Ray Blades of Alpine/Luxman; Moira Wright and Tom Smith of General Electric; Thomas Roscoe and Eddie Motokane of Hitachi; Everett Sheppard, Ron Smith, and Jeff Harris of Mitsubishi; Deborah Fee of N.A.P. Consumer Electronics (Magnavox, Sylvania, Philco); John Lostroscio of NEC Home Electronics; Bruce Dorfman of Nagaoka and Microfidelity; Thomas Lauterback of Quasar; Dave Gunzel, Hy Siegel, and Ted Rosenberg of Radio Shack; J. W. Phipps of RCA; Donald Woolhouse of Sanyo; T. Kimura, Theodore Zrebiec, Richard Wheeler, J. Philip Stack, Ralph White, and Jason Farrow of Sony; and Justin Camerlengo, Gerry Eramo, and John Lissner of Technics.

The author extends his gratitude to Tim McEwen, Rosemary Mahoney, Andy O'Hearn, Melissa Haiverstadt, Leon Liguori, Greg Burnell, Dave Boelio, Tony Caruso, Hank Kennedy, John Davis, Matt Fox, Diane Spina, Barbara Cassel, Jerry Slawney, Art Rittenberg, Ellen Denning, Beverly Vill, Mary O'Brien, Karen Fortgang, Lisa Schulz, Kathryn Pavelec, Irene Springer, Dave Amerman, and Don Schaefer of Prentice-Hall, and Marie Barlettano of P-H International. Their faith in the author has given him encouragement, and their editorial/marketing expertise has made many of the author's books best sellers. The credit must go to them. The author also wishes to thank Joseph A. Labok of Los Angeles Valley College for his help and encouragement throughout the years.

John D. Lenk

INTRODUCTION to COMPACT DISC (CD) PLAYERS

This chapter is devoted to the basics of compact disc (CD) players. Before we get into these basics, let us establish a few common terms.

First, let us resolve the *disc* versus *disk* question. The author generally spells disk with a *k* rather than a *c*. There are those who feel *disc* should be used for consumer audio/video products, and *disk* for magnetic data devices. Still others feel that *disc* should be used only with laser recordings, and *disk* for other video/audio recording. As a practical matter, most audio player manufacturers have settled on *disc,* so we do the same.

Next, compact disc or CD players are also called *compact audiodisc players, digital audiodisc players,* or simply *disc players* in some literature. However, the terms *CD player* or *compact disc player* are now in the most common use.

In this book, we cover CD players designed to reproduce sound from *digital compact discs* or *digital CDs.* Such discs are not to be confused with conventional analog LP records, or with PCM (pulse code modulation) records (so-called "digital recordings"). The compact discs described here are not interchangeable (electrically or physically) with either analog LP or digital PCM discs (or with videodiscs, for that matter).

2 Introduction to Compact Disc (CD) Players

1-1 THE CD PLAYER

The CD players shown in Fig. 1-1 are a very specialized form of phonograph, record player, or turntable. A CD player plays prerecorded discs (carrying music, speech, etc.) through a conventional hi-fi or stereo system (amplifier and loudspeakers). The disc is single-sided, 4.75 in. (120 mm) in diameter, and can contain up to 60 min. of hi-fi stereo sound. The compact disc spins at a high rate of speed compared with a conventional audio record, and uses a *light beam/optical pickup* instead of the standard stylus/needle and pickup arm. In addition to superior sound (to either analog LP or digital PCM recordings), CD players can provide immediate access to audio at any part of the disc. It is also possible to program CD players to play only selected portions of the audio material.

Figure 1-2 is the block diagram of a typical CD player. We describe each of the blocks and their functions throughout the remainder of this book. Before we get into such details, let us consider some basic differences between CD and LP players. If you are familiar with conventional record players of any kind, even those capable of reproducing digital recordings, you will see that a CD player is quite different (although the overall purpose is the same).

1-1.1 Pickup System and Drive Motors

One basic difference between a phonograph and a CD player is in the pickup. Phonograph records are played with a needle on top of the record. The beginning of the record is at the outside edge, and the needle moves inward as the music is played.

A compact disc is played from the underside with a light beam. The beginning of the CD is near the center. The light beam moves outward toward the edge as the program plays.

The beam is focused up onto the bottom or underside of the CD through an *objective lens* (also called the *object* lens). This lens is located in the player on the underside of the CD. As the CD is played from beginning to end, the lens is driven by a *servo-operated pickup motor* across the disc. The light beam reflects off microscopic *pits* on the underside of the disc. These pits are coded with music or other audio, as well as synchronization and identification data.

Note that the lens is part of a *pickup assembly* (also called the *actuator*). As shown in Fig. 1-3, there are two basic types of pickups. In one configuration, the optical system (including the objective lens) is mounted at the end of a *rotating arm*. The arm and lens are rotated (by the servo drive motor) so that the lens moves from the disc center to the edge. In the other configuration, the optical system is part of a *slide* assembly (also called the *sled*) which is driven across the disc underside by the motor.

While on the subject of motors, there is also a servo-operated *turntable*

1-1 The CD Player 3

FIGURE 1-1a Magnavox FD1000SL Compact Disc Player (Courtesy of N.A.P. Consumer Electronics Corp.—Magnavox Audio-Video Product).

FIGURE 1-1b Magnavox FD2020SL Compact Disc Digital Audio Player (Courtesy of N.A.P. Consumer Electronics Corp.—Magnavox Audio-Video Product).

FIGURE 1-1c Magnavox FD3030SL Compact Disc Digital Audio Player (Courtesy of N.A.P. Consumer Electronics Corp.—Magnavox Audio-Video Product).

4 Introduction to Compact Disc (CD) Players

FIGURE 1-1d Mitsubishi DP-103 Compact Disc Player (Courtesy of Mitsubishi Electric Sales America, Inc.).

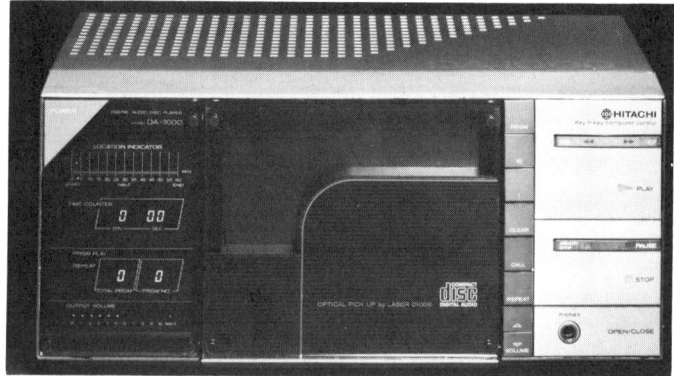

FIGURE 1-1e Hitachi DA-1000 Compact Disc Player (Courtesy of Hitachi Sales Corporation of America).

FIGURE 1-1f Quasar CD8994 Compact Disc Player (Courtesy of Quasar Company, Franklin Parks, Illinois).

1-1 The CD Player   5

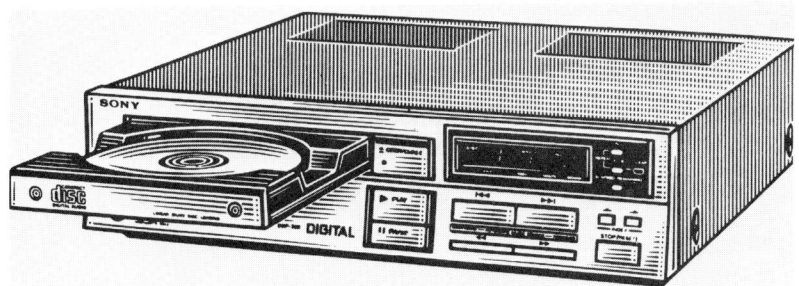

FIGURE 1-1g Sony CDP-200 and CDP-400 Compact Disc Players (Courtesy of Sony Consumer Service Company, a division of Sony Corporation of America).

FIGURE 1-1h Realistic CD-1000 Compact Disc Digital Audio Player (Courtesy of Radio Shack, A Division of Tandy Corp.).

6   Introduction to Compact Disc (CD) Players

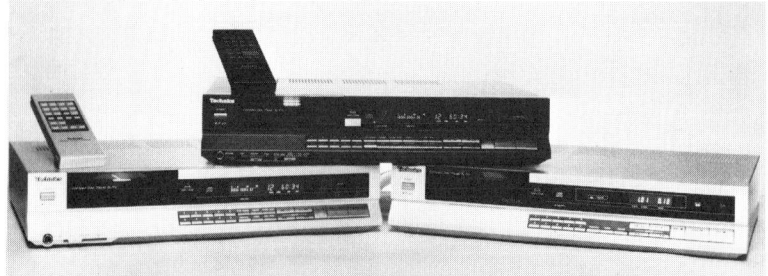

FIGURE 1-1i   Technics SL-P1, SL-P2, and SL-P3 Compact Disc Players (Courtesy of Technics).

FIGURE 1-1j   Luxman D-405 Duo-Beta Digital Audio Compact Disc Player (Courtesy of Luxman Division of Alpine Electronics of America, Inc.).

FIGURE 1-1k   NEC CD-705E Digital Compact Disc Player (Courtesy of NEC Home Electronics [U.S.A.] Inc.).

1-2 Compact Discs versus LP Records

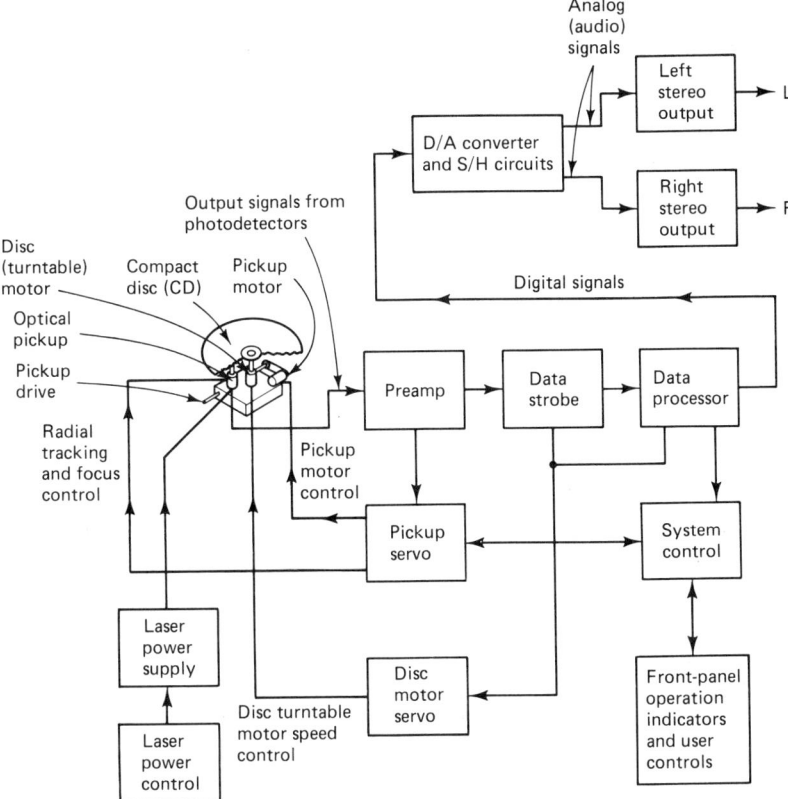

FIGURE 1-2 Block diagram of typical CD player.

drive motor in all CD players (to spin the disc), and usually a *loading motor* (to insert and remove the disc from the player).

1-2 COMPACT DISCS VERSUS LP RECORDS

Figure 1-4 shows a comparison of the grooves in a conventional LP record and the pits of a compact disc. With conventional analog records, the amplitude or depth of the groove is a direct representation of an audio signal. Analog record players reproduce the audio signal by tracing the grooves in the record.

The CD player reproduces audio signals by extracting signal information from a disc using a *laser optical readout* with no physical contact between the disc itself and the signal pickup mechanism. The audio signals stored on CDs are in a *high-density digital format*. Conversion of an audio signal into the digital information used for CDs eliminates the problems of signal deterioration (caused either by signal storage techniques or by mechanical limitations

8 Introduction to Compact Disc (CD) Players

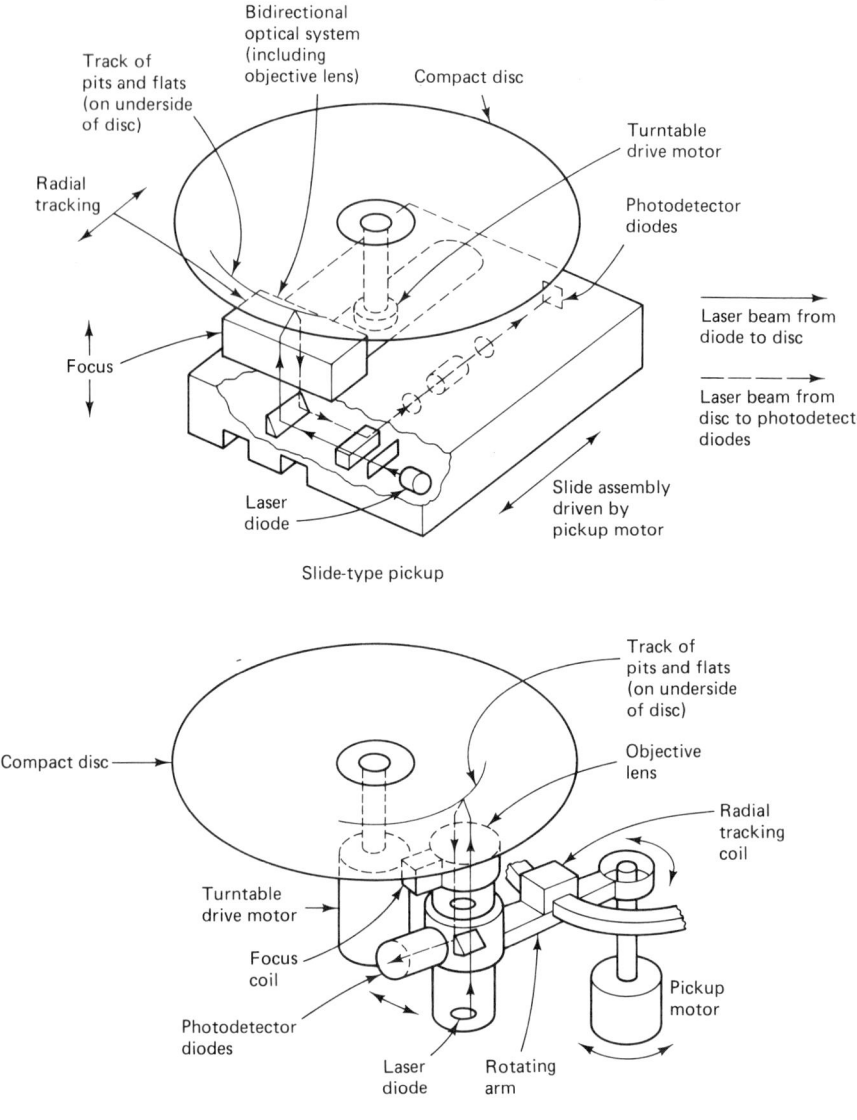

FIGURE 1-3 Basic types of pickup systems.

of analog playback). As a result, signal transmission and reproduction with the digital format provides extreme accuracy and superior reproduction.

The optical readout uses a *laser beam*. A laser (Light Amplification by Stimulated Emission of Radiation) is a special light source that produces a concentrated light beam. The laser used in CD players is generated by a small, low-power, semiconductor diode, made of aluminum gallium arsenide (Al-GaAe), which emits an invisible infrared light. The laser beam is focused onto

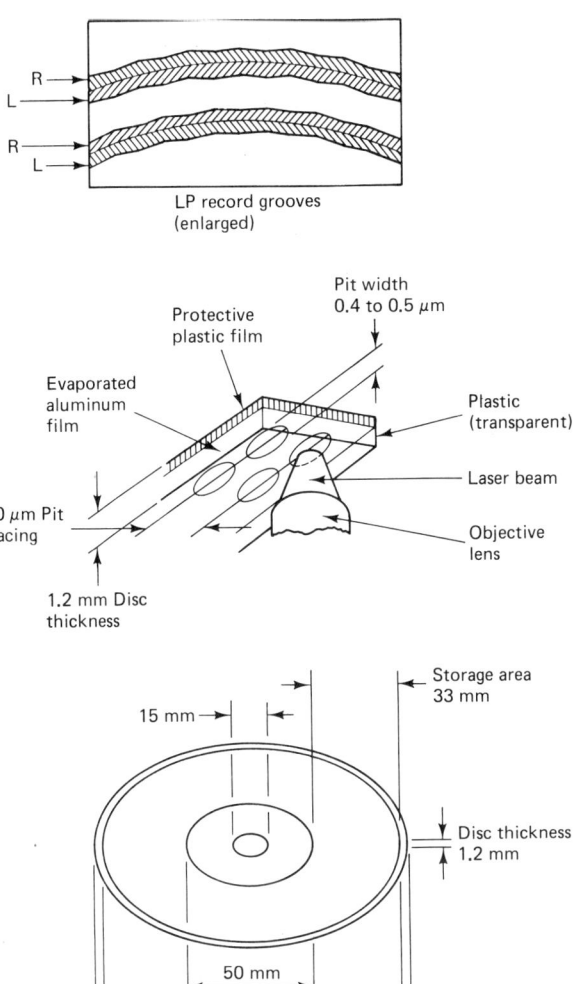

FIGURE 1-4 Comparison of the grooves in a conventional LP record and the pits of a compact disc.

the disc by the objective lens, which acts like the lens of a microscope and focuses the laser beam into a spot slightly less than 1 µm in diameter. The spot is then used to retrieve the information contained on the disc.

Figure 1-5 shows a magnified view of a compact disc. As shown, the disc is composed of thousands of circular "tracks" made in a continuous spiral from *the inside to the outside* of the disc. The tracks are similar to grooves in a conventional LP record. However, the tracks on a compact disc are not true grooves. Instead, CD tracks consist of tiny pits or indentations in the disc

10 Introduction to Compact Disc (CD) Players

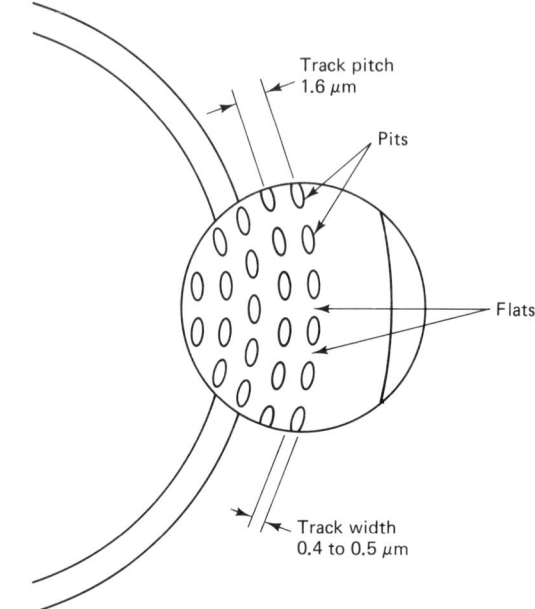

FIGURE 1-5 Magnified view of compact disc tracks.

material. The width of the pits is 0.4 to 0.5 μm, with a depth of 0.1 μm. The distance between the spiral tracks is held constant at 1.6 μm, and is called the *track pitch*. (This is not to be confused with *pit spacing*, which is about 2.0 μm from the centerline of one track to the centerline of the next track.) The combination of *pits* and *flats* (area between the pits) is used to reproduce the digital recorded information.

Each groove of an analog LP record contains two signals, one each for the left and right stereo channels, which must be simultaneously read and reproduced by conventional turntable pickup systems. The compact disc carries left and right channel information separately, with two sets of information aligned successively on the disc. There is a *fixed time interval* between the two sets of information. As a result, only one information-carrying track is required, and crosstalk between left and right channels is reduced to zero (in theory). In actual practice, channel separation of 90 dB (and better) is quite realistic.

In forming signals contained on the disc, the original music or other audio is divided into 44,100 separate signals per second. That is, the original audio is *sampled 44,100 times per second*, using a sampling frequency of 44.1 kHz. The composition (frequency, level, etc.) of each separate signal sample is then converted into a *binary format* such as that used in computers (a series of 1s and 0s). This form of storage is called *pulse code modulation*, but is not to be confused with the PCM of other digital recorders.

The CD signal composition is measured on a scale of 2^{16}, or 65,536 gradations, and the result is expressed as a 16-place binary number (combination of 1's and 0's). The 16-bit system offers a wider range in which to express the divided signal level than other PCM digital recordings (which generally use a 13-bit system). Theoretically, the dynamic range that can be expressed by the 16-bit system is about 98 dB. However, most CD player manufacturers claim about a 90- to 95-dB dynamic range.

1-3 COMPACT DISC STRUCTURE

Figure 1-6 shows the cross section of a compact disc, while Fig. 1-7 shows the basic steps involved in CD manufacture. As shown, the CD consists of a reflective evaporated aluminum layer covered by a transparent, protective plastic coating. Handling a CD presents far less problems than handling analog LP records. For example, even if the disc is dirty, the laser beam can still operate properly because the beam is directed at the reflective aluminum layer beneath the surface (rather than at the surface). The only possible surface contamination on a CD that could affect playback is something with reflective properties (which could reflect and distort the laser beam).

As shown in Fig. 1-7, the manufacturing process of a CD requires several steps. The first step is making a *disc master*. A glass disc, optically ground, polished, and spotlessly cleaned, is coated with 0.1 μm of *photo-resist* (which is evenly distributed by a spin-coating technique). This forms the *resist-master disc* (comparable to a photographic film) from the recording process. The encoded digital information is cut on the master using a high-power recording laser, modulated by the signal from a tape master. The recording laser writes a pattern of pits into the photo-resist.

The exposed part of the disc is developed to generate the final pattern of pits. After a silvering process, the master is electroplated with nickel. When the nickel plating is separated from the master, a metal "negative" is formed. This metal negative is called the *father,* and is the master tool used to produce one or more positive *mothers*. In the final plating stage, each mother produces a number of *sons* or *stampers*. These stampers are then used to mold the information into the disc.

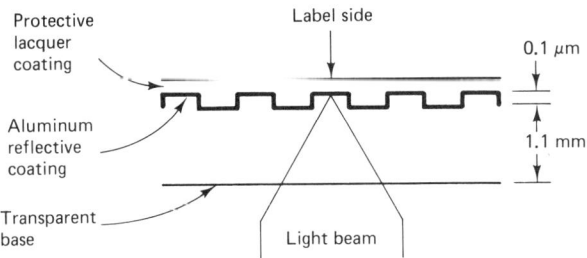

FIGURE 1-6   Cross section of compact disc.

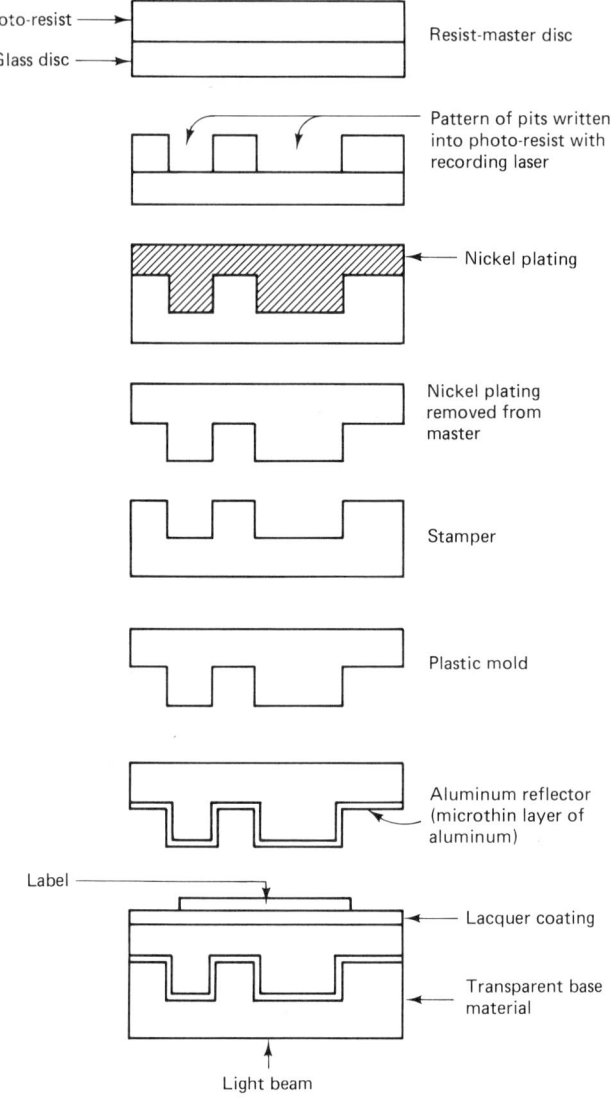

FIGURE 1-7 Summary of manufacturing process for compact discs.

A CD is pressed in essentially the same way as conventional records, using compression or injection-molding techniques. The stamper is placed into an injection-molding machine, and a clear liquid plastic is injected under high pressure and allowed to cool. The clear disc is then removed and the surface containing the pits is coated with a microthin layer of aluminum to provide the reflective coating (Fig. 1-6). The fragile "mirror" layer is protected by a lacquer coating, with the label printed on top (on the side opposite the light beam).

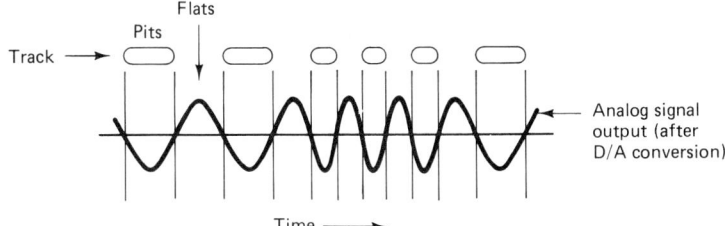

FIGURE 1-8 Track of pits and flats.

As shown in Fig. 1-6, the pits and flats representing the digital information are located 1.1 mm from the transparent surface or base of the disc. The light beam passes through the transparent base material to retrieve the information. The light reflected by the pit is not as bright as the light reflected by the flat area. The rotation of the disc, combined with the pits and flats passing over the light beam, create a series of "on" and "off" flashes of light being reflected back into the system, thus modulating the light beam.

Figure 1-8 shows a track of pits and flats. As shown, the *length* of the pits and flats determines the information contained on the track. The pits and flats can vary in length from about 1 to 3 μm. The analog waveform shown below the pits and flats represents the decoded signal after ditigal-to-analog (D/A) conversion. The pits reflect less light than the flat area, and the length of the two vary to recreate the original analog signal.

1-4 OPTICAL PICKUP SYSTEMS

Figure 1-9 shows the basic elements of the optical pickup (also called the *optical readout*) used by most CD players with the slide-type pickup. We discuss optical pickups (in boring detail) throughout Chapter 2. As you will find out, there are three common types of optical systems. For now, let us consider the basics.

The laser beam is developed by the laser diode and is applied to the reflective surface of the disc through an optical system (a series of lenses, prisms, gratings, and possibly mirrors, depending on the type of optics). With all three systems, the beam is then reflected back through the optics to a photodiode detector (typically six diodes). The detector produces an output that corresponds to the *audio stored on the disc*. The detector also produces *tracking* and *focus* signals.

1-4.1 Radial Tracking

With the system shown in Fig. 1-9, the disc spins in a horizontal plane. In many CD players, the disc spins vertically. Either way, it is essential that the laser beam *follow the track of pits and flats* as the optical pickup is drawn

14 Introduction to Compact Disc (CD) Players

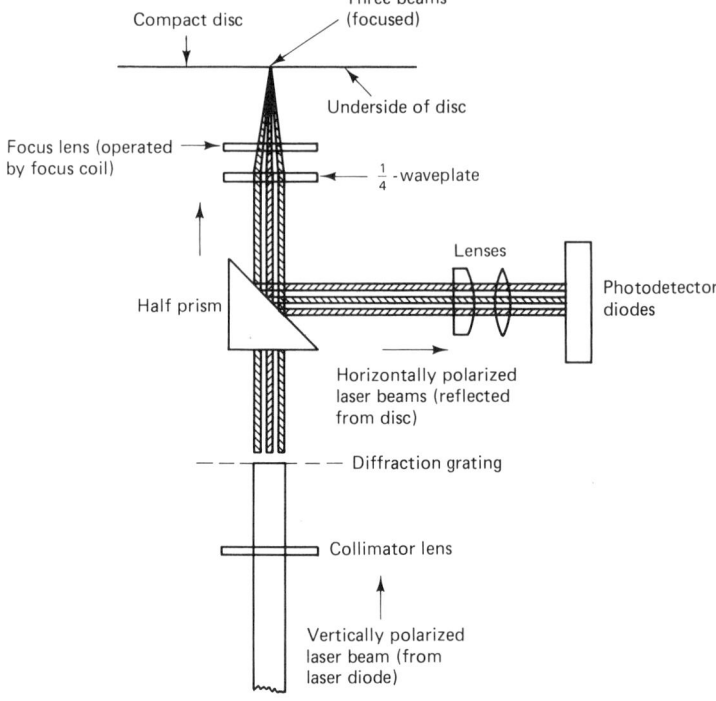

FIGURE 1-9 Basic elements of the optical pickup (optical readout).

across the disc by the pickup motor, regardless of any possible disc eccentricity. This is called *radial tracking,* and usually involves a *radial tracking coil,* which is operated by a *tracking servo* to move the lens (and beam) as necessary. The radial tracking system uses the *three-beam principle* shown in Fig. 1-10. The three-beam technique uses *two sub-beams* to detect tracking errors, and the *main beam* as the audio signal detector. The sub-beams are produced by routing the laser beam through a glass *diffraction grating,* which creates several images on the same object.

As shown in Fig. 1-10, the two sub-beams are located ahead of and behind the main laser beam. Also, the sub-beams are shifted slightly to the left and right of the main beam. After being reflected by the disc, each laser beam is routed through the optical system to corresponding photodetectors. The error signal from the two sub-beams is converted into an electrical signal and then fed to an error-signal amplifier.

As long as disc tracking is precise, the output of the error-signal amplifier is zero. However, if even the slightest radial tracking error is detected, the input differential between the two error signals (right and left) produces an output. This output is then fed to the radial tracking servo and coil, which move the objective lens (at right angles to the track) as necessary to correct the position of the main laser beam.

1-4 Optical Pickup Systems 15

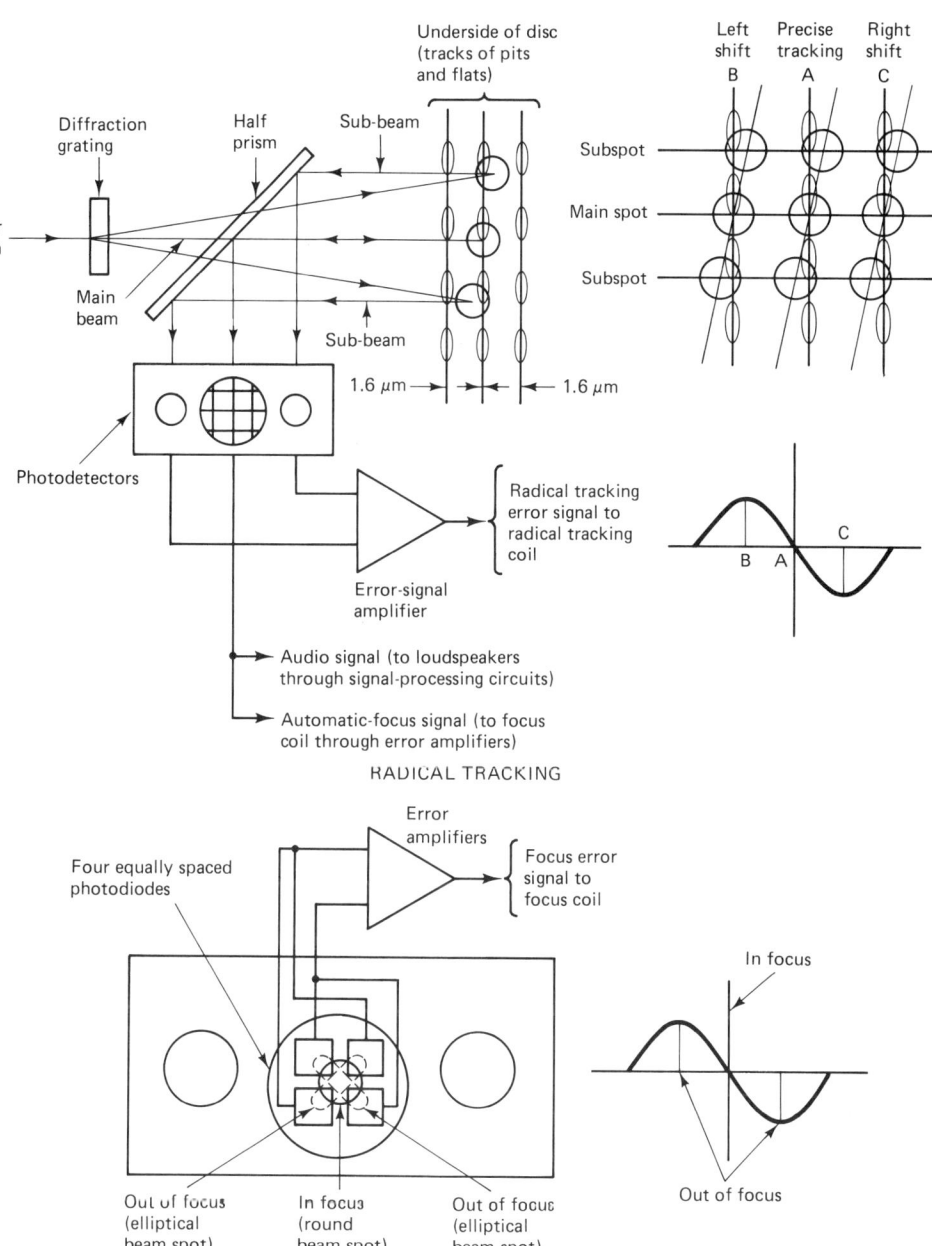

FIGURE 1-10 Basic principles of radial tracking and automatic focus.

In the rotating-arm type of pickup (Fig. 1-3), the radial tracking coil moves the entire arm and pickup as necessary to restore proper tracking. In most slide-type pickups, the radial tracking coil moves the optical system (lenses, etc.) in relation to the remainder of the pickup assembly to restore tracking.

In a third system, the tracking coil operates a *rotary mirror*. This mirror is placed between the laser and lens so that the beam makes a 90° turn when reflected by the mirror. The tracking-error signals cause the tracking coil to rotate the mirror (ever so slightly) and direct the beam back to the track.

It is interesting to note that manufacturers using the rotary mirror claim improved performance over the other two systems (both of which require that the radial error signals move the entire optical system). From a troubleshooting standpoint, it makes little difference, since you must replace the entire pickup assembly as a a package (on most CD players). That is, you can trace error signals from the pickup diodes, through the servo, and back to the pickup radial tracking coil. Then you must replace the entire assembly if: (1) the diode signals are missing to the servo, or (2) if signals from the servo are available, but the radial tracking coil does not move the lens (or mirror). About the only replaceable parts on the pickup are the drive motor, drive belt, and possibly some of the drive gears. The optics are rarely replaceable (or even adjusted, in most cases).

1-4.2 Automatic Focus (AF)

In addition to radial tracking (keeping the beam centered on the track), the optical pickup also provides for *automatic focusing* of the beam to compensate for vertical movement of the disc. This focusing system moves the objective lens (toward or away from the disc) if the laser beam is not focused precisely (within ± 1 µm) on the pits.

The focusing mechanism uses the *astigmatism* principle (Chapter 2). In the simplest of terms, the main laser beam is detected by four equally spaced photodiodes, shown in Fig. 1-10. (These same diodes also reproduce the audio signal.) If the main beam is properly focused, the beam spot is round, and all four diodes receive the same amount of light (and produce signals of the same strength). If the beam is not properly focused, the beam spot is elliptical, and the four diodes receive different amounts of light (and produce different outputs).

The outputs from the four diodes are summed in error amplifiers. The output from the amplifiers represents the focus error. This error (if any) is fed to a focus coil or actuator that moves the objective lens up or down as necessary to correct the focus. As discussed in Chapter 2, the focus coil is similar to a loudspeaker coil, and the objective lens is operated somewhat like a loudspeaker cone.

1-5 SIGNAL PROCESSING

The block diagram of Fig. 1-2 shows the sequence of signal processing within a CD player. We discuss all these circuits and more (in fascinating detail) throughout Chapter 5. For now, let us run through the signal sequence quickly.

Since the output signal originating at the optical-pickup photodetectors is very low, the signal is amplified in a *preamp stage* to a usable level. The signal then enters a *data strobe* circuit to discriminate between the 1's and 0's. The data strobe extracts and separates *synchronization* or *sync signals* from the music and other audio signals. These sync signals are encoded on the disc, along with the music, at the time of disc manufacture. (The sync signals make it possible for the CD player to reproduce audio at particular points on the disc track, among other functions.)

The next stage is the *data processor* or *signal processor,* which has multiplex functions: demodulation of the signal data, error detection and correction, determination of 1 or 0 status, compensation for possible missing part of the sync signal (performed in conjunction with the data strobe circuit), RAM control, rearranging of data for temporary storage in the RAM, and overall control of the signal-processing circuit.

Although the signal-processing circuits for all CD players are not identical, they all include some form of *interleaving* or the rearrangement (scrambling) of signal data. When a compact disc is recorded, the music or other audio is interleaved before recording on the disc. A typical interleaving sequence is shown in Fig. 1-11. The interleaving process is especially useful when a relatively large part of the signal is missing. With interleaving, the effects of dropouts in the audio (from any cause) can be minimized.

In the simplest of terms, interleaving involves dividing the audio to be recorded into a series of random sections, and then lining up the sections in a new, fixed order before actual recording. During playback, the sections are rearranged by the opposite process to recreate the original music or other signal. The playback rearrangement processing is done by temporarily storing the data in a RAM (usually part of the signal processing IC), and then retrieving the data in the original order.

Thanks to interleaving, even if a relatively large part of the signal is lost, the losses are distributed over various smaller "gaps" in the recreated, final music signal. Because the signals adjacent to the gap are still present, it is easier to compensate for the loss by inserting what are presumed to be the missing parts. For example, as shown in Fig. 1-11, the gap created by the missing 2 (letter *N*) is easily replaced, since both 1 (letter *I*) and 3 (letter *T*) are not affected by the dropout.

Note that the interleaving or scrambling is done by the recording equipment during compact disc manufacture, and cannot be changed by the CD player. It is the player's function to restore the original signal condition according to information recorded on the disc.

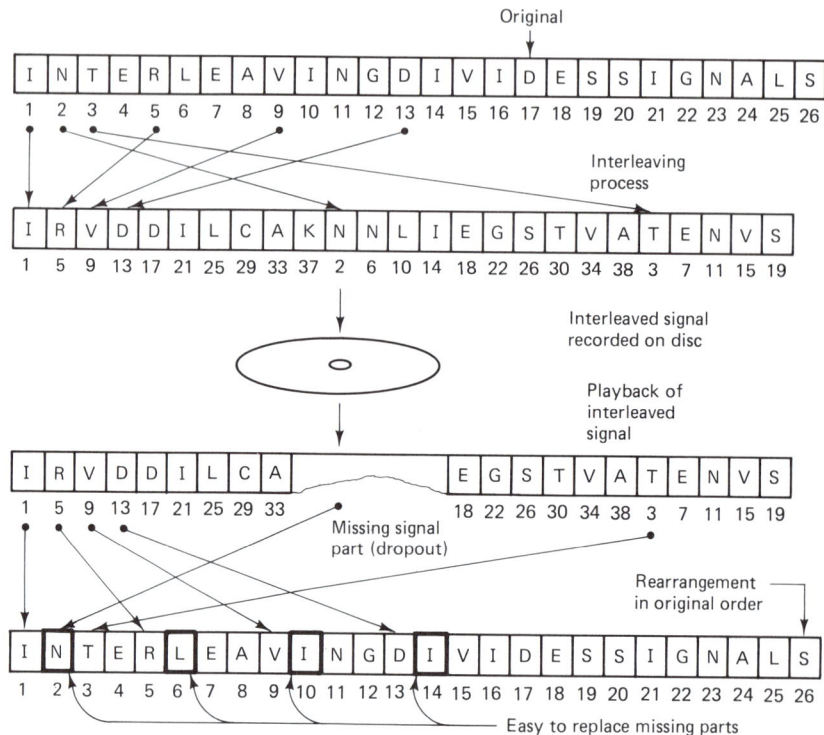

FIGURE 1-11 Typical interleaving sequence.

The *D/A converter follows* the signal-processing circuits. The function of the D/A converter is to transform the digital signal back into an analog signal. The converted analog signal is then restored to pure two-channel audio by a *sample-and-hold* (S/H) circuit, and applied to the left and right *stereo output* (and to a headphone jack in most CD players).

In addition to the signal circuits shown in Fig. 1-2, most CD players have *two servo circuits.* One servo controls disc turntable motor speed (to maintain a *constant linear velocity,* or CLV, as discussed in Sec. 1-7) by locking motor speed to signals recorded on the disc. (This function is sometimes called *tangential tracking.*) The other servo controls both radial tracking and focus of the optical pickup, as well as control of the pickup motor.

In most CD players, the laser used in the optical pickup has separate *laser power supply* and *power control* circuits. The *system control* circuits shown in Fig. 1-2 control overall operation of the player by accepting commands from the user controls and displaying operating functions on front-panel operation indicators. Generally, the system control functions are produced by a microcomputer/microprocessor IC as discussed in Sec. 1-9.8.

1-6 DIGITAL SOUND REPRODUCTION BASICS

Figure 1-12 shows the sequence of conversion from analog-to-digital (A/D) and from digital-to-analog (D/A) that occurs within a CD player. The analog

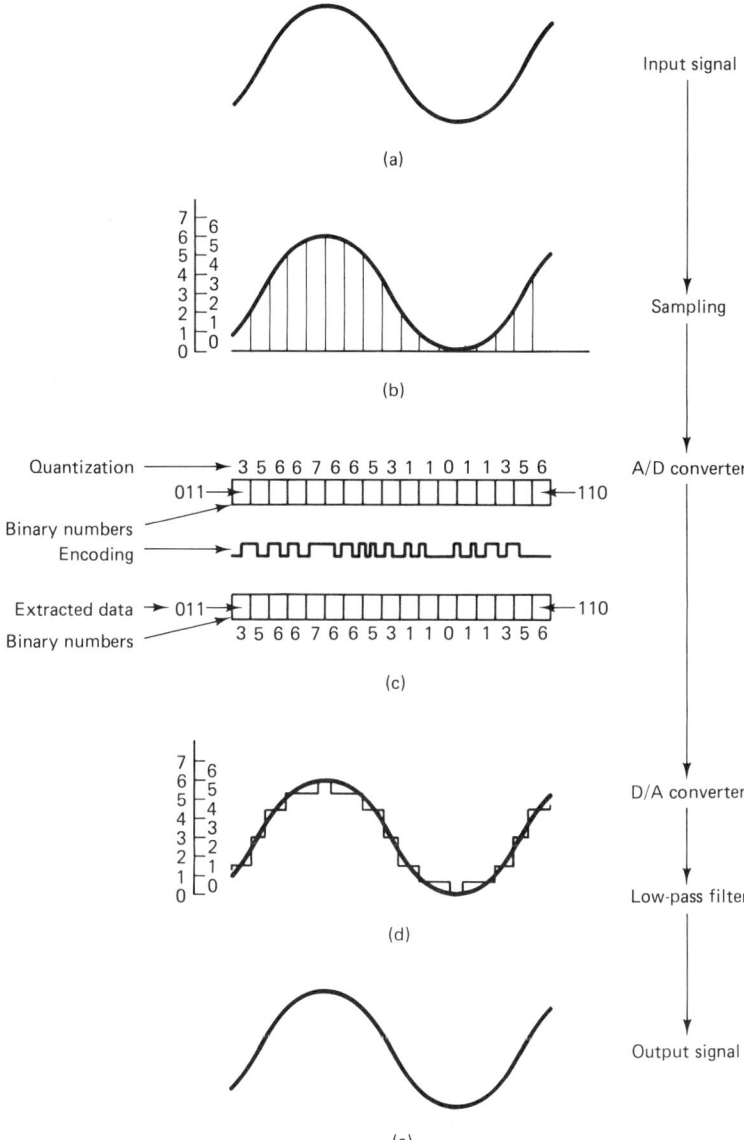

FIGURE 1-12 Sequence of conversion from A/D and from D/A.

waveform-A (original music, speech, etc.) is sampled and measured at short intervals as shown in waveform-B. The measured values are converted into binary numbers and encoded into a pulse train as shown in waveform-C. This process involves *quantization*. That is, the maximum signal amplitude that may occur is divided into a number of levels equal to the available number of binary codes. The real value of the analog signal is then *rounded to a quantized value* that comes closest to the analog value.

The pulse train shown in waveform-C is placed on the CD in the form of pits and flats. The reflected beam is modulated by the pits and flats to create the pulse train of digital information. The detected pulse train is applied to the D/A converter, as shown in waveform-D. The detected information is converted back to the original waveform by the D/A converter as shown in waveform-E.

To summarize, the audio waveform is sampled at 44.1 kHz, and the value of each sample is measured and converted to a binary number (using quantization). The string of successive binary numbers is the digital equivalent of the audio waveform. As long as the binary numbers maintain their true values, the waveform is expressed with an accuracy that depends only on the sampling speed of the binary number. The advantage of the binary code, in this respect, is that binary has two conditions, 0 and 1, which can be easily represented by electrical circuits being switched on and off. As long as digital circuits can detect the difference between these two conditions, the string of numbers is perfectly preserved.

1-7 CONSTANT LINEAR VELOCITY

The information density of the CD is 50 to 100 times greater than that of conventional LP records. The CD is scanned by the servo-controlled optical pickup at a constant linear velocity (CLV) of 1.3 m per second. To get this scan rate, the rotational speed of the disc is progressively changed from 500 rpm at start-up to 200 rpm at the outside edge of the disc.

The data stream of digital information taken from the disc is kept at a constant rate by a *memory*. The memory is allowed to fill to half capacity. Then data bits are taken from the memory at the same rate as incoming data, thus maintaining the half-full condition. If incoming data bits are received at too fast a rate, the memory exceeds the half-full condition and an error signal is developed. This error signal is applied to the turntable motor (through a servo), and disc speed is reduced until the memory remains at the half-full condition. If the disc slows down so that the memory falls below the half-full condition, the error-signal polarity is reversed. This causes the disc motor to speed up, increasing the incoming data-bit rate and restoring the memory to the half-full condition. By using the half-full memory circuit, the rotational speed change of the disc has no effect on the rate of speed that the data bits are removed from memory. As a result, the disc speed changes are not detected in the reproduced sound.

1-8 THE ADVANTAGES OF DIGITAL RECORDINGS

We will not stress the advantages of digital recording in this book. (This is a handbook, not a sales brochure!) However, it can be of benefit to the technician to understand the advantages (particularly if they also sell CD players).

The most obvious advantage of a CD player is discussed in Secs. 1-2 and 1-6. If the player can tell the difference between a 1 and a 0, the player reproduces the sound exactly as encoded, rounded off to the nearest bit in a range from 0 to 65,536 bits. No analog system can match that precision, no matter how the components are selected and matched.

Not quite so obvious is the fact that it is possible to insert extra information or to manipulate the sequence of numbers in a digitally encoded signal (which consists only of a series of numbers). Such insertions and/or manipulation can be done without affecting the original information. (The information can be deleted and/or restored to the original sequence of numbers by means of a microprocessor.) This makes it possible to insert *automatic error-correcting bits* (such as *parity bits*) into the series of numbers. Automatic error correction can compensate for signal losses resulting from marks or scratches on the disc or from temporary losses in the electronic circuits (dropouts). The interleaving described in Sec. 1-5 and shown in Fig. 1-11 is an example of such correction.

The digital recording technique has extremely low *harmonic* and *intermodulation* distortion, when compared to an LP record. *Wow* and *flutter* are virtually nonexistent in a CD player, since disc speed is locked to a crystal-controlled reference signal or timing reference.

Figure 1-13 shows a comparison of "typical" compact disc specifications to a 12-in. LP record. Keep in mind that the manufacturers of most present-day CD players claim much better characteristics than those shown in Fig. 1-13.

1-9 TYPICAL FEATURES OF A CD PLAYER

Again, we are not trying to sell CD players in this book. However, the following paragraphs describe the features found on most present-day CD players, and should be of interest to technicians who are facing CD players for the first time.

	Compact disc	12-in. LP record
Frequency range	20 Hz to 20 kHz	30 Hz to 20 kHz
Dynamic range	> 90 dB	< 55 dB (1 kHz)
S/N ratio	> 90 dB	≈ 60 dB
Channel separation	> 90 dB	25 to 35 dB
Harmonic distortion	< 0.01%	0.2%
Wow and flutter	0	0.03%
Playing time	60 minutes	20 minutes per side

FIGURE 1-13 Comparison of "typical" compact disc specifications to a 12-in. LP record.

1-9.1 Top-load Versus Front-load

As shown in Fig. 1-1, CD players are available in both *top-load* and *front-load* models. The top-load models (Figs. 1-1a and 1-1b) are best suited as stand-alone components, but can also be mounted as top-rack components in an audio system. On most top-load models, the disc compartment cover or lid is opened by a control (push button), but must be closed by hand. Top-load CD players generally do not require a *loading motor,* and are thus simpler than front-load models.

Front-load CD players can be used as stand-alone components, or can be *operated at any location* in an audio-system rack. There are two basic versions of front-load models: horizontal and vertical.

With *horizontal front-load,* you press a front-panel button to open a drawer or tray, insert the disc, and close the drawer (manually) or tray (with a control).

In the *drawer* version of horizontal front-load (Fig. 1-1c), the entire turntable and optical pickup are mounted in a drawer and are moved in and out of the front panel. With this system, you operate a front-panel control, the disc drawer slides out automatically, and a *disc pressure plate* raises. You then position the disc on the turntable and push the drawer back into the player. This pulls the pressure plate over the disc and places the player in a ready-to-play condition.

Note that, in general, the top-load and drawer-type front-load players use the rotating-arm pickup (Fig. 1-3), whereas the horizontal-tray and vertical front-load players use the slide-type pickup.

With the *tray version* of horizontal front-load (Figs. 1-1d and 1-1f), the turntable and pickup are in the player, and the disc is inserted and removed by means of the front-panel tray. The tray is operated by a loading motor in response to a load/unload (or open/close) control. One touch of the control moves the tray out to a position where the disc can be inserted (or removed). Another touch of the control causes the tray to be pulled in and positions the disc over the turntable.

With *vertical front-load* (Fig. 1-1e), the turntable and pickup are in the player. A loading motor opens and closes a vertical door (hinged at the bottom) so that the disc can be inserted and removed.

On virtually all CD players, there are circuit breakers (CBs) and safety switches that prevent operation of drive motors and the laser when the disc drawers/trays/covers are open. We discuss these CBs and switches, and the wondrous mechanisms they control, in Chapters 5 and 6, respectively.

1-9.2 Random Memory Programming

With a CD player capable of this programming, you can preset up to 15 programs (individual selections on the disc) for playback in any order. Typically, you enter the number of the desired programs by first pressing a program button; then you use buttons marked 1 and 10. If the first program you want to hear is the third program on the disc, you press the program button and enter the number 3 by pushing the 1 button three times. The program indicator displays the number 3 for confirmation. Pushing the play button after the full sequence has been entered starts playback of the program sequence entered.

1-9.3 Self-program Search

During playback, CD players with self-program search let you skip forward and backward to locate the beginning of each program on the disc. In a typical CD player, you press the FF (fast forward) control once, and the optical pickup advances to the beginning of the next program (and begins playing the disc at that point). When you press the FB (fast backward) control once, the pickup moves back to the beginning of the current program to begin play. If you press the FB control twice, the pickup moves back to the beginning of the previous program on the disc to begin play.

1-9.4 Disc Scanning

On CD players equipped with disc scanning, the player is placed in the scan mode when the play control and the FF or FB control are operated simultaneously. This causes a brief sample of the current program to be played. Then the pickup advances to a point approximately 30 seconds ahead (or behind) in disc play time, and another brief sample is played. This process continues as long as the FF or FB controls are engaged.

1-9.5 Memory Stop

On CD players with memory stop, you can mark any point on the disc for instant location with the FB control. In either play or pause modes, you mark the current disc location (the beginning of a favorite program, for example) by pushing the memory stop control. The point can then be returned to while in either play or pause modes by pushing the FB control. The pickup moves back to the memory stop location, and the player automatically goes into the pause mode. You then push the play control to start play from the memory stop point.

1-9.6 Repeat Play

Play of the entire disc, or play of a random memory programming sequence (Sec. 1-9.2) can be repeated continuously on most CD players. For play of the entire disc, you push the repeat control at any point prior to or during play of the disc. After the full disc is played, the pickup returns to the beginning and begins play again. Repeat play of a random memory programming sequence is generated in the same way.

1-9.7 Calling Out Display Information

On some CD players, there is a call control which determines what display is shown on the front-panel indicators. Typically, there are indicators on the front panel that show such conditions as *total disc playing time, elapsed playing time, number and total time of programs entered* (via random memory programming), and possibly the *track or index numbers* being played. We go into typical operating procedures for CD players in Chapter 3.

1-9.8 Computer Control

Most CD player manufacturers claim that their player is "computer controlled" or "under control of a built-in computer." In reality, the "computer" is a microprocessor IC (or possibly more than one IC). Likewise, some manufacturers use the terms *microcomputer* (μC) and *microprocessor* (μP) interchangeably. So do not be surprised at any term you may find in CD player literature.

The microprocessors used in CD players make possible all the features described thus far in this section. We will not go into all these features here, since such functions are described in Chapters 5 and 6. However, it is important to note that one major function of the μP is to provide for random memory programming.

As discussed in Sec. 1-9.2, microprocessor control allows the user to program and store in memory up to 15 individual program selections. The player normally plays from the beginning of the disc to the end. However, if only certain selections are desired by the user, these parts of the program can be selected, stored, and played as many times as desired.

CD discs are digitally encoded at the beginning of the program material so the player will know the length of the program. Also encoded at the beginning of each selection is an individual code that identifies the location of that particular selection. This system of identification (sometimes called the *disc directory*) allows each selection on the disc to be accessed (by the system-control microprocessor) on command.

1-9.9 Typical CD Player Specifications

The following specifications are for a "typical" CD player, and are included here for reference.

Audio	
Number of channels	2
Frequency response	5–20,000 Hz ±0.5 dB
Dynamic range	93 dB
Signal-to-noise ratio	94 dB
Harmonic distortion	0.003% (at 1 kHz)
Channel separation	92 dB (at 1 kHz)
Wow/flutter	Less than measurable limits (crystal accuracy)
Output voltage	2.1 V rms (with full scale) (0 dB into 50-k load)
Headphone output	20mW (0 dB into 8-Ω load)
Discs Used	
Playing time	60 min on one side
Diameter	120 mm
Signal Format	
Sampling frequency	44.1 kHz
Quantization number	16-bit linear/channel
Transmission bit rate	4.32 Mb/sec
Pickup	
System	Objective lens drive system (optical pickup)
Objective lens drive system	Two-dimensional parallel drive
Optical source	Semiconductor laser
Wavelength	7900 Å
General	
Power requirements	AC 120 V 60 Hz; 220V 50 Hz
	240 V 50 Hz
	120/220/240 V 50,60 Hz
Power consumption	25 W (AC 120 V 60 Hz; 220 V 50 Hz, 240V 50 Hz)
	28 W (120/220/240 V 50,60 Hz)
Dimensions (mm)	320(W) × 145(H) × 234 (D)
Weight	5.6 Kg
Functions, Displays, and Outputs	
Functions	Random memory search (15 tracks maximum), self-program search system, skip play, memory stop, pause, repeat, output volume adjust.
Displays	Play position (5-min steps), number of tracks, playing track number, elapsed play time, output volume level.
Outputs	Two sets of output terminals (variable and fixed level) on rear panel
	Variable-level headphone jack on front panel.
Accessories	Connecting pin cords for connection to hi-fi/stereo system
	Demonstration disc (part of the user operating instructions package)

2

ENCODING, DECODING, and OPTICAL READOUT

In this chapter we discuss the process involved for *encoding* the original audio (music, etc.) onto the compact disc in the form of pits and flats, and then *decoding* the tracks of pits and flats back to hi-fi/stereo audio suitable for reproduction on amplifiers and loudspeakers. Keep in mind that the encoding takes place at the time of disc manufacture, and cannot be altered. It is the job of the CD player to decode the disc signals. However, to understand operation of the CD player decoder circuits, it is most helpful (if not essential) that you understand the encoding process. We also describe the basic *optical readout* principles in this chapter. Keep in mind that there are many optical readout configurations now in use, and more being developed. However, the basic principles apply to all optical readout systems used in CD players.

2-1 ENCODING THE COMPACT DISC

Figure 2-1 shows a simplified block diagram of the encoding process, and is typical for the equipment used in CD recording. To produce a CD, the audio signals must be digitized and encoded before any other processing takes place. The first step in the process involves the use of low-pass filters.

2-1.1 Low-pass Filters

Both left and right input audio signals are passed through sharp-cutoff, low-pass filters as shown in Fig. 2-1. These filters limit the bandwidth

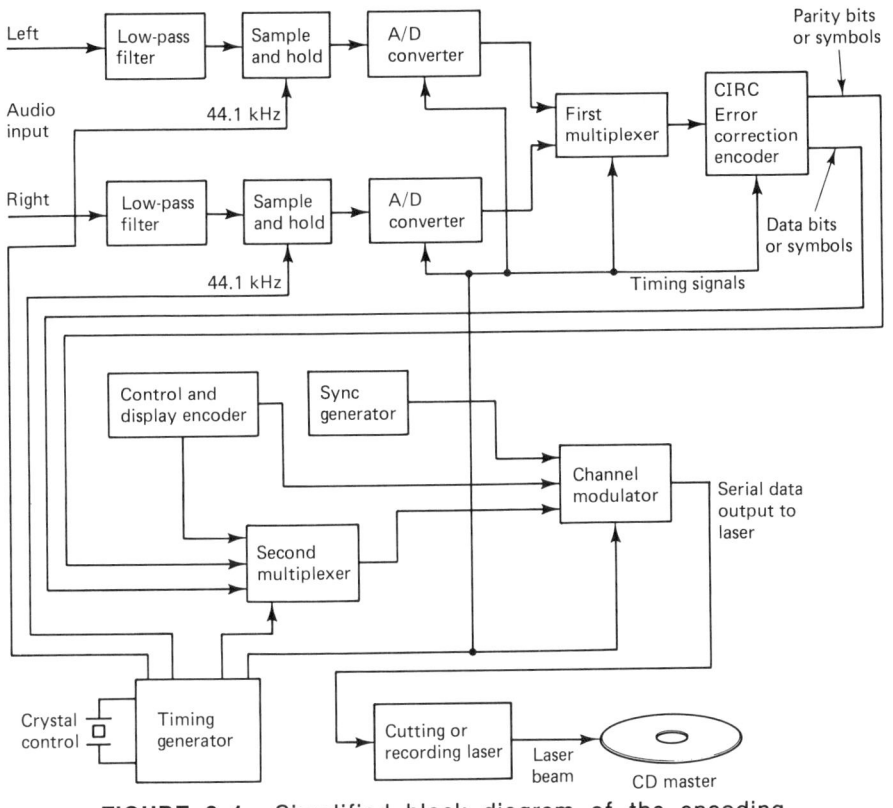

FIGURE 2-1 Simplified block diagram of the encoding process.

to a maximum frequency (f_m) equal to or less than the sampling frequency (f_s) of 44.1 kHz. If the audio frequency to be sampled is greater than the sampling frequency, *intermodulation distortion* can occur due to *frequency fold-over*, as shown in Fig. 2-2.

2-1.2 Sample-and-hold

Before the stereo audio signals are recorded on the disc, the signals are converted into a digital format. One of the first conversion steps is to sample the audio signals at fixed intervals or *time points* (also called *sampling times*). This sampling is done by the sample-and-hold (S/H) circuits shown in Fig. 2-1. Figure 2-3 shows the waveform produced when a single cycle of audio is sampled.

In addition to sampling, the S/H circuits also measure the values for each sample of the audio signal as shown in Fig. 2-3b. The measured value

28 Encoding, Decoding, and Optical Readout

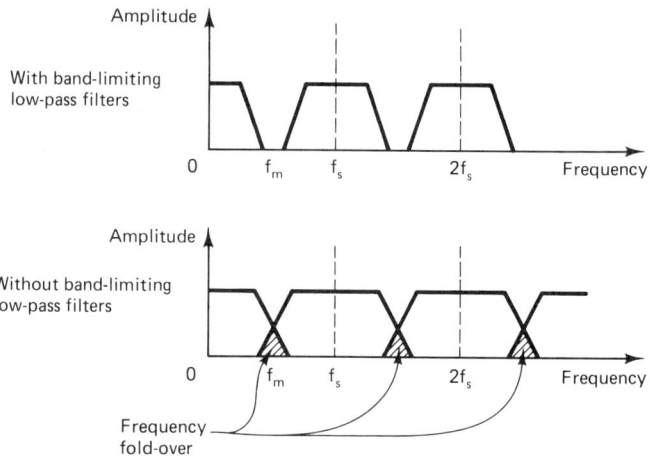

FIGURE 2-2 Filtering to prevent frequency fold-over.

is held for a moment to permit conversion to a *binary-coded waveform* as shown in Fig. 2-3c. The procedure for such action in the S/H circuits can be compared to charge and discharge of a capacitor through a switch, as shown in Fig. 2-3d.

The switch is activated by a sampling pulse of relatively short duration. When the audio signal appears at the input of the switch, and the sampling pulse closes the switch, the capacitor charges to the instantaneous value of the signal amplitude. When the switch is reopened, the capacitor retains the previous value until the switch is closed again. The capacitor then adds to, or subtracts from, the previous value when the next sampling pulse closes the switch.

The maximum audio signal frequency that can be sampled in this way is *one-half the sampling frequency*. The sampling rate of 44.1 kHz is more than sufficient for the typical audio range of 0 to 20 kHz.

2-1.3 Analog-to-digital Conversion

After sampling the analog signal, the next step is to convert each sample into a 2's-complement binary code as shown in Fig. 2-4. One of the problems in this process is that audio signals can assume an infinite number of levels, whereas the number of binary codes available to reproduce the levels are finite. To overcome this problem, the sampled signal is *quantized*. That is, the maximum value that occurs is divided into a number of levels equal to the available number of binary codes. This process occurs in the A/D converters, which produce a number of binary bits representing the quantized level of each sample.

2-1 Encoding the Compact Disc 29

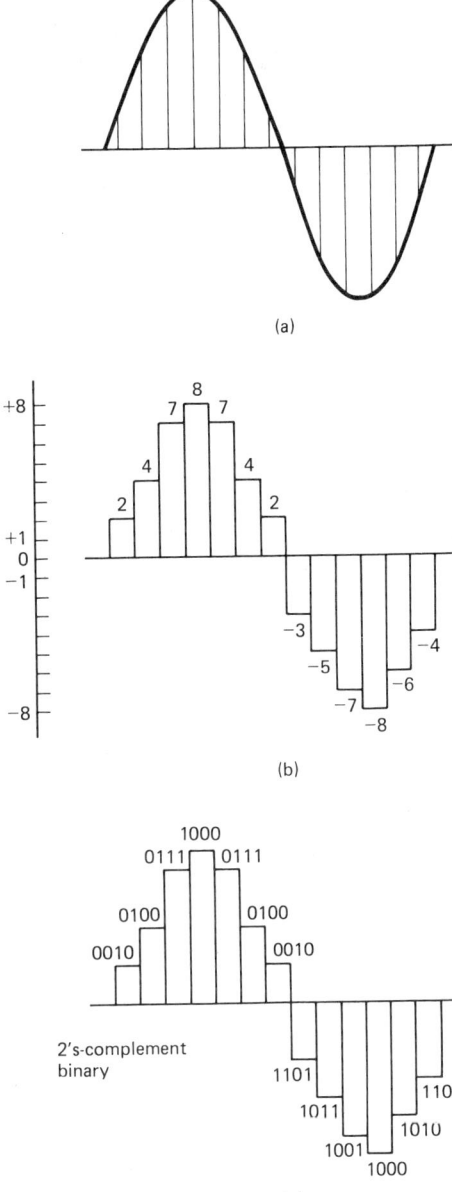

FIGURE 2-3 Waveform produced when a single cycle of audio is sampled.

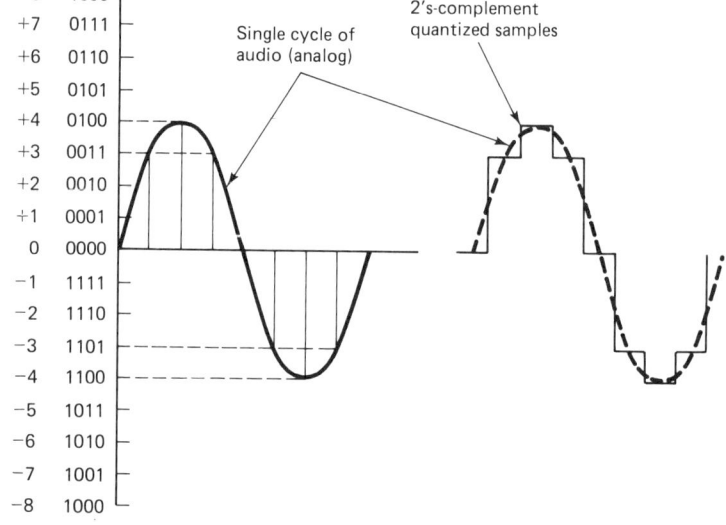

FIGURE 2-4 A/D conversion process used to convert a single cycle of audio into 2's-complement quantized samples.

2-1.4 Multiplexing

Sampling, quantization, and conversion to binary code are operations performed separately for the left and right channels. However, both channels are ultimately stored on the disc, *one after the other on a single track*. To accomplish this, the *first multiplexer* circuit is used to pass the information, in sequence, to the CIRC error-correction encoder circuit.

2-1.5 Error Correction (CIRC)

The error-correction circuit processes the digital signal (binary bits from the multiplexer) by a method called Cross Interleaved Reed-Solomon Code (CIRC), which involves both *parity bits* and *interleaving*. There are two outputs from the CIRC encoder. One output carries data and the other carries parity bits. The two outputs are applied to a *second multiplexer* which, in turn, feeds the signals in sequence to the *channel modulator*. It is at this point in the process where the control and display encoding is mixed with the data and parity bits.

2-1.6 Control and Display Encoding

The control and display encoding provides operating features for the CD player which cannot be found in conventional record players. At the beginning of each disc is encoded the number of selections contained on that disc. Each musical selection is identified separately so that the selection can be readily accessed. Indentification codes that identify the pause between two musical selections can be used to implement the search and repeat functions of the CD player. Encoding can be used to identify whether or not the recording is made with preemphasis. (This makes it possible to switch the deemphasis circuits of the player on or off automatically.) Timing information can be encoded for displaying elapsed time or the time played of a particular piece of music.

Control and display information is nonaudible and is encoded separately. The control and display encoder outputs 8-bit symbols, permitting the implementation of eight different information channels. The control and display information is usually referred to as *subcoding,* and is added to the data and parity bits in the second multiplexer.

2-1.7 Sync Generation

The output of the second multiplexer is fed (serially) to the channel modulator, with the data arranged in blocks. In order to recognize the blocks of data, the *sync generator* is used to generate a unique pattern (which is not contained in the normal data). The sync pattern is passed to the channel modulator, which adds the pattern to the data at intervals based on timing pulses received from the *timing generator.*

2-2 CHANNEL MODULATION (CUTTING THE MASTER)

Now that we have gone through the basic encoding process, let us go back through the encoding circuits using some typical audio signals. We will see how the circuits in Fig. 2-1 are used to modulate the cutting or recording laser to produce a corresponding track of pits and flats on the master (Fig. 1-7).

Figure 2-5a shows the left (L) and right (R) channels of a stereo recording to be encoded on a compact disc. The information created from these two channels during the sampling period is used to convert the signals to a binary code. The code is then used to control the cutting laser by modulating the laser beam during the manufacture of the CD master.

Note that the right-channel signal is somewhat lower in amplitude than the left-channel, and is almost twice as long (lower in frequency). However, both L and R channels are *sampled six times*. This configuration is called a *frame,* as discussed next.

2-2.1 Frame Organization

As discussed in Chapter 1, a compact disc is composed of billions of tiny pits, which represent the digital encoded data. In order for the CD player to recognize this data, it is necessary to organize the data into patterns. In all CDs,

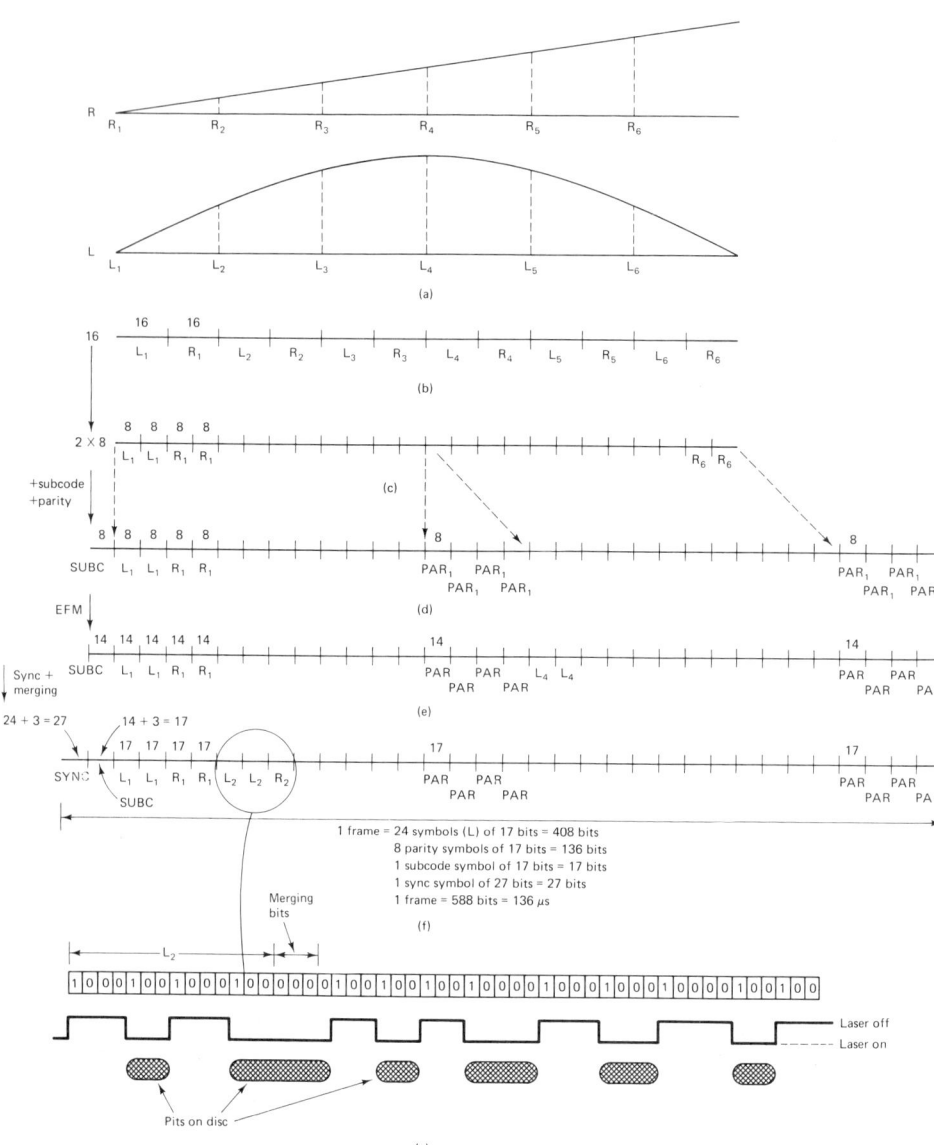

FIGURE 2-5 Conversion from analog to EFM to pits and flats on the disc.

the pattern is organized into a block structure called the *frame*. The frame is a period of time that contains six audio samples (of both channels) as shown in Fig. 2-5a.

The six audio samples of the frame are made up of six sample periods of both left- and right-channel audio so as to equal 12 sample periods. The two channels of audio are applied through separate low-pass filters to the S/H circuits (Fig. 2-1). The two S/H circuits measure (or sample) the voltage level of the analog signals in short (22.7 μs) intervals at a frequency of 44.1 kHz. This measurement is then converted into a binary code by the A/D converter.

The output of the A/D converter is a 16-bit binary code representing that sampling period of the audio signal in digital form. Note that the 16-bit code is in *2's-complement* form (as shown in Fig. 2-4) to accommodate both positive and negative swings of the audio signal. Also, in most CD literature, each 16-bit number is called a *word,* and each word is split into two *symbols* of 8 bits each.

No matter what it is called, the conversion of the audio signal to a 16-bit binary code is done separately (from each other) by two channels containing the same circuitry (and synchronized to each other by the timing generator). The two channels of data (each containing six sample periods of sequential data) are applied to the first multiplexer, which switches the two data streams into one sequential data stream as shown in Fig. 2-5b.

The output of the first multiplexer is one single data stream containing the 12 sample periods (words) of both L and R channels intermixed with each other so that the L sample period is followed by an R sample period. The sequential data stream from the first multiplexer is applied to the error-correction circuit where interleaving takes place.

2-2.2 CIRC Interleaving

One function of the error-correction circuit is to break each 16-bit word into two 8-bit symbols as shown in Fig. 2-5c. During this process, the two 8-bit symbols are interleaved (rearranged or scrambled) as shown in Fig. 1-11. However, to simplify the explanation at this point, we show the words and symbols without interleaving in Fig. 2-5. (Do not worry, we get to interleaving in our discussion of the decoding process in Sec. 2-3.)

After interleaving of the data stream, the next step is to provide a method of checking for errors in the data stream by the CD player. This is done by use of *parity bits* generated in the error-correction circuit. The parity bits are generated as 8-bit data words, and are called a *parity symbol.*

2-2.3 Parity Symbols

Two channels of information are produced by the CIRC error-correction circuit as shown in Fig. 2-1. One channel contains the data symbols representing the audio samples; the second channel represents the parity symbols. The data and parity symbols are clocked out of the error correction to the second multiplexer at intervals determined by the timing generator. The multiplexer adds the parity symbols to the correct location in the data stream so that the decoder in the CD player can check for errors in the data symbols.

There are 8 parity symbols (each containing 8 bits) generated by the error-correction circuit. Four of the parity symbols are placed in the middle and four at the end of the data stream. This allows the data stream to be checked for errors by the CD player every 12 data symbols, as shown in Fig. 2–5d. The illustration of Fig. 2–5d also shows the addition of a *subcode* to the data stream. This subcode is added to provide a means of identifying the data stream.

2-2.4 Subcode Data Symbol

The subcode data symbol (often referred to simply as the subcode) not only provides identification of the entire frame of data symbols, but also provides a *sync pattern* used in processing of the data symbols by the CD player. The subcode is processed by a microprocessor in the player, and provides the system with updated information as to where the optical pickup is located (in its travel across the disc). This information is displayed on the player front panel. The subcode also provides control information to aid the microprocessor in locating that particular frame on the disc.

The output of the second multiplexer, containing the subcode (8 bits), 24 data symbols of audio (8 bits each), and 8 parity symbols (8 bits each), all as shown in Fig. 2–5d, is applied to the input of the channel modulator.

2-2.5 Channel Modulator and EFM

The frame, as shown in Fig. 2–5d, is applied to the channel modulator which, in turn, provides modulation to the cutting or recording laser. Design of CD players would be much simpler if the data stream could be placed directly on the CD in the 8-bit format shown in Fig. 2–5d. Unfortunately, this is not the case. Instead, the 8-bit code is converted into a 14-bit code called *Eight-to-Fourteen Modulation,* or EFM. As the name implies, each group of 8 data bits is converted into a 14-bit data symbol as shown in Fig. 2–5e. The process, in effect, "stretches" the distance between adjacent pits and flats as shown in Fig. 2–6. The "stretching" from 8 to 14 bits prevents the laser beam (in the player) from converting two adjacent transitions (from pit to flat, and vice versa) at the same time.

There is no direct relationship between an 8-bit and a 14-bit code in their natural state. So, to make the two codes compatible with each other, two conditions are placed on the 14-bit code. First, there must always be at least two zeros between successive ones. Second, there must be no more than 10 consecutive zeros in a 14-bit run of the code. When these two conditions are applied, all but 277 possible combinations are eliminated. The 277 codes remaining can be further reduced by eliminating 21 codes containing the long-

2-2 Channel Modulation (Cutting the Master) 35

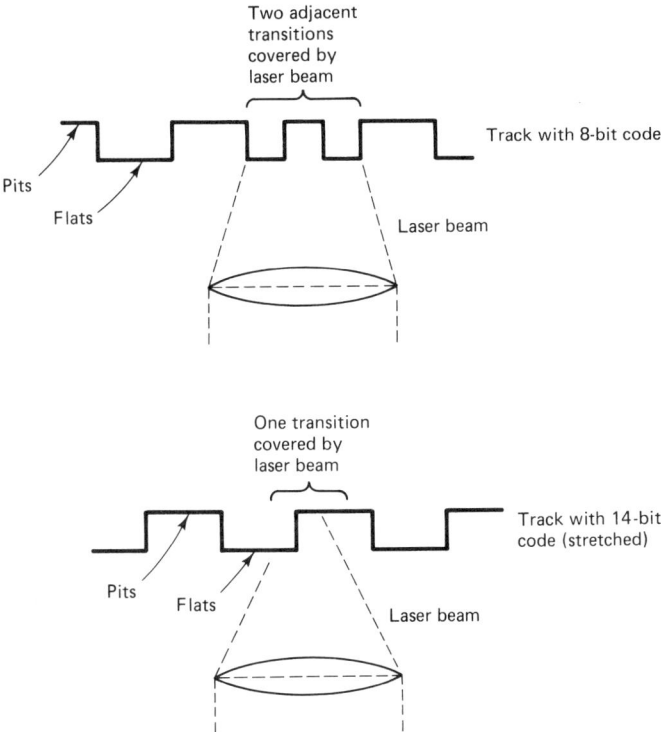

FIGURE 2-6 Effect on pits and flats when an 8-bit code is converted to a 14-bit code (8-to-14 modulation, or EFM).

est runs of zeros, which leaves 256 possible combinations. An 8-bit code contains 256 combinations in the natural state ($2^8 = 256$), so the two codes (8-bit and conditioned 14-bit) have a direct one-to-one relationship.

The EMF process is reversed in the CD player to provide correct decoding. Typically, this is done by placing the 8-bit code in a lookup table in a ROM (which is part of the CD player's decoder IC).

2-2.6 Symbol Sync and Frame Sync

In addition to EFM conversion, the channel modulator adds a unique sync pattern, created by the *sync generator,* to the EFM data stream. The sync pattern generated by the subcode (Sec. 2-2.4) is used to process the data symbols during error correction, and is called *symbol sync*. The 24-bit sync pattern placed at the beginning of the frame, as shown in Fig. 2–5f, is used to provide clock and timing signals for the player decoding system, and is called *frame sync*.

Figure 2–5f also shows three *merging bits* added to the end of each symbol. (24 sync bits plus 3 merging bits equals 27 bits. 14 L1 bits plus 3 merging bits equals 17 bits.) Without the merging bits, the symbols would violate the two conditions placed on the 14-bit code, since the symbols are linked together serially. The merging bits contain no audio or other information, and are therefore skipped by the decoding system in the CD player. The d-c content of the modulation can also be controlled by the merging bits. This is done by inserting or omitting an extra transition in the three merging bits. The decision to insert or omit the bit is based on the knowledge of one or more future symbols, and is known as the *look-ahead method*. (Keep in mind that the merging bits are not the concern of the CD player circuits, but are used by the encoding circuits.)

2-2.7 Conversion to Pits and Flats

Figure 2–5g shows conversion of three samples (L2, L2, R2) to corresponding pits and flats on the disc. In this case, each symbol has 14 EFM bits, plus 3 merging bits, for a total of 17 bits. Note that the transition from pit to flat occurs when there is a transition from 1 to 0 and 0 to 1.

The output of the channel modulator provides the data stream of Fig. 2–5g to the control circuit of the cutting laser. The signal modulates the laser beam, thus cutting pits into the master (sequentially, in a spiral pattern from the beginning to the end of the master).

2-2.8 Controlling the Cutting Laser

A study of the pattern shown in Fig. 2–5g illustrates how the data symbol and merging bits control operation of the cutting laser (how the laser is turned on and off to cut pits of the proper length and sequence).

The digital sequence of the data stream representing the left-channel second sample period (L2) contains the EFM data. This represents the first half (8 bits) of the L2 sample period, and is merged to the second half of L2 which, in turn, is merged to the first half of the sample period for the right channel (R2).

The beginning of the 14-bit code for L2 starts at the left with a 1 at the beginning of the L2 data symbol. The 1 is used to provide the transition in the data stream, and acts as a switching pulse to turn the cutting laser beam off. The laser beam remains off due to the next three bits containing 0s. The fifth bit of the data symbol of L2 contains the next transition in the data stream. The 1 then turns on the laser beam, cutting a pit into the disc. The length of the pit is determined by the bits following the bit containing the transition.

The eighth bit of the data stream contains a transition (0 to 1), which turns off the laser. The laser remains off for the next 3 bits, leaving a blank space (or flat) for this period of time. The twelfth bit of the data stream turns on the laser beam. The beam is held on by the zeros in the next 6 bits of the data stream (making a long pit). Two of the 6 bits complete the 14-bit data symbol for the first half of L2. This is followed by 3 merging bits (all 0s) and then the first bit (a 0) of the second half of L2. The laser beam is turned off by the transition contained in the second bit of L2. This procedure is continued throughout the encoding process until the complete selection of music (or other audio) is digitally encoded onto the master.

2-2.9 Subcode Information

At the beginning of the encoding of a master, the subcode contains information indicating the *number of selections* recorded on the disc. This information is encoded in the same frame structure as all other data, except that the subcode data symbols in the frame contain no audio information. This is done by placing all zeros in the subcode data symbols.

The subcode also contains a bit (known as the *pause* bit) to provide information as to *when a selection is about to begin*. The pause bit is placed at the beginning of each selection of music in an area containing no audio. The pause bit is used to tell a microprocessor in the CD player that a selection is ready to begin. This allows the microprocessor to read the subcode and determine if the selection is correct (as determined by the front-panel controls).

2-2.10 System Frequency

The frequency of the system is based on the six audio samples containing the 12 sample periods of left- and right-channel audio. There are 588 channel bits in one frame. The frame can then be divided into six audio samples, which equals 98 channel bits per audio sample. The 98 channel bits are then multiplied by the sampling frequency of 44.1 MHz to produce a system frequency of 4.3218 MHz. Note that system frequency is sometimes referred to as *high frequency,* or HF, in CD player literature.

2-3 DECODING THE COMPACT DISC

Figure 2-7 shows the simplified block diagram of the decoding process. If you compare this to the block diagrams in Chapter 5, you will see that Fig. 2-7 is essentially a block diagram of the complete CD player, but with the focus and radial tracking functions omitted.

As shown in Fig. 2-7, the high-frequency signal retrieved from the disc by the optical pickup is amplified and filtered in the *high-frequency amplifier.* The output signal of the amplifier is a frame-structured data stream containing the EFM format. The amplified high-frequency signal is applied to the EFM *demodulator,* which forms the front end of the decoding system. The EFM demodulator supplies the demodulated data and timing signals to the *error-*

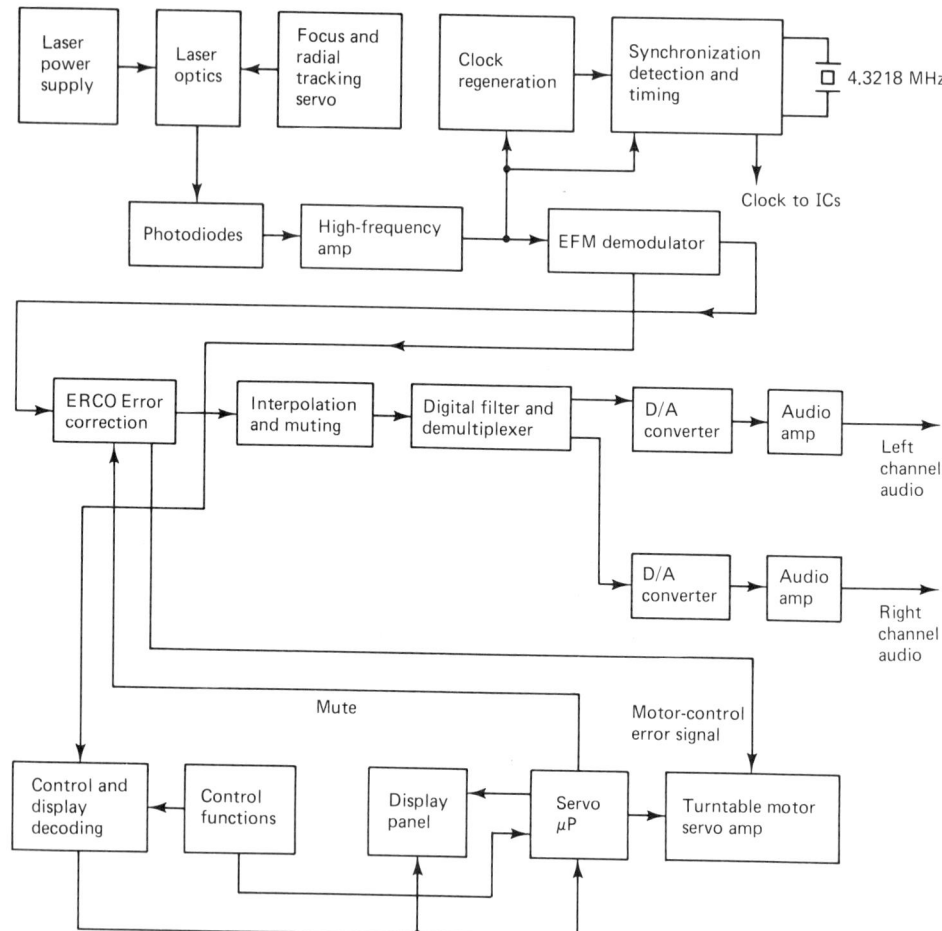

FIGURE 2-7 Simplified block diagram of the decoding process.

correction (ERCO) circuits, as well as to the *control and display decoder*. The high-frequency signal is also applied to the *clock regeneration* and *synchronization detecting and timing* circuits to recover the bit clock and sync pattern from the data stream (which, in turn, provides timing for the system).

2-3.1 Error Correction During Decoding

The error correction IC performs the task of error detection and correction. This information is supplied to the *interpolation and muting* IC, together with a flag signal indicating if a concealment action is to be performed. The ERCO compares the derived clock signal to a reference frequency (crystal controlled) to detect any discrepancy in the data stream. As discussed in Sec. 2-2.10, system frequency is 4.3218 million bits per second (or 4.3218 MHz). If an error is detected in the data stream by a comparator in the ERCO, an error-correction signal (the motor-control error signal) is applied to the *turntable motor servo amplifier*.

If the *data rate* coming into the ERCO is less than 4.3218 million bits per second, the error signal increases the turntable motor speed. If the rate is greater than 4.3218 MHz, the error signal slows the turntable motor speed. The motor-control error signal controls speed of the disc as play continues from the inside of the disc to the outside edge. Since the tracks get bigger in diameter as play continues, the tracks contain more information, and the system receives this information at a faster rate. So the disc motor speed is decreased from 500 rpm (at start-up) to 200 rpm on the outside edge of the disc. This process is called *constant linear velocity,* or CLV.

2-3.2 The Effects of Interleaving on the Decoding Process

The majority of errors that may occur during playback of a compact disc results from scratches, dust, and dirt that may reflect the laser beam (producing erroneous bits). Because of the high density of information on CDs, such defects or reflections can easily wipe out several adjacent bits or samples on the track. If all the affected samples belong to the same frame, a great many *multiposition errors* would occur inside each frame. *Interleaving* is used to avoid multiposition errors in a frame during playback.

Interleaving is based on the fact that analog signals are continuous signals that usually do not change abruptly. The amplitude of the signal during the first sample does not differ greatly from that of the second sample. The amplitude during the third sample does not differ much from the second sample, and so on. If the value of the second sample is lost, but the value of the first and third samples is known to be good, than an approximation or interpolation can be made to compute the second sample.

The principles of interleaving and de-interleaving are shown in Fig. 2-8. Keep in mind that interleaving is done by means of *delay lines* (having different delay times) allocated to specific samples during the encoding process (at the time of disc manufacture). De-interleaving occurs in the CD player at the time of playback.

In Fig. 2-8a, the sequence of signal processing is shown without interleaving. The audio signal is first sampled at time points 1, 2, 3, and so on, and is digitized and recorded onto the disc. If there is a dropout during playback of the disc, there are some symbols missing in the received data. In the example used, three symbols (5, 6, and 7) are missing, producing a serious dropout.

In Fig. 2-8b, the same sequence of signal processing is shown with interleaving. Again, the audio signal is sampled, but with the samples being

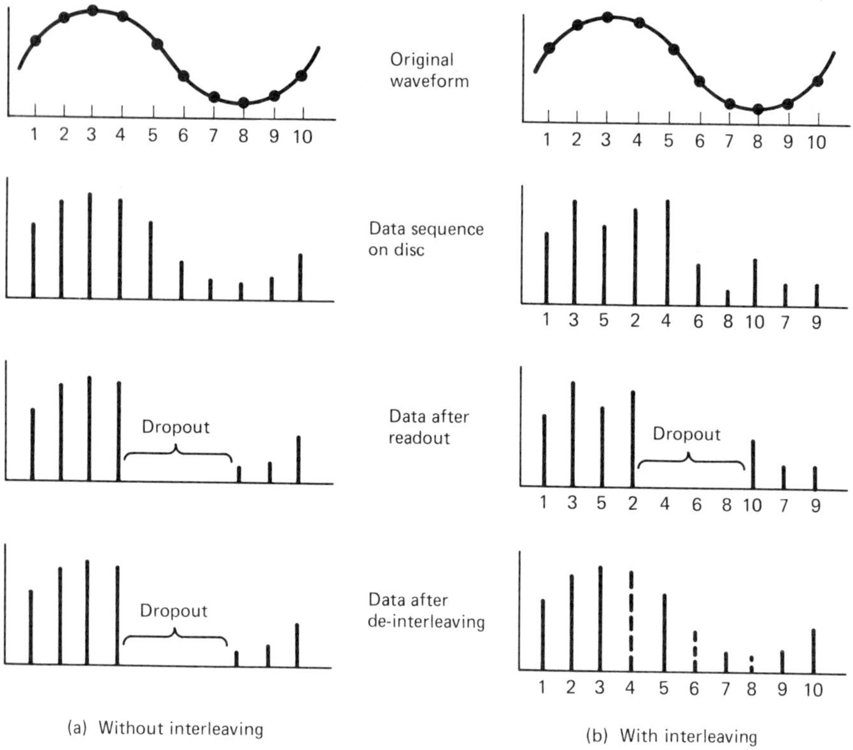

FIGURE 2-8 Principles of interleaving and de-interleaving.

rearranged prior to disc recording. Such interleaving results in the recording of data in a sequence which does not represent an increasing time scale. During reading of the disc, the same dropout occurs, and again results in three missing data symbols (4,6, and 8). De-interleaving is then performed in the CD player to restore the original sequence of data symbols.

It can be seen that with interleaving there are no multiposition errors, and that the single missing data bits can be approximated by interpolation. For example, symbol 4 can be interpolated as a value between symbols 3 and 5 (less than symbol 3, but greater than symbol 5).

2-3.3 Digital Filter and Demultiplexer

The de-interleaved and interpolated data stream is applied to the digital filter and demultiplexer IC where the stream is filtered and separated into left- and right-channel data. Digital filtering provides a higher reproduction quality than is found in conventional record players. However, to get this quality, the sampling signal frequencies must also be filtered out. If the series of binary numbers representing quantized samples were simply converted to analog values,

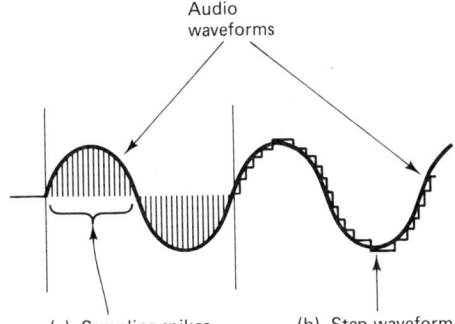

FIGURE 2-9 The basic sample-and-hold function.

a series of *sampling spikes* would occur as shown in Fig. 2-9a. Although the outline of this series resembles the audio waveform, the constant on/off switching produces an infinite series of frequencies. To overcome this problem, each sample is held until the next sample arrives. This produces a *step waveform* as shown in Fig. 2-9b. The step waveform is much nearer the shape of the original audio waveform than the series of spikes. The sample-and-hold function occurs in the digital-to-analog (D/A) converters.

2-3.4 D/A Converters

D/A conversion is the last step in the processing sequence before stereo audio amplification. The right and left D/A converters transform the 16-bit digital code into an analog signal that has the same shape as the original audio signal. Simultaneously, the converters use *oversampling,* which acts as a preliminary filter, to refine the step waveform shown in Fig. 2-10a to a step waveform resembling that of Fig. 2-10b. The oversampling or preliminary filtering is done by digital filters that operate at four times the sampling frequency (4 × 44.1 kHz = 176.4 kHz). Because of the oversampling, a relatively simple low-pass filter is used following the D/A conversion process. (Very elaborate filtering of the audio signals would be required were it not for the preliminary filtering provided by the oversampling process.)

2-3.5 Stereo Audio Amplifiers

All CD players include some form of audio amplification after the S/H and low-pass filter circuits. Generally, the audio amplifiers are in IC form and raise the left and right audio channel signals to a level of about 2 V. In some cases (particularly the early-model CD players), the audio output level is fixed. However, most later-model CD players have an adjustment (volume control) to set the audio output level. Also, most CD players have some form of stereo headphone output (usually adjustable).

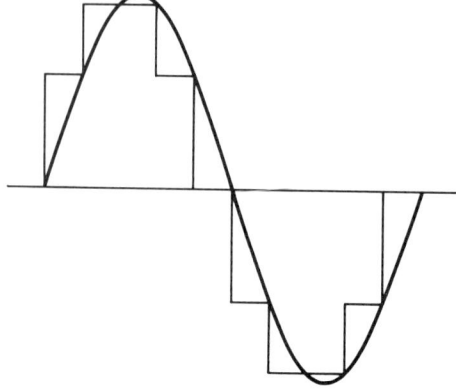

(a) Audio waveform sampled at 44.1 kHz

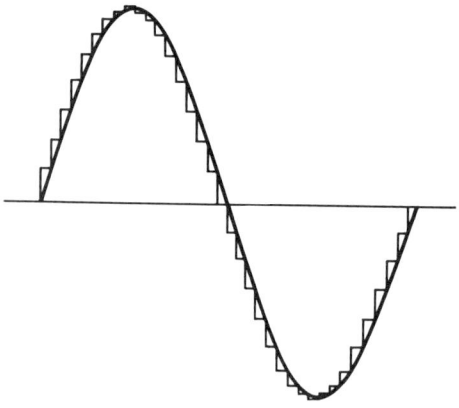

(b) Audio waveform sampled at 176.4 kHz

FIGURE 2-10 The effect of oversampling and preliminary digital filtering on the audio output waveform.

2-4 OPTICAL PICKUP OR READOUT

As discussed in Chapter 1, digital information contained on the compact disc is retrieved by means of a laser which generates a light beam to detect the track of pits and flats on the disc. The laser beam is applied to, and reflected from, the track through an optical pickup or readout (a series of lenses, prisms, etc.).

We conclude this chapter with a description of the optics used in both the rotating-arm and slide-type readouts. Keep in mind that there are several types of optical readouts for CD players currently in use, and new systems are being developed. However, as discussed in Chapter 1, the optics are part of a pickup or readout assembly that must be *replaced as a package*. We describe some typical replacement procedures in Chapter 6.

2-4.1 Rotating-arm Optics

The laser diode for a typical rotating-arm-type optical pickup is mounted in a *light-pen assembly* as shown in Fig. 2–11. The upper section of the light pen contains the photodiodes and collimator lens. The lower section contains the laser diode, a single photodiode, and the prism.

The laser generates two light beams as shown in Fig. 2–12. The main beam emerges from one end of the laser diode and is used to retrieve information from the disc. The secondary beam emerges from the other end of the laser diode and is used to control the intensity of the laser beam. For best performance, the amount or intensity of the light falling on the disc must be held constant. The beam intensity depends on laser current (and temperature). In most rotating-arm systems, laser beam intensity is held constant by controlling the laser current.

There is a fixed relationship between the intensity of the main beam and the secondary beam, so the secondary beam is used for measurement of the main beam. This is done by a photodiode (called the *monitor diode*) mounted below the laser diode, as shown in Fig. 2–13. The signal from the monitor diode is applied to the laser power supply, and it controls the amount of current supplied to the laser diode. If beam intensity is low, the monitor diode signal increases laser diode current/intensity, and vice versa.

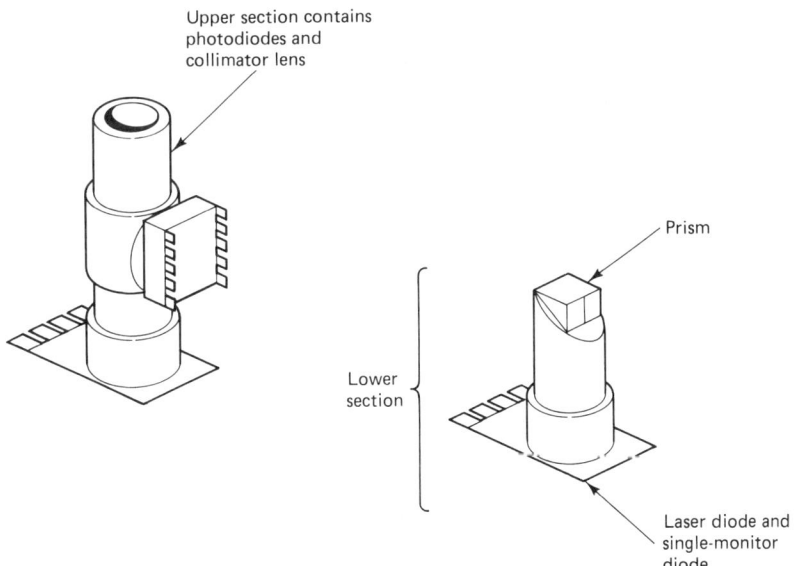

FIGURE 2–11 Light-pen assembly used in rotating-arm-type optical pickup.

44 Encoding, Decoding, and Optical Readout

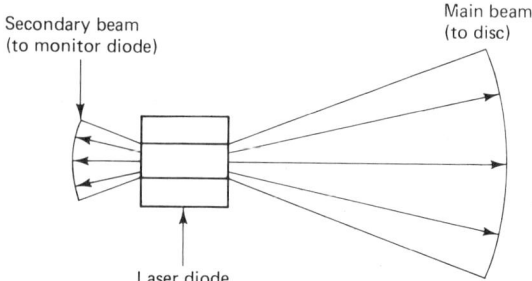

FIGURE 2-12 Laser beams in rotating-arm-type optical pickup.

As shown in Fig. 2-14, the light leaving the laser diode passes through a *semireflective prism,* which allows light coming from the laser to pass through. The reflected light returning from the disc is deflected by the prism onto the photodiodes (which provide the high-frequency signal output, focus signal, and radial tracking signal). As shown in Fig. 2-15, the prism is a wedge-shaped optical glass that splits the returning beam into two beams. The photodiodes convert both beams into electrical signals.

Typically, four diodes are used in rotating-arm optics. The diodes are arranged as shown in Fig. 2-16. The prism splits the beam so that one-half lands on one pair of diodes, while the other half of the beam hits the other pair of diodes.

The four diodes shown in Fig. 2-16 are located on one silicon chip. The large area around the four diodes is used as a *guard diode.* The function of

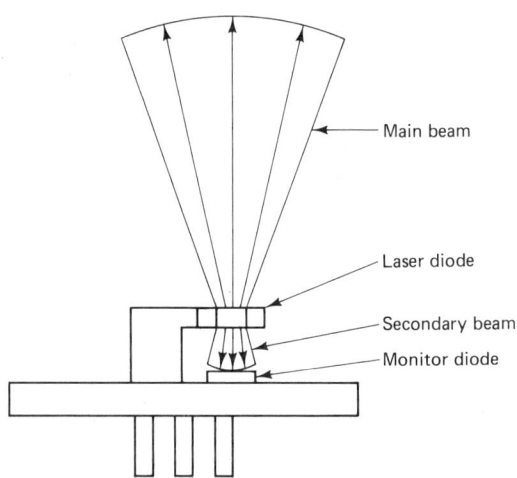

FIGURE 2-13 Monitor diode used in rotating-arm-type optical pickup.

2-4 Optical Pickup or Readout   45

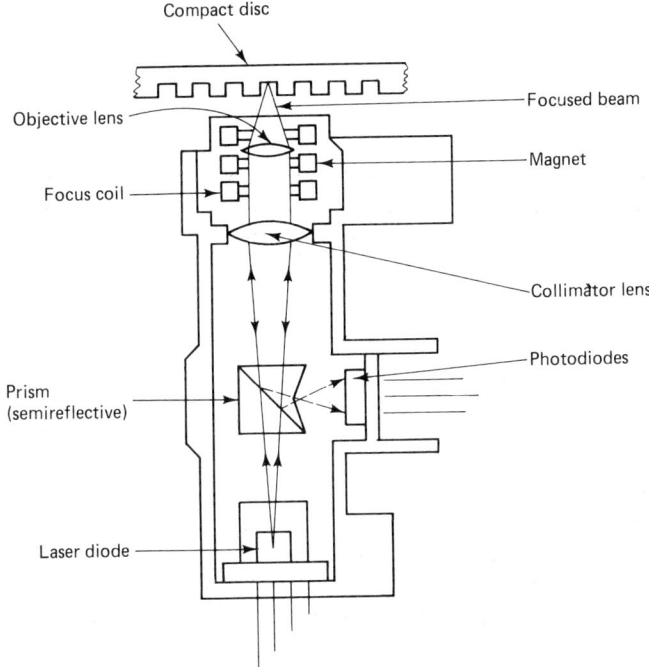

FIGURE 2-14   Typical optics in rotating-arm-type pickup.

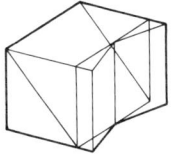

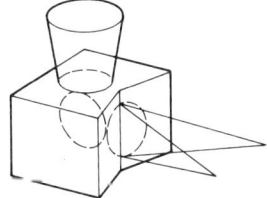

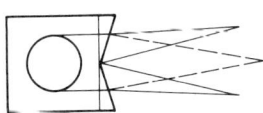

FIGURE 2-15 Typical prism used in rotating-arm-type optical pickup.

46   Encoding, Decoding, and Optical Readout

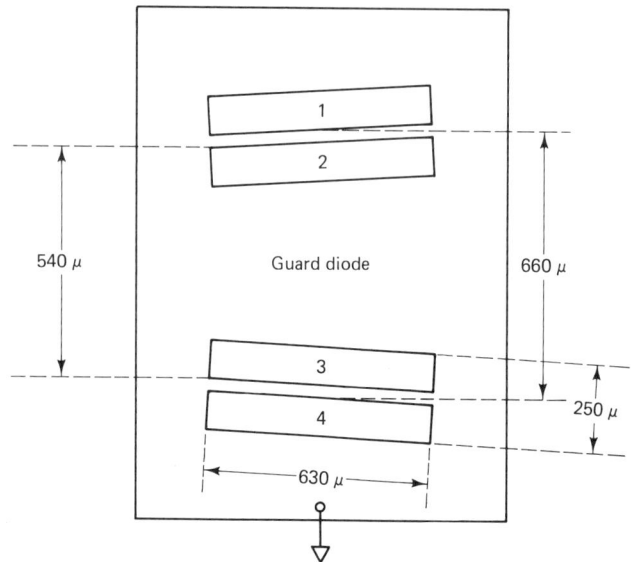

FIGURE 2-16 Typical detector diode arrangement used in rotating-arm-type optical pickups.

this guard diode is to conduct any stray current (created by stray light landing on the diodes) to ground. Such stray light could cause electron-hole pairs (in the silicon chip) which might recombine before they reach the four signal diodes. This could result in damage to the diodes, or interference, or both.

The purpose of the *collimator lens* shown in Fig. 2-14 is to diverge the light beam into a parallel beam. Light tends to spread out in all directions as the distance from one point to another becomes greater. The collimator lens diverges the light beam into a parallel path to fill the aperature of the objective lens.

Figure 2-17 shows a cutaway view of the objective lens and other optical components used to track the up-and-down movement of the disc. The objective lens is mounted on a ring of magnetic material, and is connected to the housing by two leaf springs. These springs provide tension and keep the barrel of the objective lens straight in the cylinder as the lens moves. The housing contains the focus coil, which produces a magnetic field when an electrical current (the focus error signal) is applied. The magnetic field moves the objective lens up or down, depending on the polarity and magnitude of the coil current (focus error).

Figure 2-18 shows the light beam returning from the disc and split into two beams by the prism. The beams can be in one of three conditions, as far as focus is concerned. The first condition is when the objective lens is focused perfectly on the disc, and both beams land directly on the center of the two pairs of diodes. The second condition is when the objective lens is too far

2-4 Optical Pickup or Readout 47

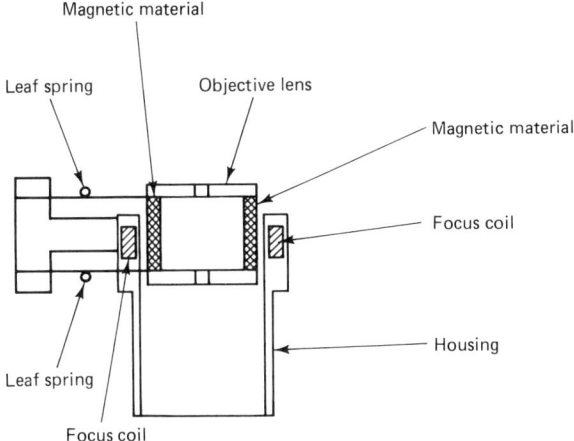

FIGURE 2-17 Cutaway view of objective lens used in rotating-arm-type optical pickup.

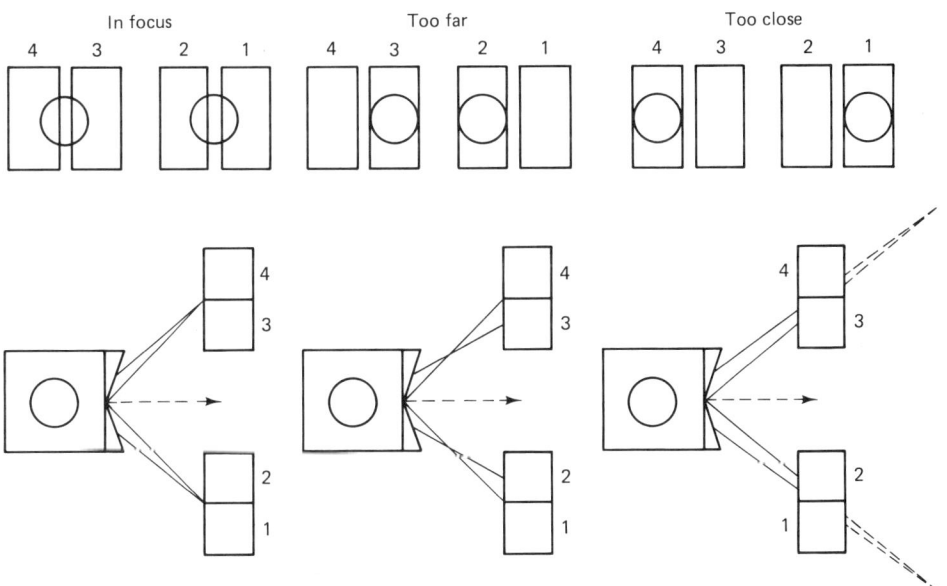

FIGURE 2-18 Three conditions of the objective-lens focus when the beam returning from the disc is split by the prism.

from the disc, and the two beams land on the inside diode of each pair. The third condition is when the objective lens is too close to the disc, and the two beams land on the outside diode of each pair. (Compare this diode arrangement to that shown in Fig. 1-10 and described in Sec. 1-4, for the slide-type optics.)

In the focused condition of Fig. 2-18, a zero error exists from the photodiodes, and the objective lens remains at the normal (focused) position. In the too-far condition, an error signal is created to return the objective lens to the normal position by applying the error signal to the focus servo control circuits. In the too-close condition, the opposite error signal is created, and applied to the focus servo to move the objective lens back to the normal position (thus establishing a zero error once again).

The photodiodes of Fig. 2-16 also provide *radial error signals*. As discussed in Chapter 5, there are two radial error signals, 1 and 2. Both signals are derived by summing the photodiode currents. Radial error-1 is the sum of the currents of diodes 3 and 4 ($i3 + i4$) with radial error-2 being the sum of diodes 1 and 2 ($i1 + i2$). The composite radial error signal is derived by subtracting the sum of one pair from the other pair: composite error = ($i3 + i4$) $-$ ($i1 + i2$). This composite error is applied to the radial tracking coil (through the radial tracking servo) to control the rotating arm (keeping the beam centered on the track of pits and flats).

2-4.2 Slide-type Optics

Figure 2-19 shows the components for typical slide-type optics. When the laser diode is activated, light is emitted and passes through a *collimator lens*. The function of this collimator lens is to take the light rays of the laser beam and make them parallel, as shown in Fig. 2-20. (In this case, the laser is considered as a point source.) The parallel rays from the collimator lens enter the *diffraction grating*. A diffraction grating is a screen containing a very large number of very narrow slits, uniformly spaced at distances only a few times the wavelength of the laser beam. When a beam of light passes through narrow slits, the exiting beam not only continues in a straight line, but also diffracts at different angles, as shown in Fig. 2-21. (If you were to focus the exiting beam on a screen, you would see a row of bars or dots with the center dot or bar being the brightest, and the dots on both sides decreasing in intensity.) For our purposes, think of the diffraction grating as a device that splits the beam into many different beams.

In the optics of a CD player, we are concerned with the main center beam (central image) and the two beams (first-order image) that are to the immediate right and left of the center beam. The center beam is used for reproduction of the audio, tracking, and focusing, while the two first-order beams are used for radial tracking only.

The three beams from the diffraction grating go through a *beam splitter*

2-4 Optical Pickup or Readout 49

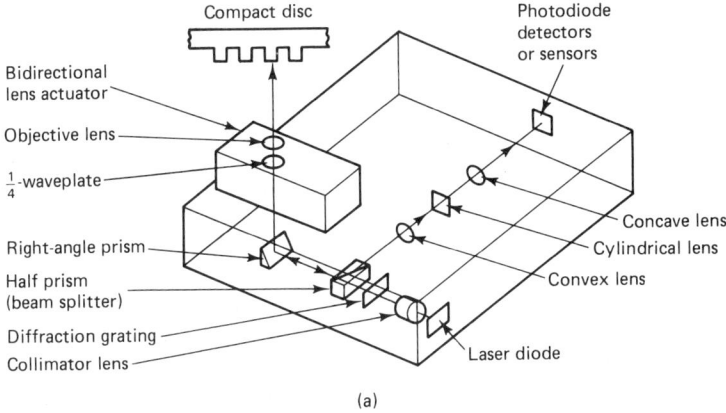

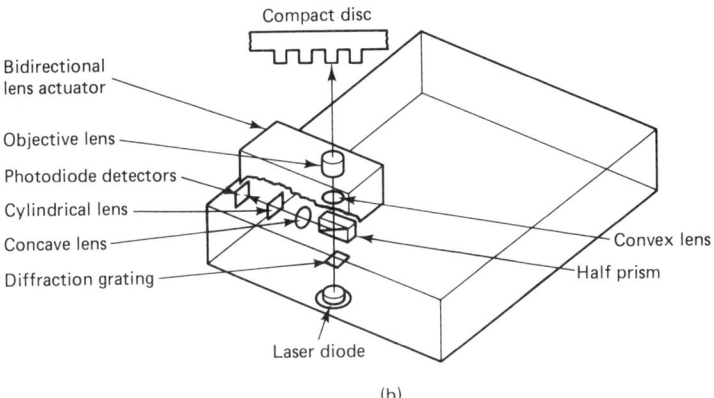

FIGURE 2-19 Components for typical slide-type optical pickups.

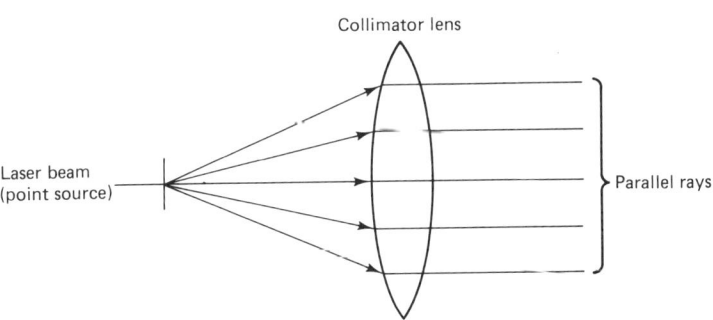

FIGURE 2-20 Function of collimator lens.

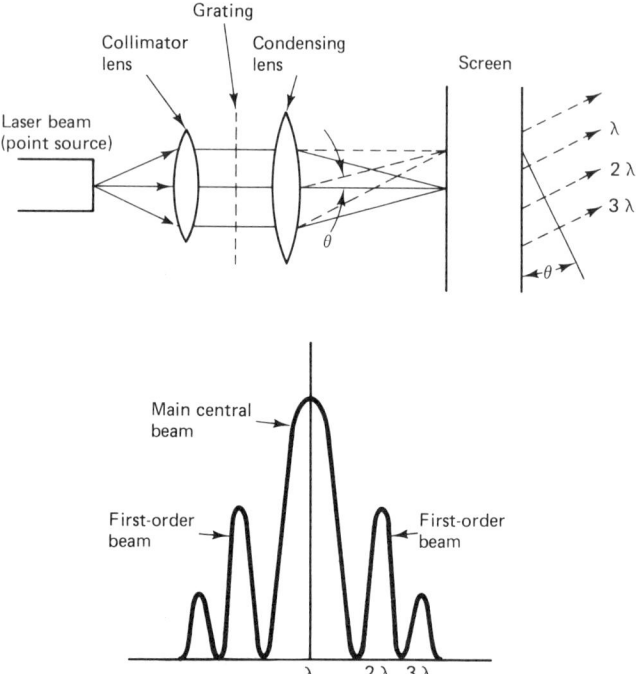

FIGURE 2-21 Function of diffraction grating.

(also called a *half prism*). The beam splitter is like a one-way mirror/window mounted at 45°. When the three beams approach the beam splitter, one side looks like a window. To the beams returning from the disc, the splitter looks like a mirror. The beams from the beam splitter are reflected (at a 90° angle) to the optics in the bidirectional lens actuator or servo by a *right-angle prism*.

The next device in the path from laser diode to disc is the ¼-*waveplate*. A ¼-waveplate is an optical device that produces and detects circularly polarized light. (This is the physics definition of the ¼-waveplate.) For our purposes, consider the ¼-waveplate as a device that changes some of the properties of the beam to distinguish which beam is being reflected from the disc, and which beam is coming from the laser diode.

Following the ¼-waveplate, the beams enter the objective lens which is used to focus the beams (all three) onto the pits and flats. As discussed, the objective lens is mounted on a mechanism that allows for two-axis mobility (up/down and side-to-side).

The beams reflect, or do not reflect, depending on the absence or presence of a pit. The reflected beam returns to the beam splitter (half prism) via the objective lens, ¼-waveplate, and right-angle prism. At the beam splitter, the beams reflect off the mirrored surface and are applied (at another 90°

angle) to the photodiodes through a series of lenses (typically convex, cylindrical, and concave).

Note that Fig. 2-19 shows two optical-pickup configurations. In Fig. 2-19a, the right-angle prism is required to reflect the beam up to the disc, since the laser diode is mounted on the side of the pickup assembly. In Fig. 2-19b, the right-angle prism and collimator lens are omitted since the laser diode is mounted directly in line with the objective lens. The configuration of Fig. 2-19b also has a different placement for the convex, concave, and cylindrical lenses.

No matter what configuration is used, the photodiodes provide the high-frequency signals, as well as the focus and tracking signals, to the CD player circuits. The focus and radial tracking functions for the slide-type optics are shown in Fig. 1-10 and described in Sec. 1-4. These are not repeated here. However, descriptions for both types of focus and tracking circuits (rotating-arm and slide-type) are included in Chapter 5.

3

USER CONTROLS, OPERATING PROCEDURES, and INSTALLATION

Although CD players are not difficult to operate or install, the basic procedures are quite different from those of a typical LP player or phonograph. This chapter describes the basic user controls and operating procedures for a cross section of CD players, both top-load and front-load. We also discuss typical installation procedures and precautions. A careful study of these procedures will help you to understand operation of the CD player circuits (which are discussed in Chapter 5) and mechanical assemblies (Chapter 6).

Keep in mind that you must study the operating controls and indicators for any CD player you are troubleshooting. This book describes "typical" controls and indicators, but there are subtle differences in operation you must consider. For example, the disc compartment of some players must be closed manually, while most others are automatic. In some players, the compartment closes automatically when the PLAY button is pressed. In other players, you must push the OPEN/CLOSE button (to close the compartment) before you press PLAY. There is nothing more frustrating than troubleshooting a failure symptom when the player is supposed to work that way!

3-1 LEAKAGE CURRENT TESTS

Before placing a CD player in use (for service or normal home use) it is recommended that you measure possible leakage current. Such leakage indicates that the metal parts of the player are in electrical contact with one side of the power line. If the leakage problem is severe, it can result in damage to the player, or possible shock to anyone touching the exposed metal parts. There are two recommended current tests: *cold check* and *hot check*. You should perform at least one of these safety checks before releasing the player to a customer (after service or when the player is first sold).

3-1.1 Cold Leakage-current Check

With the a-c plug removed from the power source, place a jumper across the two a-c plug prongs as shown in Fig. 3-1. Set the a-c power switch to on. Using an ohmmeter, connect one lead to the jumpered a-c plug, and touch the other lead to each exposed metal part (metal cabinet, screw heads, metal overlays, control shafts, etc.), particularly any exposed metal parts having a return path to the chassis. Most player manufacturers recommend that you always check from the power plug to the outside of the output connector on the rear panel.

For a typical CD player, exposed metal parts with a return path to the chassis should have a minimum resistance reading of about 500 kΩ. Any resistance substantially below this value indicates an abnormality that requires corrective action. There are exceptions, of course. For example, the center terminal of the output connector (both L and R terminals) could possibly be 50 kΩ to match the input of the stereo amplifier.

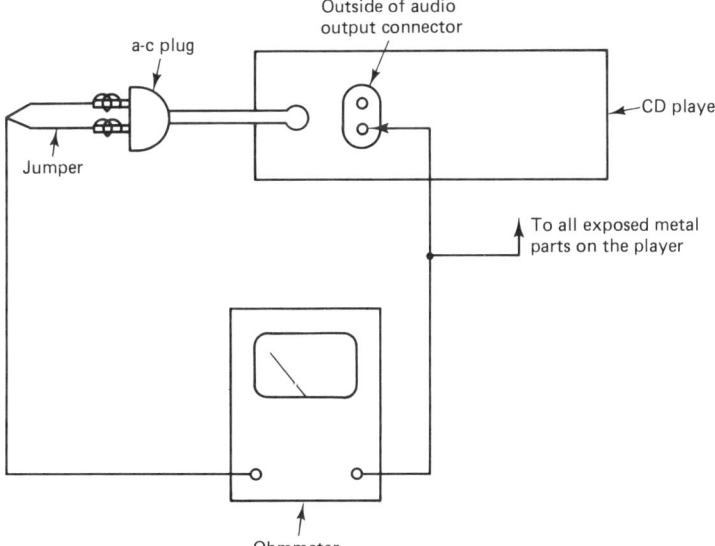

FIGURE 3-1 "Cold-check" circuit for CD player leakage-current tests.

54 User Controls, Operating Procedures, and Installation

At the other extreme, exposed metal parts that do not have any return path to the chassis are usually an indication of an open circuit. Generally, any reading above about 5 to 6 MΩ should be suspect.

3-1.2 Hot Leakage-current Check

Using the diagram of Fig. 3-2 as a reference, measure a-c leakage current with a milliammeter. Leave switch S1 open and connect the player power plug to the test connector. Immediately after connecting the player, measure any leakage current with switch S2 in both positions. Set the player switches (at least the player power switch) to on when making the leakage current measurements. Now close switch S1 and immediately repeat the leakage current measurements in both positions of switch S2 (and with the player switches on). Allow the player to reach normal operating temperature and repeat the leakage current tests. In any of these tests, the leakage current should not exceed about 0.5 mA (for a typical CD player).

If possible, check the stereo amplifier and loudspeakers to be used with the player for possible leakage. Use the same procedure as described for the player. To avoid shock hazards, do not connect a CD player to any stereo amplifier or loudspeakers that show excessive leakage current.

3-1.3 Alternate Hot Leakage-current Checks

If you do not want to use the procedures of Sec. 3-1.2, there are three practical alternatives.

First, you can use a commercial leakage tester, such as the Simpson 229 or RCA WT-540A. Be sure to follow the manufacturers' instructions to use these instruments.

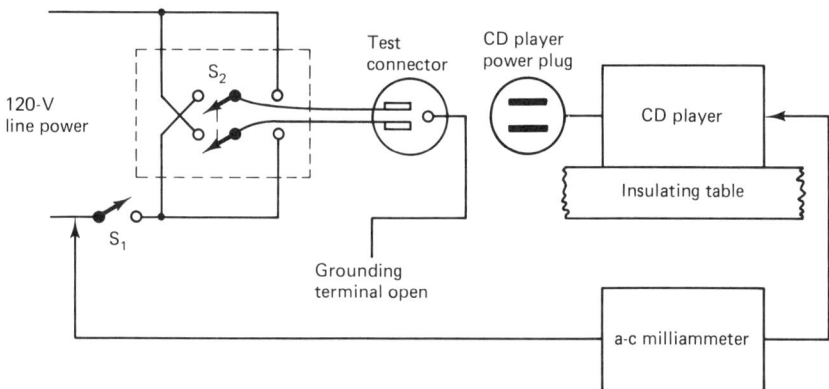

FIGURE 3-2 "Hot-check" circuit for CD player leakage-current tests.

Second, you can use a battery-operated a-c milliammeter. The Data Precision 245 digital multimeter is suitable for this job.

Finally, you can measure leakage current by measuring the voltage drop across a resistor as shown in Fig. 3-3. If you use an analog meter, the meter must have an accurate low-voltage scale, since the voltage indication should not exceed 0.75 V (across a 1.5-kΩ resistor). The Simpson 250 or Sanwa SH-63Trd are examples of passive VOMs that are suitable. Nearly any battery-operated digital multimeter (with a 2-V a-c scale) should also be suitable.

3-2 TRANSIT OR SHIPPING SCREW

Most CD players have a transit or shipping screw used to hold the optical pickup in place when the player is moved or shipped. Without such a screw, the rotating arm or slide can move back and forth, causing possible damage to the delicate optics. Typically, the transit screw is accessible from the bottom of the player, as shown in Fig. 3-4.

Before using the player (for normal home use or service), turn the player on the side and remove the transit screw. In some players, the screw is captive and cannot be removed (the screw is to be loosened only). In other players, the screw is supposed to be left in place (after it is loosened), but can be removed if you keep turning the screw. In other players, the screw is supposed to be removed. Be sure not to lose the screw. (It is the customer's job to lose the screw.)

When transporting or shipping the player, make sure the screw is properly installed. Typically, the screw can be installed only when the optical pickup is in one position (the at-rest or secured position). For example, you must turn on the power, make sure there is no disc installed, and then shut the tray,

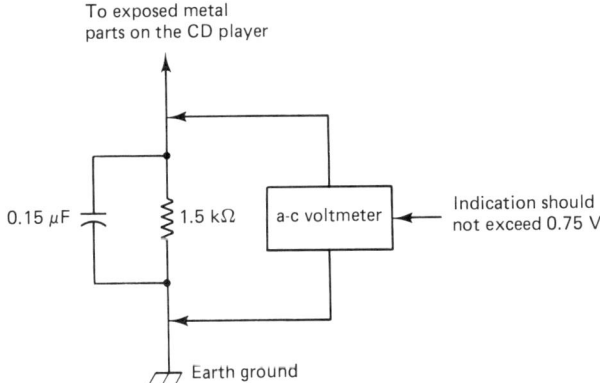

FIGURE 3-3 Using an a-c voltmeter to measure leakage current.

56 User Controls, Operating Procedures, and Installation

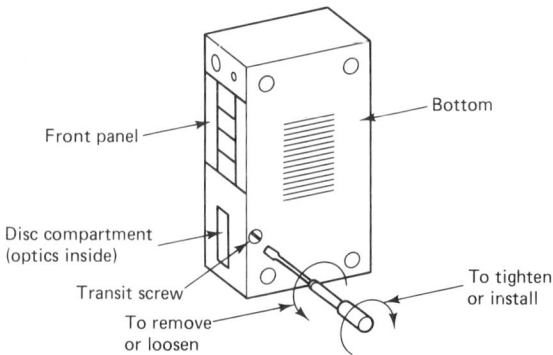

FIGURE 3-4 Removing and tightening or installing the transit screw (shipping screw).

drawer, lid, or door electrically. With the optical pickup in this secured position, turn off the power, stand the player on end, and then install the screw as shown in Fig. 3-4. Typically, the screw must be rotated two or three turns to be removed and tightened.

The transit screw (also called the shipping screw) brings up an obvious problem. When the customer brings in a CD player to the shop for service, he or she will probably forget the screw, or not tighten it, possibly damaging the optics. The opposite occurs if you tighten the screw upon returning the player to a customer. When they get the player home, they will promptly call you with a complaint that the player "no longer works after you fixed it!" You must patiently explain these facts to the customer. Good luck!

3-3 EXTERNAL CONNECTIONS

External connections between the CD player and stereo amplifier are usually made at the back of the player as shown in Fig. 3-5. Typically, a *pin cord* is supplied with the player for the connections between the player's L and R stereo outputs and the amplifier's inputs. Although the connections are very simple, certain precautions must be observed for all players. *Always connect the player output to the amplifier CD/AUX input or the TAPE PLAY input. Never connect the player to the PHONO input of the amplifier.*

The output from the player is about 2V. This audio voltage could damage the amplifier and/or speakers, and will overdrive the amplifier. Even on those CD players where the output is adjustable, the impedance of the player (typically 50 kΩ) is best matched to the CD/AUX inputs of the amplifier.

Make certain to connect the L output of the player to the L input of the amplifier (and the R output to the R input). Usually, the pin cord is color-coded, but even you can make a mistake.

Always switch off the power before making or breaking connections be-

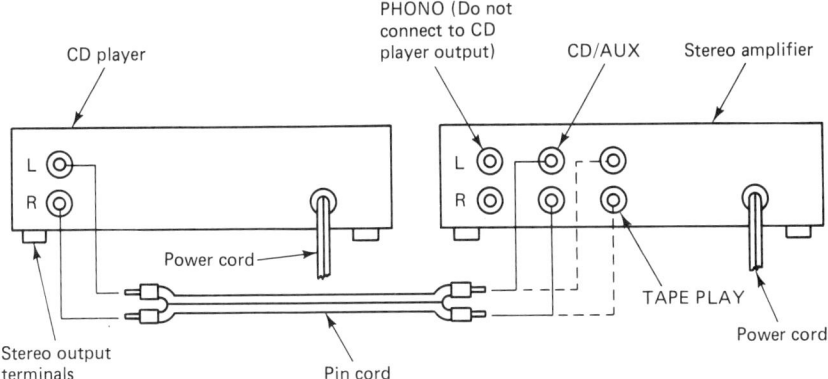

FIGURE 3-5 Typical external connections between the CD player and stereo amplifier.

tween the player and amplifier. Connect the power cord to the auxiliary power outlet on the rear panel of the stereo amplifier, or to any power outlet, whichever is convenient.

3-4 GENERAL OPERATING AND INSTALLATION NOTES

The following precautions and tips should be followed when operating any CD player. Chapter 4 also includes a series of precautions and tips that applies primarily to service and handling.

Check that the operating voltage of the CD player is identical with the voltage of the local power supply. Some CD players can be operated at 120, 220 and 240 V, while other players must be operated at one specific line voltage. Usually, there are special connections, or switch settings, required for dual-voltage players. Always check the service and/or operating literature for such connections or settings. Figure 3-6 shows the power-line connections for a CD player with a rear-panel voltage selector switch. Note that the correct tap on the player power transformer is selected by the switch.

When the CD player is not in use, turn off the power. This conserves energy and extends the life of the player. Unplug the player from the power outlet if the player is not to be used for an extended period.

The player produces strong magnetic fields. Do not place video or audio cassettes on or near the player.

Do not install the player near heat sources such as radiators or air ducts, or in a place subject to direct sunlight, excessive dust, mechanical vibration, or shock.

Good air ventilation is essential to prevent internal heat buildup in the player. Place the player where adequate air circulation is assured. Pay particular attention to the top ventilation holes (which should never be obstructed).

58 User Controls, Operating Procedures, and Installation

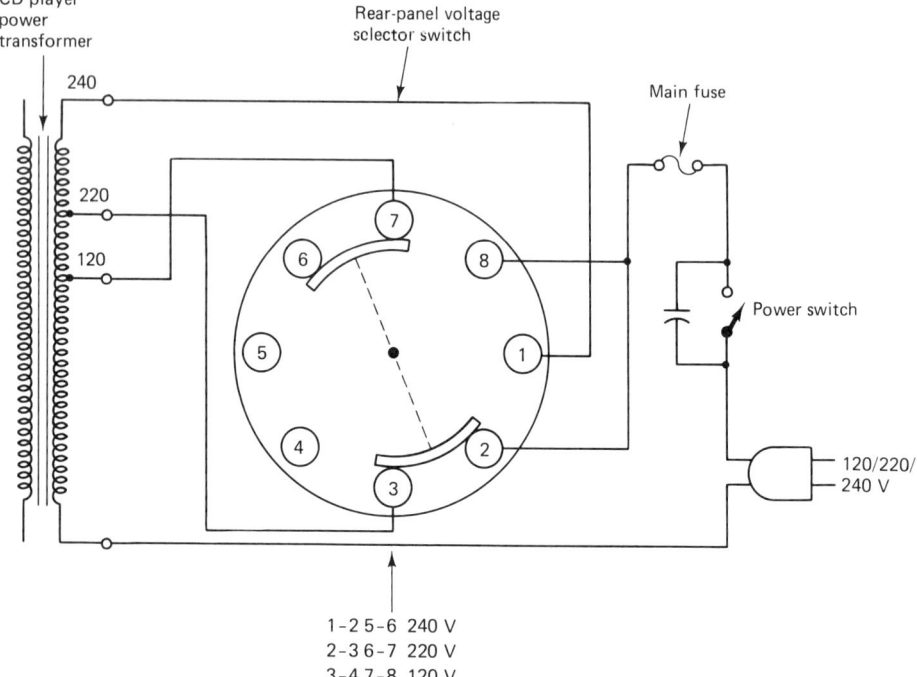

FIGURE 3-6 Typical power-line connections for a CD player with a rear-panel voltage selector switch (shown in 220-V position).

Do not place the player on a soft surface, such as a rug, which might block the bottom ventilation holes.

If the player is brought directly from a cold to a warm location, or is placed in a very damp room, *moisture may condense on the optical-pickup lenses.* The player will not operate properly (if at all) should the lenses become fogged. In such a case, remove the disc and leave the player turned on for about an hour to evaporate the moisture.

Although the compact discs are not delicate, and should last forever, they should be handled with some care. For example, always handle the disc by the edges as shown in Fig. 3-7. Try to avoid touching the rainbow-colored surface. Smudges or other dirt on this surface can reflect the laser beam and cause dropouts or other undesired performance. Do not stick paper or tape on the labeled surface. While such paper or tape will not hurt the disc, the paper/tape can get caught on the disc clamp or drive. Do not expose the disc to direct sunlight or heat sources such as hot-air ducts, or leave a disc in a car parked in direct sunlight (where there can be considerable rise in temperature). Before playing, clean the disc with a soft cloth. Most CD players include a

3-4 General Operating and Installation Notes 59

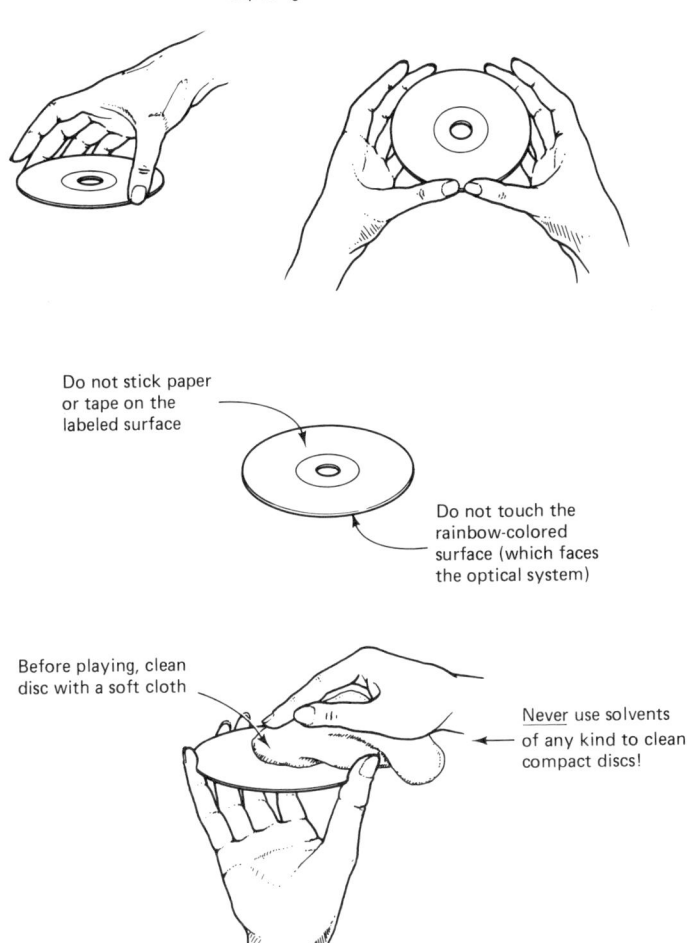

FIGURE 3-7 Handling compact discs.

cleaning cloth (usually packaged along with the pin cord and operating instruction manual). After playing, store the disc in its case.

Never use solvents such as benzine, thinner, commercially available cleaners, or antistatic spray intended for LP records. Any of these can eat through the sealant and destroy the disc. However, there are cleaners specifically designed for compact discs, as discussed in Sec. 4-4.

Some CD players cause interference to radio and television reception.

Usually this problem can be eliminated if the player is moved a few feet away from the radio or TV.

3-4.1 Setting the Volume Controls

Probably the most important operating precaution to those not familiar with CD players involves setting the volume controls. The dynamic range of a CD player is much greater (90 dB or better) than any LP record player or phonograph, and the peaks are recorded with hi-fi. Also, you get a much greater signal-to-noise ratio (also 90 dB or greater) with a CD player. Background noise is practically eliminated in most CD players.

If you turn up the volume, either on the player or the stereo amplifier, while listening to a portion of the disc where no audio signals (or very low-level signals) are recorded, the speakers may be damaged when that portion of the disc with peak signals is played. Likewise, if you are listening with stereo headphones connected to the front panel of the player, and set the player volume in an attempt to hear background noise, you can drill a hole from ear to ear when you get to the audio peaks!

3-5 TYPICAL TOP-LOAD OPERATING CONTROLS AND INDICATORS

Figures 3-8 and 3-9 show the operating controls and indicators for two typical top-load CD players (similar to those shown in Figs. 1-1a and 1-1b). The following paragraphs describe the control and indicator functions.

3-5.1 Controls and Indicators for the Players of Figs. 3-8 and 3-9

The ON/OFF key or button is used to switch the player on and off.
   The PAUSE LED lights when the PAUSE key is pressed.
   The PROGRAM DISPLAY is an LED-bar display that indicates the number of selections on a disc. It is also used as an aid in compiling a program.
   The TRACK DISPLAY is an LED-bar display in which the LEDs light one at a time to indicate the selection in play, and is also used to locate selections for compiling a program.
   The REPEAT LED lights when the REPEAT key is pressed.
   The ERROR LED flashes to indicate an operating or programming error.
   The PLAY/NEXT key starts PLAY, and moves the player to the next selection when pressed.
   The PAUSE key is used for short-term interruptions during normal play.

3-5 Typical Top-load Operating Controls and Indicators 61

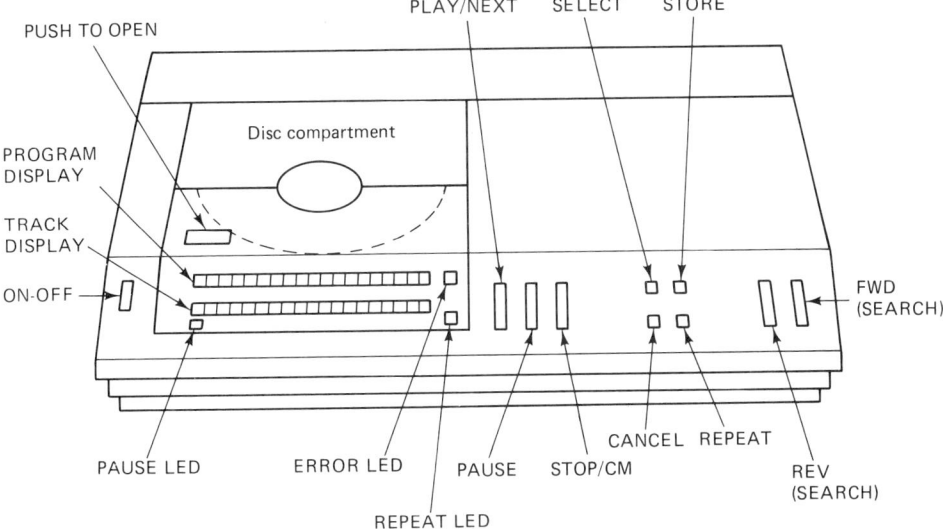

FIGURE 3-8 Operating controls and indicators for typical top-load CD player (similar to Fig. 1–1a).

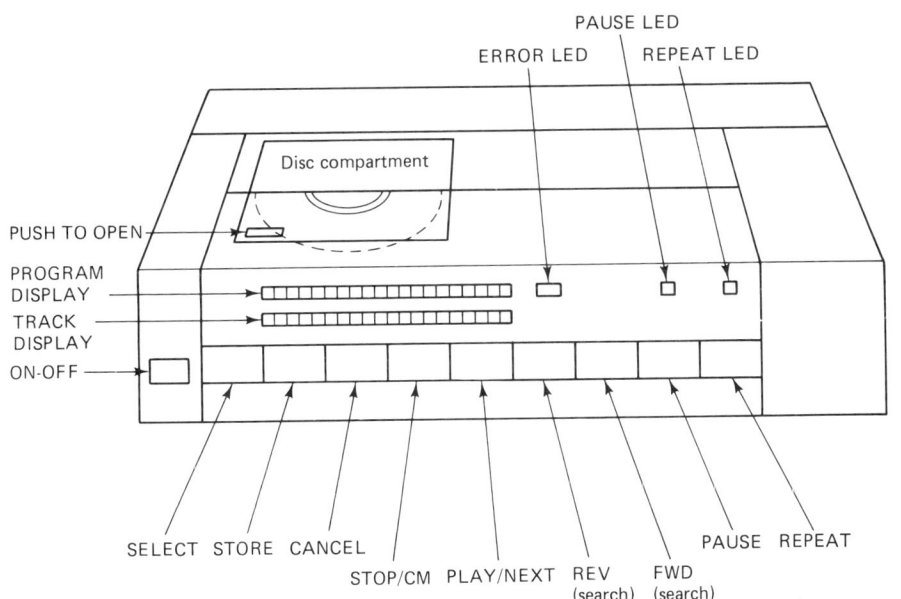

FIGURE 3-9 Operating controls and indicators for typical top-load CD player (similar to Fig. 1–1b).

When the PAUSE key is pressed, the sound stops but the disc motor continues to rotate.

The STOP/CM key is used for stopping the play during playback (STOP) and for erasing the memory for any program stored (CM, or clear memory).

The REPEAT key is used for repeating a disc or a programmed selection.

The FWD key is used for searching forward for a particular passage in a selection.

The REV key is used for searching backward for a particular passage in a selection.

The PUSH-TO-OPEN button (a rectangular boss on the cover of the disc compartment) is used to open the lid.

The SELECT key is used for selecting the number of the program at which play is to start, or for choosing certain selections in compiling a program.

The CANCEL key is used for canceling the selections not required for playback.

The STORE key is used for storing the selections into memory when compiling a program.

3-5.2 Typical Top-load Operating Functions

Note that the following operating functions and sequence apply to the players of Figs. 3-8 and 3-9, even though the front-panel configurations of the two players are quite different. Also note that both players have *two transit screws* rather than one. Both transit screws (located on the bottom) must be removed for normal operation and replaced when transporting the player. The transit screws should be stored in the documentation package along with other important documents that accompany the player. (Of course, every customer will follow this instruction!)

ON/OFF. Pressing the ON/OFF key turns the player on (all of the display LEDs turn on). Pressing the ON/OFF key again removes power from the player (all LEDs turn off).

PUSH-TO-OPEN. To open the disc compartment, press the PUSH-TO-OPEN button. The lid should open automatically. Remove the disc from its package or case and place the disc onto the turntable with the *reflective side down* (rainbow side down). Close the lid cover by pressing down on the cover (which will automatically lock when the normally closed position is reached).

PLAY/NEXT. With power on and a disc installed, press the PLAY/NEXT button. The disc should start to rotate, and the first TRACK LED should turn on. Play should continue from the first track to the last track (in order, unless the player is programmed to do otherwise). Typically, there are 15 (or less) tracks on a compact disc.

As soon as the contents of the disc is read and decoded by the player, the number of program LEDs change to correspond with the number of programs on the disc. For example, if there are only 10 programs on the disc, only 10 PROGRAM LEDs will turn on.

The PLAY/NEXT button can also be used to end the play of any program in progress. If the PLAY/NEXT button is pressed during a program, the player automatically moves to the next program. If there is no "next program" to be played, the ERROR LED flashes, and the player returns to the first track or program and begins play (unless programmed to do otherwise).

SELECT. To start the player at any location other than the beginning track or program, press and release the SELECT button. The TRACK LED will flash. Press and release the SELECT button again to move the TRACK LED one location forward. Successively pressing and releasing the SELECT button continuously moves the TRACK LED through the 15 program positions.

When the desired position is reached, the TRACK LED continues to flash for 10 seconds, after which time the flashing stops and the player returns to the normal start position (typically to track 1).

The PLAY/NEXT button must be pressed *before the end* of the 10-s time period to start the play at the selected program. When the PLAY/NEXT button is pressed (after SELECT has been used), the PROGRAM LEDs turn off one at a time until the selected program is reached. Play then begins at that point.

STORE. The STORE button is generally used in conjunction with the SELECT button. Once the track or program is reached with the SELECT button (as just described), the track can be stored into memory by pressing the STORE button. All of the PROGRAM LEDs turn off, except the one LED for the program stored in memory. Repeat the SELECT and STORE procedure for each track to be played.

Each time a program is stored into memory, the corresponding PROGRAM LED turns on so that the programmed tracks are progressively displayed. A track may be programmed into memory as many times as desired, up to the limit of the memory (15). The track stored in memory has the corresponding PROGRAM LED on continuously.

CANCEL. The CANCEL button is also used in conjunction with the SELECT button to allow for cancellation of programs stored in memory. This is done by moving the flashing TRACK LED (by pressing the SELECT button) to the corresponding PROGRAM LED, and then pressing the CANCEL button. For example, assume there are 15 programs on the disc (all 15 PRO-

GRAM LEDs are on), and you want to delete program 6. You press the SELECT button until the TRACK LED moves to program 6. You then press the CANCEL button. If you change your mind, or if a program is inadvertently canceled, you simply return the TRACK LED to the corresponding program (using the SELECT button) and press the STORE button. This restores the program back into memory.

STOP/CM. The STOP/CM button stops all operation of the player and clears the memory completely. The TRACK LED turns off, and all PROGRAM LEDs turn on. The player returns to the normal start position, and the disc stops rotating. You can then use the PLAY/NEXT, SELECT, STORE, and CANCEL buttons as described.

REV FWD. The REV (reverse) and FWD (forward) buttons allow the user to locate quickly a particular passage of a selection (track or program) being played. When the FWD button is *held down,* the optical pickup moves from the inside of the disc toward the outside. The opposite occurs when the REV button is held down.

Keep in mind that the REV and FWD buttons move the optical pickup within a program or track, but are not to be used when going from one track to another. For example, say that you are in the middle of program 3 and you want to play a passage somewhere near the beginning of program 3. You press and hold the REV button until you reach the desired passage. You then release the REV button, and play continues to the end of program 3. At that point, the player goes on to program 4 (or to whatever has been programmed next).

This points up the advantage of an elapsed-time display such as shown in Figs. 1-1b and 1-1c, compared to the basic LED-bar display shown in Figs. 3-8 and 3-9. With an elapsed-time display, it is relatively simple to find a particular passage within a track or program.

PAUSE. The PAUSE button is used to interrupt the program in progress for a short period of time. When PAUSE is pressed, the disc continues to rotate, but the audio is muted. Play is halted at the *last track played,* and the PAUSE LED turns on. Pressing the PAUSE button again, or pressing the PLAY/NEXT button, causes play to resume at (or near) the point of interruption. PAUSE should not be used if you want to interrupt play for an extended period.

REPEAT. The REPEAT button allows for complete play of the entire disc. However, the REPEAT button must be pressed *before the end of play.*

Programming sequence. On the players shown in Figs. 3-8 and 3-9 (and on most CD players), the user can select specific programs, play only those selected, and decide the playing sequence of those selected, instead of playing the complete disc. This is done by programming into memory the selection and sequence of play desired. The memory of the players shown in Figs. 3-8 and 3-9 accepts a maximum of 15 selections. Individual selections can be programmed to play more than once as long as the maximum of 15 plays is not exceeded.

In most players, programming the player is easier when the disc is stationary and the title list from the disc package or case is used. Of course, it is possible to program the player during normal operation, but this can interrupt the smoothness of playback.

There are two methods for programming the players of Figs. 3-8 and 3-9: the add-on method (SELECT and STORE) and the take-out method (SELECT and CANCEL).

With the add-on method of programming, the user stores the selections desired for play into memory. Add-on is best when only a few selections are desired or when changing the sequence of play.

With take-out programming, the user can erase the selections from memory that are not desired for play. Take-out is best when the majority of the selections on the disc are to be played and the sequence of play does not change.

3-6 TYPICAL FRONT-LOAD OPERATION (WITHOUT PROGRAMMING)

Figure 3-10 shows the operating controls and indicators for a typical front-load CD player (that shown in Fig. 1-1d). Note that this player does not include a program function. However, the player can skip from track to track in both forward and reverse directions and can move in both directions at fast speed. The player can also repeat play, if desired. The following paragraphs describe the control and indicator functions.

When you press the POWER button, power is applied to the player and all the indicators turn on. Power is removed and all the indicators turn off when the POWER button is pressed again.

When you press the OPEN/CLOSE button, the disc holder (tray) moves to the open or extended position (as shown in Fig. 1-1d). The disc tray moves back to the closed position (with a disc installed, hopefully) when the OPEN/CLOSE button is pressed again. The DISC SET indicator turns on when the disc is loaded. Note that the OPEN/CLOSE function cannot be used with the power off (since the tray is operated by a motor, as discussed in Chapter 6.

When you press the PLAY button (with power on and a disc in place), play starts at track or program 1 and continues to the last program, unless interrupted.

Press the PAUSE button for *temporary interruption* of play. Then press the PLAY button to resume play. If you press the PAUSE button when entering a selection of tracks, the pickup *moves to the start of the track selected*

66 User Controls, Operating Procedures, and Installation

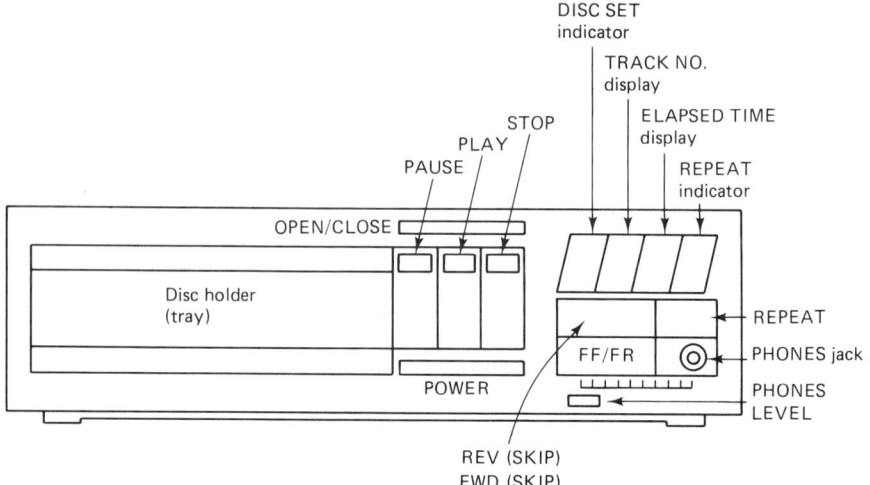

FIGURE 3-10 Operating controls and indicators for a typical front-load CD player, shown in Fig. 1-1d.

just before pushing. You can then begin play immediately at that point on the disc when you press the PLAY button.

When you press the STOP button, play stops, the disc stops spinning, and the pickup returns to the start position (over the innermost track, generally called track or program 1). So, if you want to resume play at any point other than at the beginning of the disc, use the PAUSE button rather than the STOP button.

The TRACK NO. display shows the number of the track or program, under the following conditions:

When the disc is first loaded, the TRACK NO. display shows the total number of tracks for the disc (typically up to 15).

During normal play, the TRACK NO. display shows the number of the track or program being displayed.

During fast forward (FF), fast reverse (FR), or PAUSE mode, the TRACK NO. display shows the track number for the current pickup position.

When the SKIP buttons are being used, the TRACK NO. display shows the track number being selected.

The ELAPSED TIME display indicates disc time, under the following conditions:

When the disc is first loaded, the ELAPSED TIME display shows the *total recorded playing time* for the disc (typically up to 1 hour).

During play, the ELAPSED TIME display shows the time elapsed from the start of the track being played to the current pickup position.

During FF, FR, and PAUSE modes, the ELAPSED TIME display shows the elapsed time within the track for the current pickup position.

When you press the REPEAT button, the REPEAT indicator turns on, and the disc is played again.

When you press the FWD (forward skip) button, the pickup skips forward to the *start of the track following the one to which you are listening*. Play resumes immediately at that point on the disc. If you press the FWD button again, the pickup moves to the start of the next track. You can repeat this process and move to the start of any desired track (after the one currently in play).

When you press the REV (reverse skip) button, the pickup skips back to the *start of the track to which you are listening*. Play resumes immediately at that point on the disc. If you press the REV button again, the pickup moves to the start of the track just prior to the current one. (If you are on track 4 when REV is pressed, the pickup moves to the start of track 3.) You can repeat this process and move to the start of any previous track.

When you press and hold the FF or FR buttons, the pickup is moved over any selected part of the disc. Play resumes immediately at the selected part of the disc. The FF/FR buttons are used to move to any point on the disc, not just to the start of a track or program.

The PHONES jack provides for connection of 8-Ω stereo headphones to the front panel. The PHONES LEVEL control sets the listening level for the stereo headphones (but *not* for the line output to the stereo amplifier).

3-7 TYPICAL FRONT-LOAD OPERATION (WITH PROGRAMMING)

Figure 3-11 shows the operating controls and indicators for a typical front-load CD player with programming functions (the Hitachi DA-800). Note that this player also includes an *antishock function* (controlled by a switch located on the rear panel). The following paragraphs describe the control and indicator functions.

When you press the POWER button, power is applied to the player and all the indicators turn on. Power is removed and all the indicators turn off when the POWER button is pressed again.

You press the OPEN/CLOSE button when loading or unloading a disc. The power must be on for the OPEN/CLOSE button to operate.

The PLAY button is pressed to begin disc play. During play, the PLAY indicator lights. Unless otherwise programmed or interrupted, play continues from program 1 to the last program.

Press the PAUSE button for temporary interrupt of play. The PAUSE indicator then lights. Press the PLAY button to resume play.

Press the STOP/CLEAR button to stop play and to simultaneously clear the memory of any program.

To select a program sequence, press the PROGRAM button and then

68 User Controls, Operating Procedures, and Installation

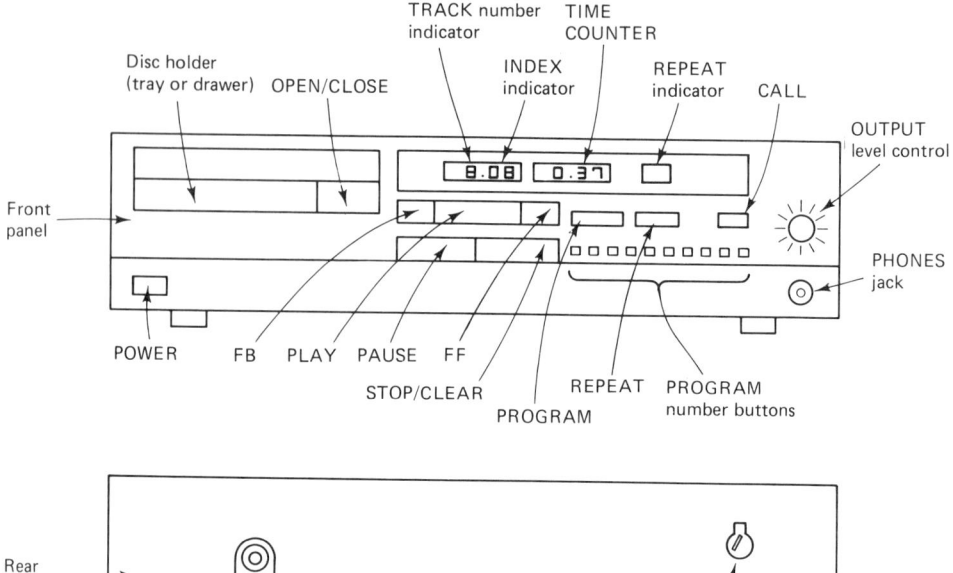

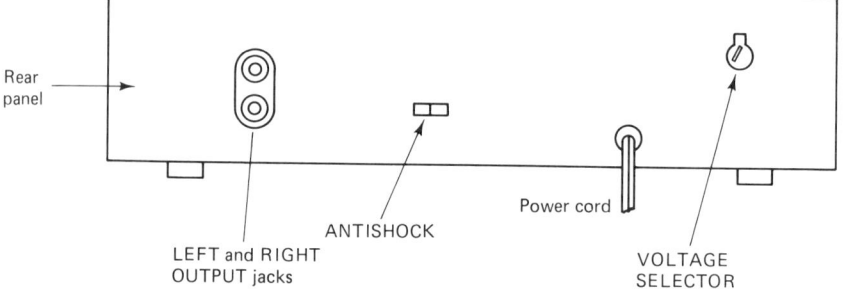

FIGURE 3-11 Operating controls and indicators for a typical front-load CD player with programming functions.

select the desired program sequence by pressing individual PROGRAM number buttons (0 to 9).

Press the FB (fast back) button to reverse play quickly. Press the FF (fast forward) button for quick forward play.

Connect stereo headphones to the front-panel PHONES jack. Connect the rear-panel RIGHT and LEFT OUTPUT jacks to the stereo amplifier's input terminals (CD, AUX, or TAPE PLAY). *Do not* connect to the PHONO input of the stereo amplifier. The front-panel OUTPUT level control sets the output level to *both* the headphones and the rear-panel OUTPUT terminal. This permits you to adjust the volume level to match that of other audio components that may be played through the stereo amplifier (such as an LP turntable, tape deck, cassette deck, etc.).

Press the CALL button to check the programmed numbers or, during play, to check the next program to be played.

Press the REPEAT button to perform repeat play. The REPEAT indicator then lights.

The TRACK number indicator shows the track number being played or, during programming, the track numbers of programmed selections. The INDEX indicator shows the index number of the selection being played. The TIME COUNTER shows the playing time in minutes (MIN) and seconds (SEC).

The rear-panel VOLTAGE SELECTOR permits the player to be operated on either 120 or 240 V. Make sure that the VOLTAGE SELECTOR is in the proper position before connecting the rear-panel power cord.

The rear-panel ANTISHOCK switch is normally set to off. The antishock function is used when the player is in a location with large amounts of vibration, or when the disc has excessive eccentricity. Sound skipping can occur in players operated under either of these conditions. With the ANTISHOCK switch on, the antishock circuits (described in Chapter 5) compensate for vibration and disc eccentricity. However, the antishock circuits can actually increase sound skipping if the disc is badly scratched. So, when troubleshooting a sound-skipping system, always check the ANTISHOCK switch setting.

3-8 TYPICAL REMOTE-CONTROL OPERATION

Figure 3-12 shows the operating controls and indicators for a typical remote-control unit (the Sony RM-101 Remote Commander used with the Sony CDP-101). The following paragraphs describe the control and indicator functions. Note that the front-panel operating controls and indicators for the CDP-101 are similar (but definitely not identical) to those for other players described thus far. So remember what we discussed in the introduction to this chapter. *Study the operating controls and indicators for the CD player you are servicing.*

When using the remote control of Fig. 3-12, you must apply power to the player (using the front-panel POWER button), and then install a disc (using the front-panel OPEN/CLOSE button). With one touch of the OPEN/CLOSE button, the disc compartment opens for loading. The indicator on the OPEN/CLOSE button lights while the compartment is opening. Another touch of the OPEN/CLOSE button closes the disc compartment (with a disc inside, if you are on your toes). The DISC SET indicator in the front-panel display window flickers when the disc compartment is moving. When the disc compartment has closed with a disc in place (in the standby mode), and during disc play, the DISC SET indicator stays on steadily. The player can be turned off at any time by pressing the POWER switch.

Once power is applied and a disc is in place, you can take control of the player using the remote unit. However, there are certain precautions to be observed.

First, point the remote unit toward the front-panel REMOTE SENSOR and indicator at the angles shown in Fig. 3-12. Note that the shorter the dis-

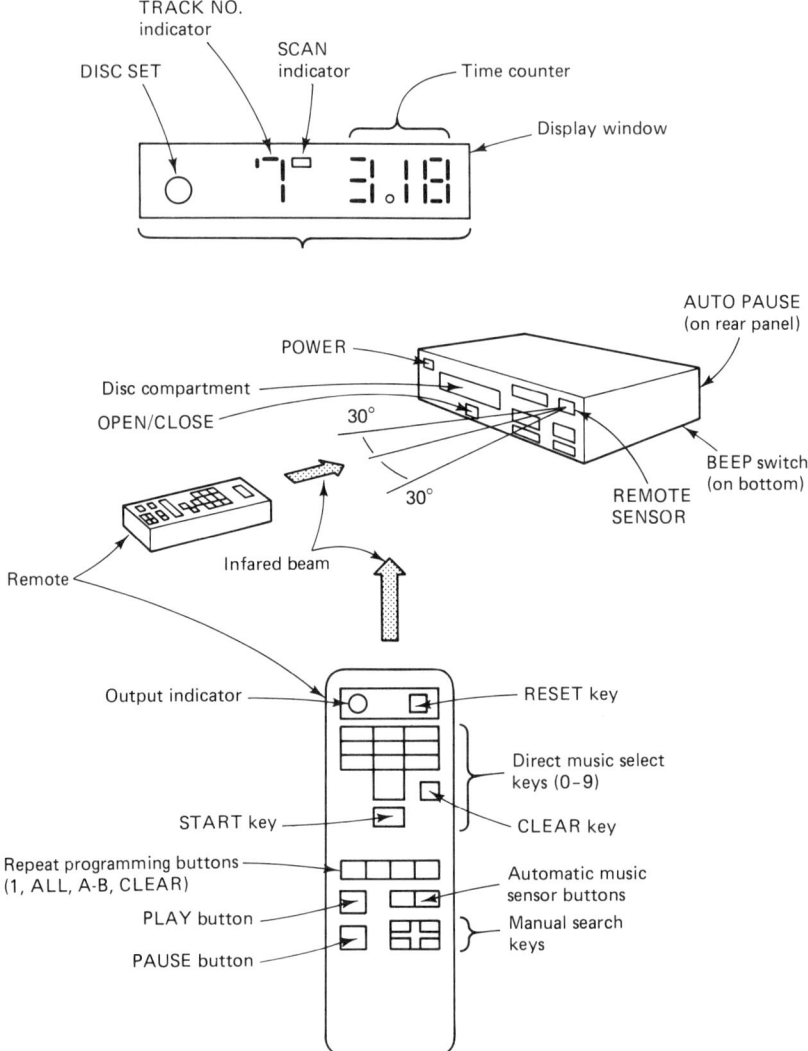

FIGURE 3-12 Operating controls and indicators for a typical remote-control unit.

tance between the remote unit and the sensor, the wider the angle within which the player can be controlled. The infrared beam transmitted by the remote is picked up at the REMOTE SENSOR. The sensor indicator blinks to indicate that a function key on the remote unit has been pressed.

The player has a BEEP switch located on the bottom. When the BEEP switch is set to ON, a signal tone (an annoying buzz) is sounded each time a signal from the remote unit is received. You can eliminate the buzz by setting the BEEP switch to OFF.

3-8 Typical Remote-Control Operation

The player also has an *automatic pause function* (controlled by a rear-panel AUTO PAUSE switch) which operates when the player is used with an optional microphone amplifier. The AUTO PAUSE switch is normally set to OFF. When set to ON, the player pauses automatically after each selection. The automatic pause mode is released when the remote unit START key is pressed. Keep this in mind when troubleshooting a "the player stops after each selection" symptom. Set the AUTO PAUSE switch to OFF.

Press the PLAY button to start normal disc play. Press the PAUSE button to pause during play. When the RESET button is pressed, disc play is reset to the beginning of the first selection, and the player stands by. The *output indicator* lights when the remote commander is operating.

The *manual search keys* permit you to move rapidly forward or backward across the disc to find a particular selection. You can monitor the disc sound reproduced in forward or in reverse (at a high speed) while searching (during play). When you release a manual search key, normal-speed play resumes (during play) or the player returns to the pause mode (during pause).

The *automatic music sensor buttons* permit you to go back to the beginning of the previous selection, or forward to the beginning of the next selection.

The *repeat programming buttons* permit you to repeat all or part of the disc. Press the 1 button to repeat the selection being played. Press the 1 button again to release the repeat function. Press the ALL button to repeat all selections on the disc. Press the ALL button again to release repeat. Press the A-B button to repeat play between two specific points on the disc. One touch of the A-B button establishes the "A" or start point of repeat play. Another touch of the A-B button sets the "B" or end point of repeat play. Press the CLEAR button to cancel this form of repeat play.

The *direct-music-select keys* permit you to select a particular program using the remote commander. These keys are similar to the corresponding program keys on the player front panel and produce corresponding track-number indications on the display window. However, the remote keys operate somewhat differently. During remote operation, you first select the desired track number by pressing the corresponding 0-9 keys. For example, if you want selection of track 8, press the 8 key. If you want a selection with a number higher than 9, press the corresponding two keys. For example, if you want track 14, press keys 1 and 4. If you press the wrong number key when selecting a particular track with the remote commander, press the CLEAR key, and that number is erased (cleared). (Note that this direct-music-select CLEAR key is not to be confused with the repeat-programming CLEAR button.) Once the track is selected, press the START key immediately to start play. If you do not press the START key within a few seconds, or if you press any other key, the selected number is automatically cancelled. Also, if you select a track number not available on the disc, the selected number is canceled when the START key is pressed.

4

TEST EQUIPMENT, TOOLS, and ROUTINE MAINTENANCE

This chapter describes the test equipment and tools you will need for CD player service. We also discuss routine maintenance for CD players. Keep in mind that the information in this chapter is general in nature. If you are going to service a particular player, get all the service information you can on that player. Likewise, if you plan to go into CD player service on a large scale, study all the applicable service literature you can find; then, when all else fails, you can follow instructions. We discuss adjustments (both mechanical and electrical) using the tools and test equipment in Chapters 6 and 7. We also discuss use of the tools and test equipment for troubleshooting in Chapter 7.

4-1 SAFETY PRECAUTIONS IN CD PLAYER SERVICE

In addition to a routine operation procedure (for both test equipment and the player), certain precautions must be observed during operation of any electronic test equipment during service. Many of these precautions are the same for all types of test equipment; others are unique to special test instruments, such as meters, oscilloscopes, and signal generators. Some of the precautions are to prevent damage to the test equipment or to the circuit where the service operation is being performed. Other precautions are to prevent damage to you.

4-1.1 General Safety Precautions

The following general safety precautions should be studied thoroughly and then compared with any specific precautions called for in the test-equipment or player service literature and in the related chapters of this book.

Warning symbols on test equipment. There are two standard international warning symbols found on *some* test equipment. One symbol, *a triangle with an exclamation point at the center,* advises the operator to refer to the operating manual before using a particular terminal or control. (This same symbol is used in player literature to signify a circuit location or part that is critical for safety.) The other symbol, *a zigzag line simulating a lightning bolt,* warns the operator that there may be dangerously high voltage at a particular location, or that there is a voltage limitation to be considered at that point. Always observe these warning symbols. Unfortunately, use of the symbols is not universal, particularly on older test equipment.

Metal cases. Many service instruments are housed in metal cases. These cases are connected to the ground of the internal circuit. For proper operation, the grounded terminal of the instrument should always be connected to the ground of the player being serviced. Make certain that the player chassis is not connected to either side of the a-c line, or to any point above ground, by using the leakage current check of Sec. 3-1.2.

High voltages. Remember that there is always danger in servicing players that operate at hazardous voltages, especially if you pull off covers with the player cord connected. Fortunately, most player circuits operate at potentials well below the line voltage, since the circuits are essentially solid state. Even the laser beam in a CD player is generated by a solid-state diode. (This is in contrast to videodisc player laser beams, which are generated by a laser tube and require high voltage.) However, a line voltage of 120 V is sufficient to cause serious shock and possibly death! Always make some effort (such as reading the service literature) to familiarize yourself with the player before servicing it, bearing in mind that high voltage may appear at unexpected points in a defective player.

Remove power. It is a good practice to remove power before connecting test leads to high-voltage points. It is preferable to make all service connections with the power removed. Since this is generally impractical, be especially careful to avoid accidental contact with player circuits. Keep in mind that even low-voltage circuits may be a problem. For example, a screwdriver dropped across a 12-V line in a solid-state circuit can cause enough current to burn out a major portion of the player, possibly beyond repair. Of course, this problem is nothing compared to the possibility of injury to yourself! Working with one hand away from the player and standing on a properly insulated floor lessens the danger of electrical shock.

Capacitors may store a charge large enough to be hazardous. Discharge filter capacitors *before* attaching test leads. (Please make sure that you have turned off the power before you discharge the capacitors!)

Remember that leads with broken insulation offer the additional hazard of high voltages at exposed points along the leads. Check test leads for frayed or broken insulation before working with them.

To lessen the danger of accidental shock, disconnect test leads immediately after the test is completed.

Remember that the risk of severe shock is only one of the possible hazards. Even a minor shock or touching a hot spot can put you in danger of more serious risks, such as a bad fall or contact with a source of higher voltage.

The experienced service technician guards continuously against injury and does not work on hazardous circuits unless another person is available to assist in case of accident.

Even if you have considerable experience with test equipment used in service, always study the service literature of any instrument with which you are not thoroughly familiar.

Use only shielded leads and probes. Never allow your fingers to slip down to the metal probe tip when the probe is in contact with a "hot" or "live" circuit.

Isolation transformer. Use an isolation transformer for all service procedures.

Avoid vibration and mechanical shock. Most electronic test equipment is very delicate. Likewise, the mechanical portions of a CD player are vulnerable to any kind of shock or vibration. Not only can the mechanical parts be damaged, but the parts can also be thrown out of adjustment by rough handling. This is particularly true of the *optical components in CD players,* and is the primary reason for the transit screw described in Sec. 3-2. Although the optical and pickup components are designed to be operated continuously, these components are not designed to be in contact with tips of screwdrivers, Allen wrenches, and the like.

Study the circuit being serviced before making any test. Try to match the capabilities of the instrument to the circuit being serviced. For example, if the circuit under test has a range of measurements to be made (ac, dc, RF, modulated signals, pulses, or complex waves), it is usually necessary to use more than one instrument. Most meters measure d-c and low-frequency signals. If an unmodulated RF carrier is to be measured, use an RF probe. If the carrier to be measured is modulated with low-frequency signals, a demodulator probe must be used. If pulses, square waves, or complex waves are to be measured, a peak-to-peak reading meter can possibly provide meaningful indications, but an oscilloscope is the logical instrument. Or you can try a really novel approach and use the test instrument recommended in the player service literature!

4-1.2 Leakage Current Tests

Before placing a CD player in use for service (or normal home use), it is recommended that you measure possible leakage current, as described in Sec. 3-1.

4-1.3 Basic Handling and Service Precautions

The following precautions apply to all types of CD players, and are to be observed *in addition* to any precautions described in the service literature.

Handling and storage. Avoid using the player in the following places: extremely hot, cold, humid, or dusty areas; near appliances generating strong magnetic fields (or ones that are affected by such fields); places subject to vibration; and poorly ventilated places. Do not block the ventilation openings. Do not place anything heavy on the player. Do not place anything that might spill on the top cover of the player. Use an accessory cover (if available) to prevent dust and dirt from accumulating on the player. Use the player in the horizontal (flat) position only. Do not lubricate player motors or any point not recommended for lubrication in the service literature. (*Generally, very little lubrication is required for CD players.*)

When reassembling any player, always be certain that all the protective devices (nonmetallic control knobs, shield plates, etc.) are put back in place. When service or testing is required, observe the original lead dress (wire routing, etc.). *Pay particular attention to the wiring associated with the disc compartment, doors, and optics (slide or rotating arm).* Since all these components are subject to constant movement, *wire routing is critical.* For example, wires can be caught in gears or subjected to excessive strain if not properly routed.

Always follow the packing/shipping instructions found in the service literature. Always use the transit or shipping screws described in Sec. 3-2 to hold the optics in place during transit. Figure 4-1 shows some typical packing instructions.

Moisture condensation. Try to avoid using a player immediately after moving the player from a cold place to a warm place, or soon after heating a room where it was cold. Either of these conditions can cause moisture condensation. Excessive condensation (which is rare) can cause possible damage

76 Test Equipment, Tools, and Routine Maintenance

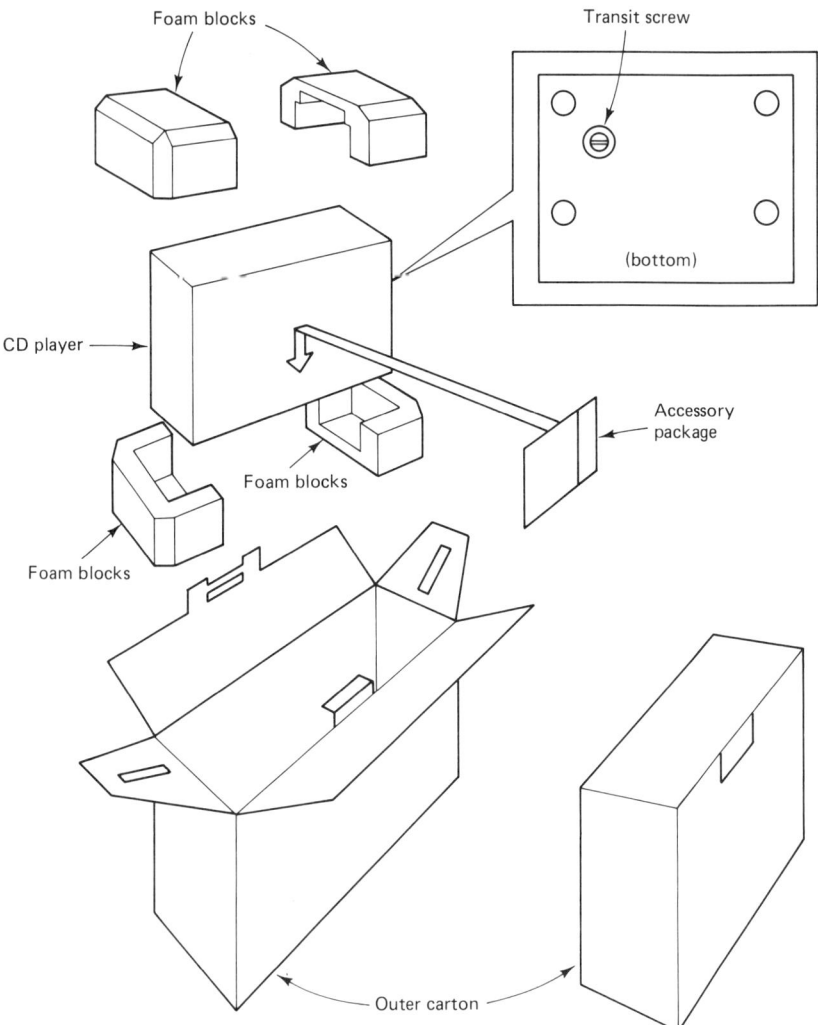

FIGURE 4-1 Typical packing instructions for a CD player.

to circuits. More likely, condensation can fog the lenses in the optical system. You can clean the surface of the objective lens (with a clean, soft, dry cloth), but the remaining lenses are not accessible. You must wait until the condensation evaporates from the internal lenses.

Interlocks. Do not defeat any type of interlock on a player (at least not permanently). If you must override an interlock during service (try to avoid this), *do not permit the player to be operated by others without all protective* *devices correctly installed and functioning.* Servicers who defeat safety features or fail to perform safety checks may be liable for any resulting damage.

Design alterations. Do not alter or add to the mechanical or electrical design of a CD player. Design alterations, including (but not limited to) addition of auxiliary audio output connections, cables, accessories, and the like, might alter the safety characteristics of the player and create a hazard to the user. Any design alterations or additions may void the manufacturer's warranty and make the servicer responsible for personal injury or property damage resulting therefrom.

Product safety notices. Many electrical and mechanical parts in CD players have special safety-related characteristics, some of which are often not evident from visual inspection, and the protection they give cannot necessarily be obtained by replacing parts with components rated for higher voltage, wattage, and so on. The manufacturers often identify such parts in their service literature. One common means of such identification is *shading on the schematics and/or parts lists,* although all manufacturers do not use shading, nor do they limit identification to shading. For example, some manufacturers use a *dark black pattern* on those areas of their printed-circuit-board copper patterns that require special care in repair. Other manufacturers use an *exclamation point within a triangle* for critical parts.

Always be on the alert for any special product safety notices, special parts identification, and the like. Use of a substitute part that does not have the *same safety characteristics* (not just the same electrical or mechanical characteristics) might create shock, fire, and/or other hazards. A simple way to solve the problem is to use the part recommended in the service literature.

Good electronic service practices. The author assumes that you are already familiar with good electronic service practices (removing or disconnecting the power cord before replacing circuit boards and modules, installing heat sinks as required on solid-state devices, connecting test-instrument ground leads to chassis ground before connecting the test instrument, and so on). The author also assumes that you can handle electrostatically sensitive (ES) devices (such as FETs, MOS and CMOS chips, etc.); that you can solder and unsolder ICs, transistors, diodes, and the like; and that you can repair circuit-board copper foil as needed. If any of these seems unfamiliar to you, please, please do not attempt to service any CD player, especially the author's.

4-1.4 Laser Safety

CD players have a laser diode which creates two possible service hazards. First, the laser produces a *potentially dangerous light beam.* As in the case of any other very intense light source, direct exposure to a laser beam can cause *per-*

manent eye injury or skin burns. Second, the *light beam produced by the laser diode is invisible* (in contrast to the red light beam produced by a laser tube used in videodisc players). Since the diode beam is invisible, you are never quite sure when the beam is present.

CD players are designed to be operated without any exposure to the beam by the operator. This is essentially true for the servicer, with one major exception. If you gain access to the laser (by removing covers, opening the disc compartment, etc.), and keep power on the laser diode (by overriding interlocks, etc.) the beam may get you! None of this should frighten you, but the problems should keep you on your toes when servicing. It is still the servicer's job to exercise all caution to avoid any direct exposure to the laser beam.

U.S. federal law (and the laws of most countries) requires that servicers be advised of possible laser dangers. There is at least one warning label on all players, and often more than one (typically one on the outer cover, and one in the disc compartment near the objective lens). The label reads something like "CLASS 1 LASER PRODUCT; Product complies with DHHS rules CRF subchapter J part 1040:10 at date of manufacture; DANGER: Invisible laser radiation when open and interlock failed or defeated. AVOID DIRECT EXPOSURE TO BEAM." On CD players designed for Canadian use, the warning label is strengthened by a *light-burst pattern within a triangle.*

Always be on the alert for these warning labels when servicing a CD player. Equally important, make sure all shields and covers are in place, and that interlocks are working *before you turn over a CD player to the customer.*

In addition to producing a potentially dangerous beam, a laser diode produces strong *electromagnetic radiation.* This is not usually harmful to people, but can be disastrous to magnetic tape, some wristwatches, and anything else affected by magnetic fields. Do not bring magnetic tape reels, audio or video cassettes, or any other magnetic device near when servicing a CD player, particularly when the player covers and shields are off. To be on the safe side, keep all magnetic tape away from a CD player, even with all covers in place.

Checking and adjusting the laser diode. Most CD player manufacturers recommend some means of checking the laser diode without having to monitor the beam with a light meter. Study the service literature for the CD player you are servicing to find the recommended procedure. In the absence of any specific recommendations, here are some tips on checking the laser diode.

Even though the laser beam is invisible, the diffused laser beam is usually visible at the objective lens (the lens appears to glow when the beam is on). Also, when power is first applied to the optical servo circuits, the objective lens moves up and down (usually three times, as discussed in Chapter 5) to focus the beam on the disc reflective surface. So if you apply power and see the objective lens moving, it is reasonable to assume that the laser is on and producing enough power.

This check procedure brings up some obvious problems. First, on most players, if you open the disc compartment and gain access to the objective lens, you must override at least one interlock. Next, many players have some provision for shutting down the player optics if there is no disc in place, so you must override this feature. Most important, *never, never look directly into the objective lens with power applied! Keep your eye at least 30 cm (12 in.) from the lens!* The purpose of the objective lens is to focus the beam sharply onto the disc. The lens can also focus the beam sharply into your eye!

Figure 4–2 shows the recommended procedure for both the laser-diode check and focus-search check on a typical CD player (the Sony CDP-101). For both checks, you must remove the outer cover and locate the objective lens.

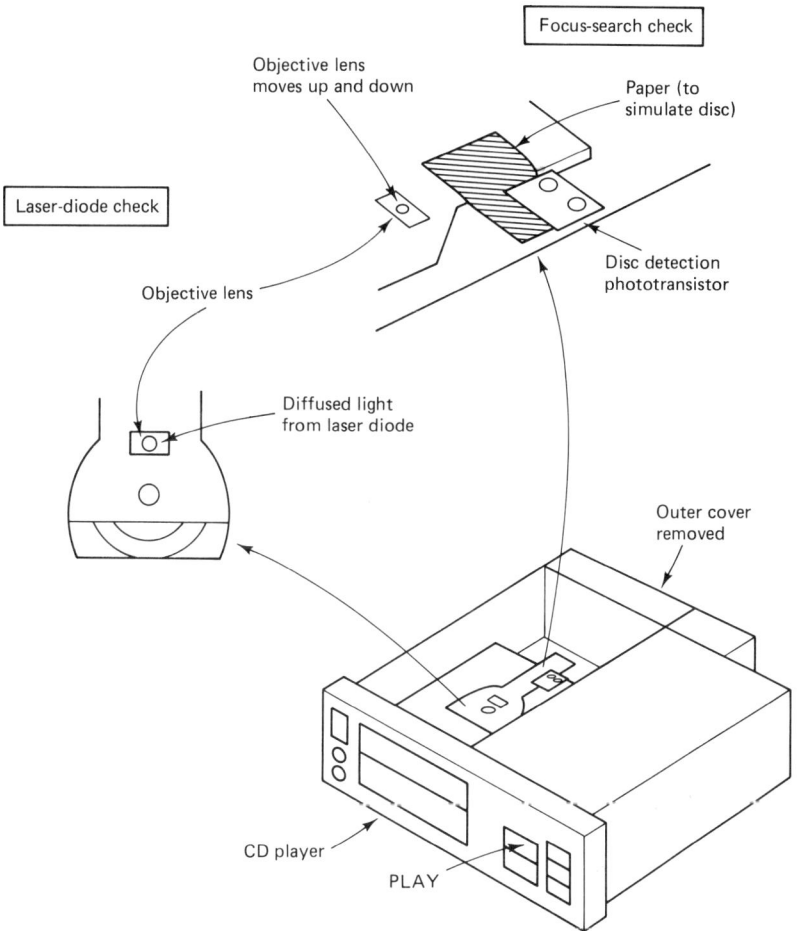

FIGURE 4–2 Laser-diode and focus-search checks for typical CD player.

To check the laser diode, you ground the LD ON (laser diode on) terminal on the system-control microprocessor (IC102) and check for diffused light at the objective lens.

To check the focus search, you block the disc detection phototransistor with paper (to simulate a disc in place), and press the PLAY button. You then check that the laser emits light, and that the objective lens moves up and down. Keep in mind that not all CD players have such a disc-detection system. Also, the objective lens may not always move the same number of times or by the same amount. (In some players you can barely see lens movements.)

Other manufacturers recommend that you monitor the EFM signal (or some similar signal) to check the laser diode. If the EFM signal is normal, or can be adjusted to a normal value, the laser diode must be functioning normally. We describe such checks and adjustments in Chapter 7.

4-1.5 Handling the Laser Diode and Optical System During Replacement

As in the case of MOS/CMOS devices, the laser diode can suffer electrostatic breakdown because of the potential differential generated by the charged electrostatic load on clothing and the human body. Keep in mind that the laser diode is usually considered part of the optical system or pickup assembly, and that most player manufacturers recommend replacement of the complete pickup assembly as a package. Most manufacturers do not supply individual parts for the optical system.

Figure 4–3 shows recommended procedures for handling the optical system of a typical CD player (the Sony CDP-101) when the entire assembly is to be replaced. The following notes supplement the procedures shown.

Place a conductive sheet on the workbench. (In the case of the CDP-101, the black sheet used as the repair parts wrapping is a conductive sheet.)

Place the player on the conductive sheet so that the chassis touches the sheet. This makes the chassis (and pickup assembly) the same potential as the conductive sheet.

Place your hands on the conductive sheet. This makes your hands the same potential as the sheet.

Remove the optical-system block from the bag (which is made of conductive material).

Perform the necessary work on top of the conductive sheet. Be careful that clothing does not touch the optical pickup block.

If practical, use a wrist strap (Fig. 4–3) with an impedance-to-ground of less than one megohm (1 MΩ). The work table and/or conductive sheet should also have an impedance-to-ground of less than 1 MΩ. Keep in mind that static electricity builds up on clothing, and is often not fully drained off, even with wrist straps and grounded work tables.

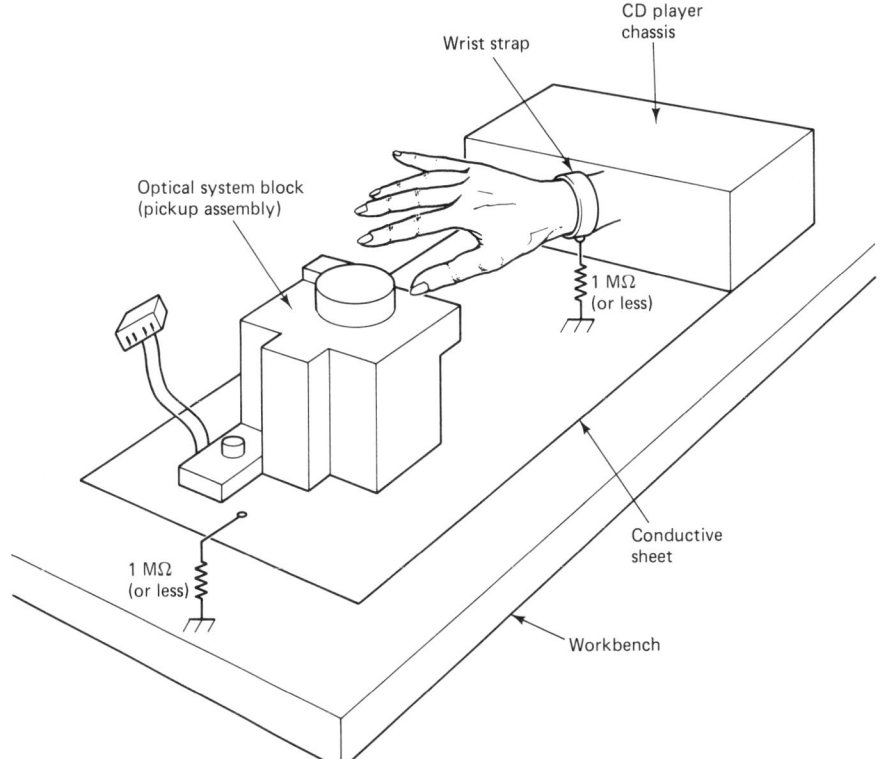

FIGURE 4-3 Handling the optical system (pickup assembly) of a typical CD player.

4-2 TEST EQUIPMENT FOR CD PLAYER SERVICE

The test equipment used in CD player service is basically the same as that used in audio service and in other fields of electronics (television, radio, etc.). That is, most service procedures are performed using meters, generators, oscilloscopes, distortion meters, power supplies, and assorted clips, patch cords, and so on. Theoretically, all CD player service procedures can be performed using conventional test equipment, provided that the generators cover the appropriate frequencies, the oscilloscopes have the necessary gain and bandpass characteristics, and so on.

For these reasons, we do not go into test equipment in this book. If you have a good set of test equipment suitable for conventional audio/stereo work, you can probably service any CD player. However, there are two items that can prove most valuable in CD player service: *test discs* and a *shop-standard stereo amplifier with speakers*. A *distortion meter* is also helpful, but not absolutely essential.

4-2.1 Test Discs

Many CD player manufacturers provide test discs (also known as *check discs, reference discs,* or *alignment discs*) as part of their recommended test equipment and/or tools. (Some manufacturers even recommend the test disc of another manufacturer!) A test disc is essentially a standard compact disc with several very useful signals recorded at the factory using very precise test equipment and signal sources. You play the test disc on a player being serviced and note the response, and/or use the signals to perform alignment and adjustment of the player. With the proper test disc, you can often eliminate the need for your own signal sources (signal generators, audio generators, etc.).

One major problem with test discs is the lack of standardization. You will probably need several test discs if you service many different models of CD players. The alignment procedures found in most service literature call for signals not available on all test discs. The only way around this problem is to *use the recommended test disc in all cases*. Of course, you can use any known good disc for a final, after-service check of the player, but this will not give you the necessary signals to perform the adjustment procedures.

4-2.2 Shop-Standard Stereo Amplifier with Speakers

If you are already in audio/stereo service work, you probably have at least one shop-standard amplifier and speaker system. Any system suitable for final checkout of turntables, tape players, and so on will do the job for a CD player. Keep in mind that the CD player output to the amplifier is about 2 V (either variable or fixed, depending on the player).

4-2.3 Distortion Meters

If you are already in audio/stereo service, you probably have distortion meters (and know how to use them effectively). This is not true for many TV service shops. As a practical matter, you can probably get by without a distortion meter in CD player service. If distortion is severe, you will hear it. If the distortion is below a level where it can be heard, you can generally forget the problem. (Of course, if you have a customer with a "golden ear," an accurate distortion meter is an excellent tool for settling "discussions" concerning his or her CD player's performance, especially after service.)

4-3 TOOLS FOR CD PLAYER SERVICE

Figure 4-4 shows some typical tools and fixtures recommended for field service of CD players. These tools are available from the player manufacturer. In some cases, complete tool kits are made available. There are other tools

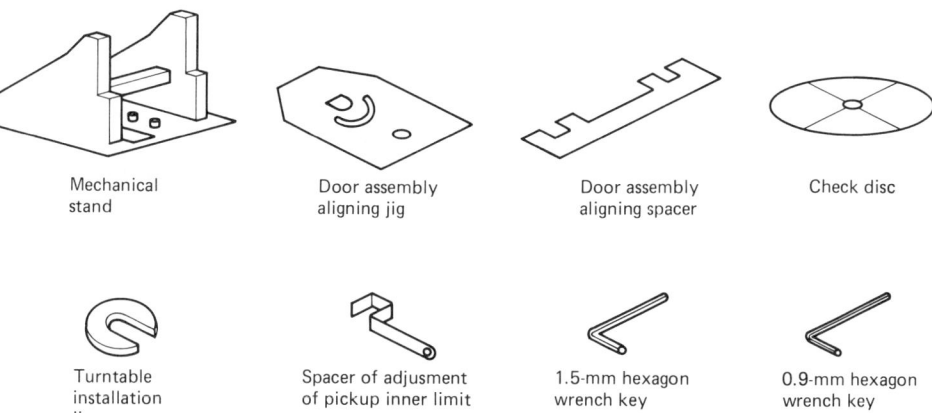

FIGURE 4-4 Typical tools and fixtures recommended for field service of CD players.

and fixtures used by the manufacturer for both assembly and service of the CD player. These factory tools are not available for field service (not even to factory service centers, in some cases). This is the manufacturer's subtle way of telling service technicians that they should not attempt any adjustments (electrical or mechanical) not recommended in the service literature.

The author strongly recommends that you take this subtle hint! There are many horror stories told by factory service people concerning the "disaster area" CD players brought in from the field. Most of these problems are the result of tinkering with mechanical adjustments, particularly in the optical-pickup system. (However, there are some technicians who can destroy a player with a simple electrical adjustment.) One effective way to avoid this problem is to use only recommended factory tools and perform only recommended adjustment procedures. We discuss some "typical" adjustment procedures, including use of special tools, in Chapters 6 and 7.

In addition to possible special tools, the mechanical sections of CD players are disassembled, adjusted, and reassembled with common hand tools, such as wrenches and screwdrivers. Keep in mind that most CD players are manufactured to Japanese *metric standards* and your tools must match. For example, you will need metric-sized Allen wrenches and Phillips screwdrivers with the Japanese metric points.

4-4 PERIODIC MAINTENANCE FOR CD PLAYERS

There is considerable disagreement among CD player manufacturers concerning the need for periodic maintenance or routine checks. At one extreme, a certain manufacturer recommends replacement of a few parts after a given number of playing hours or playing times. (They recommend that the optical pickup be replaced at 5000 hours of playing time, and all motors be replaced after 10,000 plays.) At the other extreme, another manufacturer recommends no periodic replacement, cleaning, lubrication, or adjustment of any kind. "Fix it if it breaks down" is the rule. (It is fair to say that this rule will probably be observed religiously.)

Somewhere between these two extremes, other manufacturers recommend adjustment (electrical and/or mechanical) only as needed to put the player back in service, or when certain parts or assemblies have been replaced. However, most CD player manufacturers recommend a complete checkout, using the recommended test disc, after any service.

The author has no recommendations in the area of periodic maintenance except that you follow the manufacturer's recommendations. The author also realizes that the general public regards a CD player in the same way it does an audio/stereo player or TV (that is, "bring it in for service when it breaks down"). However, there are some maintenance procedures that apply to the users of CD players, which we describe here.

Cleaning the player. Use a soft, clean cloth to wipe off dust and dirt accumulated on the player. If necessary, moisten a soft cloth with diluted neutral detergent to remove heavy dirt. *Never* use paint thinner, benzene, or other solvents, since any of these solvents react with the surface and cause color changes and melting.

Objective lens care. The objective lens is a key part of a CD player. Note that the lens surface must be clean (and free of moisture) in order to maintain the best performance. *Never* try to touch the lens surface. Keep the disc compartment closed to keep out dust and dirt. Open the disc compartment only when inserting and removing the disc. If too much dust or dirt accumulates on the objective lens, sound quality can be degraded. Dust can be removed from the objective lens with an air blower for a camera lens.

CD care. Since compact discs are played without physical contact with the playing surface, the discs do not wear out or degrade in quality. Also, light scratches or small amounts of dust or fingerprints have almost no effect on the sound. A heavy accumulation of dust and dirt, however, can reduce sound quality and should be removed by wiping both sides of the disc with a clean, soft, dry cloth. As a matter of routine cleanliness, all discs should be handled by their edges, the same as a phonograph record.

There are a variety of playability problems associated with warped CDs. Such problems including hanging (or sticking), skipping, and loss of focus. A severely warped disc can even hit the player lid or objective lens. To determine if a CD is warped, lay the disc on a flat surface and press down in the center. If no movement is detected, turn the disc over and again press down in the center. If movement is detected on either side, measure the amount of movement. The distance should be no more than about 3 mm (that is just under ⅛ in.). If the amount of warpage is over 3 mm, the disc is defective and should be replaced.

Use the following procedure to remove scratches from the surface of a compact disc:

Use a polishing compound such as Simonize Pre-Softened White Polishing Compound. *Do not use* a rubbing compound. Place a small amount of polishing compound on a dampened, soft cloth. With a light, circular motion, rub the surface of the disc until the scratched or marred area is restored to a luster.

If the compound begins to dry on the disc surface before the scratch is removed, add a small amount of water to the cloth and continue rubbing.

After the marred area has been restored, remove any residue from the disc surface with a clean, dry cloth.

If this procedure does not remove the scratch or mar, the disc is probably beyond hope.

Note that when CDs are subjected to extremely cold temperatures (try to avoid this), you should allow 45 minutes to 1 hour for the disc to return to room temperature before playing.

FIGURE 4-5 Nagaoka CD-1100K CD Cleaning System (Courtesy Nagaoka & Co., and Microfidelity Inc.).

To prevent warpage, always store CDs (in their jackets) on edge. A standard phonograph record rack is a good storage device for CDs. *Do not* stack CDs, if at all possible.

CD cleaners. The author has no recommendations for or against CD cleaners such as the one shown in Fig. 4-5. A soft, dry cloth will remove most dirt found on a CD. However, if a CD is exposed to very dirty fingers, liquids, tobacco smoke, fire and brimstone, and so on, you may need help in restoring the disc. There are even cases where a mold has started to form, or the disc surface has oxidized. Cleaners can be of great help in these extreme cases.

The CD cleaning system shown in Fig. 4-5 includes a liquid cleaning solution (dispensed from a pump-type container), a lamb's leather cleaning pad, and a brush. The liquid is dispensed on the disc surface in premeasured sprays by the pump. (A pump is used since gas-propelled sprays tend to evaporate, extracting heat from the disc. This evaporation/cooling effect can lead to the formation of surface cracks.) The lamb's-leather pad is then used to wipe the disc (from center to edge); it absorbs both the liquid and most dirt (which floats within the liquid). Finally, the cleaning brush is used to remove any solid particles picked up by the cleaning liquid. This treatment leaves the disc clean, and with some protection. The CD cleaning system of Fig. 4-5 is manufactured by Nagaoka & Co., Ltd., members of the CD group.

5

TYPICAL CD PLAYER CIRCUITS

This chapter describes the theory of operation for a number of CD player circuits. The circuits described here include power supply, laser control, error signal, high-frequency (HF) amplifier, focus servo, turntable motor amplifier, radial servo, and signal processing.

By studying the circuits found in this chapter, you should have no difficulty in understanding the schematic and block diagrams of similar CD players. This understanding is essential for logical troubleshooting and repair, no matter what type of electronic equipment is involved. No attempt has been made to duplicate the full schematics for all circuits. Such schematics are found in the service literature for the particular CD player. Instead of a full schematic, the circuit descriptions are supplemented with partial schematics and block diagrams that show such important areas as signal flow paths, input/output, adjustment controls, test points, and power-source connections. These are the areas most important in service and troubleshooting. By reducing the schematics to these areas, you will find the circuit easier to understand, and you will be able to relate circuit operation to the corresponding circuit of the CD player you are servicing.

Note that, as shown in the illustrations of this chapter, many circuit parts are contained within integrated circuits (ICs). These ICs carry reference designations such as IC1, IC181, IC6101, or possibly Q1,Q2 (although Q is generally reserved for transistors). Both the ICs and the transistors are mounted on printed circuit (PC) boards, as are other individual or discrete circuit parts. The PC boards may carry their own reference designation or be identified by some abbreviation. This arrangement, as presented in the illustrations of this chapter, is typical for many present-day CD players.

5-1 TYPICAL TOP-LOAD AND DRAWER-TYPE FRONT-LOAD CIRCUITS

The majority of the circuits described in the following sections are part of the CD players shown in Figs. 1-1a through 1-1c. It is assumed that you have already studied the basic functions of CD players, as described in Chapter 1, as well as the encoding, decoding, and optical readout system described in Chapter 2, and the operating controls and procedures of Chapter 3.

Figure 5-1 shows the major sections of the players in block form. The front-panel keyboard, in conjunction with the keyboard data-command circuits, provides the necessary commands to start the player operation.

Several sequences of events occur when the play command is received by the servo microprocessor. The first events that occur together are the laser-on and focus-on commands. The laser-on command turns the laser power supply on, but only during play operation. This prolongs the life of the laser diode. The focus-on command is applied to the focus servo and turntable motor amplifiers simultaneously. The focus servo amplifier raises the objective lens to the maximum upper limit. The turntable motor amplifier starts the turntable motor rotating.

The servo microprocessor provides commands to the focus servo to move the lens down from the maximum position, and to the radial servo amplifier to move the radial tracking control arm to the normal start position. The downward movement of the lens brings the light beam to the correct focal point to detect the pits and flats on the disc. The light beam is then intensity modulated, reflected back through the system, and detected by the prism at a 90° angle onto the photodiodes.

The light beam landing on the photodiodes is converted to electrical energy, which provides four error signals and a high-frequency (HF) signal. The four error signals are applied to the error sum amplifier, where three error signals are derived. One of the three error signals is used to control the focus servo and to maintain correct focus throughout play. The two other signals are used to control the radial servo amplifier, which controls movement of the radial tracking arm. The two radial error signals are applied to the radial AGC (automatic gain control) and offset circuit, which provides uniform gain for the radial control system and compensates for any variation in the shape of the beam spot. The error signals are converted by the AGC/offset circuit to usable levels for the servo microprocessor, which provides radial control signals to the radial servo amplifier during special functions of the player (such as when searching forward or reverse, during pause, and play/next).

5-1 Typical Top-load and Drawer-type Front-load Circuits

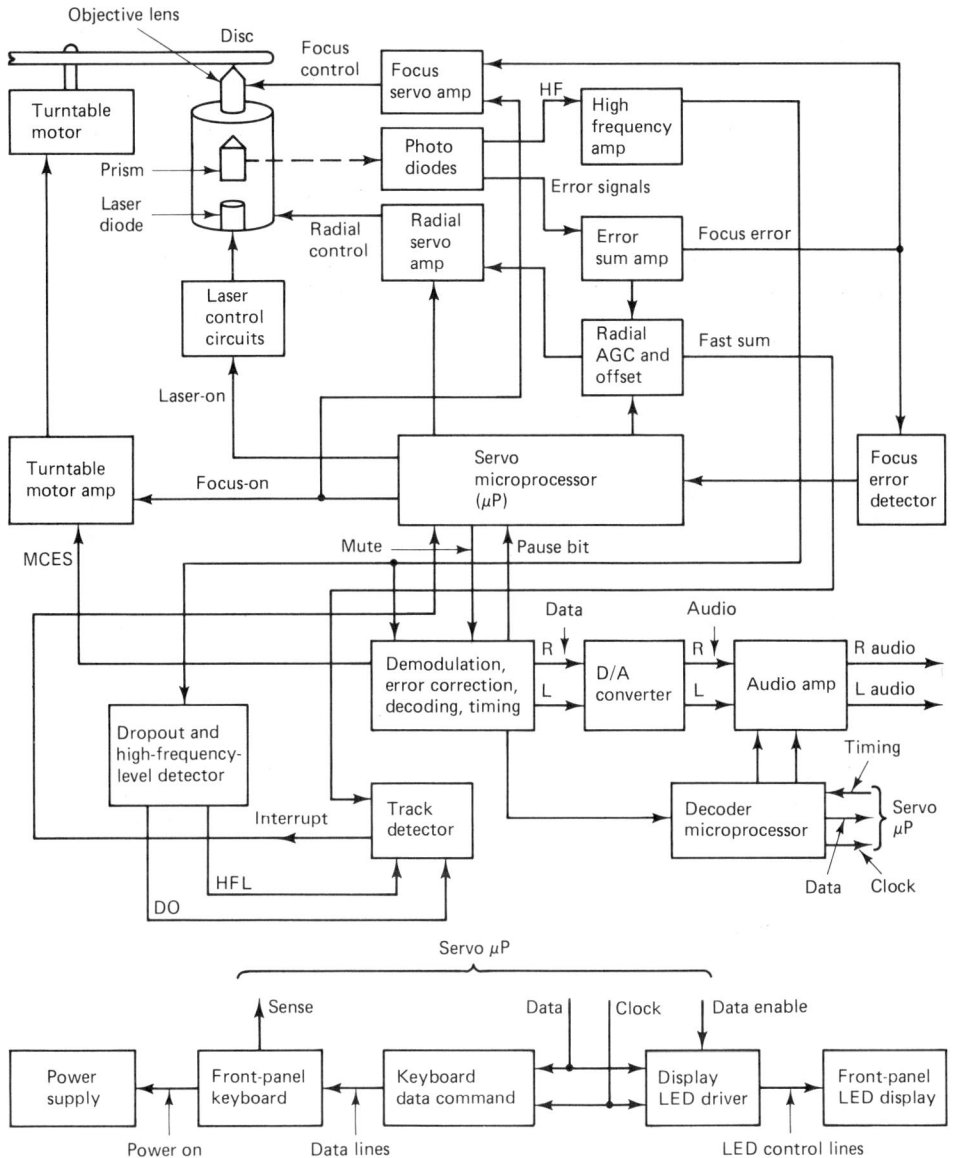

FIGURE 5-1 Major sections of top-load CD players.

The HF signal from the photodiodes is amplified and filtered. The filtered HF signal is applied to the demodulation/error-correction/decoding and timing circuits. Before the HF signal is demodulated and processed, the signal must also go through the dropout and HF level detector, which converts the HF signal to usable levels for the track-detector and demodulator circuits.

If the HF signal drops below a set level, the output of the demodulator stops demodulation of the data stream. The output to the track detector generates an interrupt signal to the servo microprocessor, which takes control of the radial tracking and keeps the tracking arm from skipping to the next track of information. At the same time, mute commands are sent to the error-correction IC and decoder microprocessor. This allows the error-correction circuits to determine if the error can be corrected. If not, the signal is muted for the period of time the HF signal is lost. Small, short-duration drops in HF signal (dropouts) are handled in the same way.

The track-detector circuit monitors the HF signal and is sampled by the servo microprocessor to determine if the HF signal is present. If an adequate HF signal is present, the interrupt signal is removed from the servo microprocessor. The radial tracking-control signals are processed by the servo microprocessor, allowing the radial servo amplifier to operate the radial control arm.

Once normal tracking and focus are obtained, the servo microprocessor removes the mute from the demodulation and decoding circuits. This allows normal processing of data to begin.

After demodulation of the HF signal, the data bits are compared to a VCO (voltage-controlled oscillator). This comparison is used to control the turntable motor speed. If the data bits are received at too fast or too slow a rate into the error-correction circuit, an error signal (MCES, motor-control error signal) is created by the error-correction circuits. This error signal is applied to the turntable motor amplifier, which corrects motor speed as necessary.

The digital data stream is processed through the D/A (digital-to-analog) converter, where the data stream is converted back to the original analog audio signal, and then is amplified by the audio amplifier stage.

The data and clock timing information, after demodulation, is applied to the decoder microprocessor. This information is decoded and applied to the servo microprocessor (for system control), to the keyboard data command, and to the display LED driver circuits (for the front-panel LED display).

5-2 POWER SUPPLY FOR TOP-LOAD CIRCUITS

Figures 5–2 and 5–3 show the power-supply circuits for one top-load player, while Fig. 5–4 shows the same circuits for another top-load player. Note that the circuits shown in Fig. 5–4 are mounted on one PC board, whereas the circuits of Figs. 5–2 and 5–3 are contained on two boards (one board for line filter and another board for main supply circuits).

As shown in Fig. 5–2, the a-c input is applied through connectors 711 and 712 of the filter PC board. The 120 V is fused by F1701 and applied through L5701 to connectors 721 and 722. Power-on switch SKO applies the

5-2 Power Supply for Top-load Circuits 91

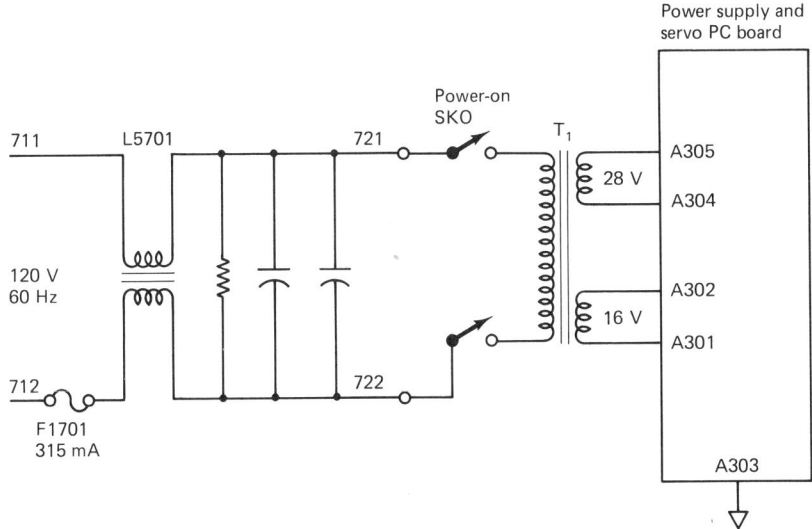

FIGURE 5-2 Filter PC board.

120 V to the primary of T1. The secondary of T1 provides 28 V and 16 V to plug A30 of the power supply and servo PC board. A30 contains five pins and is marked on the drawings as A301 through A305, which represents A30 pin 1 through A30 pin 5.

The power supply shown in Fig. 5-3 is composed of five voltage-stabilized ICs, three of which have adjustable outputs. IC6222 and IC6223 (+12 V and −12 V) do not require adjustment (and do not have an adjustment resistor to ground, as do IC6224, IC6225, and IC6226). IC6222 and IC6223 are protected by R3406, R3407, R3408, and Q6243. This protection circuit prevents the +12 V from going negative (through the loads) when the player is switched off. It takes longer for the −12 V to assume ground potential compared to the +12 V. As a result, the base of Q6243 swings negative relative to the emitter, so that Q6243 conducts. With Q6243 conducting, the −12 V through the PTC resistor R3406 is shorted to ground, and the +12 V cannot become negative.

The −18 V is developed by a voltage doubler consisting of D6267, D6268, C2290, and C2291. This −18 V provides a source voltage for the D/A converters. If the −18 V is missing, both channels of sound are made inoperative, but all other channels function normally.

The 16-V ac is applied to A30, pins 1 and 2, where the input is rectified and processed to provide the +5-V and −7-V sources. The +5 V is used throughout the player as a source voltage for most of the ICs. The −7 V is used to provide a source voltage for the laser control circuits (Sec. 5-3). This source voltage is applied through a *lid cover switch* to insure that the laser diode is off when the lid is opened.

92 Typical CD Player Circuits

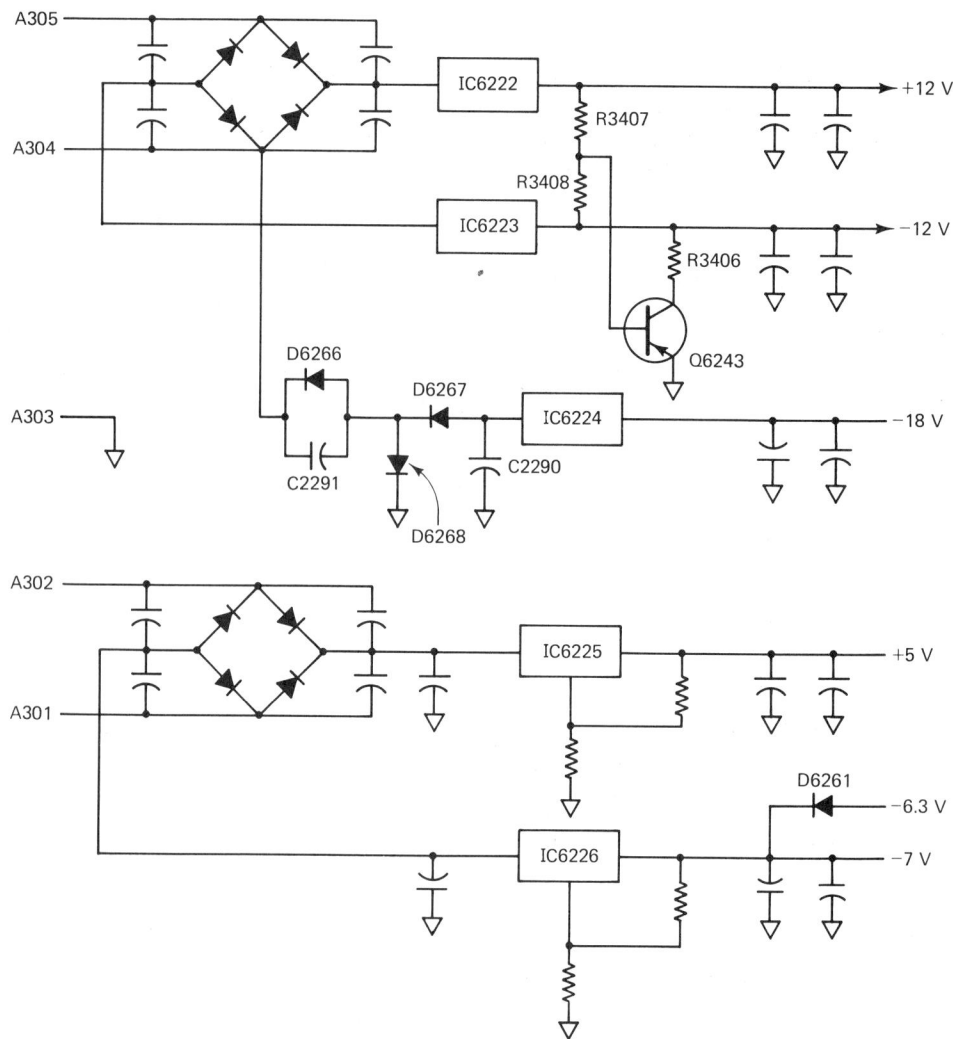

FIGURE 5-3 FD1000 power supply.

The −7 V is also supplied to the turntable motor-drive transistors (through the lid switch) to insure that the turntable drive voltage is removed when the lid cover is opened. Finally, −7 V is supplied to the D/A converters through D6261, which develops a potential of 6.3 V.

The six main voltages from the power-supply board of Fig. 5-3 are labeled +1 (+12 V), −1 (−12 V), +2 (+5 V), −2 (−7 V), −3 (−18 V), and −5 (5.3 V). Any voltages labeled differently than these are derived (on the circuit boards where the voltages are used) from one of these six voltage sources.

Besides the line filter arrangement, the main difference between the power

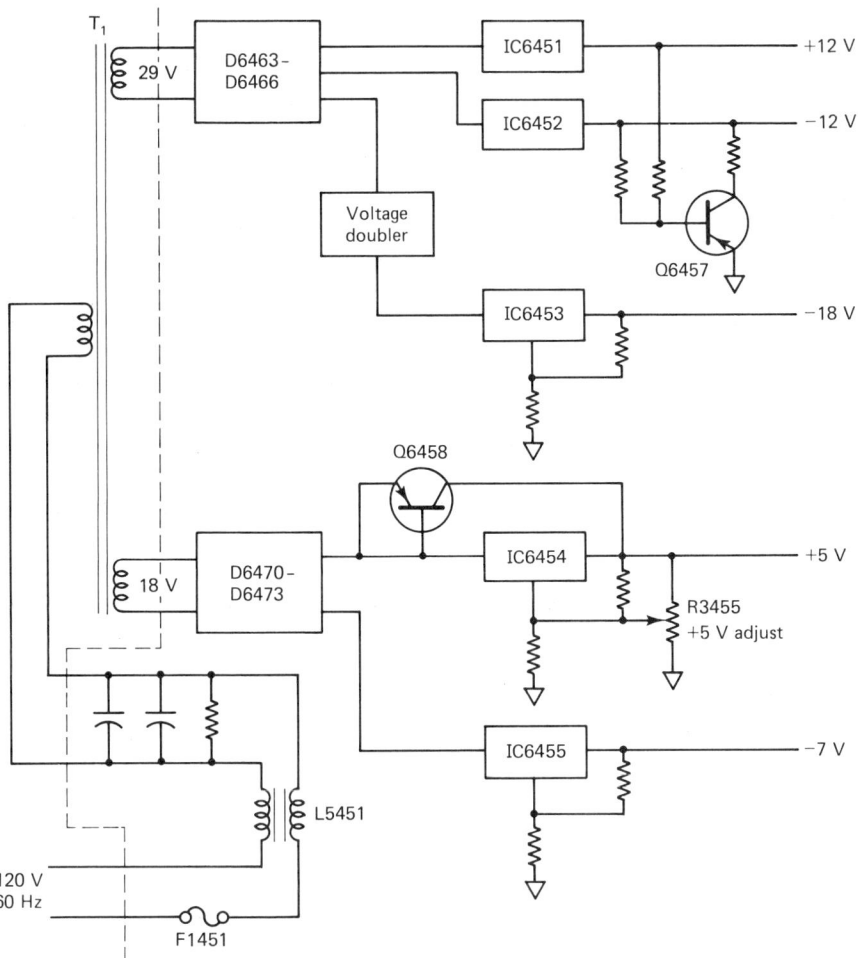

FIGURE 5-4 FD2000 power supply.

supplies of Figs. 5-3 and 5-4 is in the +5-V circuit. In the supply of Fig. 5-4, the +5-V circuit includes transistor Q6458 and R3455. These components control the level of +5-V source. All other components of the supply in Fig. 5-4 are essentially the same as those of Fig. 5-3, except for identification numbers.

5-3 LASER CONTROL CIRCUITS FOR TOP-LOAD

It is necessary to control the amount of light emitted by the laser diode to insure proper performance of the player optics. Since laser-diode resistance increases as the laser is used over time, the laser-drive current must be in-

94 *Typical CD Player Circuits*

creased so the laser will emit a *constant amount of light*. This control is provided by means of a *monitor diode* placed directed below the laser diode, as shown in Fig. 5-5. The monitor diode changes resistance value inversely to the intensity of the beam from the laser diode. (The laser diode emits two beams of light, one of which is the main beam and is used by the optical system to read information on the disc.) The secondary beam is emitted by the laser in the opposite direction from the main beam, and is applied directly to the monitor diode.

When a decrease in laser light output is sensed by the monitor diode, the monitor resistance increases. A voltage divider, made up of the fixed resistor (between 071 and 073) and the monitor diode, changes the amount of voltage applied to pin 2 of IC6114B. This negative voltage at IC6114B-2 determines the amount of source voltage supplied to the laser diode by Q6118.

Note that the laser output can be adjusted by R3180, which controls the -6 V applied to the monitor diode. The -6 V is obtained by dropping the -7 V from the power supply through R3195. The -7 V for the laser control circuits is applied through the lid switch, as discussed in Sec. 5-2. If the lid is open, the switch interrupts the -7 V source and disables the laser diode. Also note that the laser control circuits are turned on by a laser-on signal from the servo microprocessor (Sec. 5-5). This signal is applied through R3191 to pin 5 of IC6114A. With this arrangement, the laser control circuits are operative (and the laser is on) only when both the laser-on signal is present and the lid switch is closed.

5-4 OPTICAL SYSTEM PHOTODIODES, ERROR SIGNALS, AND HF SIGNALS FOR TOP-LOAD

Figure 5-6 shows the circuits of the photodiodes that receive the laser light beam after the beam has returned from the disc through the optical system. Figure 5-7 shows the circuits for the error signals generated by the photodiodes. Figure 5-8 shows the circuits for the HF signals.

5-4.1 Basic Photodiode Circuits

As shown in Fig. 5-6, the signals created by the light landing on the four photodiodes A1 through A4 are developed by the amount of current flowing through the diodes. In turn, the amount of current depends on the laser diode output and the reflectivity of the disc.

The individual outputs of the four diodes are applied to the error sum amplifier IC6101 via A10, pins 3 through 6. These outputs produce the radial and focus-error signals, as discussed in Sec. 5-4.2.

The total sum of the photodiode current is applied through 062 to the HF preamplifier via A10, pin 2. This sum output produces the HF signal, as

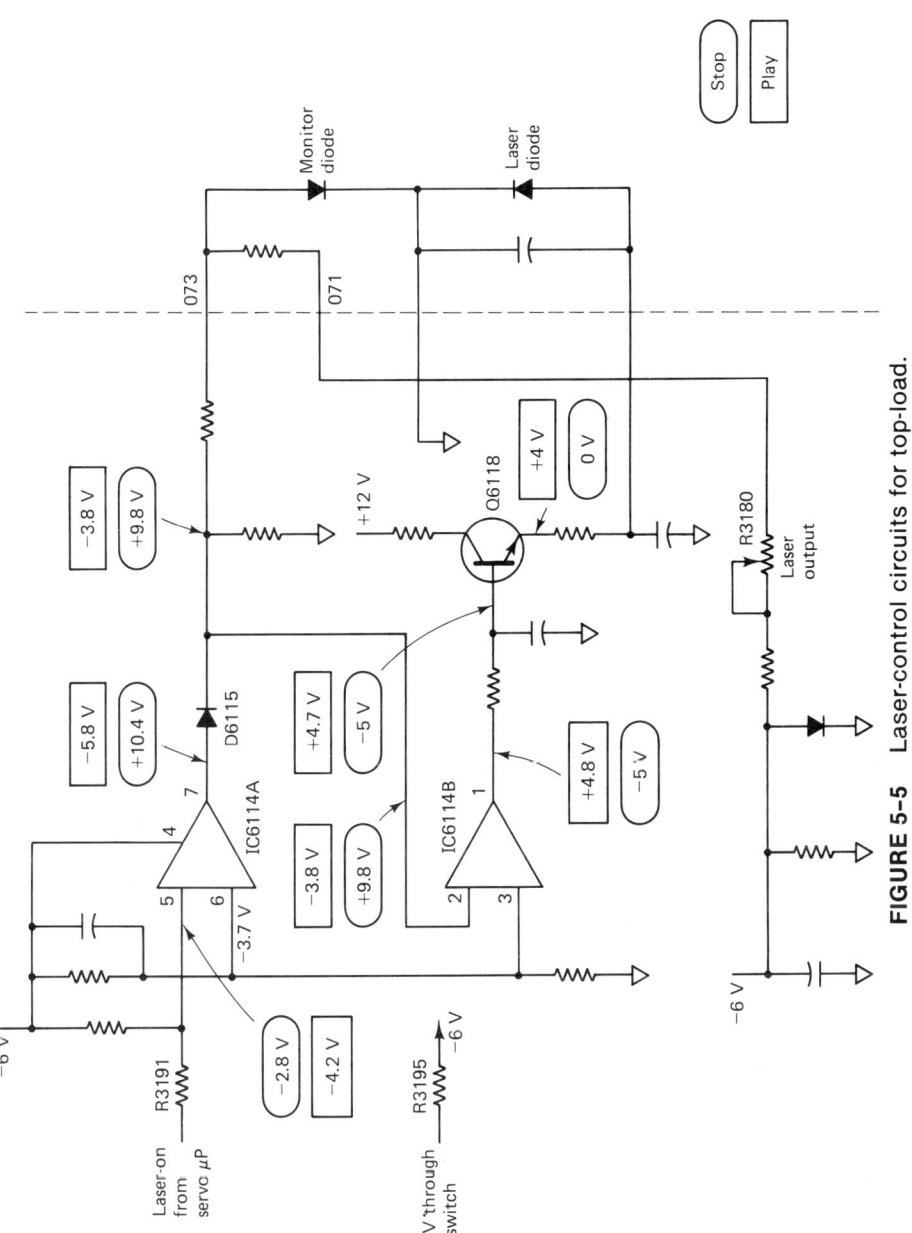

FIGURE 5-5 Laser-control circuits for top-load.

96 Typical CD Player Circuits

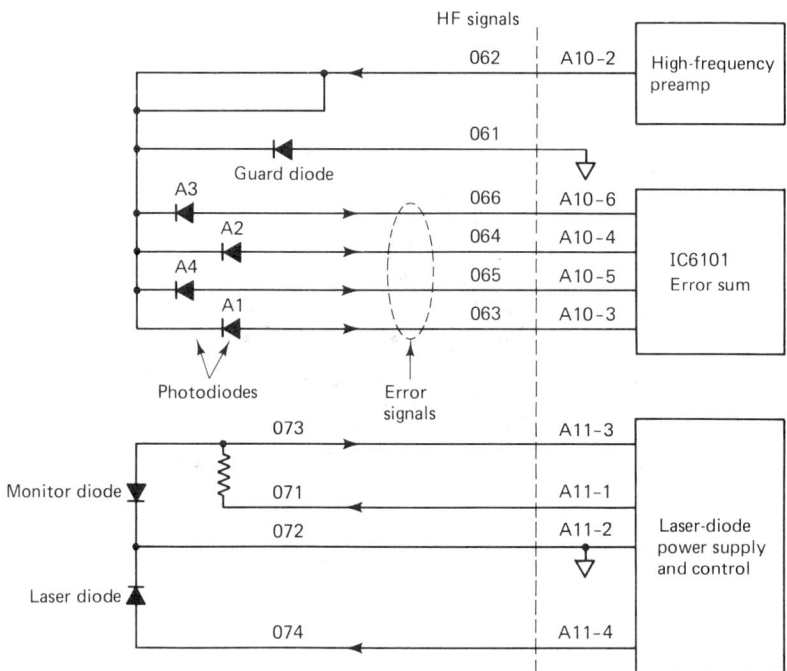

FIGURE 5-6   Basic photodiode circuits.

discussed in Sec. 5-4.3. At this point, the HF signal is in the order of 100 to 400 mV.

Operation of the guard diode shown in Fig. 5-6 is discussed in Sec. 2-4.1. The signals (shown in Fig. 5-6) passing between the laser diode, monitor diode, and the laser control circuits are discussed in Sec. 5-3.

5-4.2 Error Signals

As shown in Fig. 5-7, the error signals for focus and radial servo control are developed by summing amplifiers within IC6101. The photodiode signals are applied through the RC network to the inputs of IC6101. These inputs vary in accordance with the amount of light reflected back from the disc onto the photodiodes. The outputs of IC6101 are summed to form the error signals.

The currents from photodiodes A2 and A3 are summed by R3137 and R3138 to produce (i2 + i3). Summing of photodiodes A1 and A4 is done by R3139 and R3140 to produce (i1 + i4). Op-amp IC6107 subtracts the sum of diodes A2 and A3 from A1 and A4 to produce (i1 + i4) - (i2 + i3), which is the *focus-error signal*. The amplitude of this focus-error signal is controlled by R3158. The amplified focus-error signal is applied to the focus servo amplifier to control the position of the objective lens during play, as discussed in Sec. 5-5.

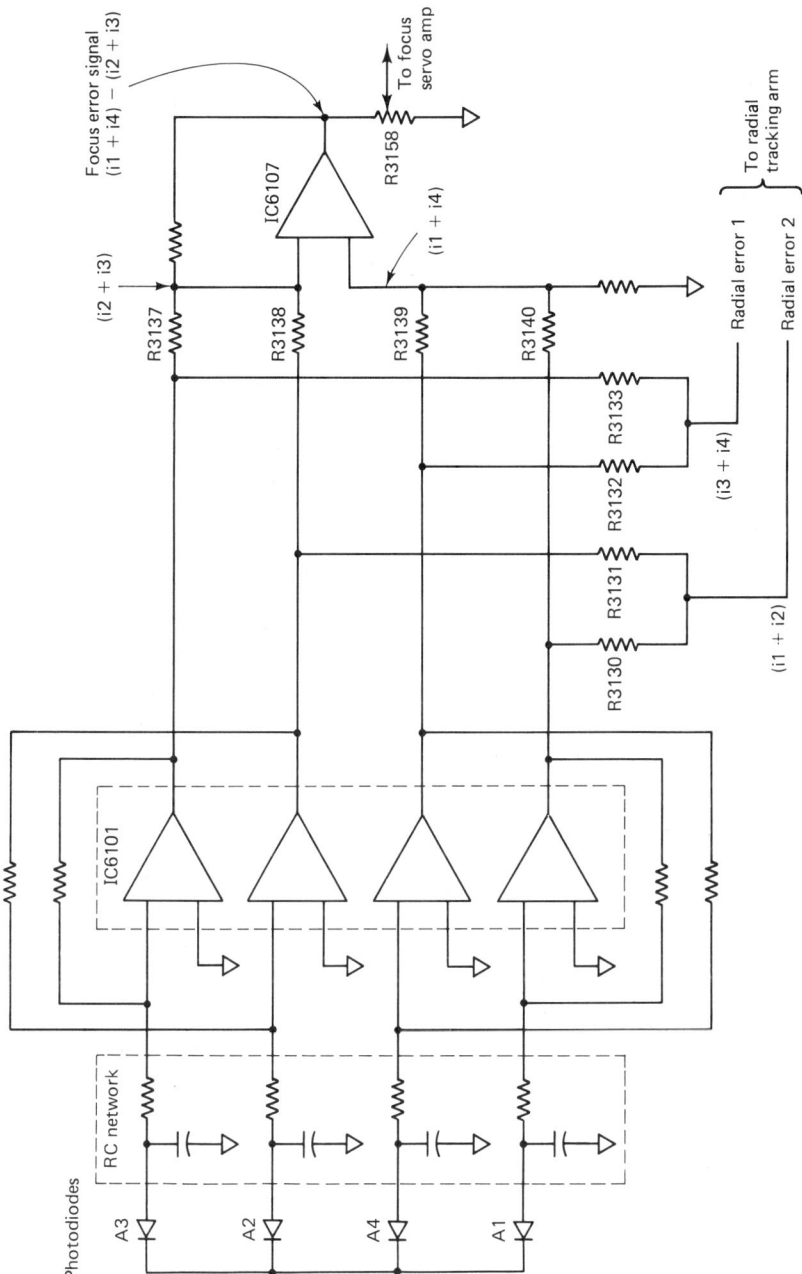

FIGURE 5-7 Error sum amplifier.

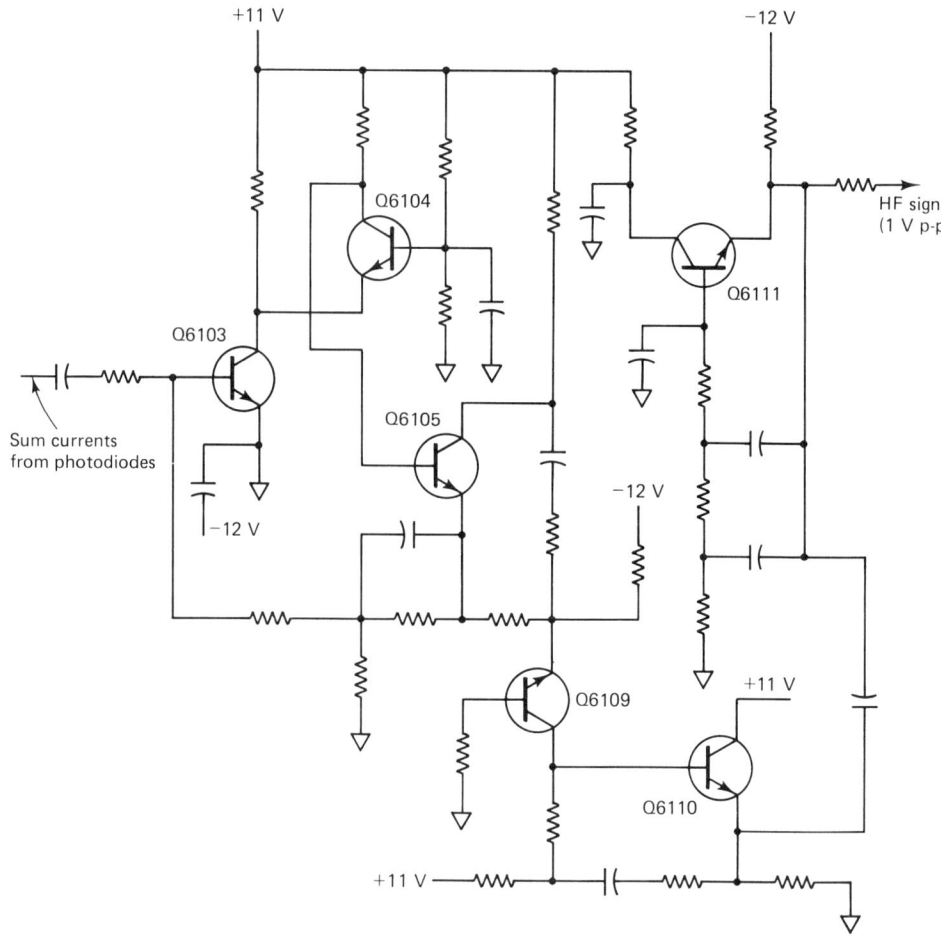

FIGURE 5-8 HF preamplifier.

The radial-error signals 1 and 2 are also derived by summing the photodiode currents. *Radial error 1* is developed across R3132 and R3133 (i3 + i4), with *radial error 2* being developed across R3130 and R3131 (i1 + i2). The output radial-error signals at A17, pins 3 and 4, are used to control the radial tracking arm, as discussed in Sec. 5-7.

5-4.3 HF Amplifier Signals

As shown in Fig. 5-8, the HF preamplifier receives sum currents from the photodiodes through A10, pin 2. The HF preamplifier performs three functions: (1) to amplify the sum currents and convert them to a voltage, (2) to produce a frequency response so that the transfer responses of the optics and disc are offset, and (3) to keep the phase response linear across the entire band.

Transistors Q6103, Q6104, Q6105, and the associated circuits form a *bandpass amplifier*. Transistors Q6105, Q6109, and the associated circuits form a *bandpass filter,* combined with a *leading-phase network*. Transistors Q6109, Q6110, and the associated circuits form a *bootstrap filter* (which is a second leading-phase filter). The HF signal from Q6110 is applied through bandpass and low-pass filters to Q6111. The output from Q6111 (approximately 1 V p-p) is the HF signal. This HF signal contains the EFM digital data stream to be converted back to the original audio analog signal. The HF signal from Q6111 is applied to various circuits (including demodulation, error correcting, decoding, and timing) as shown in Fig. 5-1.

5-5 FOCUS SERVO FOR TOP-LOAD

Figure 5-9 shows the circuits of both the focus and radial servo (Sec. 5-7) in block form. Note that most of the components are on the servo PC board. This same board also includes components of the turntable motor amplifier (described in Sec. 5-6).

As discussed in Sec. 5-4.2, the focus servo signal is derived from the sum of the currents of the photodiode pairs A2 and A3, subtracted from the sum of the other pair A1 and A4. The focus-error signal (i1 + i4) − (i2 + i3) appears on connector 27 pin 1 of the servo PC board. When the laser beam is correctly focused (zero error), the focal point of the beam coincides with the reflective surface of the disc (which coincides precisely with the plane of the photodiodes). As discussed in Chapter 2, the diodes are arranged so that each deviation from current focus is translated into an error signal. This error signal is then used by the focus coil to control up-and-down movement of the objective lens.

5-5.1 Automatic Focus Sequence

Figure 5-10 shows the focus servo circuits in more detail. In the stop mode, the objective lens is at rest and there is no current flowing in the focus coil. This is due to the positive *focus control zero* (FC0) signal from pin 18 of the servo microprocessor IC6201. The FC0 signal is applied to the base of switching transistor Q6230, and keeps Q6230 switched on. With Q6230 on, the error signal line, and the input at IC6208B-6, are shorted to ground. As a result, there is no current flowing in the focus coil, and the objective lens remains at rest. During start-up, the FC0 signal remains applied until correct focus is obtained, or until the IC6201 programming has reached a predetermined number of attempts to focus (typically two to four attempts, or up/down movements of the objective lens). These automatic-focus functions occur in a specific sequence for each CD player. The following describes the auto-focus sequence for the circuits of Fig. 5-10.

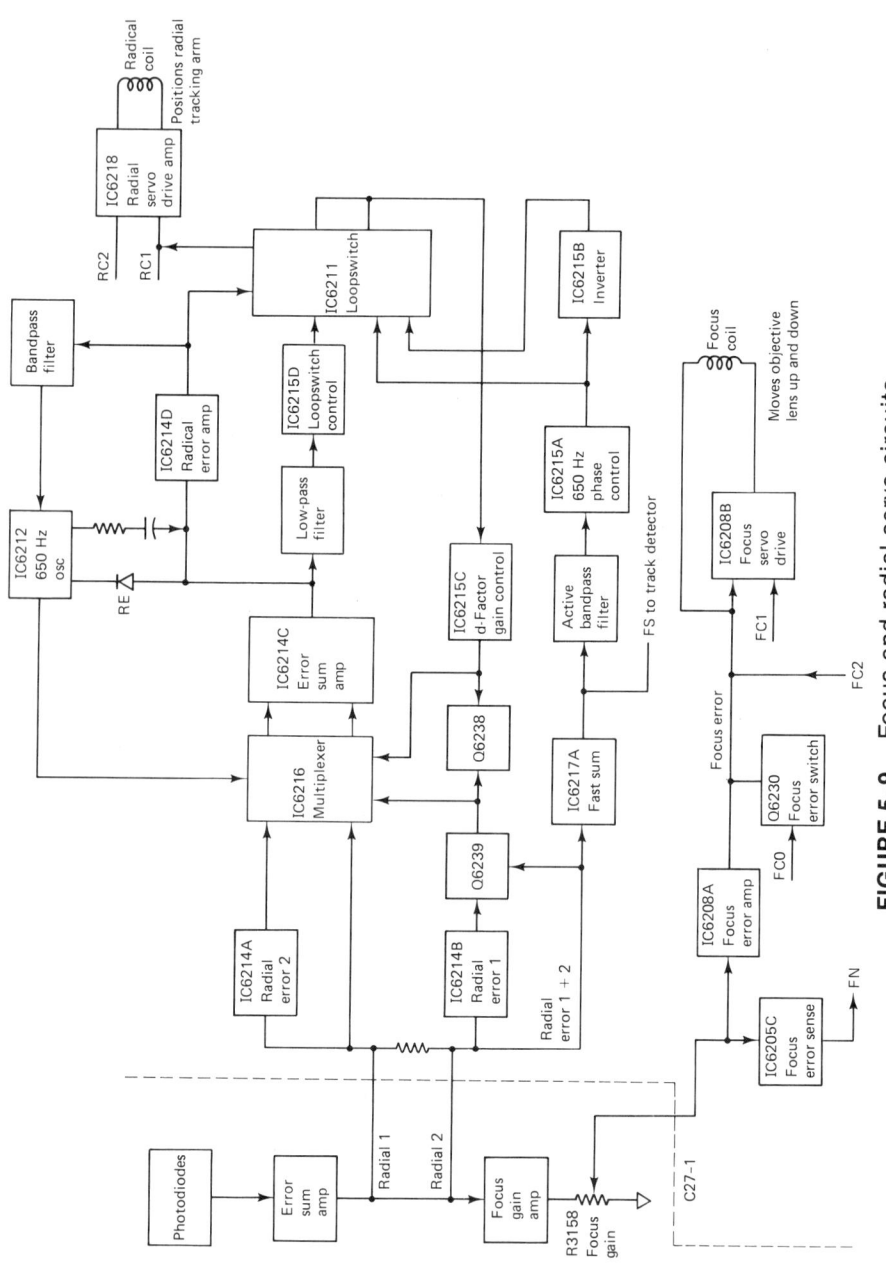

FIGURE 5-9 Focus and radial servo circuits.

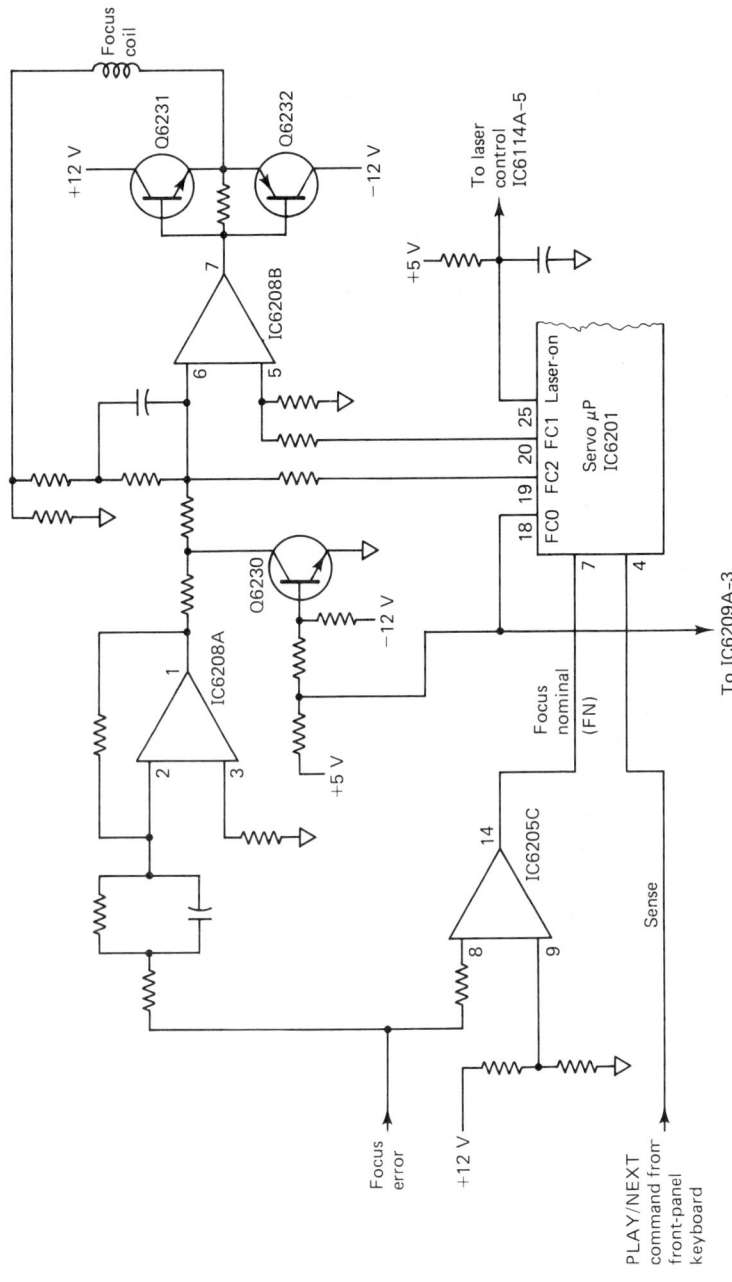

FIGURE 5-10 Focus-control circuits during automatic-focus sequence.

During the start-up sequence, the PLAY/NEXT command is received from the front-panel keyboard at pin 4 of IC6201. The laser-on command at IC6201-25 is switch on (low), and applied to the laser control circuits, as described in Sec. 5-3. The FC0 output at IC6201-18 remains positive until the *focus control 1* (FC1) at IC6201-20 goes positive. This positive FC1 signal is applied to pin 5 of IC6208B, which drives the objective lens to the maximum upward position. IC6201 then switches pin 19, the *focus control 2* (FC2) signal, positive. This positive FC2 signal is applied to pin 6 of IC6208B, and allows the objective lens to start the downward movement.

If an error signal is present during the downward movement of the objective lens, the error signal at pin 8 of IC6205C causes the output of IC6205C at pin 14 to go low (zero volts). This output is the *focus nominal* (FN) signal that tells IC6201 two conditions: (1) a disc is present, and (2) a focus error exists. At the moment FN becomes zero, IC6201 switches FC0, FC1, and FC2 to zero.

With FC0 at zero, Q6230 switches off and removes the ground from the focus-error line (permitting the focus error to be applied at pin 6 of IC6208B). Also, the FC1 and FC2 signals are removed from pins 5 and 6 of IC6208B. This allows the focus error signal to pass to the focus coil and bring the objective lens to the correct focal point on the disc (by nulling out the error signal). Any deviation from the correct focal point creates a positive or negative error, which moves the lens up or down as necessary to restore proper focus (thus decreasing the error signal to zero).

Note that the FC0 output from IC6201-18 is also applied at pin 3 of IC6209A to start or stop the turntable motor, and discussed next in Sec. 5-6.

5-6 TURNTABLE MOTOR AMPLIFIER FOR TOP-LOAD

Figure 5-11 shows the turntable motor amplifier circuits. These circuits control speed of the turntable motor. The rate at which the data stream enters the error correction IC in the signal-processing circuits (Sec. 5-8) depends on the rotational speed of the turntable and the location of the optical pickup. The speed at which the track is moving *with respect to the pickup* must be kept constant. This means that the disc speed must be varied as the pickup moves across the tracks. For example, if the disc were rotated at a constant speed, the data rate near the center of the disc would be lower compared to near the outside edge of the disc. This is due to the fact that less information is contained in the tracks near the center (inside edge of the disc) than on the outside tracks. (The diameter of the tracks becomes much larger, and can contain much more information in one revolution of the disc, on the outside edge.)

In the error correction IC (Sec. 5-8), the rate at which information enters is compared to voltage-controlled oscillator (VCO). If the incoming rate is too high or low, an error signal is created and applied to the turntable amplifier.

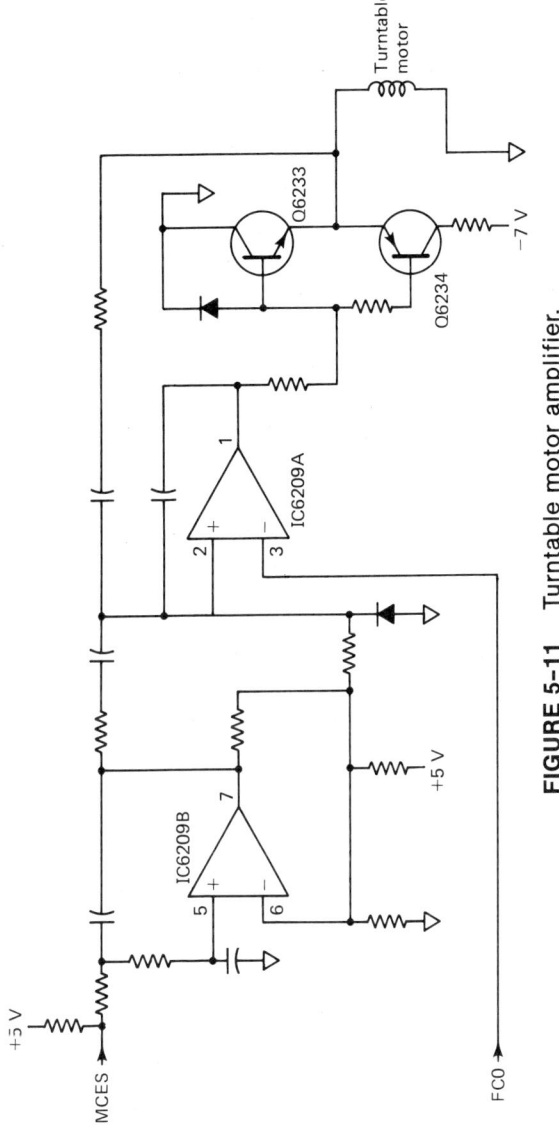

FIGURE 5-11 Turntable motor amplifier.

This error signal is called the *motor-control error signal* (MCES). The MCES has a 50 percent duty cycle that "jitters." The rate of jitter determines the amount of drive current supplied to the turntable motor.

The MCES signal is applied to the turntable motor through IC6209A, which is controlled by the FC0 signal (Sec. 5-5). During stop and initial startup, FC0 is positive. This holds the MCES line off and prevents premature operation of the turntable. Once the PLAY/NEXT command is received and focus is obtained, the FC0 line goes low, permitting the MCES line to operate the turntable motor.

5-7 RADIAL SERVO FOR TOP-LOAD

As discussed in Sec. 5-4.2, the radial-error signals 1 and 2 are derived by summing the photodiode currents. The output radial-error signals from the error sum amplifier (IC6101, Fig. 5-7) are used to control the radial tracking arm. Figure 5-9 shows the radial servo in block form. Figures 5-12 and 5-13 show the radial circuits in more detail.

The error sum signals are applied to the radial-error amplifier circuits at pins 3 and 4 of connector 27 on the servo PC board, as shown in Fig. 5-12. The radial-error signals are amplified by IC6214A and B. The amplified error signals are applied to pins 1 and 7 of multiplexer IC6216, which is used to combine additional factors to the system and to maintain stability over the radial tracking servo loop. The outputs from IC6216 are applied from pins 12 and 13 to IC6214C, pins 9 and 10. The radial error signal on pin 8 of IC6214C splits into four different paths (RE, RE1, RE2, and a path at IC6212-13), but remains the radial error signal.

The offset control R3315 offsets the asymmetry of the reflected light beam (or spot) by offsetting the d-c gain of IC6216. IC6215 is used as a switch to provide d-c control over the gain of IC6216. This d-c control of multiplier IC6216 is called the *d-Factor*.

IC6217A, pin 3, receives the sum of the radial-error signals on pins 3 and 4 of connector 27, and produces the *fast sum signal*. The fast sum is used in conjunction with the dropout and HF level to provide the servo microprocessor IC6201 with an interrupt (INT) signal during *track jumping*.

The radial-error signal (RE1) on pin 8 of IC6214C is applied through R3351 to pin 13 of IC6214D, as shown in Fig. 5-13. The amplified signal on pin 14 of IC6214D is coupled through C2259 and R3376 to pin 15 of loop switch IC6211. Diodes D6256 and D6257 limit the high excursions of the radial-error signal. The output of loop switch IC6211 is applied to radial drive IC6218, which provides the drive current to the radial tracking coil (to move the radial tracking arm). Transistors Q6240 and Q6241 provide stability and increase the dynamic range of IC6218.

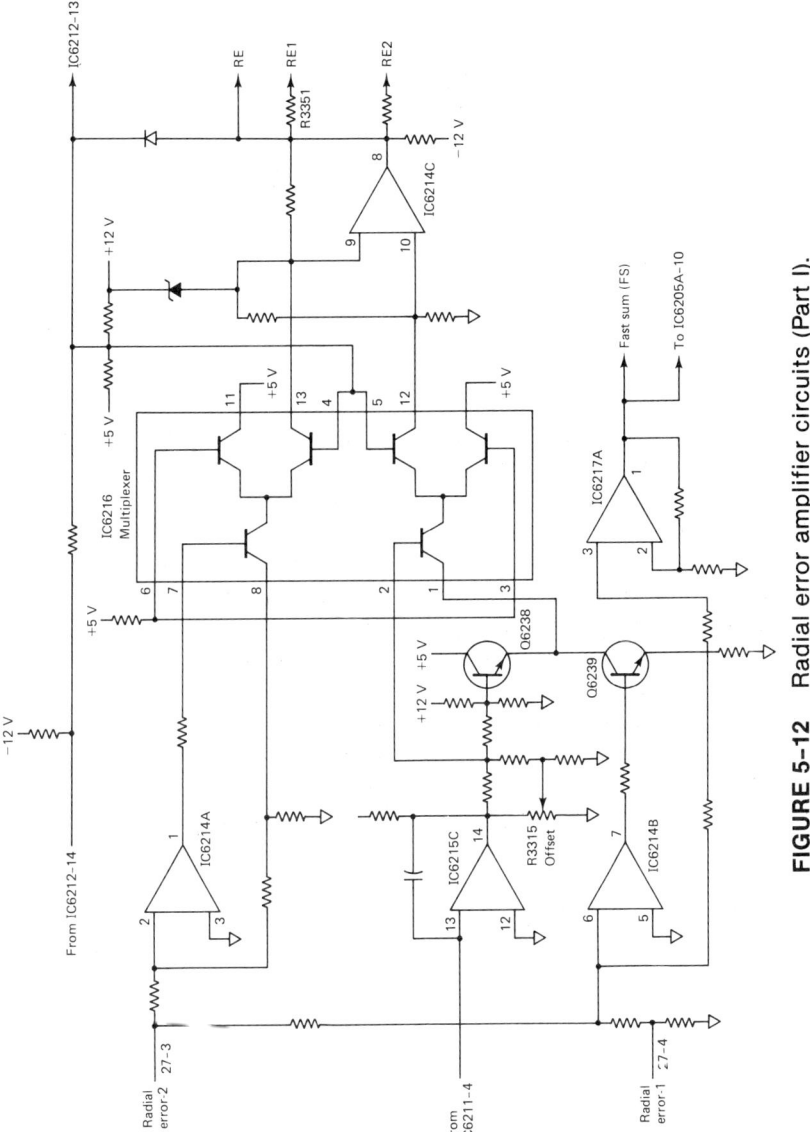

FIGURE 5-12 Radial error amplifier circuits (Part I).

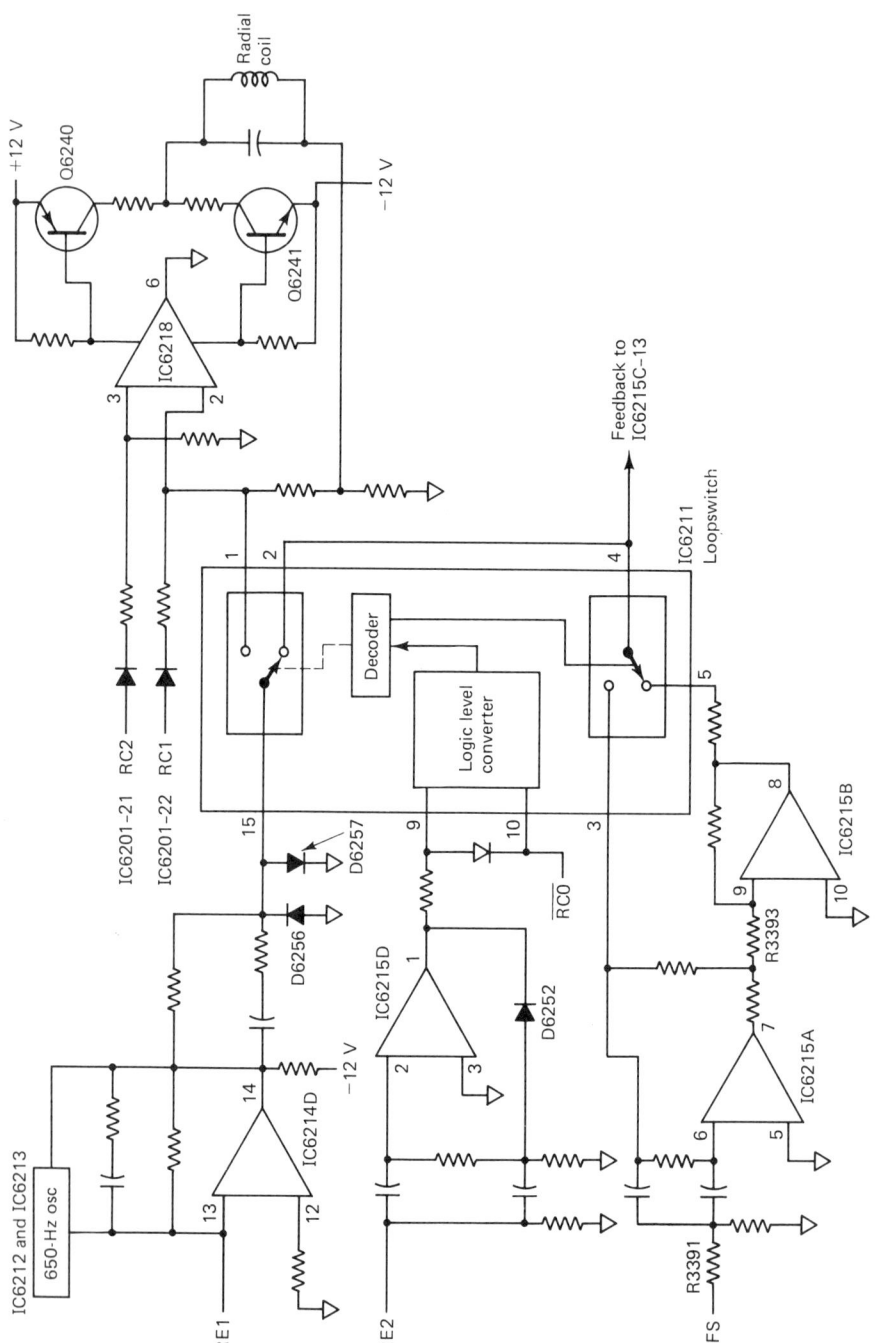

FIGURE 5-13 Radial error amplifier circuits (Part II).

5-7.1 650-Hz Sine-Wave Signal and d-Factor

As shown in Fig. 5-13, a 650-Hz sine-wave signal is injected into the radial servo loop. This 650-Hz signal is generated by IC6212 and IC6213, as discussed in Sec. 5-7.2. The 650-Hz signal is present throughout the radial servo system and causes the radial tracking arm to oscillate at a 650-Hz rate. Typically, the arm moves back and forth for a total travel of about 0.1 μm (± 0.05 μm).

The 650-Hz sine wave appears in the RE signals at pin 8 of IC6214C, shown in Fig. 5-12. The RE2 signal is applied through a low-frequency bandpass filter to IC6215D (Fig. 5-13). Because of the filter, only the 650-Hz signal passes to IC6215D. The sine wave is converted to a square-wave signal by IC6215D and D6252. The square-wave signal is applied to loopswitch IC6211 at pin 9. This opens and closes IC6211 at a 650-Hz rate.

The input to pin 10 of IC6211 is the *radial control zero* ($\overline{RC0}$) signal from the servo microprocessor IC6201. $\overline{RC0}$ is used to open loopswitch IC6211 when radial tracking is lost or when *track jumping* is required by the system. This allows the servo microprocessor IC6201 to take control of the radial tracking arm, using RC1 and RC2 signals at pins 21 and 22 of IC6201. The *radial control 1* (RC1) and *radial control 2* (RC2) signals are applied to the radial tracking coil through IC6218, Q6240, and Q6241. During normal start-up, IC6211 is held open by the $\overline{RC0}$ signal so that RC1 and RC2 can control movement of the arm from the at-rest position to the initial-start position.

The fast sum (FS) signal from pin 1 of IC6217A (Fig. 5-12) contains the sums of RC1 and RC2, plus the 650-Hz sine-wave signal injected into the system. The FS signal is applied to R3391 (Fig. 5-13), which is the input to an active bandpass filter network. IC6215A applies the 650-Hz signal to pin 3 of loop switch IC6211, and through R3393 to pin 9 of IC6215B, which inverts the sine wave before the sine wave is applied to pin 5 of IC6211.

The output on pin 4 of IC6211 is controlled by the switch control pulse on pin 9 of IC6211. This control pulse switches the output at pin 4 of IC6211 between the two inputs on pins 3 and 5 of IC6211 at a 650-Hz rate. The signal developed on pin 4 of IC6211 is the feedback to pin 13 of IC6215C (Fig. 5-12). The output at pin 14 of IC6215C is the average d-c voltage level to control the gain of the stage connected at pin 2 of multiplier IC6216.

Figure 5-14 illustrates the curve that represents the amount of reflected light from the disc. The curve shows that maximum light is reflected when the beam is directly between the tracks, and a minimum light is reflected when the beam is directly on the center of the track.

By injecting a 650-Hz signal into the radial servo loop, the tracking arm starts to oscillate at 650 Hz. Figure 5-15 shows the effects of arm oscillation on the reflected light beam. When the light beam hits the center of the track, there is a positive signal as a result of the injected 650 Hz. If a shift occurs in the beam to the right of the track, the resulting reflected beam is in phase

108 Typical CD Player Circuits

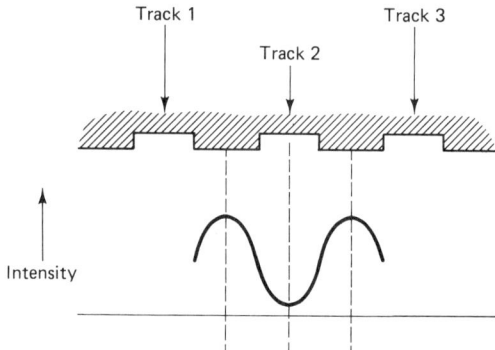

FIGURE 5-14 Curve representing the amount of reflected light from a compact disc.

with the injected signal. During a shift to the left of the track, the reflected beam is out of phase with the injected signal. By detecting the reflected signal synchronously, a d-c control signal is developed. This d-c control signal is called the *d-Factor,* and is used in conjunction with the radial-error signal to control the gain of one section of the radial servo loop.

The d-Factor corrects for an asymmetrical spot (Sec. 2-4) due to a deviation in the angle between the disc and the tracking arm. This deviation in angle causes the radial-error signals (i1 + i2) and (i3 + i4) to become unequal, even when the beam is directly on the center of the track.

Figure 5-16 shows the resulting waveforms and d-c level created from the 650-Hz signal when the light beam is directly on the center of the track. The switch-controlled square-wave signal applied to pin 9 of IC6211 switches the input signals on pins 3 and 5 of IC6211 at a 650-Hz rate. The input on pin 3 is the opposite of the input on pin 5 at any given instant. The

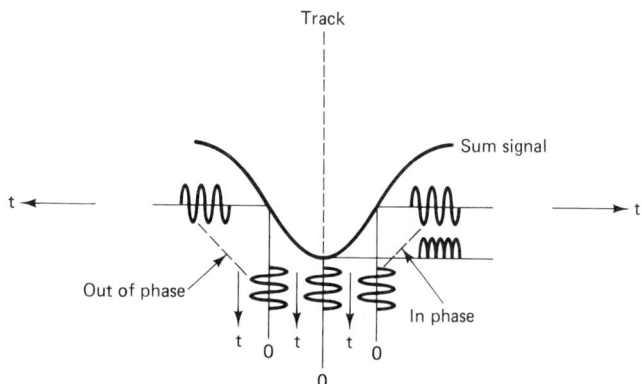

FIGURE 5-15 Effects of radial-arm oscillation on the reflected light beam.

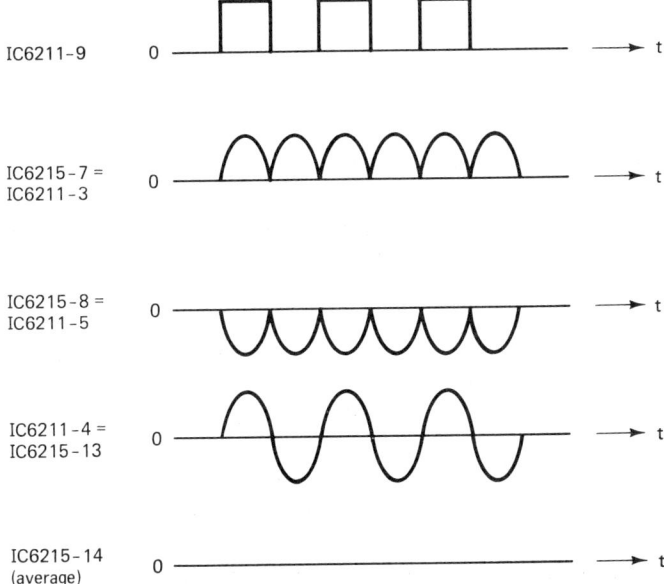

FIGURE 5-16 Waveforms and d-c level when the light beam is direct on the center of track.

output on pin 4 of IC6211 is a sine wave that swings above and below the zero reference. This signal is applied to pin 13 of IC6215C, resulting in an average d-c level of zero on the output of IC6215C, pin 14.

Figure 5-17 shows the results of the signal when the light beam is to the left of the center of the track. The input signals on pins 3 and 5 are out of phase, so both appear at pin 4 of IC6211. This causes the average d-c output at pin 14 of IC6215 to go negative.

Figure 5-18 shows the results of the signal when the light beam is to the right of the center of the track. The input signals on pins 3 and 5 are again out of phase, so both appear at pin 4 of IC6211. However, this causes the average d-c output at pin 14 of IC6215 to go positive.

5-7.2 650-Hz Sine-Wave Signal and k-Factor

As can be seen from the discussion in Sec. 5-7.1, the phase of the 650-Hz signal produces a d-Factor used to control gain of one stage in the radial servo loop. The use of the d-Factor is not sufficient to control the overall gain of the system. This is because of other factors that can be induced into the system. For example, if the output of the laser diode decreases, or the reflectivity of the disc is low, it is possible for the tracking system to become unstable. To prevent such a condition, the overall gain of the radial tracking system is controlled by reacting to any deviation from normal. Such control is provided by

110 Typical CD Player Circuits

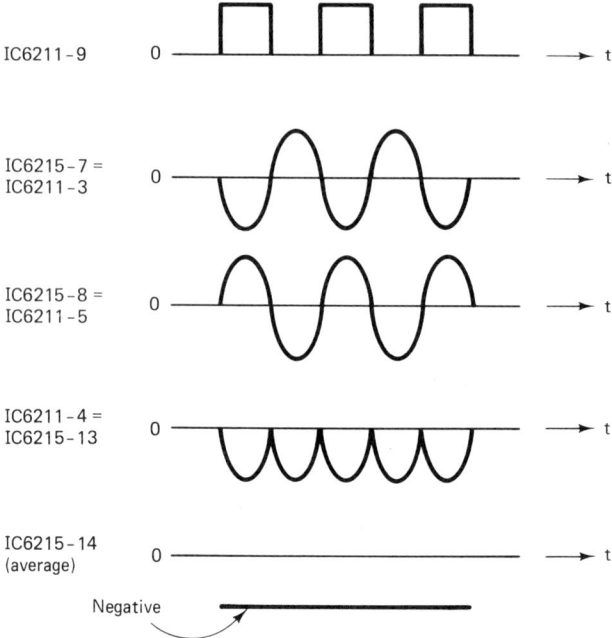

FIGURE 5-17 Waveforms and d-c level when the light beam is to the left of center.

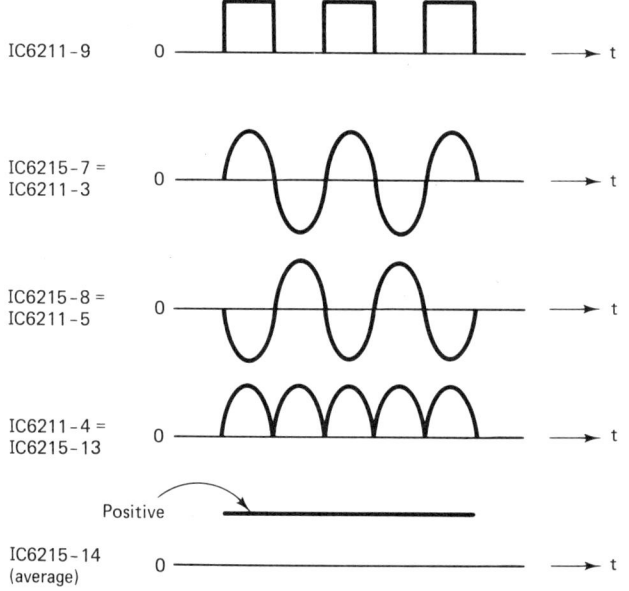

FIGURE 5-18 Waveforms and d-c level when the light beam is to the right of center.

the k-Factor, which adjusts overall gain when radial tracking signals deviate from normal for any reason.

The k-Factor also uses the 650-Hz signal. The phase of the 650-Hz signal is strongly influenced by the gain of the system. If the gain increases or decreases, the phase shift between the original and the returning signals also increases or decreases. With k-Factor, both signals (original and returning) are compared, and the resulting signal is used to control gain of the second stage of multiplier IC6216 (Fig. 5-12).

Figure 5-19 shows the 650-Hz oscillator and the d-c control generator for the k-Factor. The oscillator IC6212B injects the signal into the radial servo loop through R3322 and C2244, which act to shift the signal phase by 45°, before application to pin 13 of IC6214D (Fig. 5-13). The signal from pin 14 of IC6214D is returned to the input of bandpass filter at pin 6 of IC6212D (Fig. 5-19) through R3370.

The 650-Hz signal is extracted from the filter and applied to pin 6 of square-wave converter IC6213B. The output on pin 4 of IC6213B is applied to phase detector IC6213C. The oscillator output on pin 8 of IC6212B is applied to a reference IC6213D at pin 8. This reference converts the oscillator output to a square wave that is in phase with the generated 650-Hz sine wave. The output of reference IC6213D at pin 10 is applied to the phase detector IC6213C at pin 1. The phase of the generated signal (pin 1) is compared with the phase of the extracted signal (pin 2) in IC6213C. If the overall radial tracking loop gain increases or decreases, the phase difference or shift of the returning signal increases or decreases. The two signals are compared by IC6213C to produce a difference signal on pin 3. This difference signal is applied to pin 12 of switch IC6213A.

The RC0 is applied to pin 13 of IC6213A, and is used to control the output of IC6213A. $\overline{RC0}$ is applied to pin 13 of IC6212A through D6249 and R3281. If the player tracks properly, RC0 is positive and $\overline{RC0}$ is zero. This permits the difference signal from IC6213C to be applied to pin 13 of IC6212A.

If the reflected light is less than nominal, the phase shift of the 650-Hz signal from the servo loop decreases relative to the oscillator signal. As a result, the duty cycle of the phase detector IC6213 decreases. The input at pin 13 of integrator IC6212A becomes less positive. This causes the output at pin 14 of IC6212A to go more positive. This output is fed back to the input of multiplier IC6216 (Fig. 5-12) at pins 4 and 5, causing the transistors within IC6216 to conduct more heavily and increase the amplification factor.

If the reflected light is greater than nominal, producing a radial-error signal that is also greater, the input on pin 13 of integrator IC6212A becomes more positive. This decreases the output on pin 14 of IC6212A, causing IC6216 to conduct less, and thus returning the radial-error signal to the nominal value.

Note that when the radial tracking is switched off by the servo microprocessor IC6201, incoming information from phase detector IC6213C is also switched off. Also note that radial-error RE information from IC6214C (Fig.

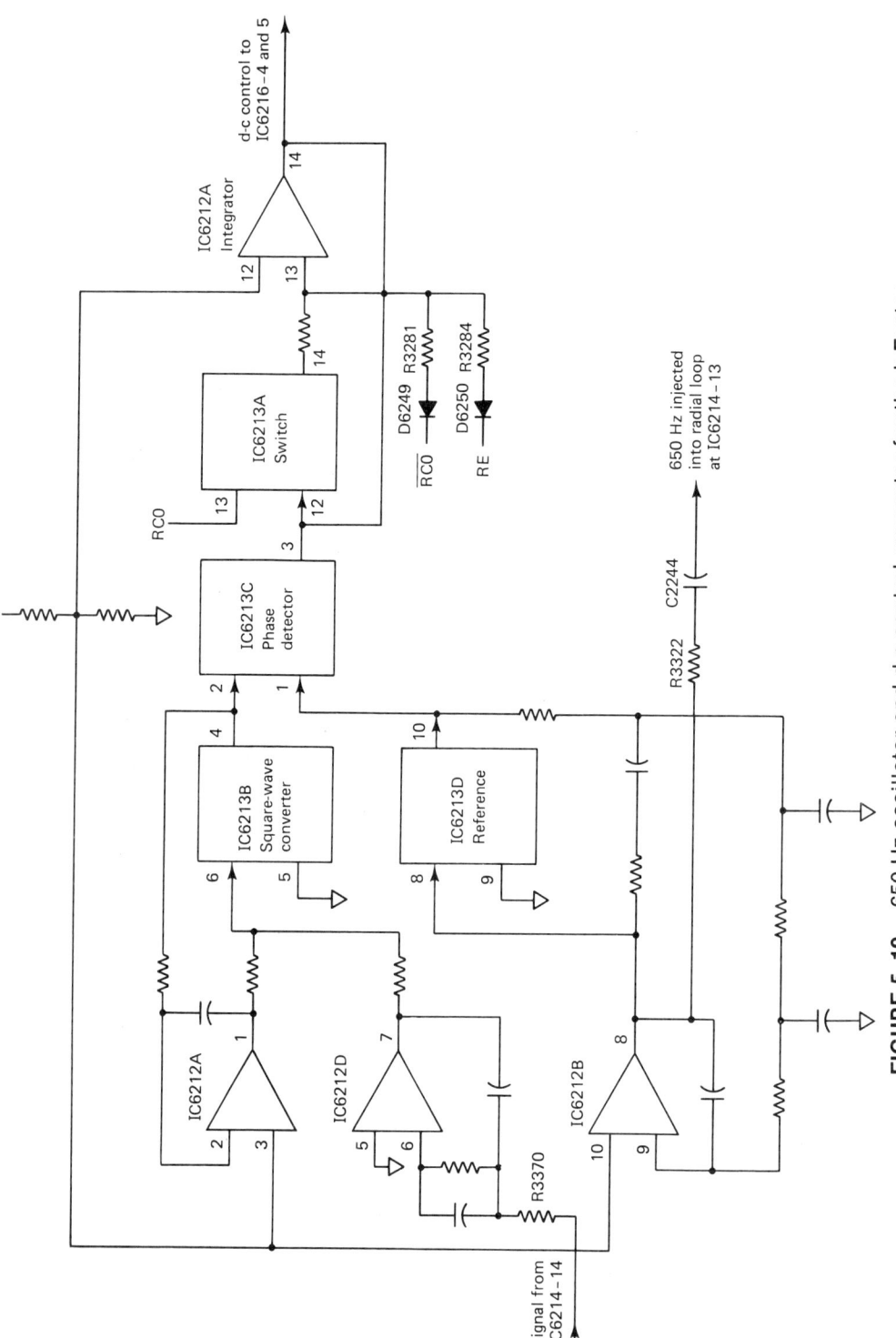

FIGURE 5-19 650-Hz oscillator and d-c control generator for the k-Factor.

5-12) is applied to input pin 13 of IC6212A through D6250 and R3284, as shown in Fig. 5-19.

5-7.3 Left and Right Motion-Detector Circuit

Figure 5-20 shows the left and right motion-detector circuits, as well as a portion of the focus-error control circuits. These circuits monitor and control movement of the radial arm with respect to motion and shock.

The radial-error RE signal from pin 8 of IC6214C (Fig. 5-12) is applied to pin 5 of IC6205B. The output at pin 2 of IC6205B is applied to pin 13 of IC6201. Servo microprocessor IC6201 measures the time between two consecutive positive-going signals (typically about 0.5 ms). If the speed of radial-arm motion across the tracks is constant, the time between the two consecutive pulses is constant. If the speed is too slow, the time between the positive-going edges of the square wave is longer than normal. If the speed is too high, the time is shorter than normal.

This monitor function is used primarily during *track jumping* (when the player has been programmed to jump from one track to another, out of the normal sequence). During such track jumping, IC6201 takes over control of the radial tracking arm. IC6201 monitors the input at pin 13 and applies a signal to either RC1 or RC2 if the rate of track jumping is too fast or slow. The signal from IC6201 is applied to RC1 or RC2 until the width of the input signal on pin 13 returns to normal. If the speed is too slow, RC2 is made positive by IC6201. RC1 is made positive if the speed is too slow. This holds track jumping at a constant rate of speed.

The monitor function is used if the player is subjected to *shock or excessive vibration*. If a shock occurs to either the left or right side of the player, the width of the signal on pin 13 of IC6201 increases or decreases. Under these conditions IC6201 acts to switch on either RC1 or RC2, and thus brakes movement of the tracking arm.

If the shock comes from the top and side at the same time, loss of focus error (IC6201-7) and radial error (IC6201-13) is possible if the shock is severe. The loss of the focus and radial-error signals causes IC6201 to shut down the system and return to the normal start position. As discussed in Secs. 5-5 and 5-6, the FC0 output on pin 18 of IC6201 is used to hold the MCES line at zero volts before start-up, thus preventing the turntable motor from rotating.

5-7.4 Decoder Circuits

Figure 5-21 shows the decoder circuits. The high-frequency HF signals from the HF amplifier (Sec. 5-4.3) are applied to the differential amplifier, consisting of Q6530 and Q6531. (The HF signal is also applied to the demodulator circuits, as discussed in Sec. 5-8.) The outputs from the differential amplifier are applied through C2520 and C2521 to two full-wave rectifier circuits (D6548,

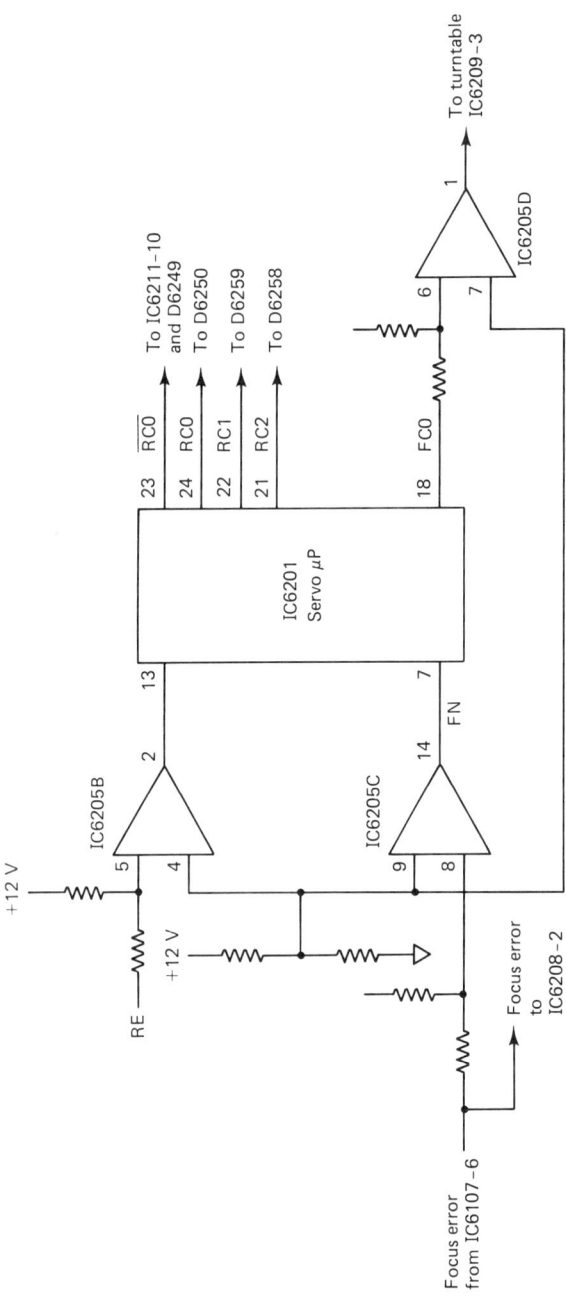

FIGURE 5-20 Left and right motion detector and portion of focus-error control circuits.

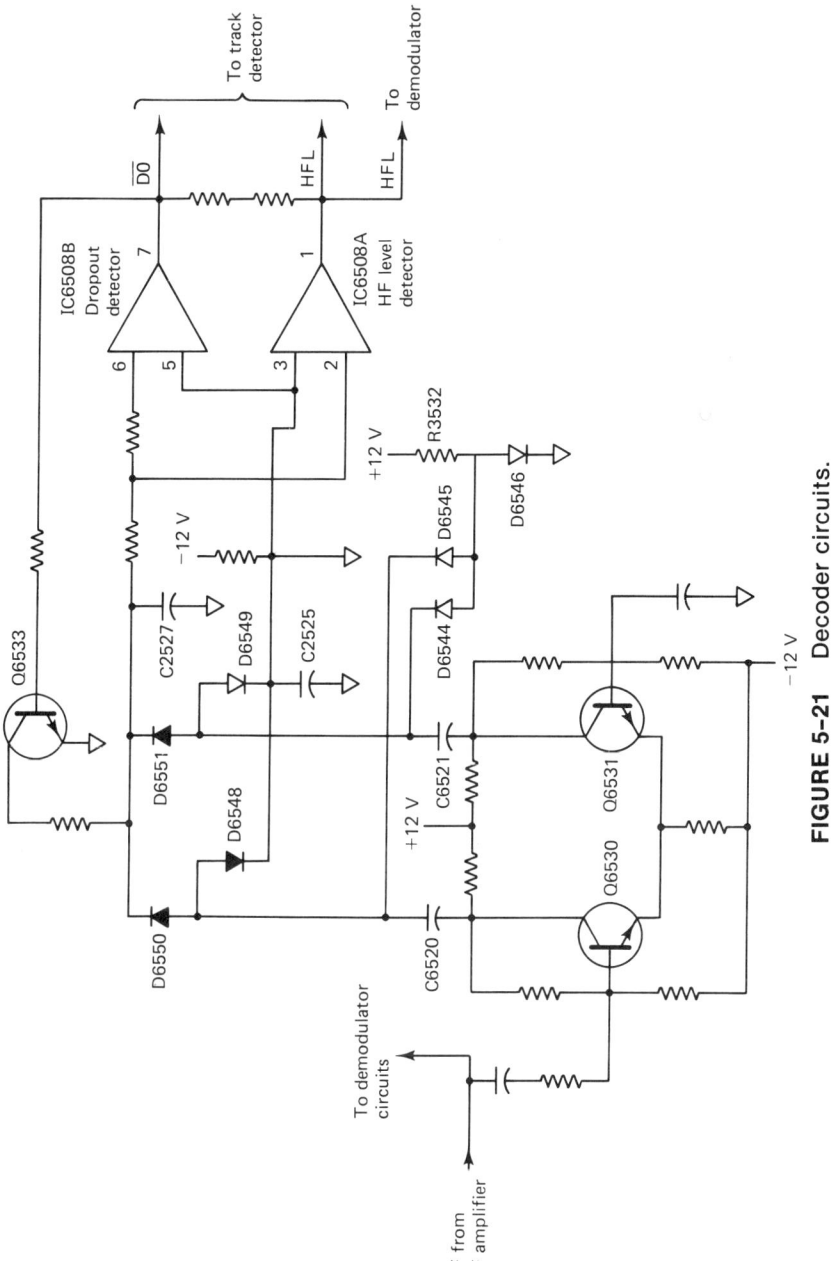

FIGURE 5-21 Decoder circuits.

D6549, D6550, D6551). Diodes D6544, D6545, and D6546, along with R3532, form a clamping circuit to clamp the output level of the differential amplifiers.

The outputs of the full-wave rectifiers are applied to the *HF level detector* IC6508A and the *dropout* (DO) IC6508B. The input on pins 3 and 5 does not vary as much as the input on pins 2 and 6. This is due to smoothing capacitors C2525 and C2527.

If the HF-signal level is nominal (about 1 V p-p), and there are no dropouts in the signal, pin 3 of IC6508 is positive in relation to pin 2, and the output on pin 1 is also positive. The voltage on pin 3 of IC6508 is also applied to pin 5. If the voltage on pin 5 is more positive than the voltage on pin 6, the output at pin 7 is also positive.

If the HF-signal level drops to about 65 percent of the nominal value, pin 3 goes negative in relation to pin 2, causing the output at pin 7 to drop to zero. This indicates a loss of HF signal. The voltage on pin 5 also goes negative, but the voltage on pin 6 is still more negative. This results in no change to pin 7.

When a dropout occurs in the HF signal, the level drops to about 10 percent of the nominal value. With dropout, pin 5 goes more negative than the voltage on pin 6, and the output on pin 7 becomes zero volts. This indicates a dropout condition in the HF signal.

The output voltages on pins 1 and 7 of IC6508 are prevented from changing rapidly by Q6533. The high-frequency level (HFL) and DO level change very rapidly when the light beam encounters fingerprints on the disc. This causes the levels to switch back and forth very quickly, and can cause the system to become unstable. Such a condition is prevented by Q6533, which feeds back a signal to cancel or retard rapid signal changes.

5-7.5 Track-Detector Servo Circuits

Figure 5-22 shows the track-detector servo circuits. Both the HFL and DO signals from the decoder are applied to the track-detector servo, along with the fast-sum FS signal from the radial servo.

When the radial tracking arm moves quickly across the disc, the radial error RE, which controls the arm, must be switched off by the servo microprocessor IC6201. Control of the radial servo system is obtained using the DO and HFL signals in conjunction with the FS signal.

When there is no dropout in the HF signal, then DO is positive. The HFL signal is positive when the HF signal is nominal (1 V p-p). The two levels (DO and HFL) reverse (both go negative) when a dropout occurs and the HFL signal drops to about 10 percent of nominal.

The FS signal from the radial servo appears on the collector of Q6242, which acts as a switch and is operated by the HFL applied to IC6217B. Q6242 conducts when the level of HFL is correct. When Q6242 conducts, the FS signal appears on pin 11 of IC6205A. The output signal on pin 13 of IC6205A

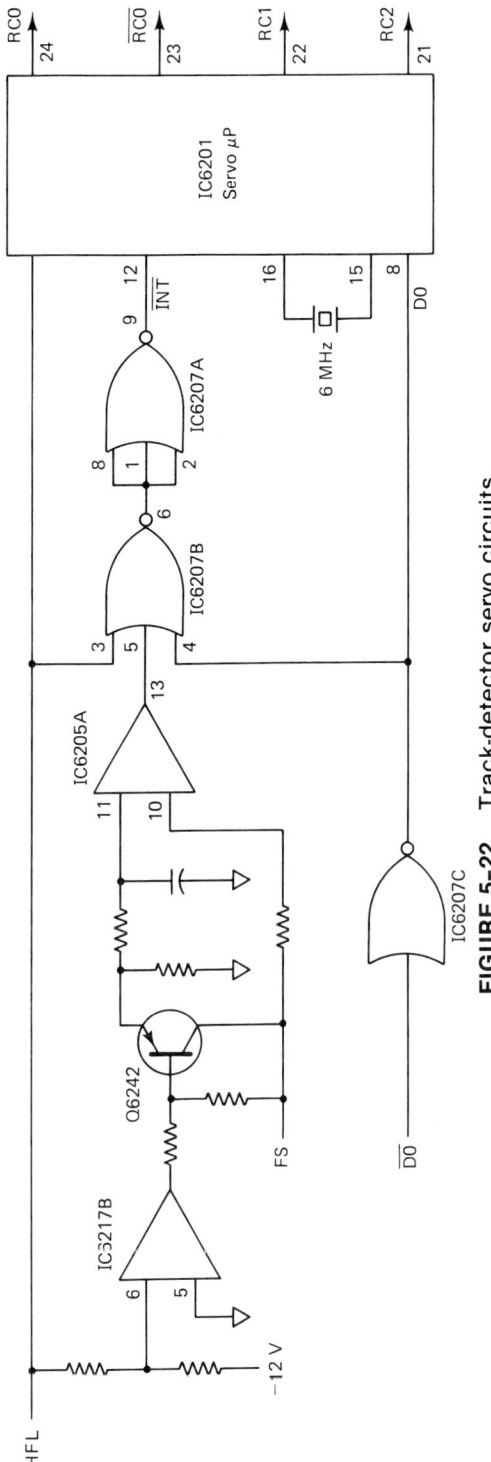

FIGURE 5-22 Track-detector servo circuits.

117

goes positive if the slow-sum (SS) signal on pin 11 is more positive than the signal on pin 10. Pin 13 of IC6205A is zero if pin 11 is more negative than pin 10.

When a loss of HF signal occurs, pins 3 and 5 of IC6207B become zero, and pin 4 (the dropout input) stays zero. Under these conditions the output of IC6207B (pin 6) and the inputs of IC6207A (pins 1, 2, and 8) go to zero. The $\overline{INT}$ output of IC6207A at pin 9 is active-low and is applied to the servo microprocessor IC6201 at pin 12. When IC6201-12 is made low (due to a dropout or other HF signal loss), IC6201 takes control of the radial tracking arm by activating the four outputs (RC0, $\overline{RC0}$, RC1, RC2) to the radial servo system.

As discussed in Secs. 5-7.1 and 5-7.3, the RC0, $\overline{RC0}$, RC1, and RC2 outputs are used to move the arm from inside to outside and back to inside during track jumping. The same outputs are used during dropout or other loss of HF signal to *hold the radial tracking arm at its last known position*. Note that dropout or HF signal loss can be caused by dirt, fingerprints, and scratched blocking passage of the light beam to a portion of the tracks (of pits and flats) on the disc. No matter what the source of signal loss, the tracking detector circuits prevent the system from becoming unstable (skip or jump tracks) each time a signal loss occurs.

5-8 SIGNAL-PROCESSING CIRCUITS FOR TOP-LOAD

Figure 5-23 shows the circuits for processing the HF signal from the photodiodes in block form. Such circuits include the HF preamp, demodulator, digital filter, error correction (ERCO), concealment by interpolation and muting (CIM), digital-to-analog (DAC), audio amp, decoder, and relay control. All the circuits are located on the decoder board except the HF preamp, which is mounted on the amplifier board.

As shown in Fig. 5-23, the HF signal from the photodiodes is about 170 mV (p-p). The level of the HF signal is increased to about 1.5 V (p-p) by the HF preamp. The amplified HF signal is applied to the various ICs on the decoder board and is processed as follows.

5-8.1 Demodulator, ERCO, and CIM

Figure 5-24 shows the circuits associated with the demodulator (IC6501), ERCO (IC6510), and CIM (IC6514) ICs for a CD player similar to that shown in Fig. 1-1a. Figures 5-25 and 5-26 show comparable circuits for a CD player similar to that of Fig. 1-1b. This brings up an important point: Although the information (audio, encoding, track numbering, etc.) is standard for all CDs, the way in which the information is taken from the disc and processed can be quite different for each CD player. The only way you can be sure of how the

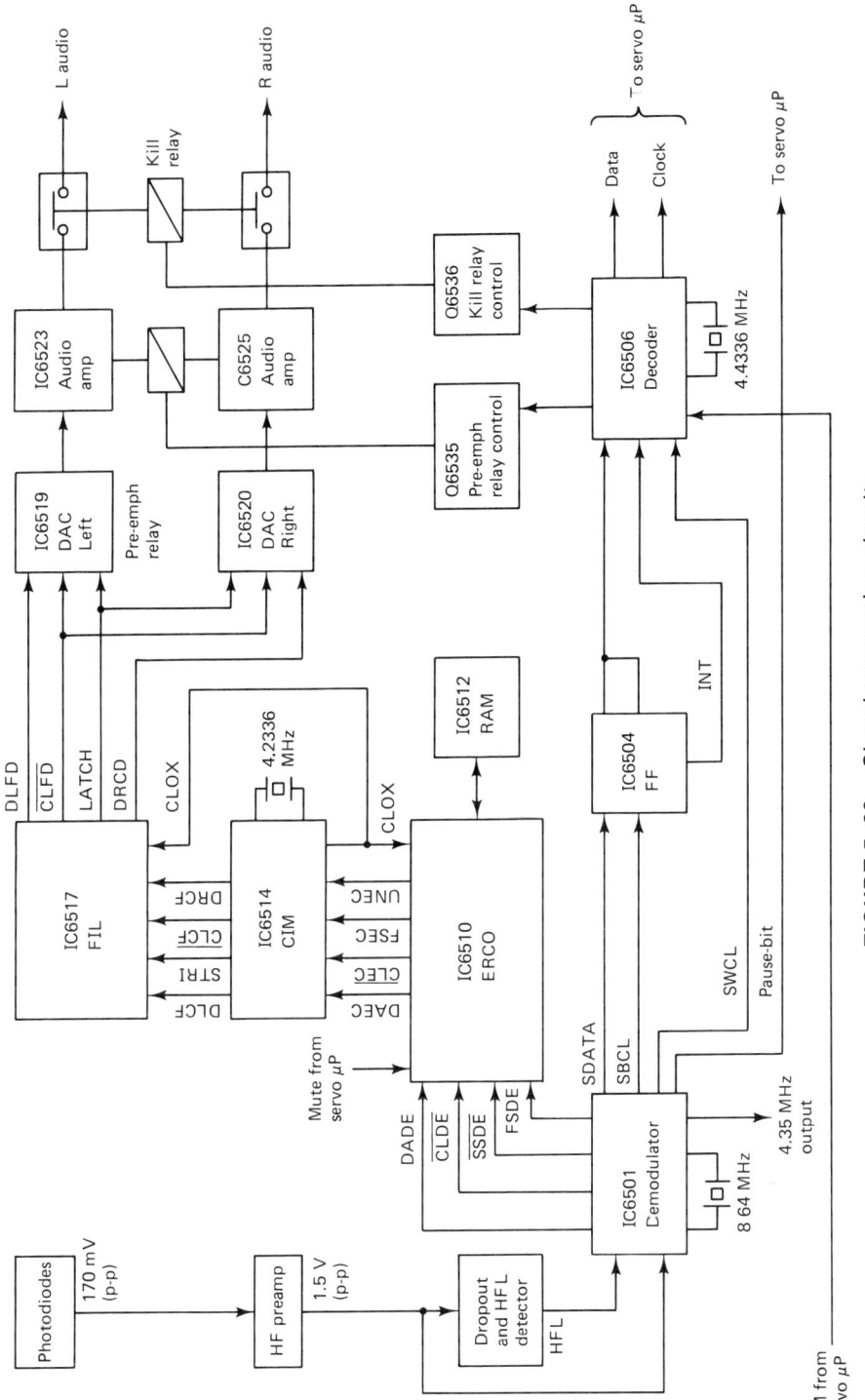

FIGURE 5-23 Signal-processing circuits.

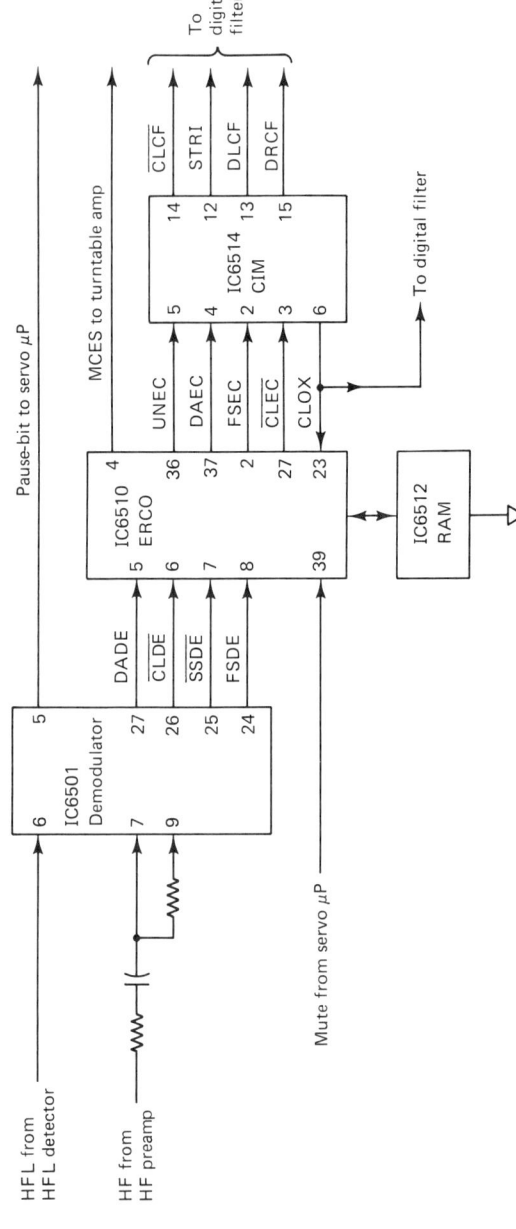

FIGURE 5-24 Demodulation and error correction for FD1000.

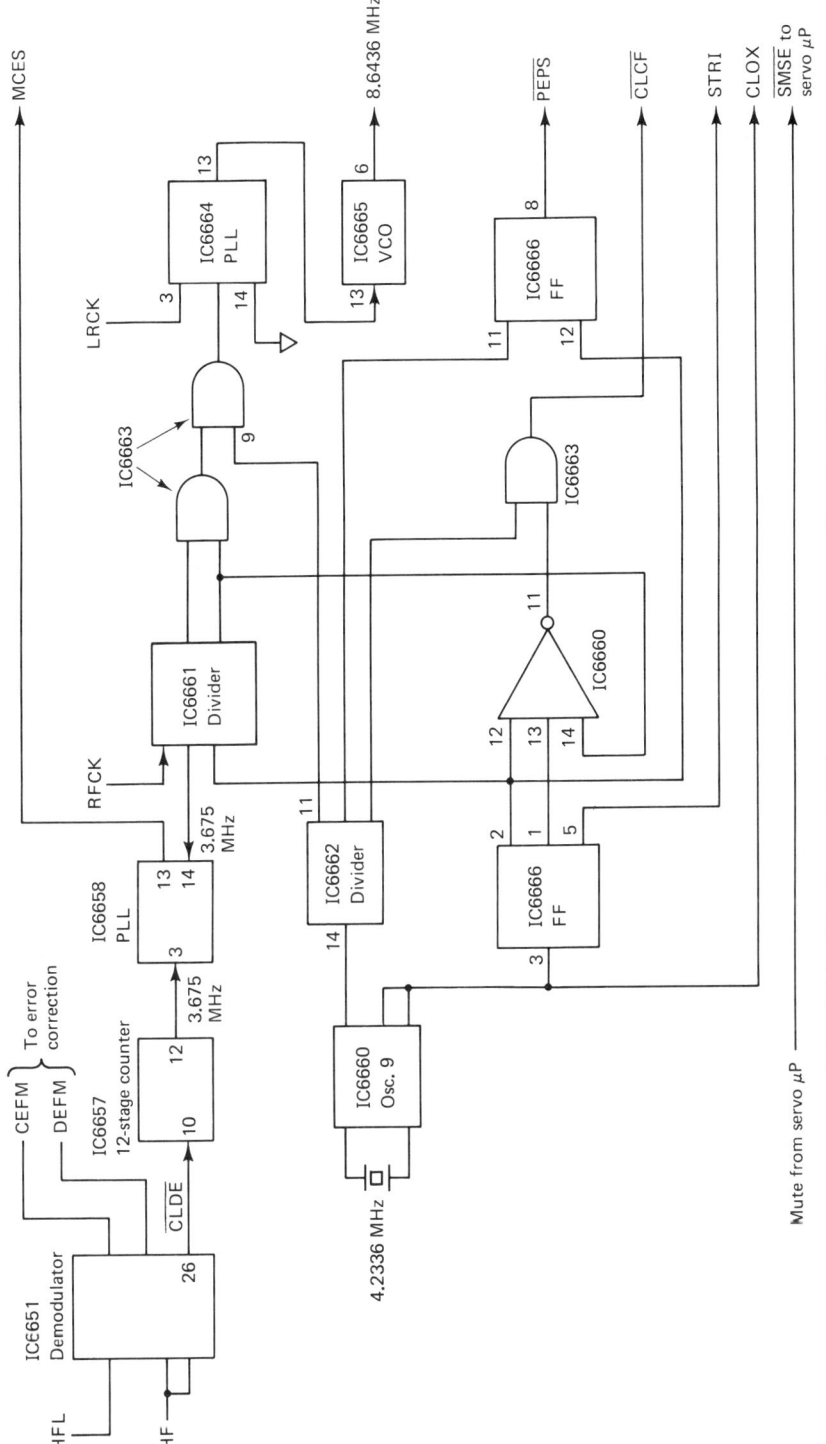

FIGURE 5-25 Demodulation and error correction for FD2000.

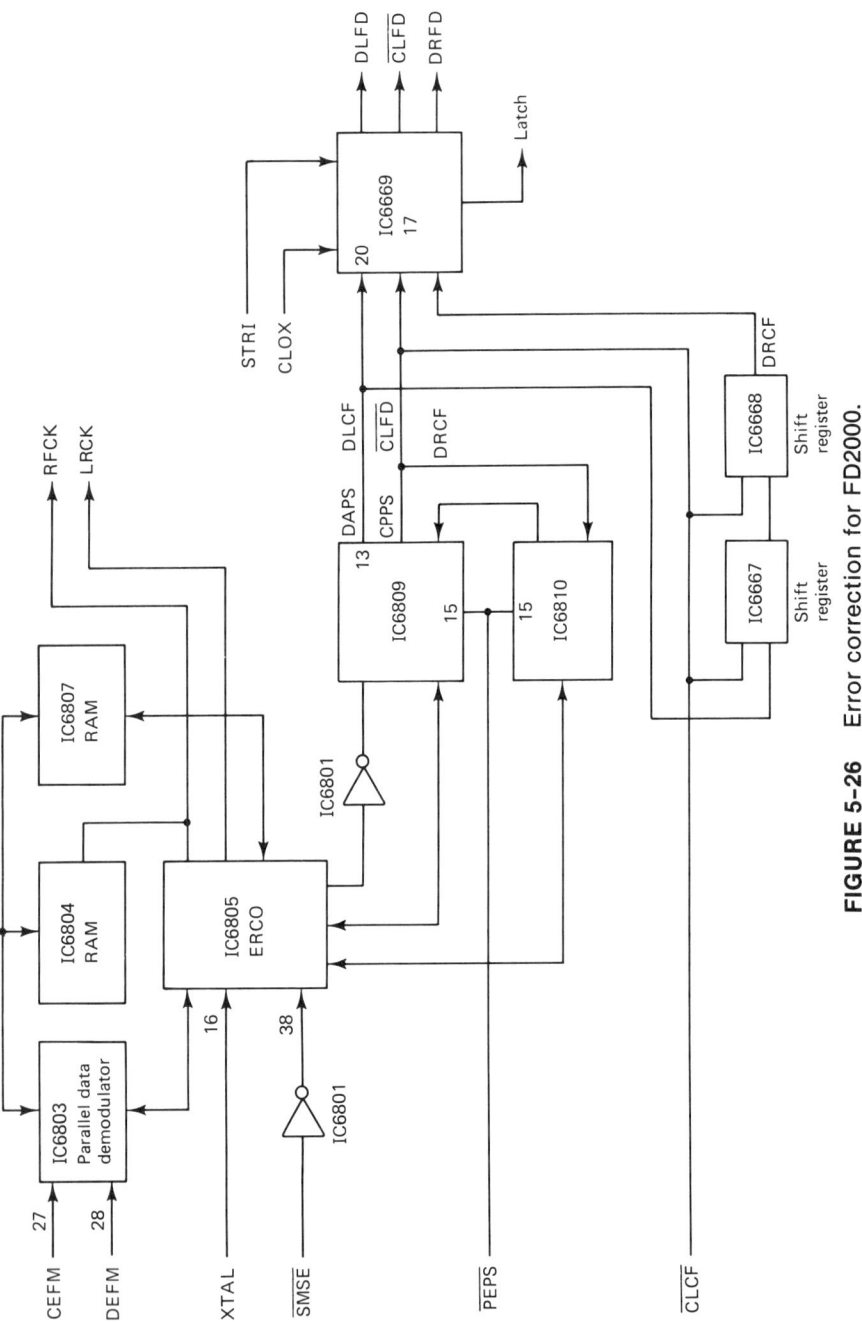

FIGURE 5-26 Error correction for FD2000.

signal-processing circuits work is to study the service schematics, using the discussions of this chapter as a guide.

As shown in Fig. 5-24, the HF signal from the HF preamp is applied to pins 7 and 9 of demodulator IC6501. The HFL from the HFL detector circuit (Fig. 5-21) is applied to pin 6 of IC6501. The main purpose of this HFL signal is to halt demodulation of data when the HF signal is too low. (If the HF signal drops below about 65 percent of the nominal value of 1 V p-p, the bit clock cannot be recovered from the data stream.)

The operating frequency of the demodulator is 8.64 MHz and is locked to the system frequency of 4.32 MHz. The 8.64 MHz is approximately 196 times the sampling rate of 44.1 kHz (actually, 196 times 44.1 kHz = 8.6436 MHz). This frequency ratio is used to aid the system in recovery of the bit clock by comparing the phase of the two frequencies (demodulator and system). Recovery of the bit clock is essential in providing timing signals for processing of the data. The data bits are organized into frames. One frame contains six complete stereo audio samples, with each sample containing 98 channel bits, for a total of 588 bits per frame. The system frequency is obtained by multiplying the 98 channel bits by the sampling rate of 44.1 kHz. This produces a system frequency of 4.32 MHz (actually, 98 times 44.1 = 4.3216 MHz).

The eight-to-fourteen modulated (EFM) data stream (Chapter 2) is demodulated by IC6501, which converts the 14-bit word back to the original 8-bit data symbol. The resultant DADE data bits are then shifted out serially on pin 27 of IC6501 to pin 5 of ERCO IC6510. The data bits are organized into frames of 32 symbols, with 8 bits per symbol. Twenty-four of the symbols are audio (one symbol is half an audio sample of 16 bits), and 8 of the symbols are parity symbols added for error correction and detection.

The data bits must be timed and synchronized to identify and process the data correctly. Timing is provided by the $\overline{\text{CLDE}}$ clock signal at pin 26 of IC6501 to pin 6 of IC6510. Synchronization is provided by the $\overline{\text{SSDE}}$ (symbol sync) and FSDE (frame sync) signals at pins 25 and 24 of IC6501.

The output on pin 5 of IC6501 is the *pause-bit* (P-bit), which is encoded at the beginning of each selection on the disc. The P-bit is used by the servo microprocessor IC6201 to determine the beginning of each selection. The P-bit is also used during the program mode of operation; it allows IC6201 to stop the search for a particular selection each time the P-bit is encountered. The system reads the subcode to determine if that selection is the one requested in the program. If not the requested selection, the search continues in forward or reverse until the correct selection is obtained.

The ERCO IC6510 performs both error detection and correction of the encoded data. The DADE data bits are applied serially to the first-in, first-out (FIFO) register within IC6510. The FIFO register acts as a jitter-reduction circuit to eliminate the effects of wow and flutter. The RAM IC6512, in conjunction with IC6510, is used for de-interleaving (rearranging) the symbols back to the original input word, as described in Chapter 2. The two ICs also check for data errors by using the parity bits encoded in the data stream.

If there are no errors detected by IC6510, the data bits are shifted out serially, along with the clock and frame sync signals, to CIM IC6514. When an erroneous word occurs in the data stream, an unrealiable data signal (identified as the UNEC signal or flag) is sent to pin 5 of IC6514. The UNEC signal notifies IC6514 to begin processing the erroneous symbol. If there are no errors in the signal, IC6510 does not change the DAEC data stream (pin 37), which is shifted out of IC6510 serially, together with the $\overline{\text{CLEC}}$ data clock (pin 27) and FSEC frame sync (pin 2).

The output on pin 4 of ERCO IC6510 is the motor-control error signal, or MCES, which is created by a combination of the memory and the rate of speed at which the incoming data is written into memory. The memory in IC6510 is allowed to fill to half-capacity before the information is removed and passed on at a constant rate to CIM IC6514. The MCES signal is developed when the memory goes above or below the half-capacity. This slows down or speeds up the turntable motor (Sec. 5-6) until the memory again reaches the half-capacity. The speeding up and slowing down of the turntable motor does not affect the rate at which data bits are shifted out of IC6510 to IC6514.

The mute input at pin 39 of IC6510 is developed by the servo microprocessor IC6201 to halt the data flow between IC6510 and IC6514. This function is active during a search or program selection by the front-panel keyboard.

The ERCO IC6510 corrects all erroneous data, if possible. However, when errors are too large for IC6510, this condition is flagged by the UNEC signal at pin 36 of IC6510. The UNEC signal at pin 5 of IC6514 causes the CIM to descramble the data. After descrambling by IC6514, the data bits are passed on to the digital filter (Sec. 5-8.2) as the data left-channel (DLCF) and data right-channel (DRCF) signals. If an error signal is received, IC6514 looks at the symbols adjacent to the erroneous symbol, computes the value of the missing symbol, and inserts the computed value in place of the missing symbol, as discussed in Chapter 2.

The crystal-controlled clock (CLOX) signal generated at pin 6 of IC6514 is used for internal timing of IC6514, as well as for synchronization of ERCO IC6510 and the digital filter. The FSCE and $\overline{\text{CLEC}}$ signals are for internal timing of IC6514, and for reset of IC6514 (which synchronizes IC6514 to IC6510).

Although the coding of information is standard for all compact discs, there are *several ways to process the information* (as you will find out by reading through the remainder of this chapter). For example, the circuit shown in Fig. 5-25 uses a demodulator (designated IC6551) similar to demodulator IC6501 shown in Fig. 5-24. The main difference between the two circuits is in the outputs for the data and clock signals.

The circuit of Fig. 5-24 must convert the EFM, which is a 14-bit word, back to the original 8-bit data symbol, and then shift the data bits out serially to the ERCO IC. The circuit of Fig. 5-25 uses the EFM signal to perform this conversion. The data eight-to-fourteen modulation (DEFM) and clock eight-to-fourteen modulation (CEFM) signals from IC6551 in Fig. 5-25 are applied to the error-correction circuit of Fig. 5-26.

The $\overline{\text{CLDE}}$ signal from pin 26 of IC6551 (Fig. 5-25) is used to generate the MCES signal. (This same $\overline{\text{CLDE}}$ signal from IC6501 of Fig. 5-24 is used to clock data into the ERCO.) The $\overline{\text{CLDE}}$ signal in Fig. 5-25 is applied to pin 10 of IC6657, a 12-stage counter that divides the signal by 512. The output frequency at pin 12 of IC6657 is 3.675 kHz. This signal is applied to pin 3 of IC6658, the PLL IC. The other input to IC6658 at pin 14 is generated by the reference clock (RFCK) from the error-correction circuit. IC6661 divides the RFCK by two to obtain a frequency of 3.675 kHz. The signal at pin 14 of IC6658 locks the MCES signal to the error-correction circuit.

Timing is very important in processing the data stream in any CD player circuit. The output at pin 9 of oscillator IC6660 is a 4.2336-MHz signal, which is applied to pin 14 of IC6662. The output at pin 11 of IC6662 is applied to pin 9 of IC6663, which is used as a gate for PLL IC6664. The output of IC6664 is applied to VCO IC6665, which generates a frequency of 8.6436 MHz. This is the operating frequency for error correction IC6805, Fig. 5-26. IC6805 divides the crystal signal and applies the signal back to PLL IC6664 (at pin 3) as the lock reference clock (LRCK). This locks the VCO to the system frequency of 4.2336 MHz.

Note that the error correction IC6805 (Fig. 5-26) serves the same purpose as the ERCO and CIM ICs in the circuit of Fig. 5-24. However, the output of IC6805 is *parallel data* instead of two channels of serial data (as is generated by the CIM).

The parallel output data from IC6508 is converted to serial data by IC6809 and IC6810. The timing of conversion from parallel to serial data is controlled by the pulse exchange parallel-to-serial (PEPS) signal on pin 8 of flip-flop IC6666 (Fig. 5-25). This is the takeover command for the conversion process. The system mute ($\overline{\text{SMSE}}$) signal at pin 38 of IC6805 mutes the processing of data during search, pause, and program modes of operation.

The primary function of the circuits of Fig. 5-26 is to convert the EFM back to the original 8-bit format. IC6803 receives the clock EFM (pin 27) and data EFM (pin 28) from the demodulator IC6651. IC6803 is the parallel data demodulator for error correction IC6805. IC6804 and IC6807 are RAMs used in storing data during the error-correction process. The outputs of IC6805 are two channels of parallel data that must be converted to serial before application to the digital filter (Sec. 5-8.2). IC6809 and IC6810 are parallel-to-serial converters that provide the data parallel-to-serial (DAPS) signal on pin 13 of IC6809. The PEPS signal on pin 15 of both IC6809 and IC6810 controls insertion of the IC6810 data serially with the IC6809 data.

The clock parallel parallel-to-serial (CPPS) signal, in conjunction with the PEPS signal, is used to clock out the DAPS signal on pin 13 of IC6809.

The DAPS signal contains the serial data for both channels, with left-channel data occurring first, followed by the right-channel data. The DAPS signal is applied to digital filter IC6669, pin 20, as the data for the left channel (DLCF). The separation of data for the right channel is done by applying the DAPS signal to the two 8-bit shift registers IC6667 and IC6668. This delays the DAPS signal for one sample (16-bit delay) to obtain the data for the right channel (DRCF). The DRCF data is applied to pin 17 of digital filter IC6669.

5-8.2 Digital Filter and D/A Conversion

Figure 5–27 shows the circuits associated with digital filtering and D/A conversion. As shown, there are five inputs to digital filter IC6669. The data for the left and right channel is clocked ino IC6669 by the $\overline{\text{CLCF}}$ clock from the CIM at pin 18. The CLOX signal on pin 19 synchronizes IC6669 to the system frequency. The DLCF data bits applied to pin 20 are received as left, right, left, and so on. The DRCF data bits at pin 17 are received as right, left, right, and so on, because of the delay. The strobe-1 (STR-1) signal at pin 21 strobes IC6669 to obtain the left-channel and right-channel data in the proper sequence.

The *data left from filter to D/A* (DLFD) and *data right from filter to D/A* (DRFD) from IC6669 are applied to pin 1 of both D/A converters IC6519 and IC6520. The data bits are clocked into the D/A converters by the *clock from filter to D/A* ($\overline{\text{CLFD}}$) signal at pin 28 of IC6619 and IC6620.

The latch output on pin 7 of IC6669 is used, in conjunction with the CLOX signal, to obtain the strobe-2 (STR-2) signal on pin 3 of IC6663. The STR-2 signal is applied to pin 2 on both IC6519 and IC6520.

The output on pin 22 of both IC6519 and IC6520 is the *original analog signal before the encoding process*. The analog signals on both channels are then amplified by IC6673 (left channel) and IC6675 (right channel) audio amplifiers.

Figure 5–28 shows the left-channel digital conversion circuits in greater detail (including the preemphasis networks and the symmetry control). The right-channel circuits are essentially the same.

5-8.3 Data Decoding

Figure 5–29 shows the data-decoding circuits. These circuits are required in decoding the control and display information encoded in the EFM format during the disc-encoding process.

The demodulator IC6501 or IC6651 demodulates the EFM data and provides the control and display information at pins 2, 3, and 4. The *subcode data bits plus subcode synchronization* (SDATA) on pin 2 is applied to pin 2 of flip-flop IC6504 or IC6552. The *subcode bit clock* (SBCL) information on pin 3 is applied to pins 3 and 11 of the flip-flop IC6504 or IC6552, and is used

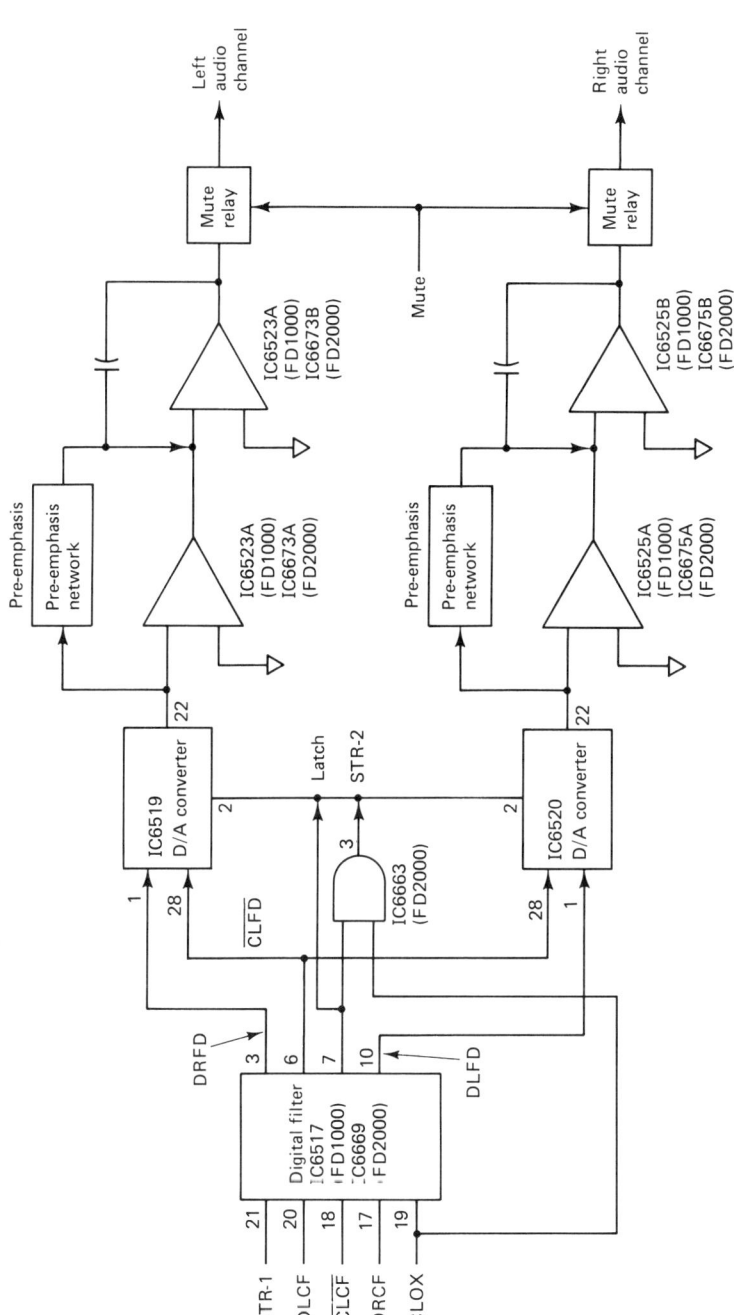

FIGURE 5-27 Digital filter and D/A conversion.

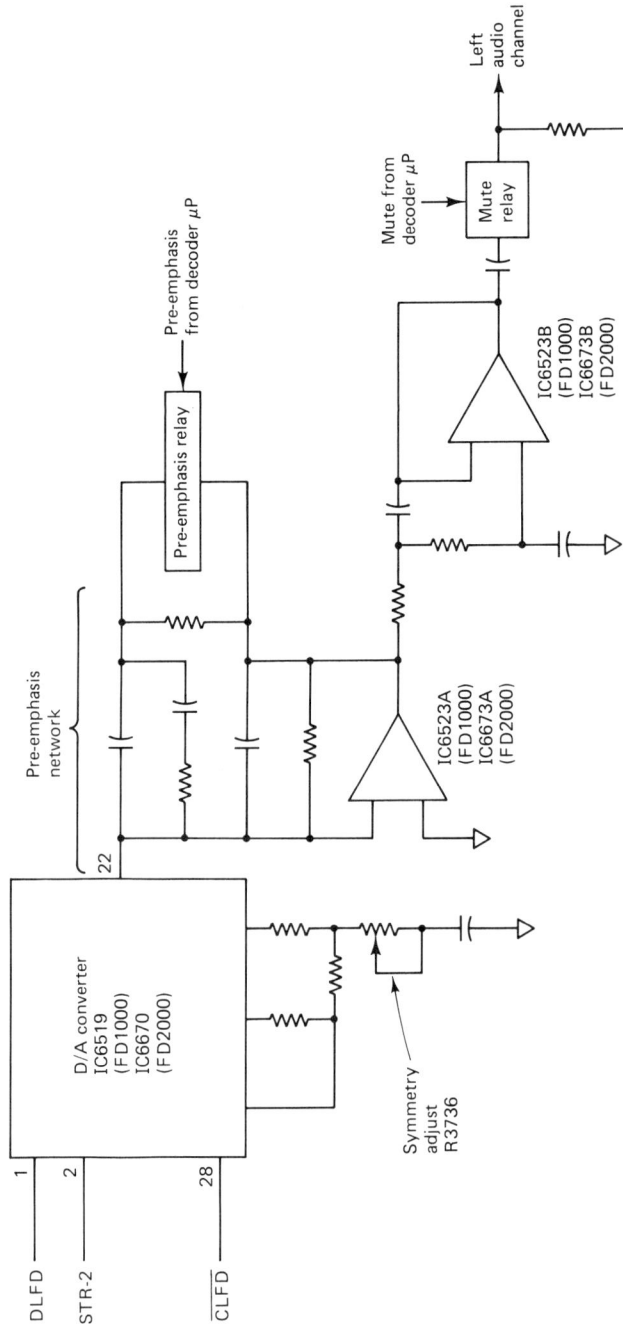

FIGURE 5-28 Left-channel digital conversion.

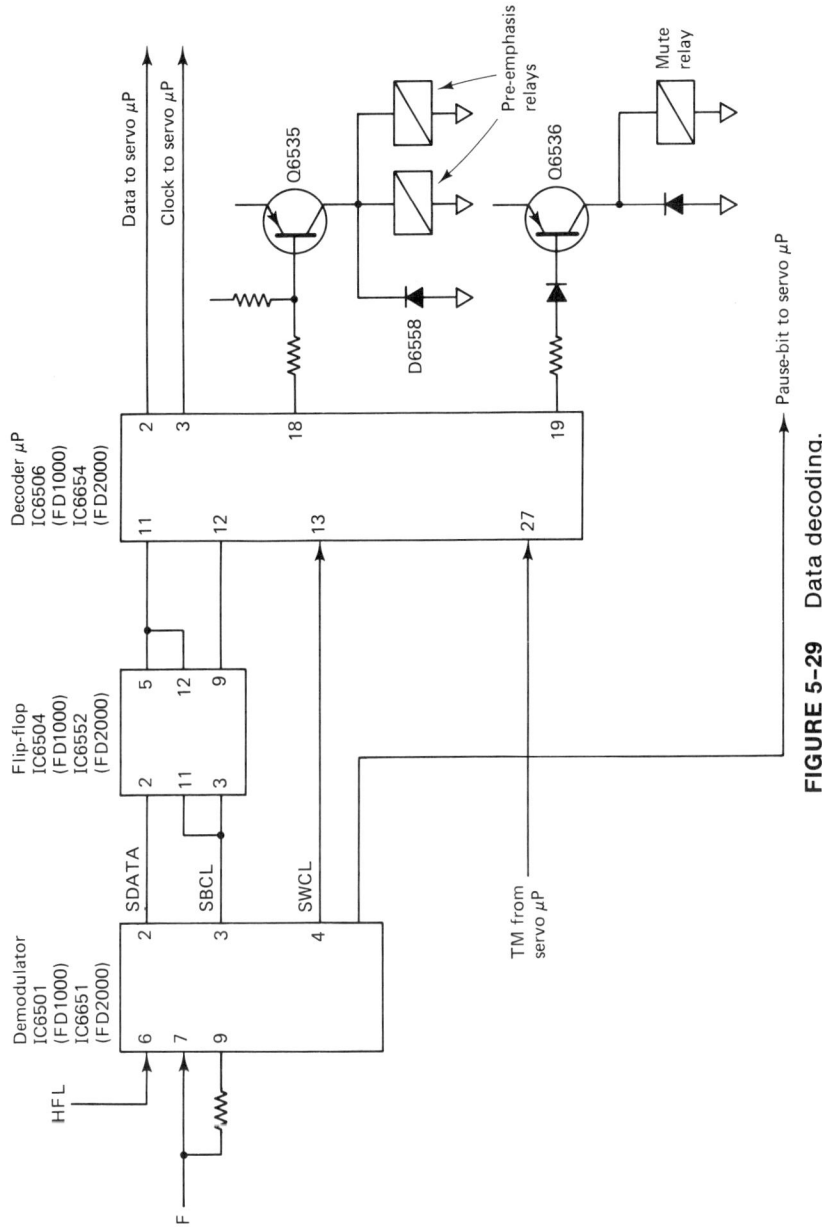

FIGURE 5-29 Data decoding.

to clock the SDATA to the decoder microprocessor IC6506 or IC6654. The *subcode word clock* (SWCL) output on pin 4 provides timing signals for the decoder microprocessor. Another timing signal (TM) from servo microprocessor IC6201 is applied to pin 27 of the decoder microprocessor. The TM signal is generated during the search and program modes of operation.

The decoder microprocessor IC6506 or IC6654 passes the data and clock signals (control and display information) to servo microprocessor IC6201 at pins 2 and 3. If the music or other audio has been recorded with preemphasis, the decoder microprocessor detects a preemphasis code (which has been encoded on the disc during recording). This causes pin 18 of the decoder microprocessor to operate the relays in the two preemphasis networks (Fig. 5–28) of the audio amplifiers.

Undesirable noise may occur when the CD player power supplies are turned on. This is prevented by the audio mute system (Fig. 5–28). Transistor Q6536 is operated by a signal from pin 19 of the decoder microprocessor. Q6536 keeps the mute relays open until the power supplies have reached their nominal value. This prevents audio from passing to the rear-panel audio output connectors.

5-8.4 Control and Command Functions

As shown in Fig. 5–30, data and clock information is supplied to the servo microprocessor IC6201, along with the pause-bit and sense commands. The pause-bit (pin 5) is encoded on the disc at the beginning of each selection to notify IC6201 that the next selection is about to begin. The sense line (pin 4) is scanned continuously by IC6201 for a command from the front-panel keyboard. IC6201 performs the commands in accordance with a built-in program.

The mute output (pin 6) and the timing or TM output (pin 27) from IC6201 are used during the search, pause, and program modes of the system. The mute command is applied to ERCO IC6805 to stop the processing of data, thus muting both audio channels. The TM line is used to signal the decoder IC6506 or IC6654 each time a P-bit is encountered (at the beginning of selections). This allows the decoder to read the subcode of the next selection and compare the selection with that of the program selected.

The data line enable ($\overline{\text{DLEN}}$) output on pin 1 of IC6201 provides the enable command to the front panel. This enable command allows data bits to be clocked into the 34-bit shift register IC6761, which drives the front-panel LED display. The data and clock bits are also applied to IC6763, an 8-stage shift register. IC6763 provides command signals to the front-panel keyboard. When keyboard switches are activated (front-panel buttons are pressed), the command for that particular switch is applied to servo microprocessor IC6201 at pin 4 (the sense line).

The lid switch is connected between the power supply and the laser control circuits, as discussed in Sec. 5-3. The lid switch controls the −7 V used

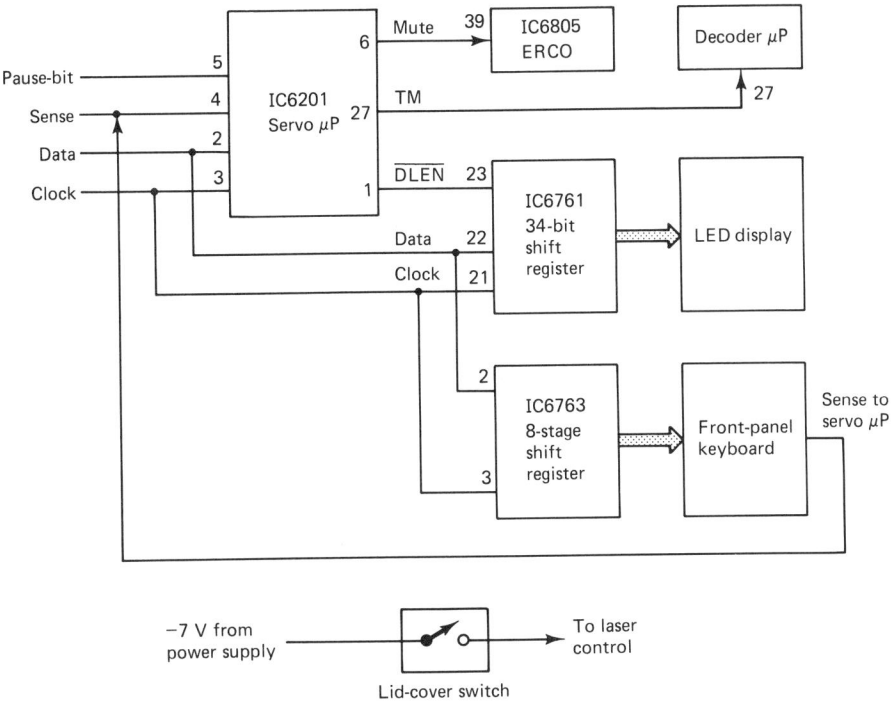

FIGURE 5-30 Control and command functions.

by the laser control circuits, and insures that the laser diode is turned off when the disc compartment lid is open.

5-9 TYPICAL FRONT-LOAD CIRCUITS

In this section we discuss the circuits for some typical front-load CD players, both vertical and horizontal. These circuits perform the same basic functions as the circuits described in Secs. 5-1 through 5-8. However, the circuits here perform their functions in quite a different manner. Also, the circuits described in this section are primarily for the *slide-type optical system* rather than the radial-arm type. Figure 5-31 shows the major sections of a typical front-load CD player in block form.

5-9.1 Front-load Focus

As discussed throughout this book, the purpose of the optics is to *detect* the disc pits while maintaining good *radial tracking* and *focus*. Focus and detection use the center beam (which is also the brightest), while tracking uses all

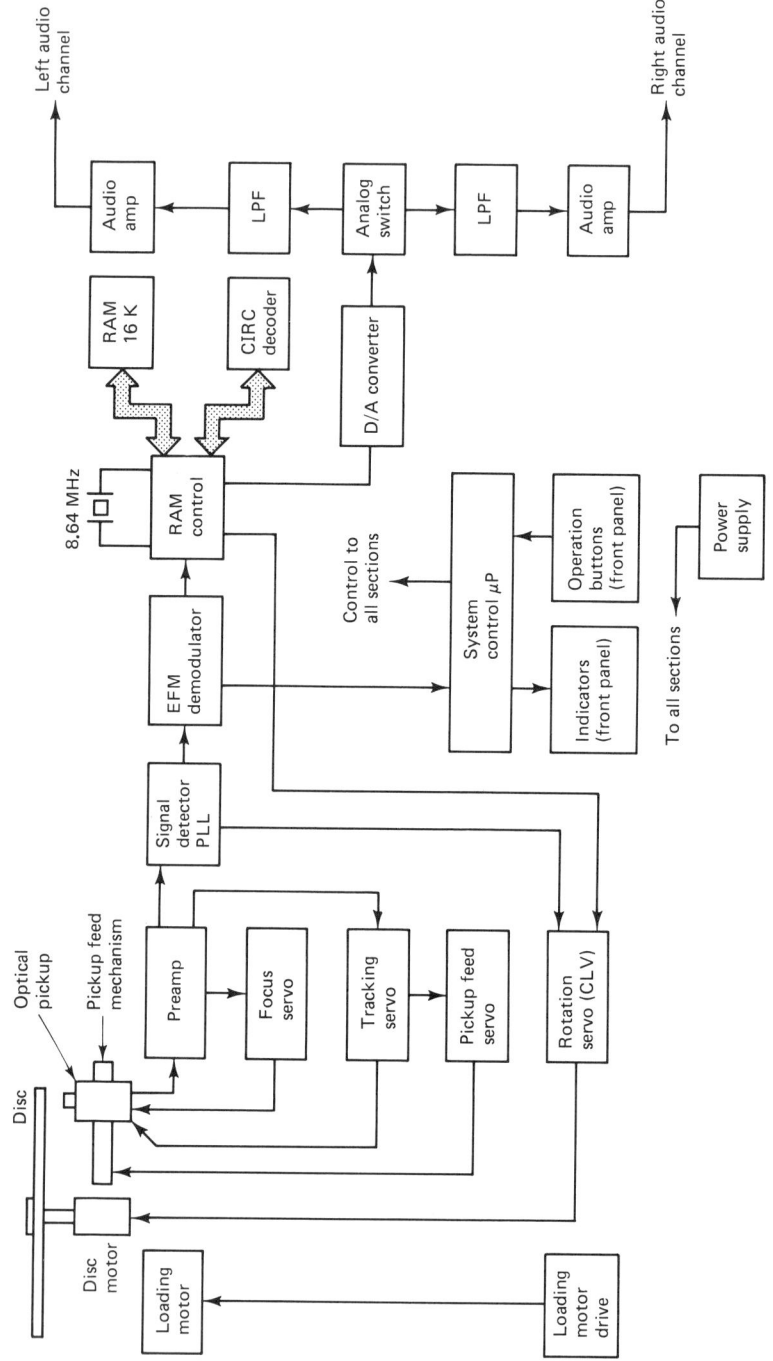

FIGURE 5-31 Major sections of front-load CD players.

three beams. Figure 5-32 shows the focus circuits (in simplified form) for some typical front-load players.

As shown in Fig. 5-32, the center beam illuminates on a four-quadrant photodiode. When the beam is focused on the track, the cylindrical lens makes the reflected beam illuminate equally on all four quadrants of the photodiode. If the beam should focus above the track, the lens makes the beam elliptical and illuminates quadrants 2 and 4 brighter than 1 and 3. If the beam focuses below the track, the reflected beam is again elliptical, but illuminates quadrants 1 and 3 brighter than 2 and 4. Depending on the illumination pattern, the focus circuits move the lens up or down to maintain good focus.

Quadrants 1 and 3 are tied together, and quadrants 2 and 4 are tied together, with all four photodiodes sharing one common connection. The two pairs of photodiodes are applied to the inverting input of two comparators. The noninverting inputs of the comparators are referenced to ground. The outputs of the first pair of comparators are applied to the inverting and noninverting inputs on a second pair of comparators. One of the second comparators is for detection, and produces a signal at pin 28. We discuss this

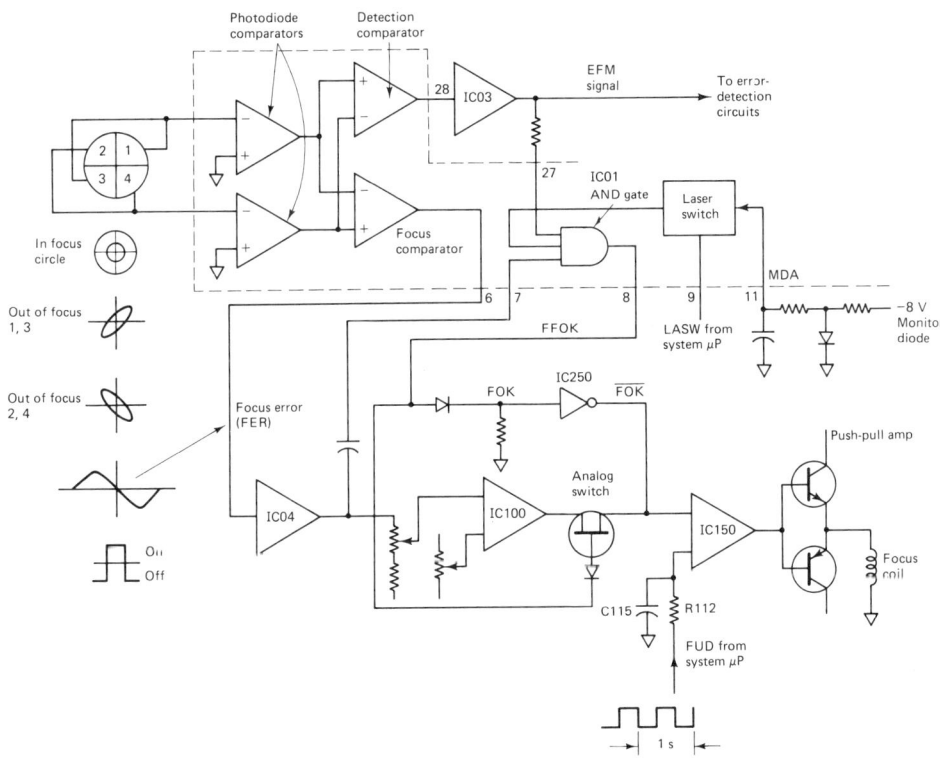

FIGURE 5-32 Front-load focus circuits.

detection signal in Sec. 5-9.3. For now, we concentrate on the focus comparator with an output at pin 6.

When the beam is in focus, it illuminates all quadrants equally. The two photodiode comparators see the same voltage at the inverting inputs, and the comparator outputs are at the same level. These equal output voltages are applied to the focus comparator. Since there are no differences between the voltages, the output at pin 6 is zero (actually the pin 6 is at a fixed d-c reference voltage).

If the beam goes out of focus, either the even (2,4) or odd (1,3) quadrants become brighter and produce a positive or negative voltage deviation from the zero reference. If you plot the voltage at pin 6 versus the amount the beam is out of focus, you get an S-curve similar to that of an FM signal. In the circuit of Fig. 5–32, the S-curve signal is called the focus-error signal or FER.

The FER signal is amplified by IC04 and IC100, and applied through a FET-type analog switch to IC150. The FET switch is turned on by a high from the *focus-ok* or FFOK output of AND-gate IC01. The AND-gate produces the FFOK output only when all three inputs are present. Two of the inputs come from the photodiode comparators. The third input comes from the laser monitor diode, and is present only when the laser beam is on and producing a suitable output.

The FER signal from IC150 is applied to the focus coil through push-pull amplifier circuits. The focus coil moves the lens up or down to achieve proper focus. This focus adjustment allows for a focus precision of about ±1 μm.

When a disc is first loaded, a *rough focus* adjustment is made possible by the focus-up/down or FUD signal from the system microprocessor. The FUD signal consists of two square-wave pulses that have a period of 1 sec. The two pulses are applied to IC150 through an integrator composed of R112 and C115. The integrated signal drives IC150 and the push-pull amplifier to move the lens up and down *two times*. The first time the lens starts to move toward the disc, the laser illuminates the disc. The lens stops when a $\overline{\text{FOK}}$ signal is applied through IC250 to IC150. If no disc is detected the first time, the lens moves toward the disc one more time (on the second FUD pulse). The system microprocessor shuts the system down if no disc is detected.

In some front-load CD players (particularly those with vertical disc loading) the analog switch shuts off and the FOK signal pulls the focusing lens all the way back to prevent contact with the disc whenever the automatic focus system is not working (door open, laser inoperative, etc.). In other front-load players (particularly those with horizontal disc loading), the focus lens retracts just enough to prevent contact with the disc. It is generally not necessary to retract the lens fully on horizontal-load players, since the horizontal loading mechanism lifts the disc up upon retraction to further prevent the possibility of contact.

5-9.2 Front-load Radial Tracking

Most front-load CD players use some form of three-spot radial tracking, which is similar to that of top-load players. Figures 5-33 and 5-34 show the radial tracking circuits (in simplified form) for some typical front-load players. As discussed in Sec. 1-4.1 (and illustrated in Fig. 1-10), the laser light is split into three beams when the light emerges from the diffraction grating. The three beams continue along the optical path and are focused on the disc surface. Under conditions of proper tracking, the center or main beam is focused directly on the correct circumference containing pits. The two tracking beams (also called *first-order beams*) are focused above and below and are slightly offset from the center beam. With proper tracking, half of each tracking beam is focused on the pit circumference, while the other half is focused on the mirrored area between pit circumferences (Fig. 1-10).

The three beams reflect off the surface of the disc and travel back through the ¼-waveplate to the half-prism, where the beams take a 90° turn. The main beam is detected by the four-quadrant photodiode. The two tracking beams are picked up by two separate photodiodes (TRA and TRC) mounted on each side of the four-quadrant photodiode, as shown in Fig. 5-33. The TRA and TRC photodiodes produce corresponding TRA and TRC tracking signals.

The TRA tracking signal is applied to op-amp IC06, which is connected as a current-to-voltage converter. Since the TRA photodiode is a current device activated by light, it is necessary to convert current changes into corresponding voltage changes. The gain of the converter is set by the *tracking servo offset* control, an adjustable potentiometer in the feedback circuit. The output of the TRA converter is applied to one input of a comparator IC01.

The TRC tracking signal is also converted to a voltage by another op-amp within IC06. However, the output of the TRC converter is not adjustable. The TRC voltage output is applied to the other input of comparator IC01 through a 30-μs time-delay network consisting of CP03 and CP04. This time delay is necessary because the tracking circuits require the TRC and TRA beams to analyze the *same point* on the disc. At one instant, the TRC beam analyzes a particular spot on the disc. As the disc continues to rotate toward the TRA beam, the same spot on the disc is analyzed by the TRA beam, but after a 30-μs delay. As a result, the voltage outputs from the TRA and TRC converters reach the input of the comparator at the same time.

If the system is tracking properly, the TRA and TRC converter outputs are equal, and the comparator output is zero. Should the main beam start drifting one way or the other, the converter outputs are different. As a result, the comparator output varies above and below 0 V, depending upon the position of the main beam on the disc. The comparator output is called the tracking-error or TER signal, and has the characteristic S-curve, as shown in Fig. 5-33 (similar to that of the focus-error system). The TER signal is further

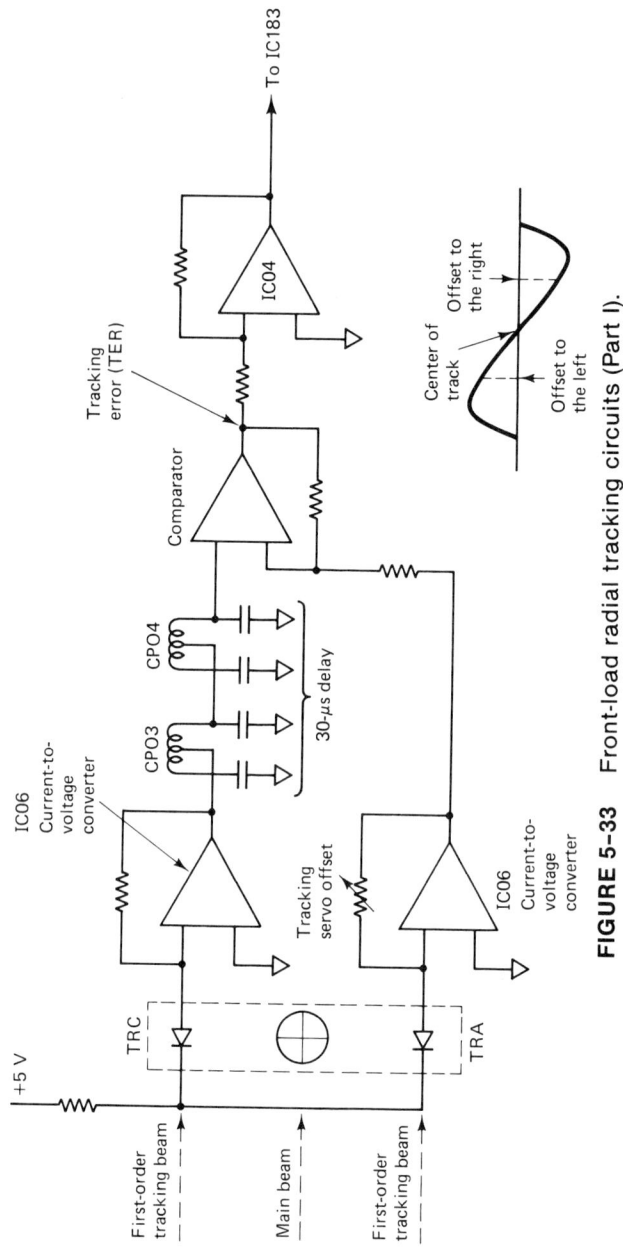

FIGURE 5-33 Front-load radial tracking circuits (Part I).

5-9 Typical Front-load Circuits 137

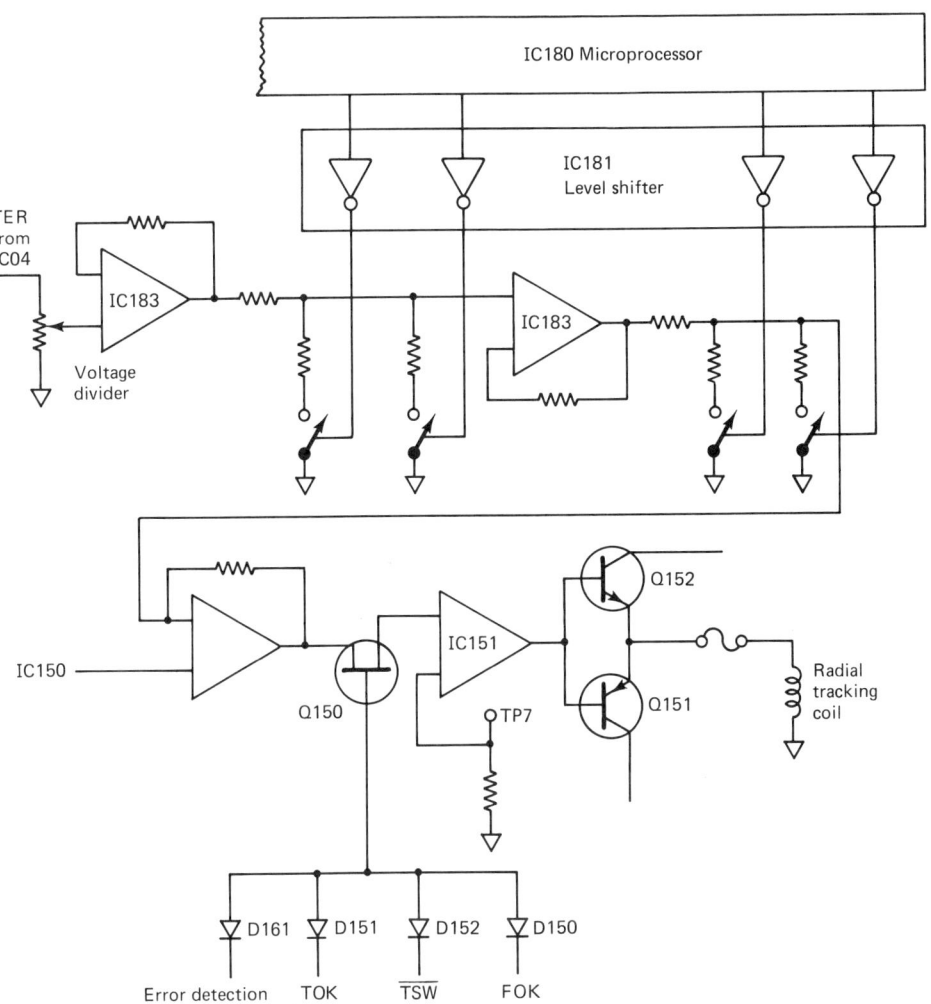

FIGURE 5-34 Front-load radial tracking circuits (Part II).

amplified by IC04, and is applied to amplifier IC183 through an adjustable voltage divider, as shown in Fig. 5-34.

In some front-load CD players (particularly those with vertical disc loading), a *variable gain* system is used in the radial tracking circuits to compensate for variances in reflectivity of the disc. In the circuit of Fig. 5-34, variable gain is provided by IC183, which is an op-amp controlled by resistors. By using microprocessor IC180 and a level shifter IC181, various resistances are switched into the amplifier circuits to vary the gain from +10 dB to −6 dB. When the gain is adjusted to a predetermined value, IC180 signals the system microprocessor. The gain adjustment is performed during the initial read of the disc, and the calculated gain remains as long as the disc is in the play mode. Once a jump or search function is initiated, the gain goes to a predetermined value, called TYP gain (generally 0 dB). Not all front-load CD players use this variable gain in the radial tracking system. Instead, the system microprocessor is programmed to compensate for gain variations.

The TER signal is gated by FET Q150 and applied to the radial tracking coil through IC151 and the push-pull amplifier Q151/Q152. (Note that the combination of Q150, IC151, Q151/Q152 and the tracking coil is sometimes referred to as the tracking servo or, in some literature, as the TAC actuator. However, this is not to be confused with the slide or pickup motor and the servo circuits that operate the motor.) FET Q150 is gated on by signals from different sources. For the TER signal to pass, it is necessary for four diodes (D150, D151, D152, D161) to be reverse-biased by various signals. In effect, the four diodes act as an AND gate. The four signals necessary to gate Q150 on are: FOK (focus-ok), TOK (tracking-ok), $\overline{TSW}$ (not-tracking switch), and damage-detection signal.

The FOK signal is discussed in Sec. 5-9.1. TSW is generated by the system-control microprocessor ($\overline{TSW}$ is the gating signal from TSW after inversion). The damage-detection signal and TOK are discussed later in this section (Sec. 5-9.6). Before going into any of these signals, let us review how the signal-processing circuits are used to take audio information from the disc.

5-9.3 Front-load Detection and EFM Signal Generation

Figure 5-35 shows the circuits used to detect the information encoded on the disc in the form of pits and flats. Besides having the responsibility of focus detection (Sec. 5-9.1), the main beam must also detect the presence or absence of pits on the disc track. When a pit is present, the main beam is absorbed and no reflection occurs. When a pit is not present (a flat), the beam reflects back to the four-quadrant diode. As discussed in Sec. 5-9.1, the quadrants are broken down in pairs (1,3 and 2,4) and are applied to two inverting amplifiers (or comparators) in IC01. The outputs of the two amplifiers are applied to the focus comparator (Fig. 5-32) and to the detection comparator or amplifier. This amplifier acts as a mixer to combine the four signals from the two comparators.

The output of the IC01 comparator/amplifier/mixer is at pin 28 of IC01. This output is amplified by an op-amp within IC03 (which has a voltage gain of about 3) and is returned to IC01 as the EFM signal. Note that the EFM signal resembles a variety of high-frequency sine waves, as shown in Fig. 5-35. (Also note that the EFM signal can be called the high-frequency or *HF signal,* the *RF signal,* or the *eye pattern.*) Although the waves of the EFM signal appear to be sine waves, they are digital signals. The designations of 3T, 4T, and so on, refer to 3 times the period required to read one pit, 4 times the period, and so on. The limits of the EFM signal, 3T-11T, are set by CD specifications.

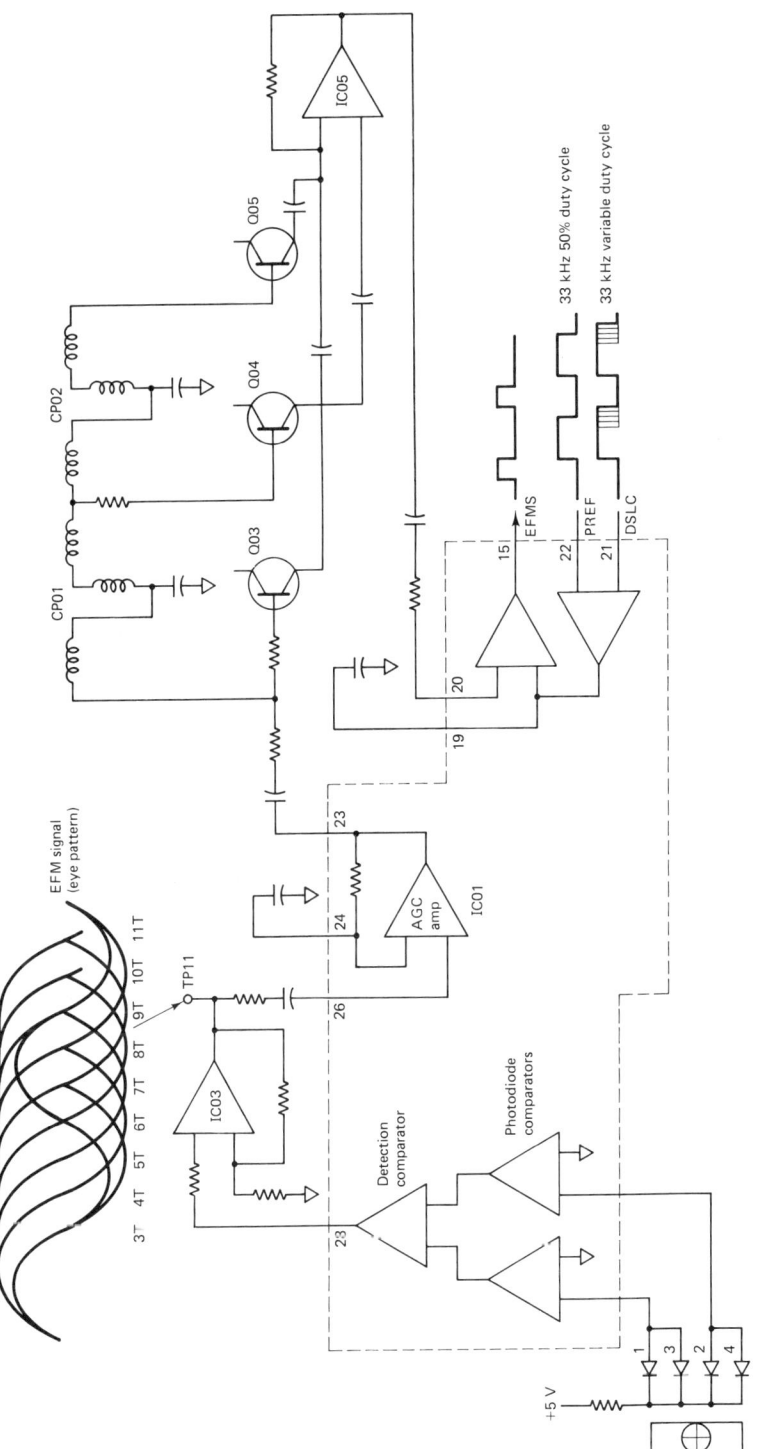

FIGURE 5-35 Front-load detection and EFM signal generation.

The EFM signal returns to IC01 at pin 26 and is applied to pin 23 through an AGC amplifier. The EFM signal exits IC01 at pin 23 and enters an equalization network (actually a transverse filter) composed of Q03, Q04, Q05, CP01, CP02, and IC05. The transverse filter is necessary to assure that the 3T signal (high frequency) is equal in amplitude with the 11T signal (low frequency). The output of the filter is applied to a comparator within IC01 at pin 20. This comparator is used to shape the EFM signal into square waves (to be more compatible with other digital circuits in the player).

The EFM signal is compared to a d-c threshold voltage developed by closed-loop circuits within IC01, IC402, and IC404. The EFM signal at pin 15 of IC01, referred to as the EFMS signal, is applied to pin 21 of IC402 through Q402. The EFMS signal is detected within IC402 and applied to controller IC404, which develops two square-wave signals. A variable-duty cycle 33-kHz square wave, called the data-slice level control or DSLC, is applied to pin 21 of IC01 through an inverter and an integrator. A 50 percent duty cycle 33-kHz square wave, called the preference pulse or PREF, is applied to pin 22 of IC01 through two inverters and an integrator. The two square waves are compared by an amplifier within IC01, and produce an error voltage. This error voltage becomes the threshold voltage for the EFM comparator. The output of the EFM comparator (at pin 15) is the EFMS in true digital form.

5-9.4 Front-load Signal Control Logic Circuits

Once the disc information has been detected and the EFM signal generated, the signal control logic circuits process the digital signal before application to the digital-to-analog converter (where the digital information is converted to audio, as discussed in Sec. 5-9.5). Typically, the signal control circuits are contained within three or four ICs. Figure 5-36 shows the overall relationship of ICs in typical signal control logic circuits. There are five ICs involved in the system of Fig. 5-36: clock IC401, RAM IC405, data strobe processing IC402, error-detection and -correction IC403, and controller IC404.

The following paragraphs describe the functions performed within the three major ICs. Keep in mind that the functions cannot be altered, adjusted, or even checked, since the circuits are not accessible. At best, you can check input and output functions at the IC pins during troubleshooting.

Data strobe processing IC402. As shown in Fig. 5-37, IC402 has many functions. However, the major function is to detect and generate sync pulses derived from the EFMS signal applied at pin 21. The sync pulses generated include:

Bit synchronization (DATAK): The DATAK pulse (pin 13) is generated in sync with the EFMS signal and is necessary to determine whether the digital information is a 1 or a 0.

5-9 Typical Front-load Circuits   141

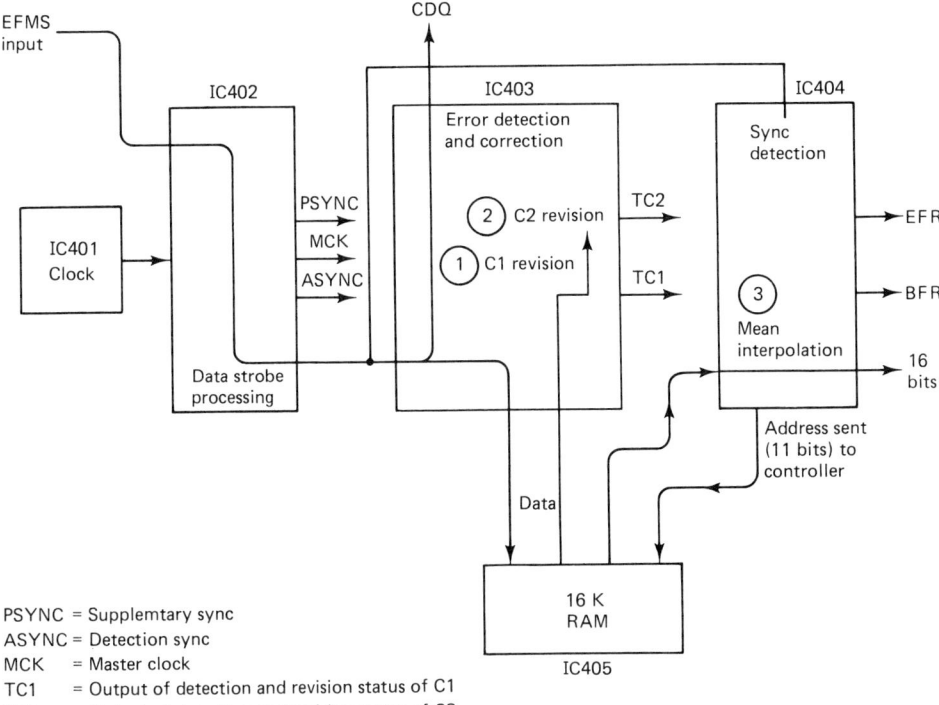

PSYNC = Supplemtary sync
ASYNC = Detection sync
MCK   = Master clock
TC1   = Output of detection and revision status of C1
TC2   = Output of detection and revision status of C2
EFR   = Output of mean interpolation and compensation status
BRF   = Output of interleave in a surpassed condition

FIGURE 5-36 Overall relationship of ICs in typical signal-control logic circuits.

Symbol synchronization (SSYNC, CDSTR, DSTR): An SSYNC pulse (pin 11) is generated for synchronizing the 33 symbols in a frame. The clock CDSTR (pin 19) and display DSTR (pin 17) strobe pulses are generated for use by IC403.

Frame synchronization (ASYNC, BSYNC): Synchronization bits are added to each frame during encoding of the disc (Chapter 2). These bits are extracted by IC402 and applied to IC403 as ASYNC (pin 3) and BSYNC (pin 1).

Just prior to the information being encoded on the disc, the NRZ (nonreturn to zero) is changed to NRZ-i. IC402 transforms the NRZ-i signal back to the NRZ format. The NRZ signal is output at pin 13 as SDATA, and is applied to IC403.

Error-detection and -correction IC403. As shown in Fig. 5-38, the main functions of IC403 are to demodulate the EFM signal and unscramble the signal back to the original 16 bits of digital data. IC403 uses a 16K RAM for

142 Typical CD Player Circuits

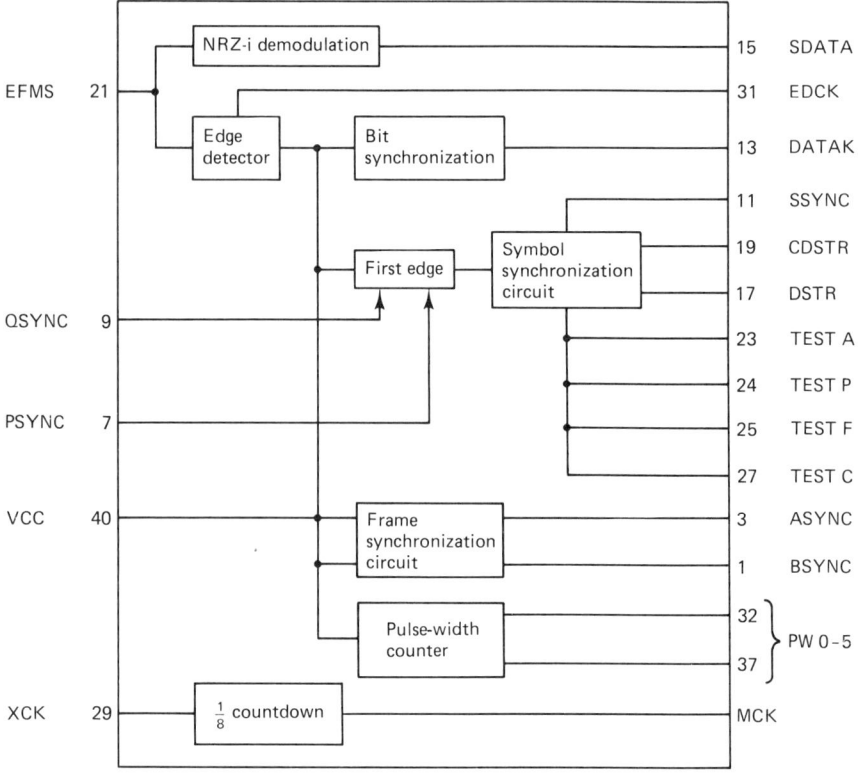

FIGURE 5-37 Data strobe processing IC402.

storage of the processed data. Transfers of the data between IC403 and memory (both internal and external) are controlled by IC404.

The EFMS signal enters at pin 28 of IC402 and is demodulated by means of a stored table. When the disc is encoded (Chapter 2), the symbols are scrambled, interleaved, and parity bits added. IC403 decodes the various processes in the reverse order. IC403 uses the internal RAM to assist in reorganization of the data. The internal ram is split into 3 columns, with a memory capacity of 3 frames.

Once the unscrambling process is complete, *P-parity* is detected and corrected. This process is called *C1-decoding*. When correction is performed, a pulse is output at TC1 (pin 1). Test point TP7, connected to TC1, permits the C1-decoding process to be monitored with a frequency counter. If the TC1 count exceeds a given amount (typically 200 pulses per second, or less), this indicates that there is a problem in the C1-decoding process. The problem will also show up (usually) as a malfunction (skipping, lack of audio, etc.). In some players the audio is muted if the C1-decoding count exceeds a certain level.

Communication between IC403 and the access microprocessor IC601

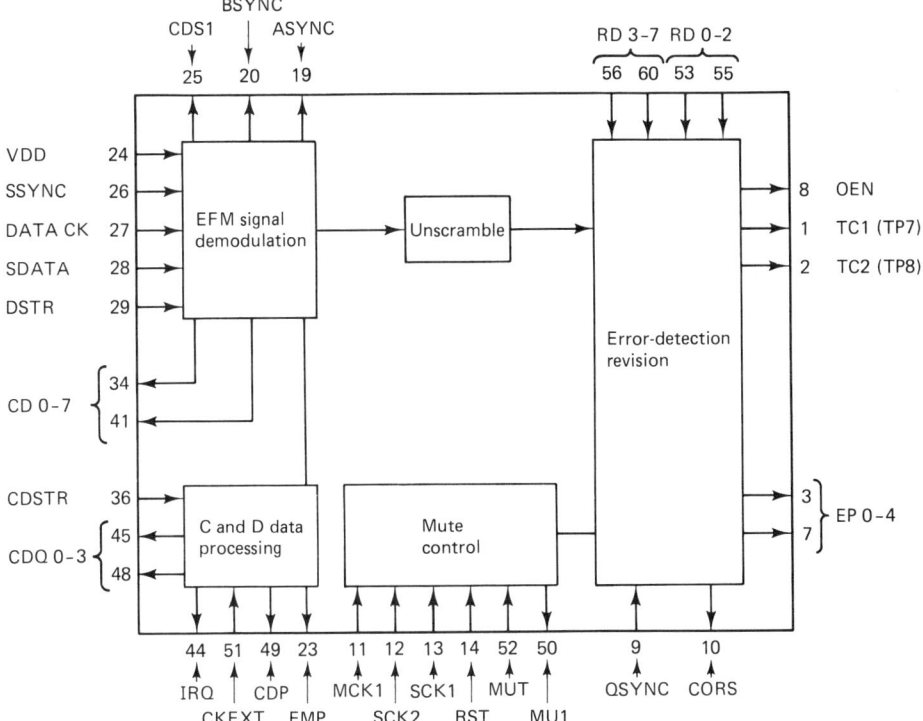

FIGURE 5-38 Error detection and correction IC403.

(which calculates the errors) is carried over MU1 (pin 50) and MUT (pin 52). Once correction has been made, the data bits are stored in external RAM IC405. Note that the data bits are stored in a special order so as to *de-interleave* the encoding process.

After the de-interleaving process is done, *Q-parity* is detected and corrected. This process is called *C2-decoding*. When correction is performed, a pulse is output at TC2 (pin 2). Test point TP8, connected to TC2, permits the C2-decoding process to be monitored. Again, if the TC2 count exceeds a given amount (typically 1000 pulses per second, or less), there is a problem in the C2-decoding, and (probably) an obvious malfunction in player performance.

After the C2-decoding process, the data bits are transferred to external memory IC405. (The bits are placed in IC405 so as to compensate for any delay in the decoding circuits.) External memory IC405 holds the digital information for conversion to the original audio by the D/A converter IC406 (Sec. 5-9.5).

IC403 also has the task of processing *control and data information* from the encoded information (in addition to demodulating the audio). Fourteen bits of control and data information are added to each frame. IC403 reads 98 frames and addresses the 14 bits of control and data information from each frame into the internal RAM to form a block. Each block is broken up into different channels controlling the time and track displays. This information is applied to the system by access microprocessor IC601, which receives the information from IC403 over CDQ0-3 (pins 45-48) and CDP (pin 49) lines.

Controller IC404. As shown in Fig. 5-39, IC404 governs many of the digital circuit functions. For example, using data from the error-pointer inputs from IC403, IC404 correctly addresses the proper location within external RAM IC405 during error detection and correction. IC404 also receives and generates sync pulses used by the servo circuits to determine DSLC duty-cycle and PREF/PWM pulses (discussed at the beginning of this section).

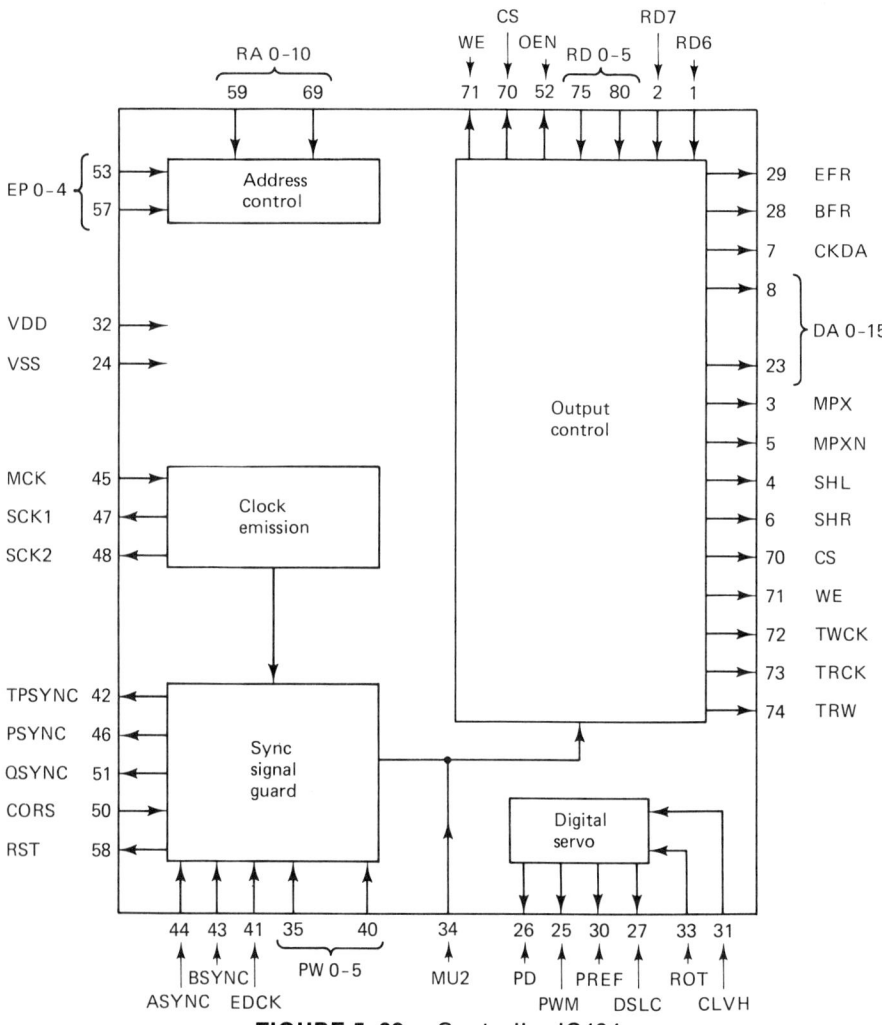

FIGURE 5-39 Controller IC404.

5-9 Typical Front-load Circuits   145

The main purpose of controller IC404 is to address memory locations in external RAM IC405, and to read information from these memory locations via the RDO-7 (pins 75–80) lines. IC404 also has the responsibility of outputting the 16 bits of digital information (representing the original audio, but in digital form) to the D/A converter (Sec. 5-9.5) over the DAO-15 (pins 8–23) lines.

5-9.5 D/A Converter and Audio Section

Figure 5-40 shows the D/A converter and audio circuits (in simplified form) for some typical front-load players. The D/A converter IC406 is a 16-bit device, using the familiar R-2R ladder configuration with an op-amp summing circuit. IC406 is capable of producing 2^{16} or 65,536 analog or audio output levels.

The audio output from IC406 is amplified by IC407 and multiplexed into

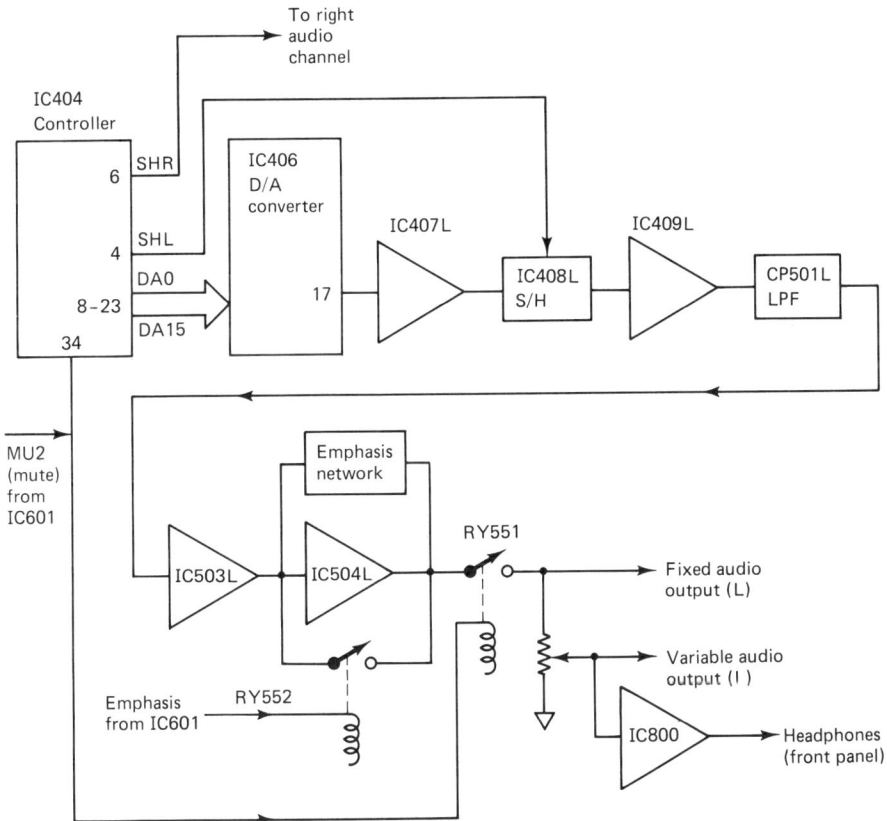

FIGURE 5-40 D/A converter and audio section (left channel).

right and left channels by special sample-and-hold (S/H) circuits within IC408, under the control of IC404. When the left channel is in the sample status (audio output from IC406 passing), the right channel is being held (audio not passing), and vice versa.

The right- and left-channel outputs from the S/H circuit are amplified by IC409 and applied through a low-pass filter (LPF) CP501 to amplifier IC503. CP501 has a very sharp drop-off between 20 and 25 kHz, so any frequencies above the audio spectrum (which might produce distortion) are rejected. Low-pass filter CP501 also smooths out the transitions between the analog voltage levels. Further filtering and amplification are performed by IC503 and IC504, both of which are preamp ICs with equalization resistors and capacitors (or emphasis circuits) in the feedback paths. In some cases, the equalization/emphasis networks are under the control of relays and switches (RY552 in the circuit of Fig. 5-40).

The outputs of the right and left channel are routed to the rear and front panels through various controls and circuits. In the player of Fig. 5-40, there are both fixed and variable outputs on the rear panel and a variable output at the front panel (for the headphones).

In most players, the audio outputs can be muted by relays (either electronic or mechanical). In the circuit of Fig. 5-40, the audio outputs are applied through RY551, which is under control of the MU2 signal (developed by IC601). This same MU2 signal is also used to mute the digital signal path (at pin 34 of IC404), as shown in Fig. 5-39.

5-9.6 Error-detection Circuits

Many CD players include some form of error-detection circuit that monitors the EFM signal for problems (skipping between tracks, defects in the disc, etc.). When such problems occur, the error-detection circuits apply signals as necessary to either correct the condition or to cut off the player. Figure 5-41 shows some typical error-detection circuits used to control the radial tracking (as discussed in Sec. 5-9.2).

The circuit of Fig. 5-41 analyzes the EFM signal (output from IC03, Fig. 5-32) and controls the radial tracking circuits by gating Q150 (Figs. 5-34 and 5-41). Under normal play conditions, the EFM signal at IC03 reaches a high level of about 850 mV (mirror level) and a low level of about 200 mV (pit level), as shown in Fig. 5-42. The EFM signal is applied to the bases of Q140, Q300, Q302, and Q304.

Transistor Q140 conducts when the EFM signal approaches the mirror level, and turns off as EFM approaches the pit level. This on/off action is bypassed by C160, resulting in a low-level signal which turns on Q141. In turn, Q141 applies 0.87 V to pin 3 (the + input) of comparator IC151. The EFM signal also turns Q300 on and off, providing drive current to Q301. In turn, Q301 applies 0.38 V to pin 7 (the + input) of comparator IC300 through

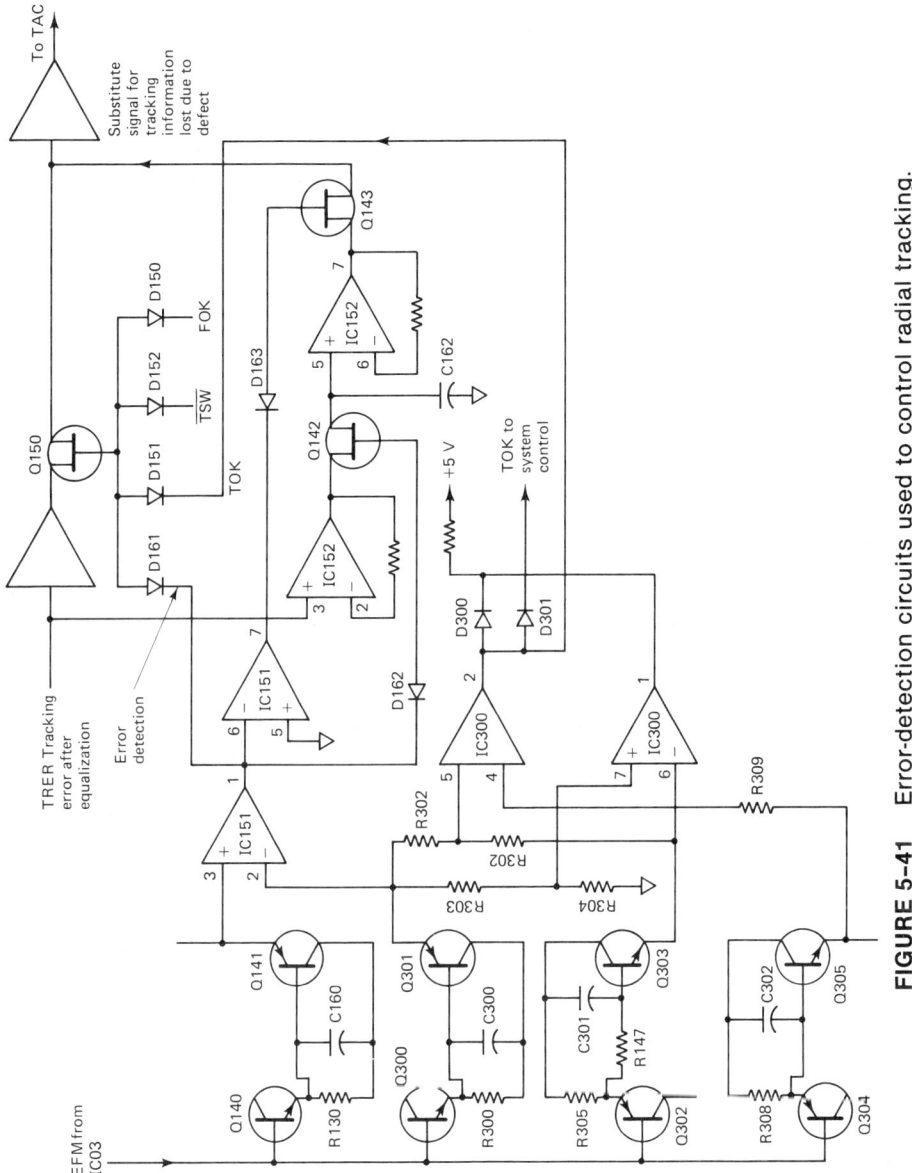

FIGURE 5-41 Error-detection circuits used to control radial tracking.

148 Typical CD Player Circuits

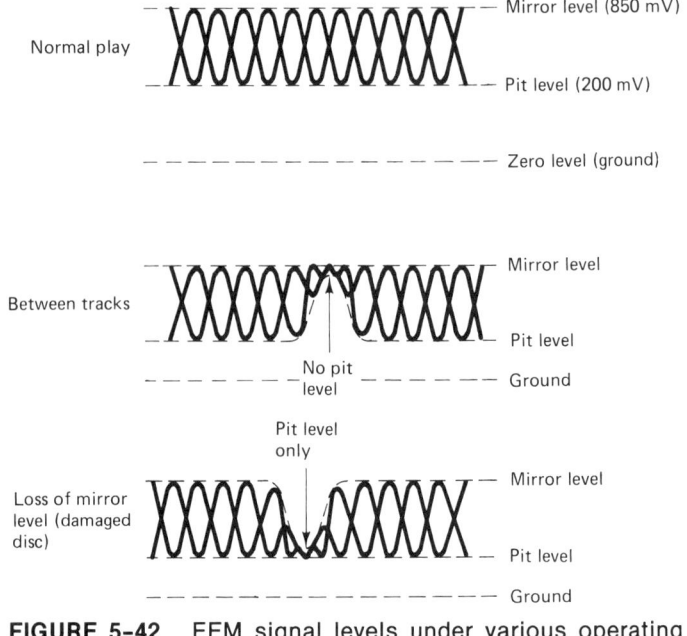

FIGURE 5-42 EFM signal levels under various operating conditions.

R303, 0.278 V to pin 5 (another + input) of IC300, and 0.278 V to pin 2 (the − input) of IC151.

With 0.87 V at pin 3 (+) and 0.278 at pin 2 (−), pin 1 of IC151 goes high, indicating that the disc is good (making normal transitions from pit to mirror levels). The high at pin 1 of IC151 is applied to D161, which is one of the enabling diodes for Q150 (as discussed in Sec. 5-9.2 and shown in Fig. 5-34).

The EFM signal is also applied to Q302 and Q304, which turn on and off during normal play operation, turning on Q303 and Q305. Q303 applies 0.1 V at pin 6 of IC300 and (in conjunction with Q301) 0.278 V to pin 5 of IC300. The output at pin 1 of IC300 goes high (to about 4.8 V), keeping D300 reverse-biased.

Q305 applies 0.083 V at pin 4 of IC300. Since pin 5 is at 0.278 V, the output at pin 2 of IC300 goes high. This high of about 4.8 V is applied to D151, which is another of the enabling diodes for Q150 (Sec. 5-9.2). The signal at pin 2 of IC300 also becomes the TOK (tracking-ok) signal, which is applied to the system control microprocessor through D301.

Figure 5-43 shows the relationship among the tracks, EFM signal, tracking error or TER, and tracking-ok or TOK signals during normal play. When play is not normal, the TER and TOK signals are interrupted. The normal

5-9 Typical Front-load Circuits 149

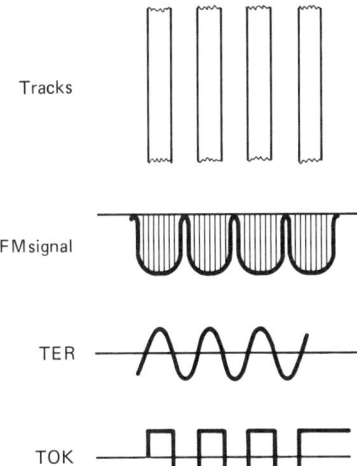

FIGURE 5-43 Relationship among the tracks, EFM signal, TER, and TOK.

tracking-error signal is replaced by a temporary substitute, and the system-control microprocessor is informed of a tracking error.

Now let us assume that the laser beam moves between tracks (Fig. 5-42) where there are no pits (only reflective material or mirror). Under these conditions, the EFM signal rises to the mirror level, and the following sequence occurs.

Q140 turns on as the EFM reaches mirror level. Q141 shuts off, and the input at pin 3 of IC151 remains high, so the output at pin 1 of IC151 stays high, as during normal play.

Q300 also turns on when the laser beam is between tracks (EFM at the mirror level). However, because C300 is fully charged, Q301 does not shut off immediately, and all voltages at the emitter of Q301 remain as during normal play. If the EFM remains at the mirror level for a prolonged time (say if the laser beam is stuck between tracks), Q301 eventually shuts off, and the emitter voltages change.

Q302 shuts off completely when the EFM rises to mirror level. However, Q303 remains on due to the action of C301/R147/R305, so the emitter voltage of Q303 says as during normal play.

Q304 also shuts off completely when the EFM rises to mirror level. However, Q305 remains on, increasing the voltage at pin 4 of IC300 to a point where the pin 4 voltage exceeds the pin 5 voltage. As a result, the output at pin 2 of IC300 goes low. The low is applied to D151 to turn off Q150. Since the output at pin 2 of IC300 is also the TOK signal, D301 is reverse-biased, and the system-control microprocessor is informed that tracking is not correct.

Now suppose that there is a defect in the disc (scratch, pin hole, gouge, etc.), resulting in the complete removal of reflective material from the surface

150 *Typical CD Player Circuits*

(Fig. 5–42). When the laser passes over such an area, there is no reflection, the EFM signal reduces to the pit level, and the following sequence occurs: Q140 shuts off and Q141 turns on, lowering the voltage at pin 3 of IC151. Q300 also shuts off completely, and C301 stays on due to the action of C300. Under these conditions, the voltage at pin 2 of IC151 exceeds the value of pin 3, producing a low at the output of pin 1. This low is applied to D161, shutting off Q151.

The low at pin 1 of IC151 also shuts off Q142 through D162. Tracking information is not passed. Instead, the tracking voltage that was present just prior to being shut off is held by C162 at the output of Q142. This prior tracking information is passed through a noninverting amplifier within IC152 and is output at pin 7.

The output at pin 7 of IC152 is applied to Q143, which acts as an analog switch. Q143 is enabled by a signal passing through D163. The low that disables Q150 and Q142 is inverted by IC151 (at pin 7) and reverse-biases D163 to enable Q143. The tracking voltage held by C162 and amplified by IC152 is passed to the radial tracking actuator as a substitute for the tracking information lost due to the defect.

5-9.7 *Antishock Circuits*

In addition to the error-detection circuits just described, many CD players include antishock circuits to minimize the effects of severe shock and/or vibration. Figure 5–44 shows typical antishock circuits. The related waveforms are shown in Fig. 5–45.

The circuit of Fig. 5–44 minimizes shock noise generated when the pickup skips a disc track as a result of vibration applied to the player. This is done by gating and holding the audio information (Sec. 5-9.5 and Fig. 5–40) at the previous level for a specific time interval (until the shock is over). The circuit also operates when there is a scratch in the disc. In fact, when there are many scratches, the antishock circuit can produce more skipping than normal. This is because the antishock circuit operates from the BFR (block error) signal generated by IC404 (Fig. 5–39). The BRF signal occurs when IC404 detects a large block error. Such an error can be from either shock or defects in the disc.

When the antishock circuits are turned on by the antishock switch (Fig. 3–11), and a BFR signal is present, the audio information is held at the previous level for a time determined by IC406–IC409, which are combined as a counter circuit. Typically, the time is about 17 ms after detection of skipping (after the BFR signal is present). Most shock noises occur during this period.

Keep in mind that a scratch also produces a BFR signal. In turn, this triggers the antishock circuits into holding the audio information for the 17 ms, even though the scratch may produce a block error of much shorter du-

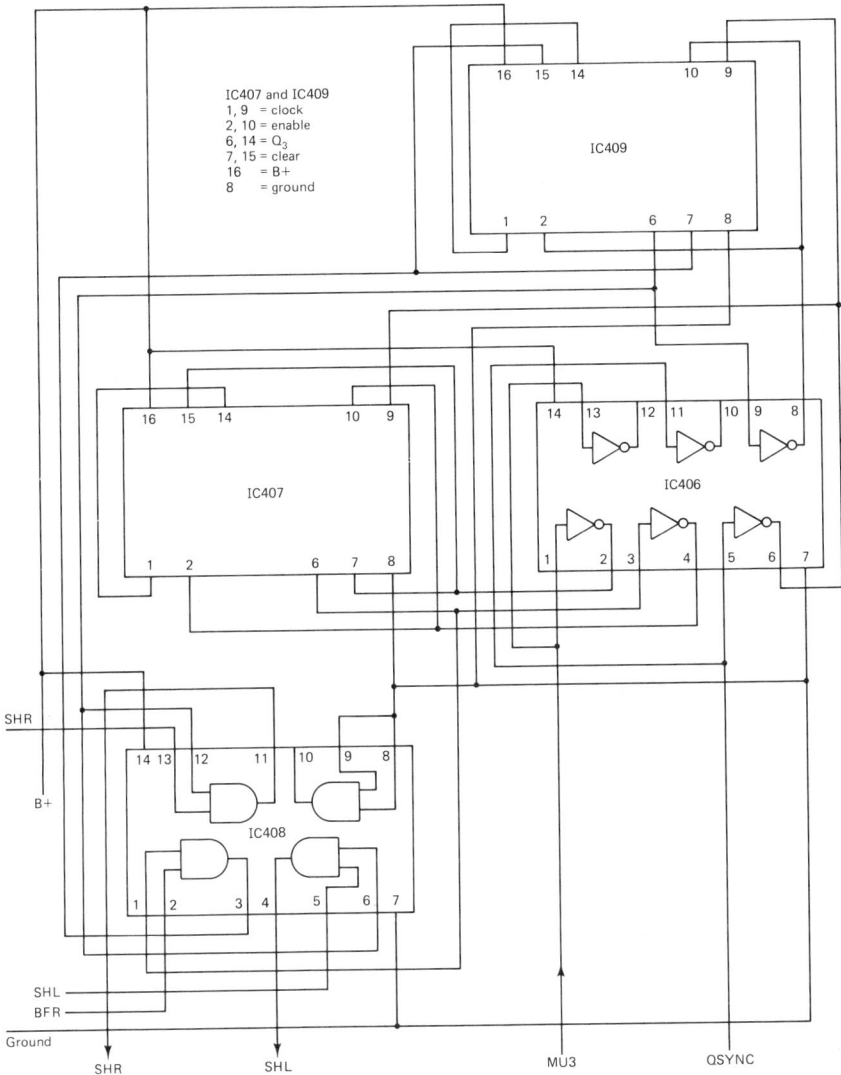

FIGURE 5-44 Antishock circuits.

ration. This is because the holding period is set by the counter circuits, and not by the size of the scratch (or the amount of block error).

5-9.8 Jump Forward and Jump Reverse

Figure 5-46 shows the jump forward (JPF) and jump reverse (JPR) circuits for some typical front-load players. Most CD players are capable of forward

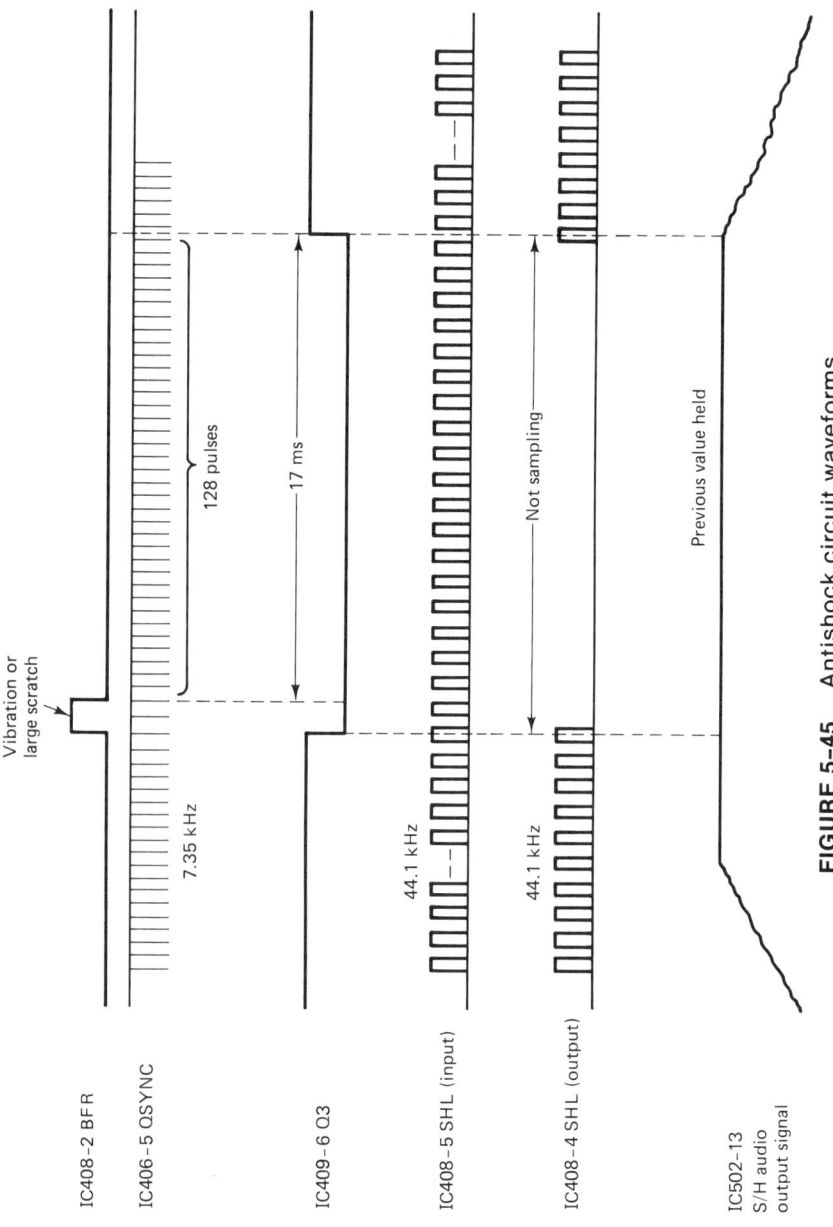

FIGURE 5-45 Antishock circuit waveforms.

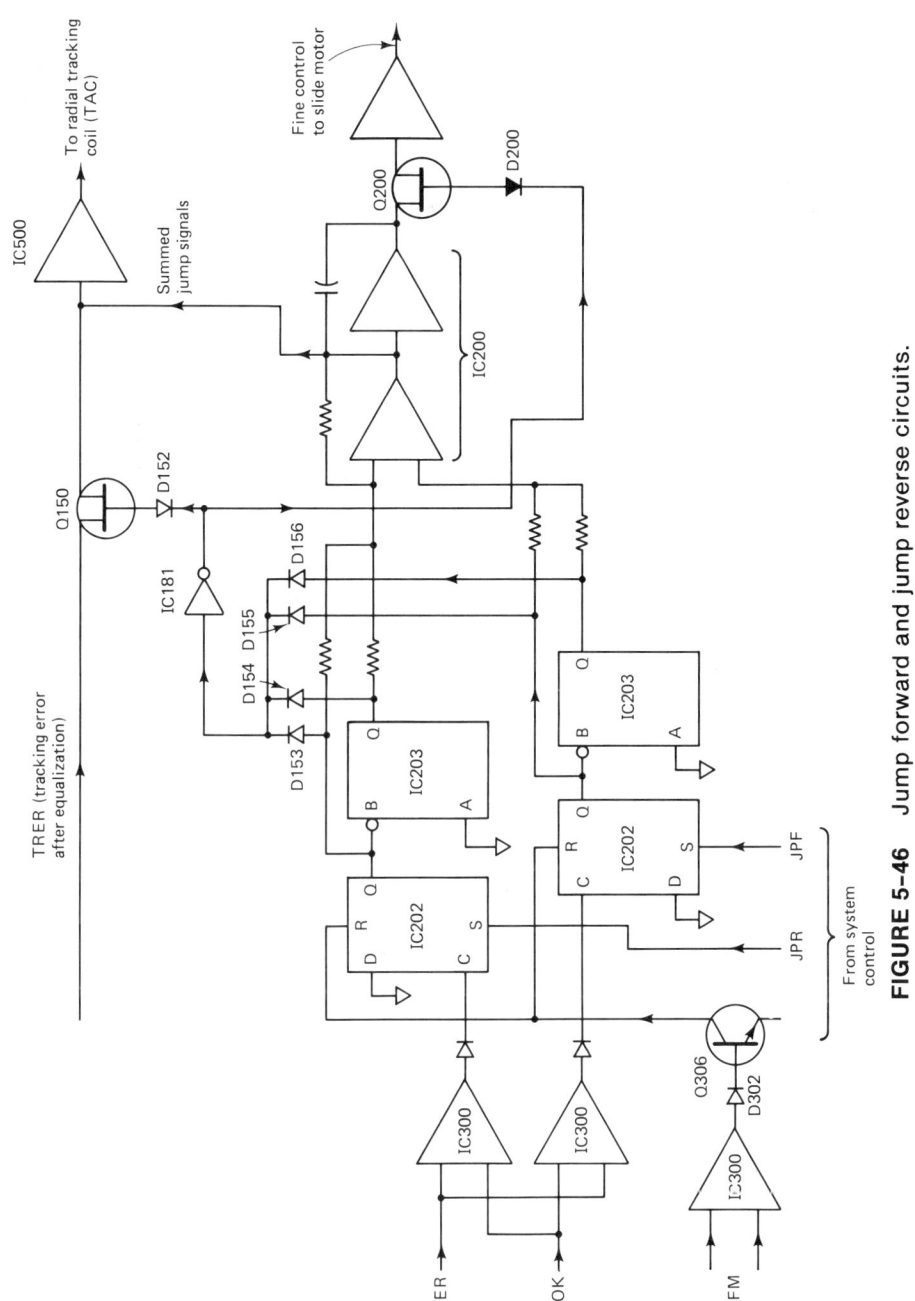

FIGURE 5-46 Jump forward and jump reverse circuits.

or reverse jumps of tracks from any point on the disc. In the circuits of Fig. 5-46, the jumps are initiated by the system-control microprocessor via the JPF or JPR signals.

When a JPF signal is sent by the system-control microprocessor, the pulse is applied to the S (set) input of a D-type FF (flip-flop) in IC202. The Q output of the FF goes high. This disables Q200 and Q150 (through D155, IC181, D152, and D200), and shuts off the tracking error or TER signal to the radial tracking coil and the slide motor (As discussed in Sec. 5-9.9, the TER signal provides control of the tracking coil as well as a fine control for the slide motor.) During jump, the slide motor receives no fine control signal, and the radial tracking coil is controlled by the output of the Fig. 5-46 jump circuits (which are summed at the output of IC200). This output drives the radial tracking coil toward the next track.

In order to notify the jump circuits when the pickup is centered on the next track, the TER and TOK signals are compared by IC300. Figure 5-47 shows the relationships among EFM, TER, TOK, JPF IC300 input/output, and the IC200 jump pulse outputs. As shown, the TER S-curve goes high and the TOK pulse goes low when the tracking beams leave the present track. TER and TOK are compared by IC300 and produce a low at the IC300 output.

As the tracking beams become centered between tracks, the TER signal passes zero (going in the negative direction). The TER signal continues in a negative direction as the tracking beams move to the next track. As soon as the TER signal drops below 0 V, the output of IC300 goes high. The low-to-high transition at the output of IC300 changes the state of the IC202 JPF FF, and triggers a one-shot FF within IC203. This pulls the output of IC200 negative for a fixed time interval as shown in Fig. 5-47. The negative-going one-shot pulse acts as a "brake" to counter the inertia of the radial tracking mechanism, causing the mechanism to stop when aligned with the next track.

The EFM signal is applied through IC300, D302, and Q306 to the reset inputs of the IC202 FFs. This restores operation to normal when the jump is complete.

Note that jump reverse or JPR operates the same way as JPF, except for the polarity of the output pulse as IC200.

5-9.9 Slide Motor (Pickup Motor) Control

Figure 5-48 shows the slide motor (also called the pickup motor) control circuits for some typical front-load players. As discussed, a motor is required to keep the optical pickup or laser beam moving across the disc at a constant rate (even though the disc speed changes, as discussed in Sec. 5-9.11). Except during track jump or search operation, the tracking-error (TER or TRER) signal is applied to the slide motor as a fine control. The TER signal is applied to the slide motor through Q150, low-pass filter IC200, analog switch Q200, amplifier IC201, and motor-drive transistor Q203/Q204. The direction of cur-

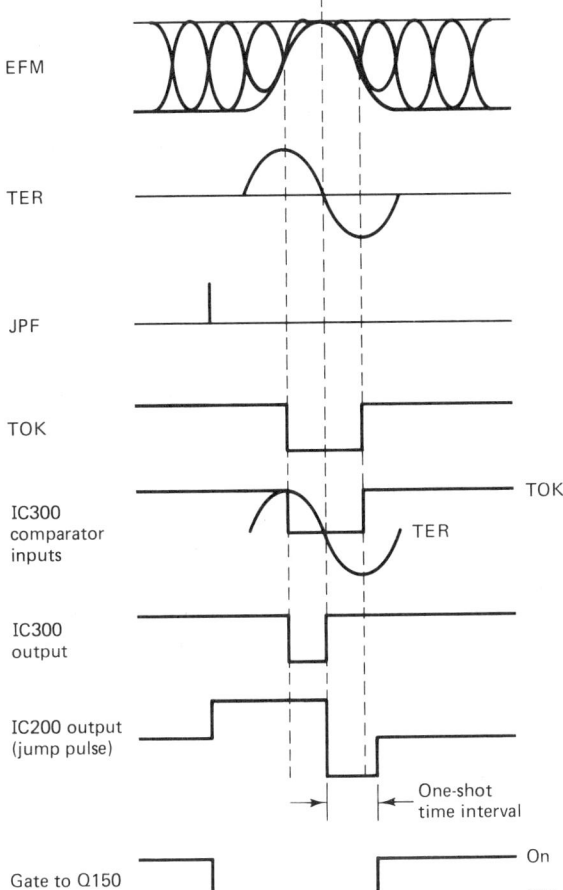

FIGURE 5-47 Waveforms associated with jump forward and jump reverse.

rent through the slide motor (and the direction of slide motor rotation) is determined by the polarity of the signal applied to Q203/Q204. If the drive signal is positive, Q203 conducts, and current passes from ground through the motor, causing the motor to move in one direction. The opposite occurs if the drive signal is negative and Q204 conducts.

Note that the TER signal is passed only when there is a TSW (tracking switch) signal from the system control microprocessor. The TSW signal is inverted by IC181 and applied to Q150 (through D152) and Q200 (through D200), permitting the TER signal to pass.

During search operation, the pickup must move at a faster rate than during play. This is done by SLR and SLF pulses from the system-control

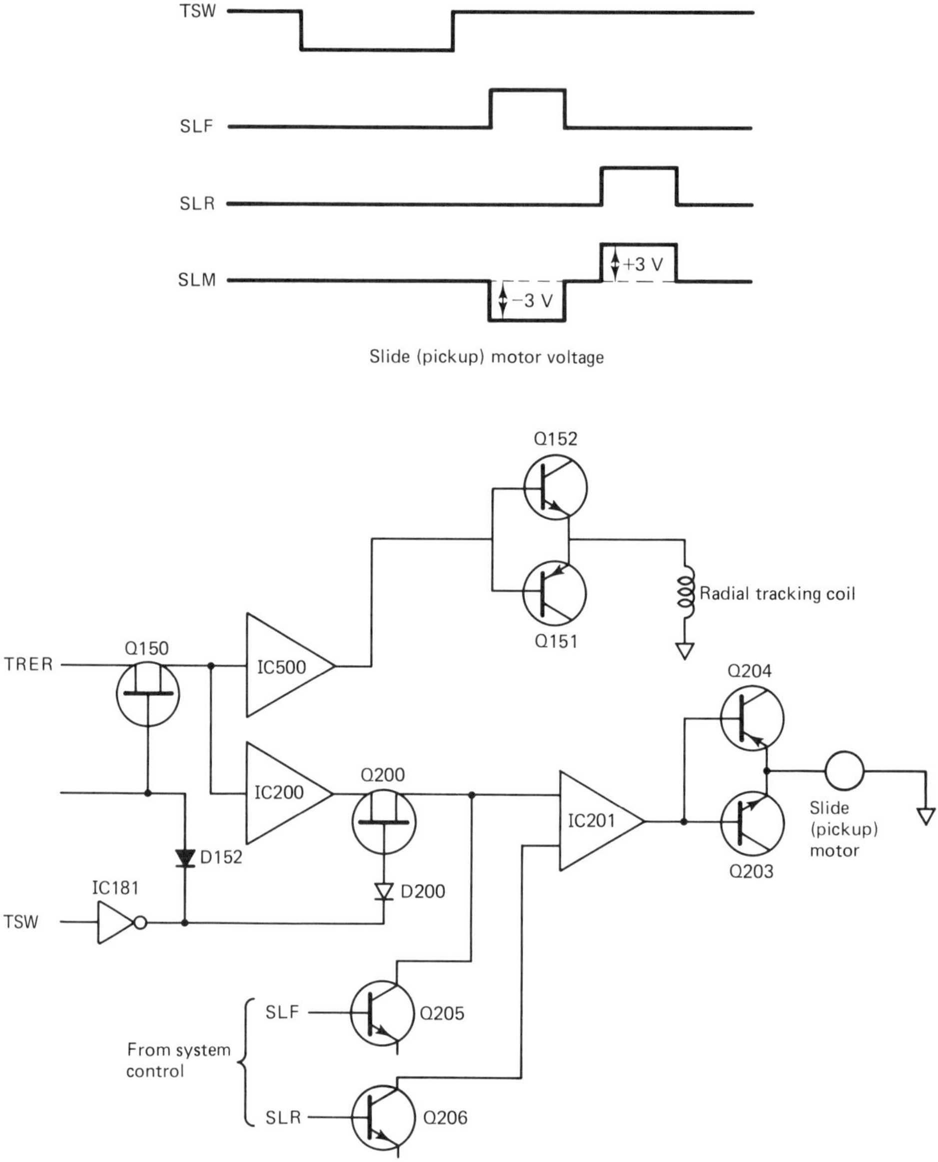

156 Typical CD Player Circuits

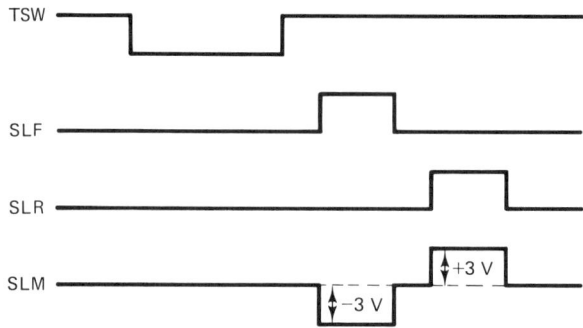

FIGURE 5-48 Slide (pickup) motor control circuits.

microprocessor. The SLR and SLF pulses, applied through Q205 and Q206, produce inputs to IC201 much larger than the inputs from Q200. This produces increased current in Q203/Q204 and increases the speed of the slide motor.

5-9.10 Laser Monitor and Control

Figure 5-49 shows the laser monitor and control circuits for some typical front-load players. As discussed in Sec. 5-3, it is necessary to monitor and control the amount of light emitted by the laser diode to insure proper performance of the player optics. In the circuit of Fig. 5-49, the output of the monitor diode is applied to the input of a comparator within IC01. The other input to the comparator receives an adjustable reference voltage. The comparator output is applied to the laser diode through drive circuits. If the laser-diode output goes above the desired reference level, the monitor-diode output increases, and the comparator output goes more positive. This reduces drive to the laser diode back to normal. The opposite occurs if the laser-diode output decreases.

Most laser-diode drive circuits have some form of adjustment control. With the circuit of Fig. 5-49, it is possible to set the amount of laser-diode output by setting the reference voltage (with R21) to the IC01 comparator.

On most front-load players (particularly those with a horizontal tray), the laser diode is cut off when the outer cover is in the extended position (ready to insert or remove a disc). This prevents the user from being exposed to laser radiation. In the circuit of Fig. 5-49, the drive circuits are controlled by two series-connected microswitches (usually called the *laser power cut switches* or

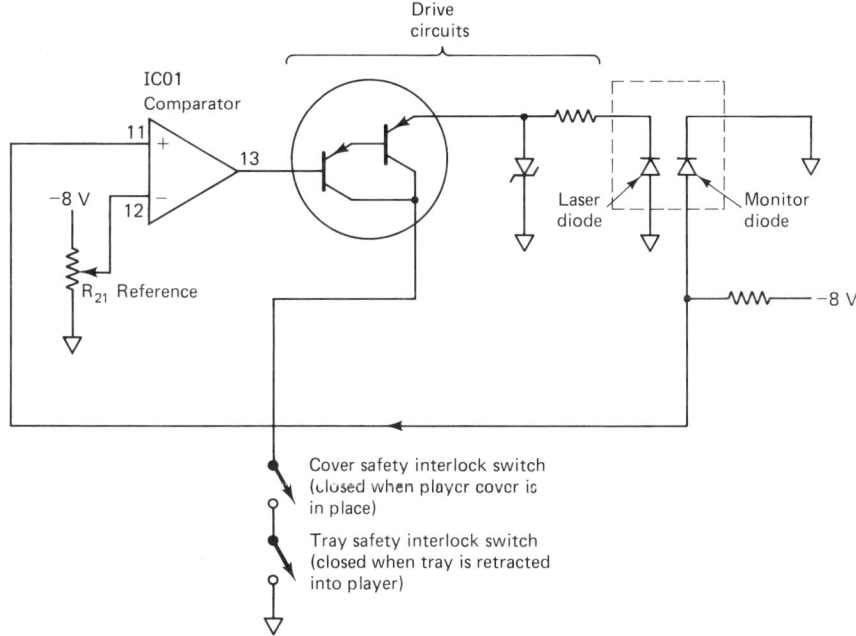

FIGURE 5-49 Laser monitor and control circuits.

the *safety interlock switches*). Both switches must be closed (player cover in place and tray retracted back into the player) before the drive circuits can pass the comparator output to the laser diode.

5-9.11 Disc Drive (Turntable) Motor

Figure 5-50 shows the disc drive motor (also called the turntable motor) control circuits for some typical front-load players. As discussed in Sec. 5-6, a CD player disc is rotated at a varying speed. This is done so that the rate at which the track is kept moving, with respect to the pickup, is constant. The variation of speed is necessary since there is less data on the tracks near the inside of the disc (start) than near the outside (end).

Most front-load CD players use some form of *unitorque motor* with *Hall-effect elements* to get the variable disc speed. Typically, the disc motor speed varies from about 480 rpm (inside) to 210 rpm (outside) so as to maintain a constant linear velocity (CLV) of about 1.25 to 1.3 meters per second.

The unitorque motors used in CD players are similar to those of tape decks and turntables. That is, the Hall-effect elements produce outputs in proportion to the magnetic fields resulting from motor rotation. The outputs of the Hall-effect elements are fed back through control circuits to the motor drive windings and thus maintain the desired speed. However, in CD players, the Hall-effect elements are also fed currents (from a controller under the direction of the system-control microprocessor) to vary the speed at the desired rate. CLV circuits within the controller monitor the EFM signal to determine the rate at which information is passing. The CLV circuits then produce the necessary signals to maintain the desired rate of speed.

In the circuit of Fig. 5-50, the signals from the system control microprocessor to controller IC404 include DMSW, CLVH, and ROT. The output from IC404 to the Hall-effect element control circuits are the PREF, PWM, and PD pulses. The relationships of these signals and pulses, as well as motor speed, are shown in Fig. 5-51. Note that PWM and PREF are both 50 percent duty cycle pulses, while PD has a 25 percent duty cycle, even though all three are produced at 33 kHz. Also note that DMSW, CLVH, and ROT are all high when the motor is off.

The outputs of the Hall-effect elements are applied to the motor windings through transistors Q252-Q255 and amplifiers within IC251. R284 and R289 provide for offset or balance adjustments of the motor-control circuit. R273 sets the gain for the motor-control circuit.

Operation of the disc motor can be divided into two phases: *start servo* and *regular servo*. (These phases are also called the *motor start* or *run-up phase* and the *stabilizing* or *holding phase*.) The start servo phase controls the disc motor operation from start to the point where the motor reaches the correct speed (or correct angular velocity, as it is described in some literature).

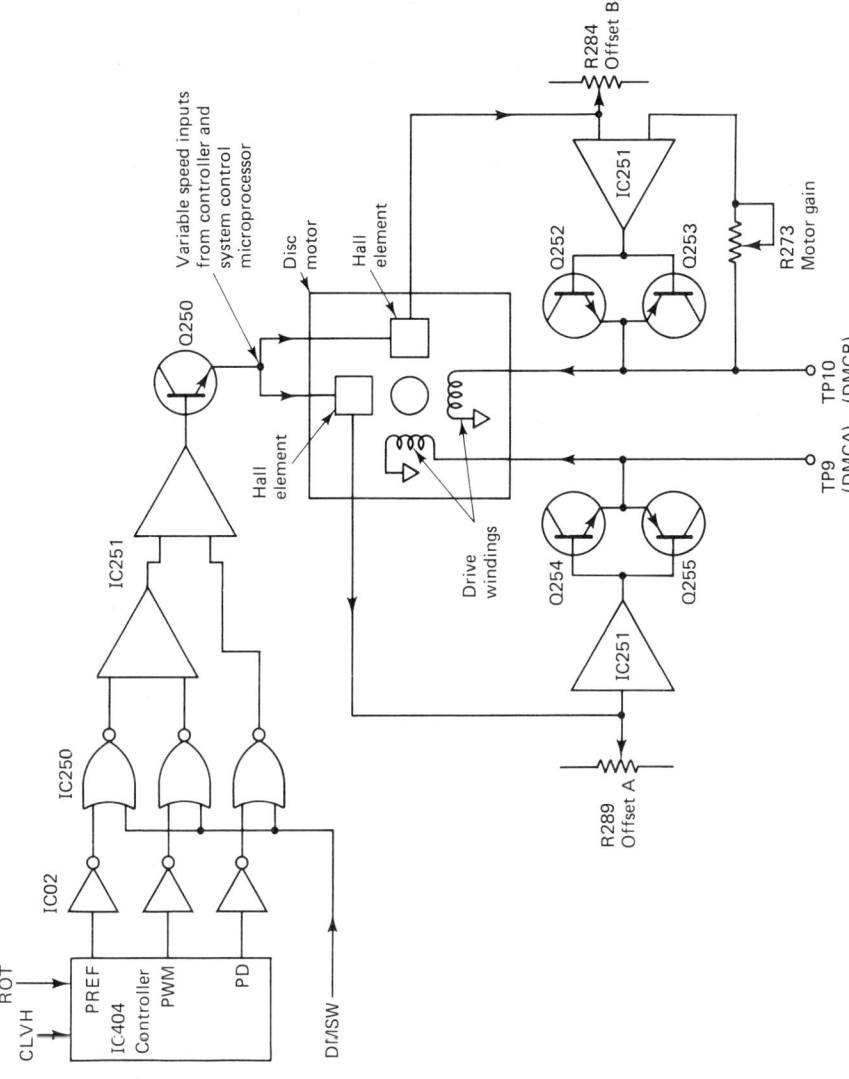

FIGURE 5-50 Disc drive (turntable) motor control circuits.

160 Typical CD Player Circuits

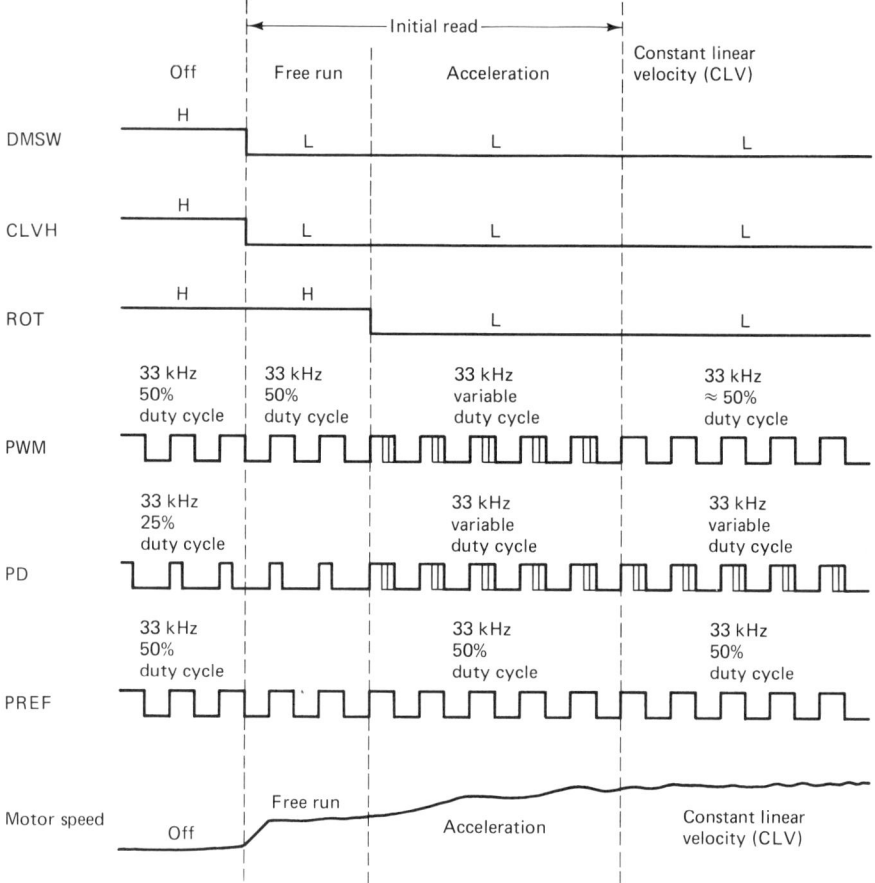

FIGURE 5-51 Relationships of disc motor control signals and disc motor speed.

The regular servo phase controls motor operation when proper speed is reached.

Start servo. During the free-run portion of the initial read period (Fig. 5-51), the DMSW and CLVH outputs are low and the ROT output is high. Under these conditions, the disc motor begins to accelerate and turn at a constant velocity. IC404 produces essentially similar outputs at PWM, PREF, and PD. After a free-run period determined by the system-control microprocessor, ROT goes low and the motor starts to accelerate. The EFM signal is reached by IC404 and analyzed. During this analysis, the 11T pit length (Sec. 5-9.3) is compared with a known reference. (As discussed, 11T is the maximum pit length recorded onto the disc.) The difference between the known reference and the 11T pit length being picked up from the disc is the PWM output from IC404.

During the acceleration portion of initial read, the PWM duty cycle (which varies above and below 50 percent according to motor speed) is compared with the PREF signal (which has a fixed duty cycle). The result of this comparison is applied to the motor circuits to control speed.

Regular servo. When the motor reaches the desired speed, the PWM signal has a 50 percent duty cycle, and the pickup reads the disc information at a constant linear velocity (Fig. 5-51). This condition is maintained with a ±1 percent accuracy by means of the PD pulse from IC404. The duty cycle of the PD pulse is determined by comparison of P-sync information and frame length (Chapter 2) to a reference standard stored within IC404. In turn, the PD signal is compared with the output of the PWM and PREF comparator. The result of this comparison is applied to the motor to maintain the ±1 percent accuracy.

6

MECHANICAL OPERATION, ADJUSTMENT, and REPLACEMENT

This chapter describes operation and adjustment/replacement procedures for the mechanical sections of typical CD players. The mechanical sections are concerned mostly with loading/unloading the disc and driving the optical pickup across the disc. Mechanical operation of top-load players is relatively simple when compared to front-load players. In most top-load players, the only true mechanical function (other than moving the optical pickup via the rotating arm and drive motor) is to open the disc compartment, install a disc (manually) on the turntable, and then close the disc compartment door. For these reasons, we do not go into the mechanical sections of top-load players here. Instead, we concentrate on the far more complex mechanical sections of front-load players.

A typical front-load player has three drive motors: one for the turntable, one for the optical pickup, and a third for opening and closing the disc compartment tray or door. With a typical horizontal front-load player (the most popular version) the tray is opened by a drive motor, a disc is inserted (manually) within the tray, the tray and disc are returned within the player (by the drive motor), and then the disc is installed on the turntable (by the same tray drive mechanism, and usually the same drive motor). Some front-load players use a fourth drive motor to clamp or "chuck" the disc onto the turntable.

We discuss the mechanical sections for all three types of front-load players (vertical door, horizontal tray with one load/unload motor, and horizontal with a separate clamping or chucking motor) in this chapter. However, we concentrate on horizontal players where both the tray and clamping operations are controlled by one motor. Most CD player manufacturers appear to be adopting this version for future production.

Since operation of the mechanical sections (drive motors, gears, etc.) are controlled by limit switches and the system-control microprocessor, the following descriptions also include diagrams and discussions of the control circuits (in simplified form). By studying the mechanical operation and circuits found here, you should have no difficulty in understanding the mechanical operations of similar CD players.

This understanding is essential for logical troubleshooting and repair, no matter what type of player is involved. For example, if you know that a particular drive motor is actuated to turn a gear in a given direction for a given mode of operation, and you can see that the motor does not drive the gear in that mode, you have pinpointed a failure. The origin of the trouble may be electronic (no actuating signal is received from the microprocessor, or the motor may be burned out), mechanical (the gears may be jammed or a belt broken, etc.), or adjustment (limit switch not opened or closed at the right time), but you have a starting point for troubleshooting. The descriptions given here should also help you to interpret the mechanical sections of CD player service literature (which are usually very good as far as adjustment procedures are concerned, but often somewhat vague as to how the mechanism operates).

We also describe adjustment and replacement procedures for the mechanical sections of CD players in this chapter. In the absence of manufacturer's instructions, and to show you what typical adjustment/replacement procedures involve, we describe complete procedures for the mechanical sections, *as recommended by the manufacturer.* The procedures covered here involve the use of special tools described in Chapter 4.

Keep in mind that these specific procedures apply directly to the CD players described in this chapter. When repairing other players, you must follow manufacturer's service instructions exactly. Each type of CD player has its own adjustment points and replacement procedures, which may or may not be different from procedures for other players. Using the examples described here, you should be able to relate the procedures to a similar set of adjustment points and replacement procedures on most similar CD players. Where it is not obvious, we also describe the purpose of the procedure.

6-1 VERTICAL FRONT-LOAD MECHANICAL SECTION

Figure 6-1 shows the location of the principal mechanical components for a typical front-load CD player with a vertical door (such as that illustrated in Fig. 1-1e). Figure 6-2 shows the associated wiring. Note that most of the components are mounted on a *unit base* to which the vertical *door assembly* (loading mechanism) is hinged (at the bottom). The door is attached to the base by *L-arms,* and is opened and closed by a *crank arm* driven by a *gear motor.* The

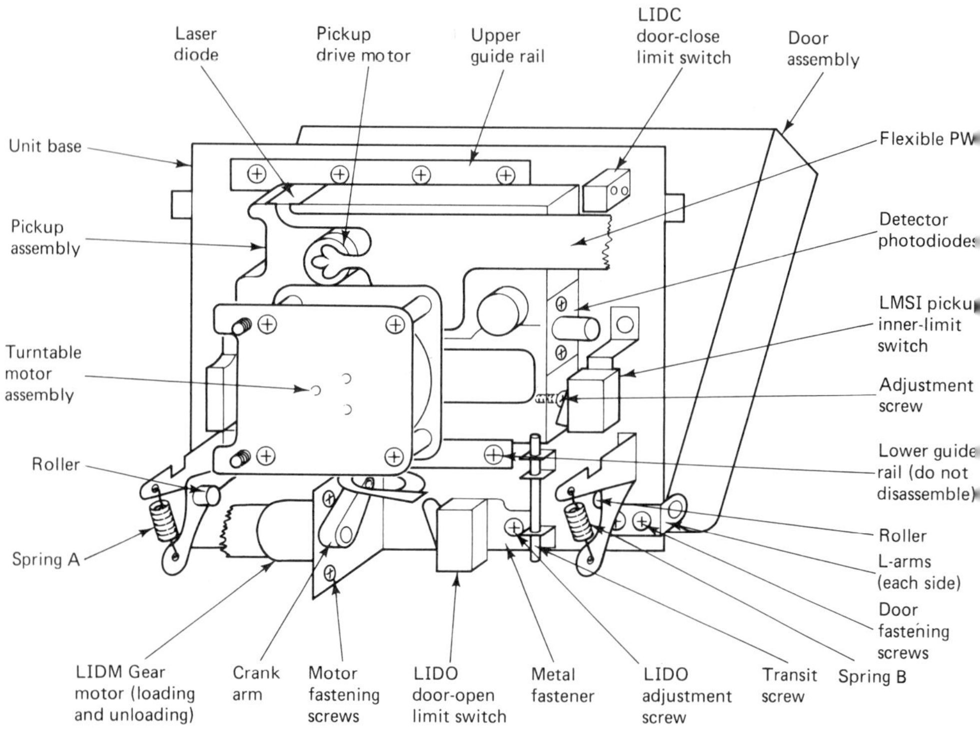

164 Mechanical Operation, Adjustment, and Replacement

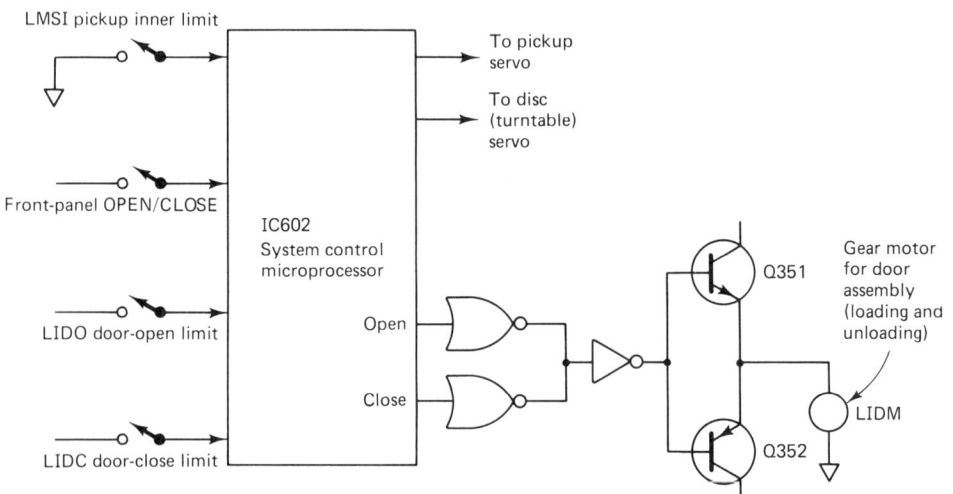

FIGURE 6-1 Location of principal mechanical components for a typical front-load CD player with vertical door.

FIGURE 6-2 Wiring for mechanical section of typical front-load CD player with vertical door.

6-1 Vertical Front-load Mechanical Section 165

door is supported by springs (A and B) and *rollers* mounted on arms which are part of the door assembly.

In use, the door is opened by the gear motor, a disc is installed (manually), and the door is closed by the motor. The disc is pressed against the *turntable motor assembly* by a disc clamp assembly on the door. The turntable motor is operated by a turntable drive servo (Sec. 5-9.11) to spin the disc at the appropriate speed.

As shown in Fig. 6-2, the gear motor for the door assembly receives open/close drive signals from the system-control microprocessor through gates and transistors. In turn, the system microprocessor receives control signals from the front-panel OPEN/CLOSE switch. The microprocessor also receives indicator signals from the door-open (LIDO) microswitch and the door-close (LIDC) microswitch. The LIDO and LIDC switches are positioned and adjusted to actuate when the door has reached the correct open/close limits, and thus cut off the door motor through operation of the system microprocessor.

The *optical pickup assembly* is secured to the unit base by upper and lower *guide rails,* and is driven across the disc by a motor (which is part of the pickup assembly). The motor is operated by a servo as described in Sec. 5-9.9. The pickup motor is connected to the pickup drive gears by means of a belt. The belt can be replaced through a cutout on the unit base, *without* removing either the pickup or the motor. The cutout is normally covered by a press-out lid or cover. The optical pickup is held in place when the *transit screw* is turned in.

The entire pickup can be replaced as an assembly, or the pickup motor can be replaced separately. (We describe both procedures in this section.) Some manufacturers supply a few additional mechanical parts (gears, etc.) for replacement on the pickup assembly. Always consult the service literature regarding such replacement parts. However, as a practical matter, you will probably replace the belt, the motor, or the entire pickup assembly. In any event, you should *never* attempt to replace the laser diode, or the detector photodiodes, unless specifically directed by the service literature (which is not likely).

As shown in Fig. 6-2, the system microprocessor receives a signal from the pickup inner-limit (LMSI) microswitch. The LMSI switch is positioned and adjusted to actuate when the pickup assembly has reached the inner limit (start) of the disc. The LMSI signal cuts off the pickup motor through operation of the system microprocessor and pickup servo.

6-1.1 Mechanical Section Servicing Precautions

Here are some precautions you should observe before performing any adjustment or replacements on the mechanical sections of a vertical front-load CD player. These precautions should be observed *in addition to* any precautions found in the player service literature.

Laser safety. Although you will probably be performing all adjustments and replacements of parts in the mechanical section with the power off (except possibly to test for proper adjustment of the limit switches), *keep in mind that the laser diode can be operating on a vertical front-load player even when the door is open. Always avoid direct exposure to the laser beam.*

Disassembly. The mechanical section is precision engineered and critically adjusted at the factory. Do not disassemble any part of the player beyond that point absolutely necessary to gain access or replace parts. This precaution applies especially to the pickup assembly (lens actuator, laser diode, optical parts, detector photodiodes), and to the *lower guide rail* (Fig. 6-1). The lower guide rail should never be removed from the unit base, since the guide rail serves as a reference standard for the pickup mount dimensions (as we discuss later in this section).

Aluminum parts. Most of the mechanical parts are made of aluminum. Be careful not to overtighten screws, and do not scratch or bend any parts by exerting excessive force. (It is very easy to strip the threads in the unit base!)

Flexible wiring. The pickup assembly has a flexible printed wiring board (PWB), since the pickup must move across the disc. While the PWB is sufficiently strong to withstand constant movement of the pickup, the PWB is not designed to be bent or twisted during service. Keep in mind that if you break even one lead in the PWB, the entire pickup must be replaced.

Dirt in moving parts. Be especially careful not to get any dirt or other foreign matter in the guide rails or the turntable assembly. The pickup assembly must be completely free to move within the rails, and the turntable must be capable of spinning freely.

Objective lens. If the player has been in service for any length of time, always check the objective lens for dirt, dust, smudges, and so on (but keep your fingers away from the lens while doing so). Use a clean, dry cloth to clean the lens. If the objective lens is dirty, the EFM signal can be weak. If you find a weak EFM signal during troubleshooting (Chapter 7), always make a quick check of the objective lens.

Wiring. Be careful to route all wiring to the original position. This is particularly important to keep any wiring from being jammed by the pickup assembly or the door open/close mechanism, since both of these sections are subject to repeated movement.

Adjustment after replacement. Always perform the associated adjustment procedures after replacement of any mechanical part. For example, if the turntable motor or assembly is replaced, the Hall-element gain and offset adjustments should be checked (as described in Chapter 7). If the pickup assembly is replaced, check the laser-diode output and tracking/focus adjustments.

Lens actuator quick check. If you suspect that the lens actuator on the pickup assembly is defective, it is possible to make a quick check of the actuator without removing the entire pickup assembly for replacement. Simply measure the resistance of focus and tracking coils with an ohmmeter, as shown in Fig. 6–3. Typically, the focus coil is about 20 ohms, while the tracking coil is 4 ohms. The actual resistance depends on the particular assembly. However, if you get an open or short indication, or a resistance that is drastically different from these values, the actuator is suspect. In some players, you can see a slight movement of the actuator when the ohmmeter is connected to the coils. This usually indicates that the actuator is good.

Transit screw. In most cases, the transit screw (Chapter 3) should be in place when performing any service procedures. This prevents the pickup assembly from moving back and forth when the player is moved about the service bench. Of course, you must loosen the transit screw for certain checks.

6-1.2 Gaining Access to the Components

This section describes the basic procedures to open the player for service. Keep in mind that these procedures are "typical" for vertical-door players. Always follow any disassembly procedures found in the service literature.

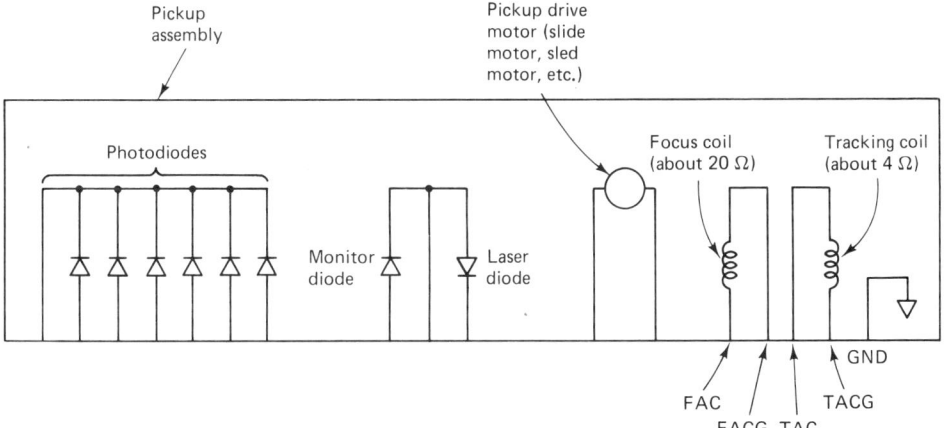

FIGURE 6-3 Measuring resistance of focus and tracking coils for a quick check of the lens actuator on the pickup assembly.

168 Mechanical Operation, Adjustment, and Replacement

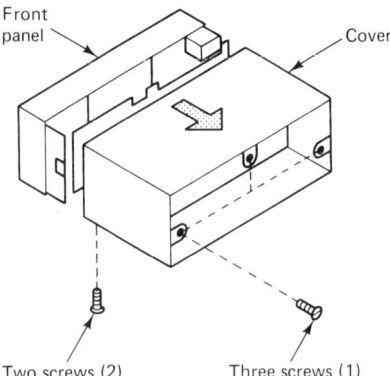

FIGURE 6-4 Procedure for removing cover of a typical front-load CD player with vertical door.

Figure 6-4 shows the procedure for taking off the cover. Slide off the back cover after disengaging the screws (1) and (2).

Figure 6-5 shows the procedure for taking off front panels A and B. Pull out the nylon rivets holding the front panels. Use a pointed object to remove the rivets.

Figure 6-6 shows the procedures for removing the unit mechanism. After taking off the cover, remove screws (3), which hold the escutcheon plate. Switch on the power, push the door OPEN/CLOSE button, and open the door. Then switch off the power and unplug the power cord. Next, after removing the escutcheon plate, remove the lead plate and disengage screws (4).

As shown in Fig. 6-6, there is a pressed protrusion on the lower part of the escutcheon. When dismounting or mounting the unit mechanism, be careful to cover the protrusion with a piece of thick paper (such as drawing paper) so as not to damage the lower part of the unit mechanism.

When the door does not open after pressing the door OPEN/CLOSE button, use a 1.5-V battery to operate the door motor, as shown in Fig. 6-7. After removing the lead-line connector, connect a 1.5-V battery directly to the motor terminals as shown. The door can be closed by reversing the battery

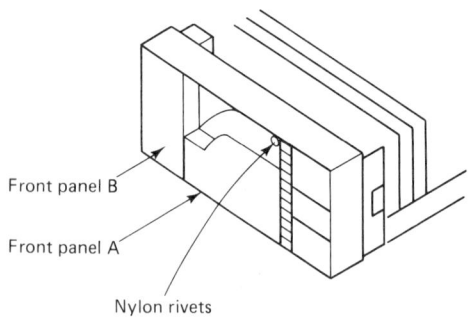

FIGURE 6-5 Procedure for removing front panels A and B of a typical front-load CD player with vertical door.

6-1 Vertical Front-load Mechanical Section 169

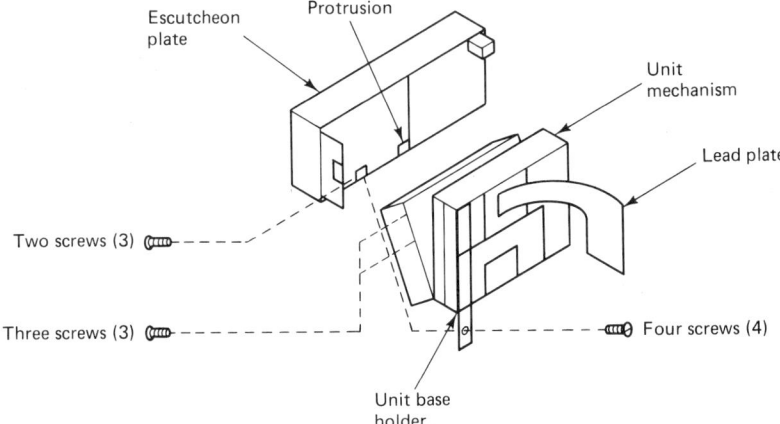

FIGURE 6-6 Procedure for removing the unit mechanism of a typical front-load CD player with vertical door.

terminals. (This same procedure can be used as a quick check of the door motor if you are having door open/close problems.)

Avoid lifting or moving the unit mechanism by the unit base holder (which can easily slip out of place).

Figure 6-8 shows the procedure for removing the console. Disengage screws (5) and move the console forward as shown. Keep in mind that the console need not be removed unless operating controls and the associated printed wiring board are to be replaced.

Figure 6-9 shows the procedure for removing the power switch and display section. Disengage screws (6) to remove the power switch. Disengage screws (7) to remove the display section. Keep in mind that the display section need not be removed unless the lamp fixture, LEDs, and so on, and the associated printed wiring board are to be replaced.

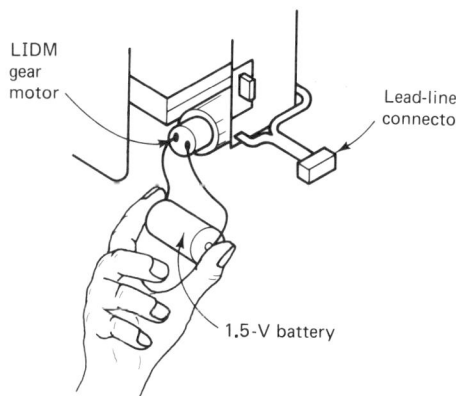

FIGURE 6-7 Procedure for operating the vertical door with a battery.

170 Mechanical Operation, Adjustment, and Replacement

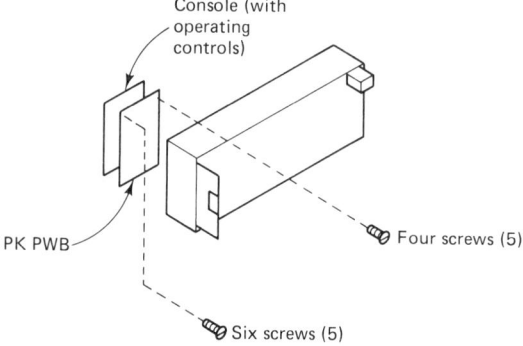

FIGURE 6-8 Procedure for removing the console of a typical front-load CD player with vertical door.

Figures 6–10 through 6–13 show the procedures for removing the various printed wiring boards (PWBs). Disengage screws (8) and the board fixture to remove the PA PWB. Disengage screws (8) and (9), and the board fixture, to remove the PP PWB. Disengage screws (10), the board fixture, and the shield plate to remove the PD and PS PWBs. After removing the escutcheon plate, and the PA, PP, PD, and PS PWBs, disengage screws (11) and (12), and then remove the rear plate (Fig. 6–12). Disengage screws (13) and remove the PC PWB (Fig. 6–13).

After removing the console (Fig. 6–8), disengage screws (5), and remove the PK PWB. After removing the display section (Fig. 6–9) and lamp fixture, remove the three pins and then remove the PI PWB.

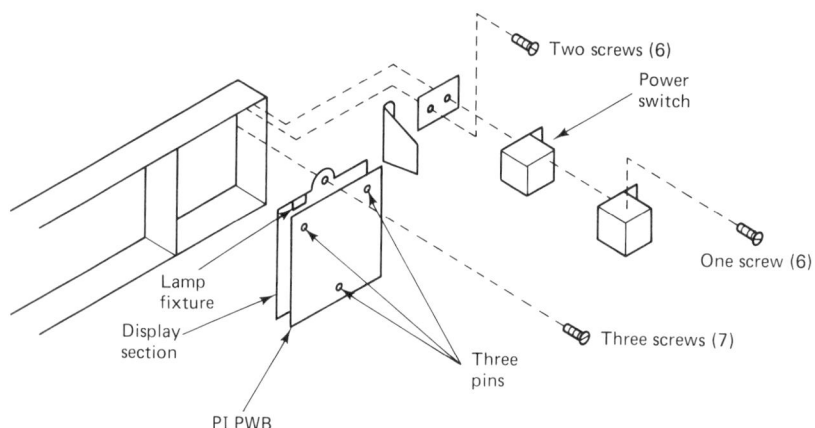

FIGURE 6-9 Procedure for removing the power switch and display section of a typical front-load CD player with vertical door.

6-1 Vertical Front-load Mechanical Section 171

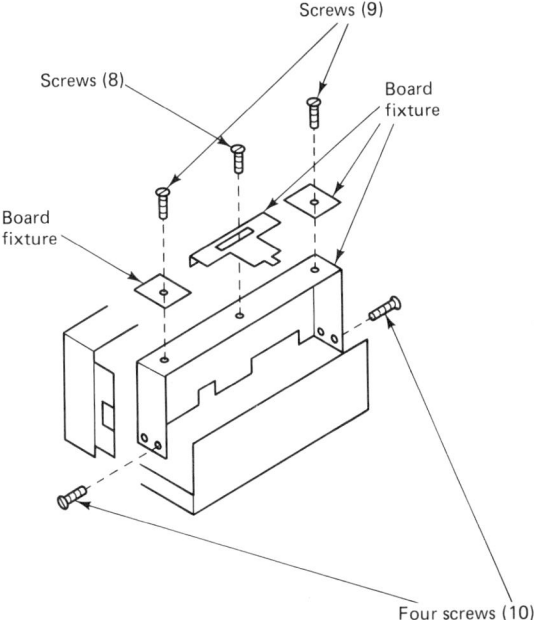

FIGURE 6-10 Procedure for removing board fixtures of a typical front-load CD player with vertical door.

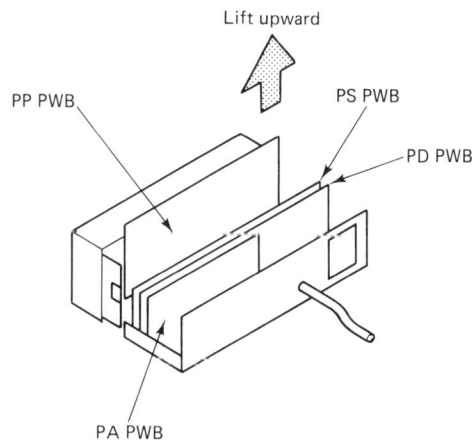

FIGURE 6-11 Removing printed-wiring boards from a typical front-load CD player with vertical door.

172 Mechanical Operation, Adjustment, and Replacement

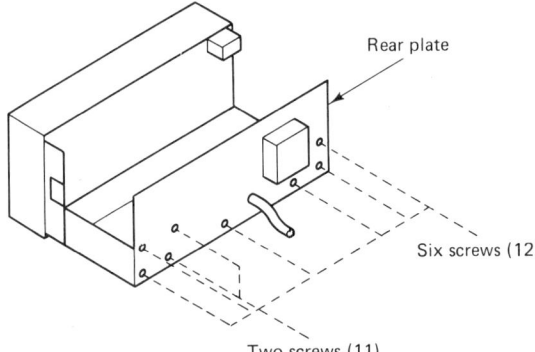

FIGURE 6-12 Removing the rear plate of a typical front-load CD player with vertical door.

6-1.3 Changing the Pickup Drive Belt

Figure 6–14 shows the basic procedures required to change the pickup assembly drive belt. Switch on the power. Press the door OPEN/CLOSE button to open the door (or use a battery, as shown in Fig. 6–7). Switch off the power and turn the left-hand side of the unit face down, as shown in Fig. 6–14. Remove the belt access cover or lid from the unit base by moving the cover in the direction of the arrows. Use tweezers to remove the old belt and to install a new belt over the motor axle and pulley as shown. Replace the access cover and close the door.

6-1.4 Removing the Door (Loading Mechanism) Assembly

This section describes the basic procedures to remove the door assembly from the unit base. This should be done *only* if the door assembly must be replaced.

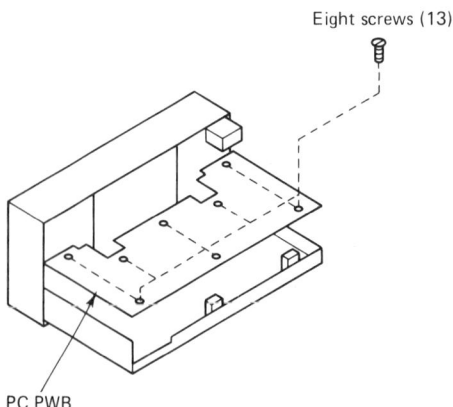

FIGURE 6-13 Removing a horizontal printed-wiring board from a typical CD player with vertical door.

6-1 Vertical Front-load Mechanical Section 173

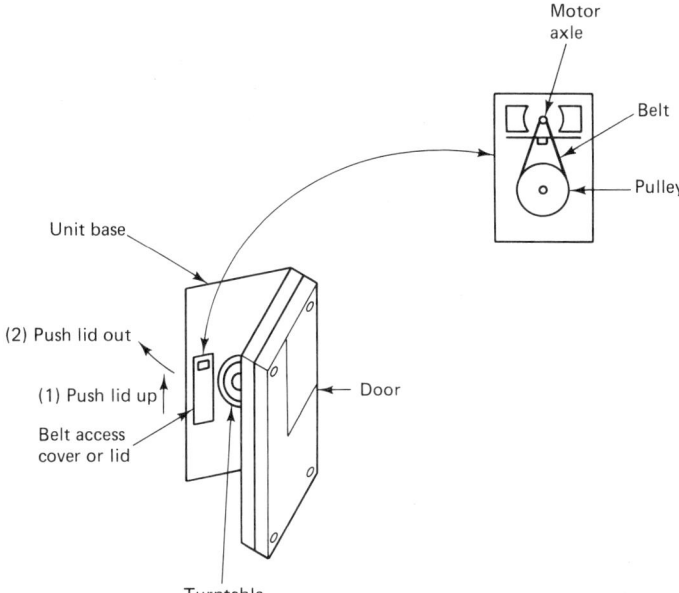

FIGURE 6-14 Procedures to change the pickup drive belt of a typical front-load CD player with vertical door.

Before performing any repairs or replacement, switch on the power, set the player in the STOP mode, and fasten the transit screw (to prevent the pickup from sliding back and forth).

Remove springs A and B from the roller shaft (Fig. 6-1). Remove the unit mechanism from the main chassis (Fig. 6-6). Close the door by connecting the motor terminals to the main chassis or by applying 1.5 V from the battery (Fig. 6-7).

Remove the four door-fastening screws from the L-arms shown in Fig. 6-1. Then remove the door assembly using the 1.5-mm hexagon wrench key (shown in Fig. 4-4), for the gear motor crank arm.

6-1.5 Reinstalling the Door (Loading Mechanism) Assembly

This section describes the basic procedure to reinstall the door assembly on the unit base. Again, the transit screw should be in place.

Before installing the door assembly, loosen (but do not remove) the gear motor crank shaft fastening screw. Insert the door assembly and temporarily fasten the L-arm with the four door-fastening screws, as shown in Fig. 6-15. Set the door assembly aligning jig (Fig. 4-4) into the disc loading area. Position the door assembly aligning spacer (Fig. 4-4) as shown in Fig. 6-15. Note that this operation cannot be performed if the gear motor crank arm fastening screws are tightened.

174 *Mechanical Operation, Adjustment, and Replacement*

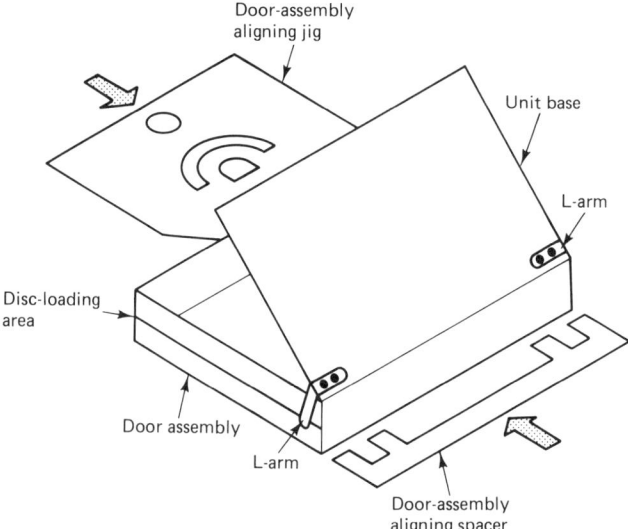

FIGURE 6-15 Procedure for reinstalling the door assembly of a typical front-load CD player with vertical door.

While pushing in the door assembly aligning jig, turn the rotor section of the turntable motor by hand, as shown in Fig. 6-16. Confirm that the turntable does not turn easily (because of the pressure from the jig). In this condition, tighten the door-fastening screws.

Remove the door assembly aligning jig and the door assembly aligning spacer. Insert the check disc (Fig. 4-4) as shown in Fig. 6-17. With the door

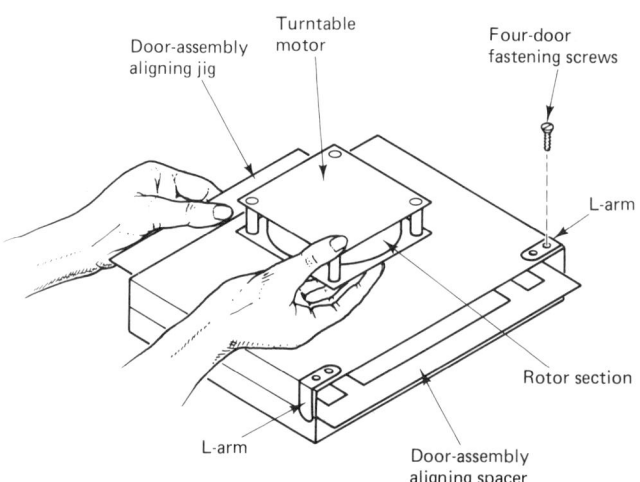

FIGURE 6-16 Confirming turntable rotation during door installation.

6-1 Vertical Front-load Mechanical Section 175

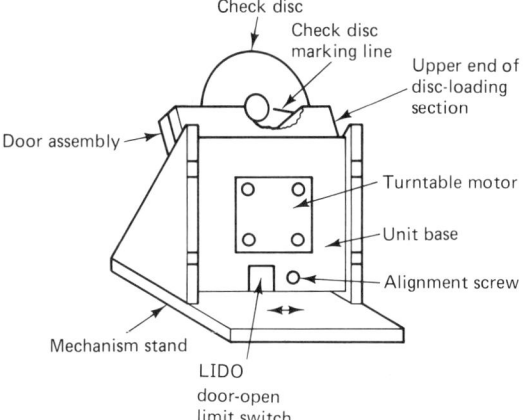

FIGURE 6-17 Confirming turntable rotation with check disc during door installation.

closed, turn the rotor section of the turntable motor and confirm that the disc turns smoothly without contacting any part of the loading area.

Set the assembled unit mechanism assembly on the mechanism stand (Fig. 6-17), and connect connector A of the unit mechanism section to the PS PWB on the main chassis. Also connect the PK PWB connector. Switch on power and open the door.

Open and close the door several times after inserting the check disc. Adjust the position of the LIDO microswitch (door-open limit) so that the check disc marking line is below the upper end of the disc loading section when the door is open, as shown in Fig. 6-17.

6-1.6 Replacement of Gear Motor (for Door Open/Close)

This section describes the basic procedure to replace the door motor without complete disassembly of the unit. Refer to Fig. 6-1 for location of parts. The transit screw should be in place.

Loosen the gear motor crank-fastening hexagon socket screw, using the 1.5-mm hexagon wrench key. Then remove the two motor-fastening screws. Disconnect the wiring. Reverse the procedure to install the motor.

It is easier to replace the door motor if you follow the guidelines shown in Fig. 6-18. The cutout section of the motor axle must be aligned when installing the motor. Correct alignment is achieved when the cutout (or flat) section of the axle makes a right angle (almost) with the emboss line on the motor face. Use a 1.5-V battery to rotate the motor axle as necessary.

176 *Mechanical Operation, Adjustment, and Replacement*

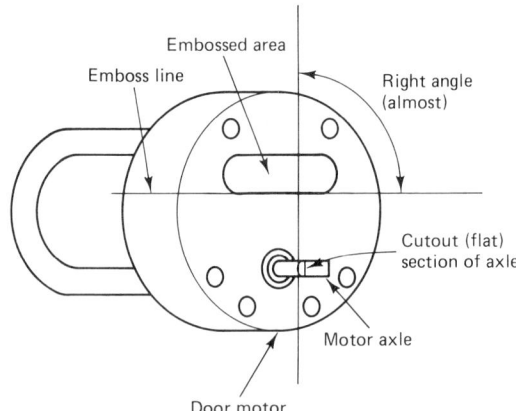

FIGURE 6-18 Guidelines for replacement of door motor of a typical front-load CD player with vertical door.

6-1.7 *Replacement of Pickup Drive Motor*

This section describes the basic procedure to replace the pickup motor without complete disassembly of the unit. Refer to Figs. 6-1 and 6-19 for location of parts. The transit screw should be in place.

Remove the lid of the belt replacement access cutout (Fig. 6-14). Unsolder the motor connections from the flexible PWB (Fig. 6-1). Remove the motor connections from the flexible PWB on the rear. Remove the two motor-fastening screws (Fig. 6-19). Remove the motor. Reverse the procedure to install the motor. Make certain to replace the belt as described in Sec. 6-1.3 after the motor is installed.

6-1.8 *Replacement of the Turntable Motor*

This section describes the basic procedure to replace the turntable motor without complete disassembly of the unit. Refer to Figs. 6-1 and 6-20 for location of parts. It is necessary to loosen the transit screw during this procedure.

Before replacing the turntable motor, try rotating the turntable by hand. The rotor section should turn smoothly. If not, the rotor portion of the motor must be replaced. If the rotor turns smoothly, but the motor does not run when power is applied, it is possible that the coil assembly is defective and can be replaced separately (on some, but not all, players). Also, some turntable motors require lubrication on the axle or drive shaft during replacement. Always check the service literature.

Start by removing the door assembly as described in Sec. 6-1.4. (In most vertical door players, you cannot replace the turntable and motor without removing the door. However, you can replace the coil assembly without removing the door.)

6-1 Vertical Front-load Mechanical Section 177

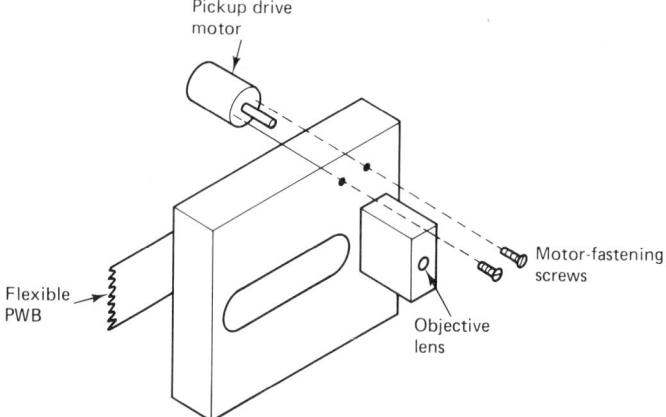

FIGURE 6-19 Removing and replacing pickup drive motor of a typical front-load CD player with vertical door.

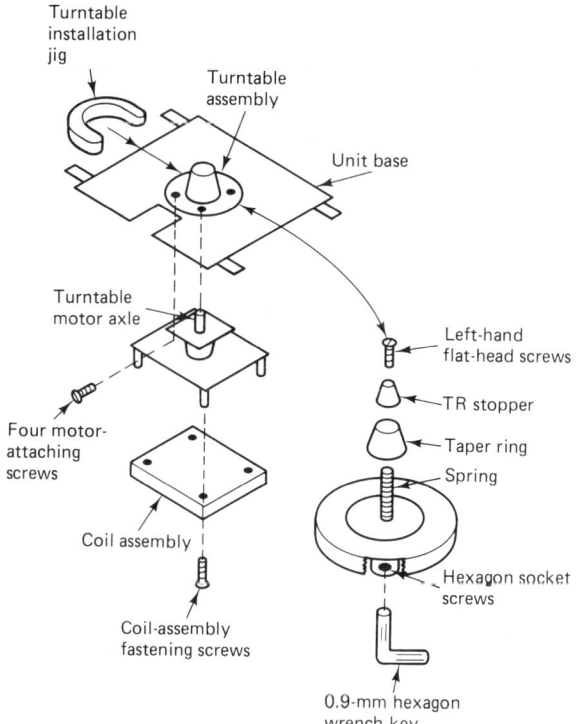

FIGURE 6-20 Adjusting turntable height for a typical front-load CD player with vertical door.

178 *Mechanical Operation, Adjustment, and Replacement*

Remove the left-hand flat-head screw and the TR stopper shown in Fig. 6-20. Loosen the two hexagon socket screws using the 0.9-mm hexagon wrench key (Fig. 4-4), and remove the turntable assembly. Be careful not to lose the screw, TR stopper, spring, and taper ring.

Now loosen the transit screw and move the pickup toward the outside. Reach through the lens actuator access hole and remove the four turntable motor-fastening screws. Position the pickup at the center of the guide rail, turn the turntable motor 90°, and then remove the motor. Reverse the procedure to install the turntable assembly and motor.

The turntable height must be properly set during installation. Use the turntable installation jig (Fig. 4-4) as shown in Fig. 6-20. Slide the turntable assembly over the motor axle or shaft, with the jig positioned between the unit base and turntable assembly bottom. Tighten the two hexagon screws with the 9-mm hexagon wrench key. Remove the jig (which should be snugly in place, but not binding), and check that the turntable rotates freely.

If the coil assembly is available as a separate replacement part (typical for many players), simply remove the four screws and disconnect the wiring (unplug the connector).

6-1.9 *Installing and Adjusting the Microswitches*

This section describes the basic procedure to install and adjust the three mechanical-section microswitches. Refer to Figs. 6-1 and 6-21 for location of parts. The transit screw should be in place.

Install the LIDC door-close limit switch so that the slider of the switch and the inside of the hole on the unit base *are not in contact*.

Turn the adjustment screw (Fig. 6-21) for the LMSI pickup inner-limit microswitch so that switch operation is triggered when the gap between the pickup inner stopper and the pickup is 1 mm. Use the spacer (Fig. 4-4) for this adjustment.

Adjust the LIDO door-open limit switch as described in Sec. 6-1.5 and shown in Fig. 6-17. Loosen the LIDO adjustment screw (Fig. 6-1) and slide the LIDO switch and metal fastener as necessary. Tighten the adjustment screw once proper adjustment is obtained. The check-disc marking line should be below the upper end of the disc loading section when the door is fully open (LIDO switch actuated).

6-1.10 *Removing the Pickup Assembly*

This section describes the basic procedure to remove the pickup assembly from the unit base. This should be done only when you are certain the pickup assembly is defective. Be sure to observe all the precautions regarding static discharge described in Chapter 4 and shown in Fig. 4-3. It is necessary to loosen the transit screw during this procedure. Refer to Figs. 6-1 and 6-22 for location of parts.

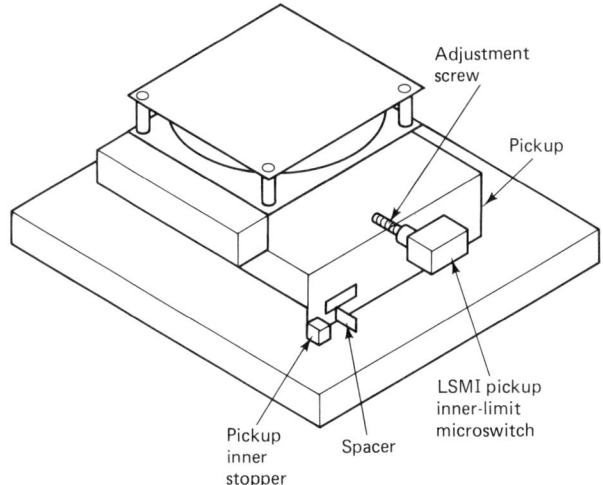

FIGURE 6-21 Adjusting the LMSI pickup inner-limit switch of a typical front-load CD player with vertical door.

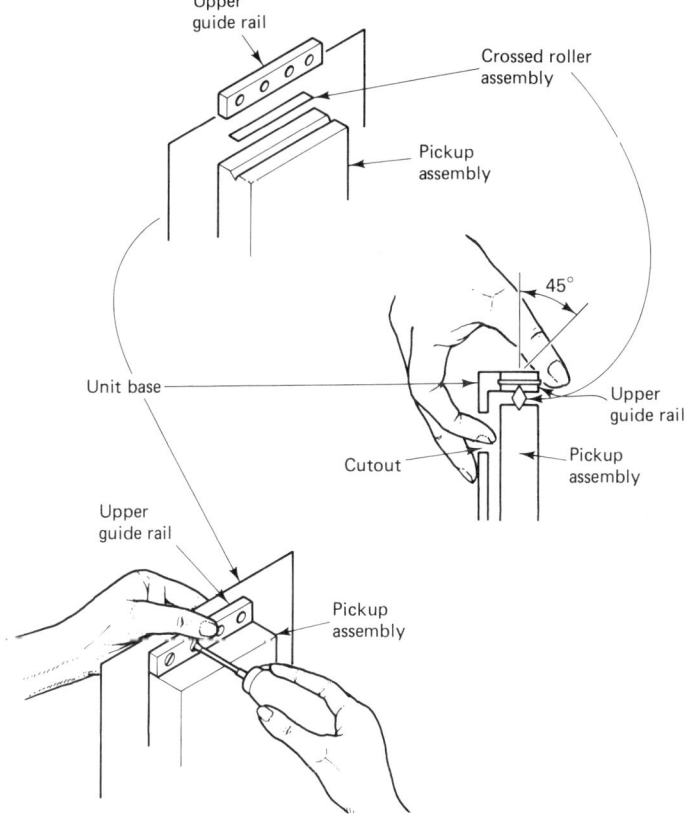

FIGURE 6-22 Reinstalling the pickup assembly of a typical front-load CD player with vertical door.

First remove the turntable motor as described in Sec. 6-1.8. Then remove the four fastening screws for the *upper guide rail* (but not the lower guide rail). Disconnect the wiring (flexible PWB) and lift the pickup assembly from the unit base. Be careful not to lose the upper and lower crossed-roller assemblies (positioned between the guide rails and pickup assembly).

6-1.11   Reinstalling the Pickup Assembly

This section describes the basic procedure to reinstall the pickup assembly on the unit base. Refer to Figs. 6-1 and 6-22 for location of parts. It is necessary to loosen the transit screw during this procedure.

Install the lower crossed-roller assembly into the V-shaped groove of the lower guide rail (making the right and left spacing equal). If specified by the service literature, lubricate the upper and lower crossed-roller assemblies (typically with silicone grease, such as HIVAC-G).

Set the pickup assembly onto the lower guide rail while aligning the outer side of the pickup with the outer side of the guide rail.

Install the upper crossed-roller asembly into the V-shaped groove on top of the pickup assembly (Fig. 6-22). Make the right and left spacing equal. Align the upper guide rail and temporarily tighten the four fastening screws so that the pickup assembly can still be moved freely.

Remove the lid of the belt replacement access cutout in the unit base (Fig. 6-14). Strongly squeeze the top and bottom edges of the upper guide rail at the center with thumb and forefinger, as shown in Fig. 6-22. Apply force at an angle of about 45° to the upper guide rail face. In this condition, first tighten the two inner screws and then the two outer screws. Move the pickup assembly and check that the pickup moves smoothly without binding (too tight) or chattering (too loose). Tighten the transit screw to lock the pickup assembly in place.

6-2   HORIZONTAL FRONT-LOAD MECHANICAL SECTION (SINGLE-LOAD MOTOR)

Figure 6-23 shows the major mechanical components for a typical front-load CD player with a horizontal tray operated by a single open/close/load/unload motor. Figure 6-24 shows the associated wiring. Note that most of the components are part of a *unit mechanism* secured to the mainframe by two *rails*.

In use, the *tray* is moved out of the player front panel by the loading motor (LIDM). This action also raises the *clamp* or *chuck*. A disc is installed manually in the tray, and the tray is pulled within the player by the loading motor. This action also lowers the clamp or chuck so that the disc is pressed against the *turntable motor assembly*. The turntable motor is operated by a turntable drive motor (Sec. 5-9.11) to spin the disc at the appropriate speed.

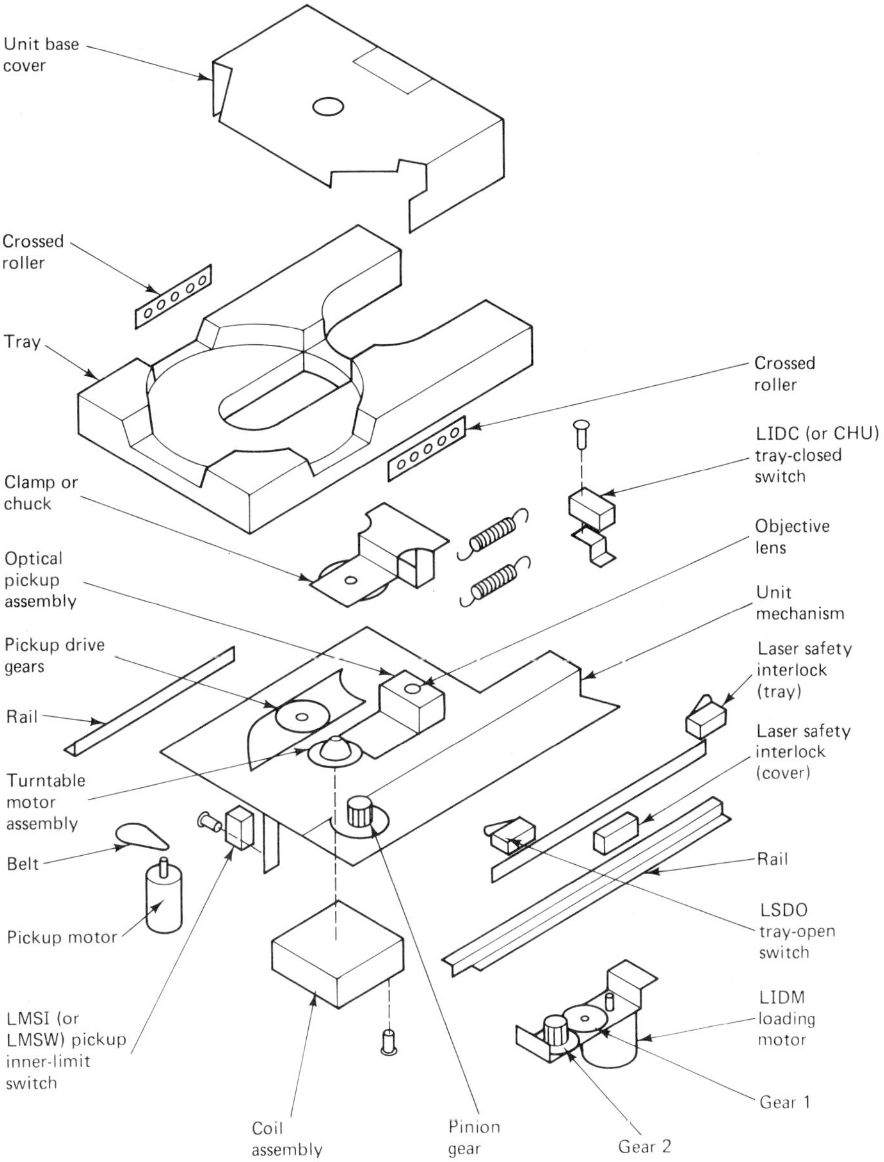

6-2 Horizontal Front-load Mechanical Section (Single-load Motor)

FIGURE 6-23 Major mechanical components for a typical front-load CD player with a horizontal tray (single load/unload motor).

182   *Mechanical Operation, Adjustment, and Replacement*

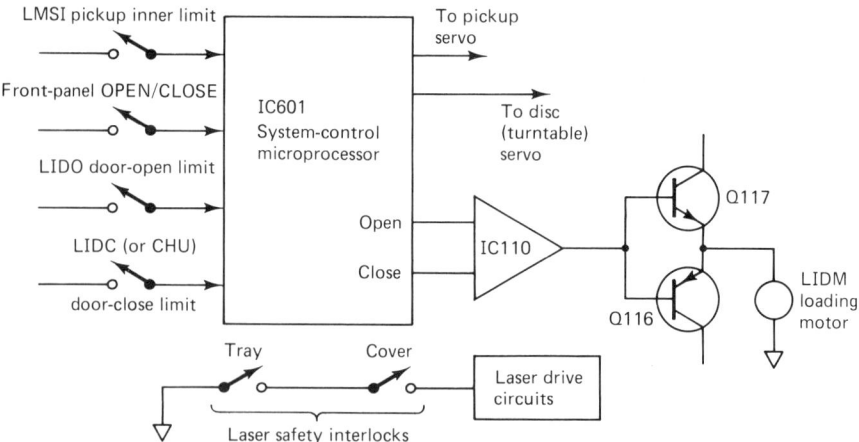

FIGURE 6-24   Wiring of mechanical section of typical front-load CD player with a horizontal tray (single load/unload motor).

In most players, the *coil assembly* can be separated from the turntable motor and replaced as a separate component.

As shown in Fig. 6-24, the two *laser safety interlock* switches (one for the cover and one for the tray) are connected in series. Both switches must be actuated (tray fully within the player, and the player cover in place) before the laser-drive circuits can operate (as discussed in Sec. 5-9.10).

As shown in Fig. 6-24, the loading motor LIDM receives open/close drive signals from the system-control microprocessor through gates and transistors. In turn, the microprocessor receives control signals from the front-panel OPEN/CLOSE switch. The microprocessor also receives indicator signals from the tray-open (LSDO) switch and the tray-closed (LIDC) switch. Note that the LIDC switch is actuated when the tray is in and the clamp or chuck is in the fully down position. (LIDC is identified as the chuck or CHU switch in some literature.)

The LSDO switch is positioned and adjusted to actuate when the tray has reached the correct open limit, and thus cuts off the loading motor through operation of the system microprocessor. No matter what it is called, the LIDC or CHU switch actuates when the tray is in and the clamp is fully down, thus cutting off the loading motor.

The *optical pickup assembly* is driven across the disc by the pickup motor, which is part of the unit mechanism. The pickup motor is operated by a servo, as described in Sec. 5-9.9. The pickup motor is connected to the *pickup drive gears* by means of a belt. The belt can be replaced when the player cover and the *unit base cover* are removed, without removing either the pickup or the motor.

As shown in Fig. 6-24, the system microprocessor receives a signal from

6-2 Horizontal Front-load Mechanical Section (Single-load Motor)

the pickup inner-limit (LMSI) switch. The LMSI switch is positioned and adjusted to actuate when the pickup assembly has reached the inner limit (start) of the disc. The LMSI signal cuts off the pickup motor through operation of the system microprocessor and the pickup servo. (The LMSI switch is called the LMSW switch in some literature.)

The entire unit mechanism can be replaced as an assembly (in most players). Some manufacturers also recommend replacement of the motors and limit switches (and they describe the procedures for replacement/adjustment in their service literature). As a practical matter, never disassemble the unit mechanism beyond that point necessary to replace or adjust a given part. Never make any adjustments unless the troubleshooting procedures lead you to believe that adjustment is required.

6-2.1 Operation of the Disc Loading/Unloading Mechanism

The following paragraphs describe how the tray is moved in and out and how the clamp or chuck is lowered and raised by the single loading motor. Keep in mind that this applies to a specific horizontal front-load player (with single loading motor), but is generally correct for most similar players.

Loading and clamping the disc. Figure 6–25 shows the sequence for loading and clamping (chucking) the disc in a horizontal front-load player. As shown, the operation can be divided into three basic steps (tray loading, moving the disc, and clamping). The *loading motor* is used as the driving force for all three steps. The loading-motor rotation is reduced through gears and converted into horizontal motion of the *rack* under control of a *latch* and link mechanism. The rack is divided into two sections. One section moves as a body with the tray. The other rack section moves separately (to move the disc up and down and to provide clamping).

The tray is loaded 150 mm into the player in about 2 seconds. The rack is then fixed to the tray with a latch. When the tray moves fully into the player, the latch is disengaged, the rack slides, the *lifters* lower, and the disc is moved down. This takes about 0.15 second. While the rack is moving 35 mm, the *clamp bar* is lowered to clamp the disc. The time required for this operation is about 0.55 second. When play is complete, the operation is reversed (the clamp bar is raised, the lifters raise the disc, and the tray moves outside the player).

The loading motor is turned off by the LSDO switch (Fig. 6–24) when the tray reaches the fully open or extended position. The loading motor is also turned off by the LIDC switch when the tray is fully in and the clamp is fully down. The time between fully open and fully closed is about 2.75 seconds. If the system microprocessor senses that the time between open (LIDO actuated) and close (LIDC actuated) is greater than about 5 seconds (say that you have

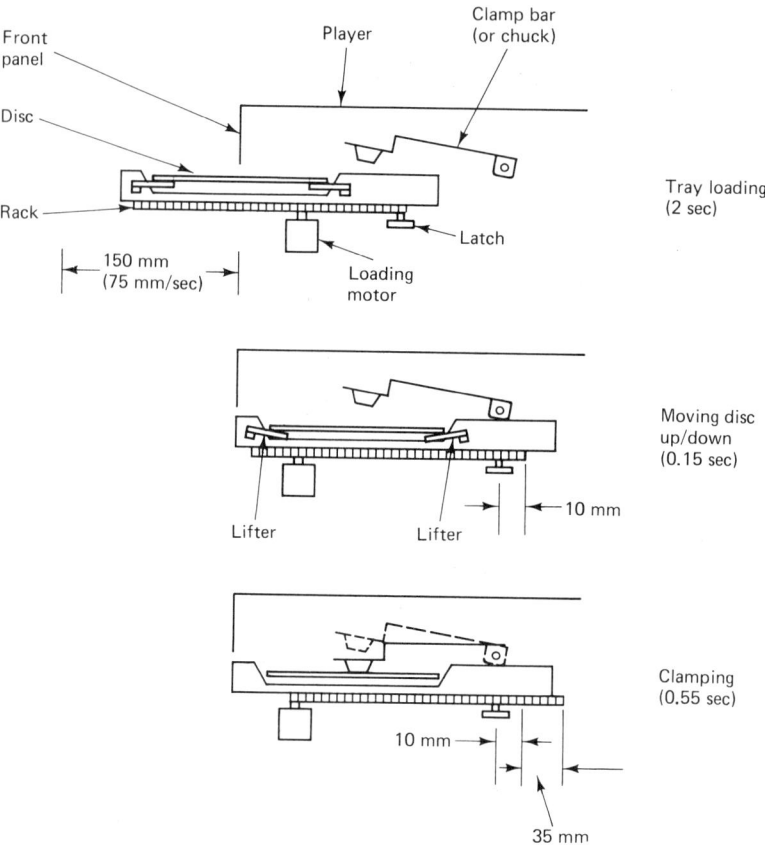

FIGURE 6-25 Sequence for loading and clamping the disc in a horizontal front-load player (single motor).

caught your finger in the tray), the microprocessor causes the loading motor to open the tray (move the tray to the fully open position).

Loading the tray. Figure 6-26 shows details of tray loading. The tray is mounted on the *tray rails* (left and right) and *unit rails* (left and right). The tray rails are part of the tray, while the unit rails are part of the *unit plate*. Power from the *loading motor* is applied to the rack through *gear-1, gear-2,* and the *pinion gear,* causing the tray to move in and out in a horizontal plane. The rack can move about 45 mm separately from the tray. However, during tray loading, the *latch* works as a stopper so that the rack and tray move as a single unit or body.

6-2 Horizontal Front-load Mechanical Section (Single-load Motor)

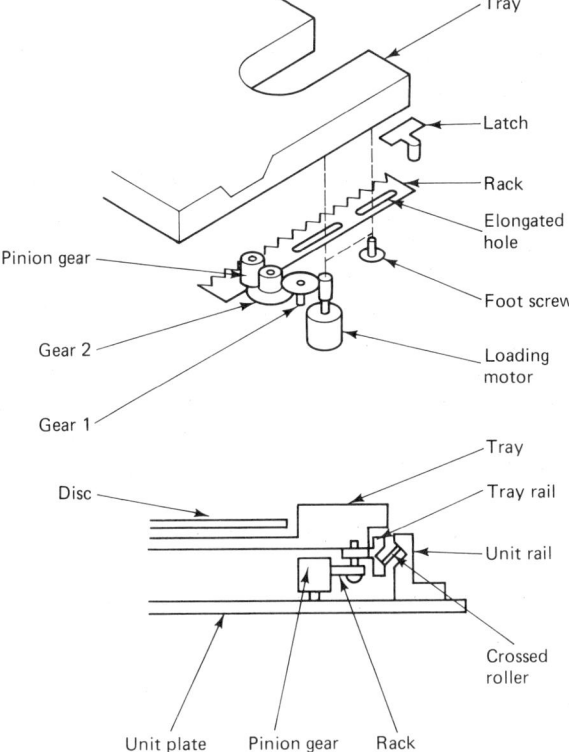

FIGURE 6-26 Details of tray loading.

Sliding the rack. Figure 6-27 shows the relationship of the rack and tray. One section of the rack slides independently of the tray to move the disc and to move the clamp up and down. During closing, as soon as the tray comes to the close position, the latch is led into the *hole* of the *latch guide* and rotates in the direction of the A-arrow, permitting the rack to slide in the direction of the B-arrow.

While the tray is opening, the rack first moves about 45 mm, and the *R-part* of the rack contacts the *foot screw* to open the tray. At this time, the latch (which has moved into the hole of the latch guide) moves in the direction of the C-arrow so that the rack and tray move as a body.

Moving the disc up and down. Figure 6-28 shows the details of disc up/down movement. The disc is moved up and down by the elevation (rotation) of the four *lifters* (which are part of the tray). The lifters are coupled to the *lifter cam assembly,* which is composed of a *lifter cam* and two *cam levers* (left and right). The two cam levers are moved (around two fulcrums) by the

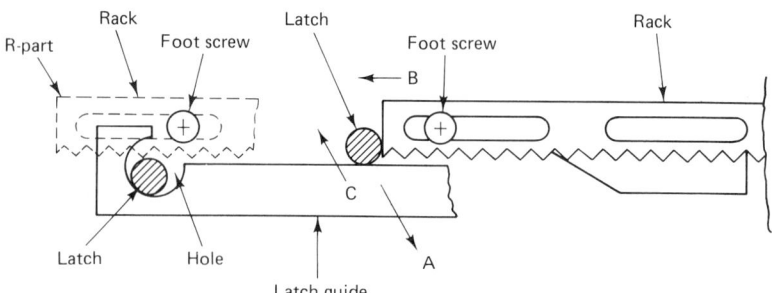

FIGURE 6-27 Relationship of the rack and tray.

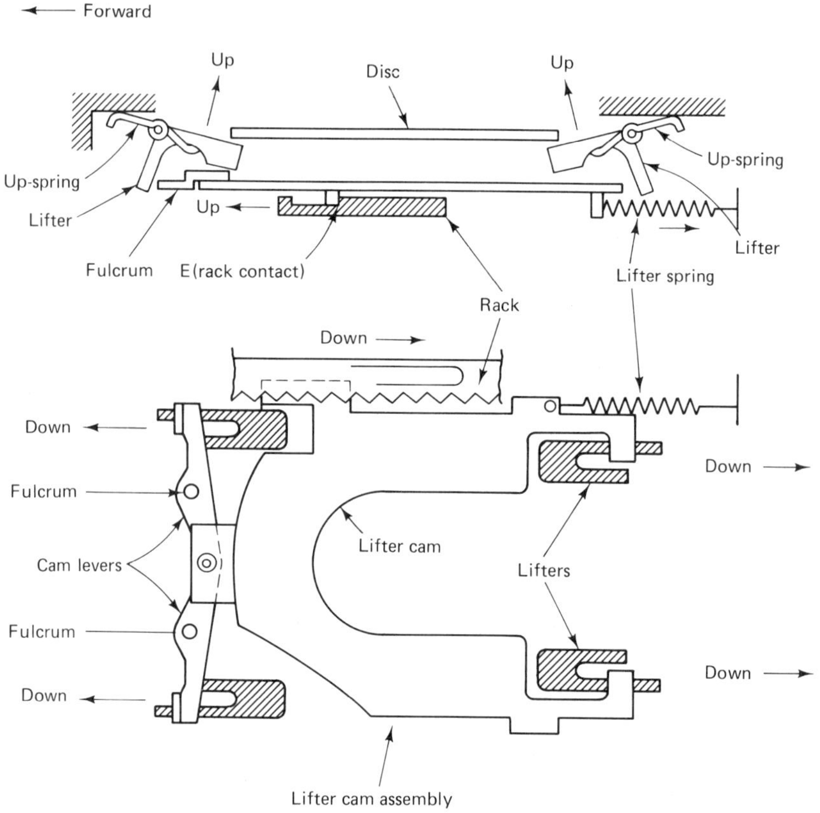

FIGURE 6-28 Details of disc up/down movement.

	Cam lever	Lifter cam	
Down	←	→	By lifter spring
Up	←	→	By rack and motor

6-2   Horizontal Front-load Mechanical Section (Single-load Motor)   187

lifter cam. In turn, the lifter cam is moved by the *lifter spring* (in the down direction), and by the *rack contact* at point E (in the up direction). Force is normally applied to the lifters in the up direction by the *up-springs.*

During load, when the disc is to be moved down, the rack moves together with the tray until the tray is within the player. During this time, the lifter cam assembly does not contact the lifters, which are held up by the lifter spring. When the tray reaches the close position, the rack starts moving backward, point E is separated, but the lifter cam is also moved backward (like the rack) by the force of the lifter spring, thus moving the lifters (and disc) down. The rear lifters are operated directly by the lifter cam, while the front lifters are moved to the down position by the left and right cam levers.

During unload, when the disc is to be moved up, the force from the loading motor which moves the rack forward is received at point E. This moves the lifter cam assembly forward to separate the lifter cam from the lifters. The rear lifters are separated from the lifter cam, while the front lifters are released by the lift and right cam levers. The lifters are moved to the up position by the up-springs.

Clamping the disc.   Figure 6-29 shows the details of disc clamping. The *disc* is clamped onto the *turntable* by the *clamp bar,* which uses the horizontal movement of the *rack* as a drive force. The rack moves about 35 mm after the disc is moved down. The rack has a *slope A,* which contacts the boss of the *C-cam.* This rotates the C-cam in the direction of the P-arrow. The C-cam motion is coupled through the *C-cam springs* to the *C-arm,* which moves the clamp bar over the disc.

During load, when the rack moves backward and the disc is clamped, slope A rotates the C-cam in the direction of the P-arrow. At this time, the C-arm is rotated in the direction of the S-arrow by the force of the C-cam spring (1), thus clamping the disc onto the turntable.

During unload, when the rack moves forward and the disc is unclamped, the boss of the C-cam is moved along slope A by the force of C-cam spring (2), turning the clamp bar up to unclamp the disc from the turntable.

6-2.2   Mechanical Section Servicing Precautions

All the precautions described in Sec. 6-1.1 generally apply to horizontal front-load players. Here are some additional precautions to consider.

In most horizontal front-load players, the laser diode does not receive drive signals (Fig. 6-24) unless the tray is fully retracted (to actuate the tray laser safety interlock switch) and the player cover is in place (to actuate the cover interlock switch). This means that you must override these interlocks during service. Try to avoid this! If you must override the interlocks (and it will be necessary), *always avoid direct exposure to the laser beam. Never look directly into the objective lens!*

188 Mechanical Operation, Adjustment, and Replacement

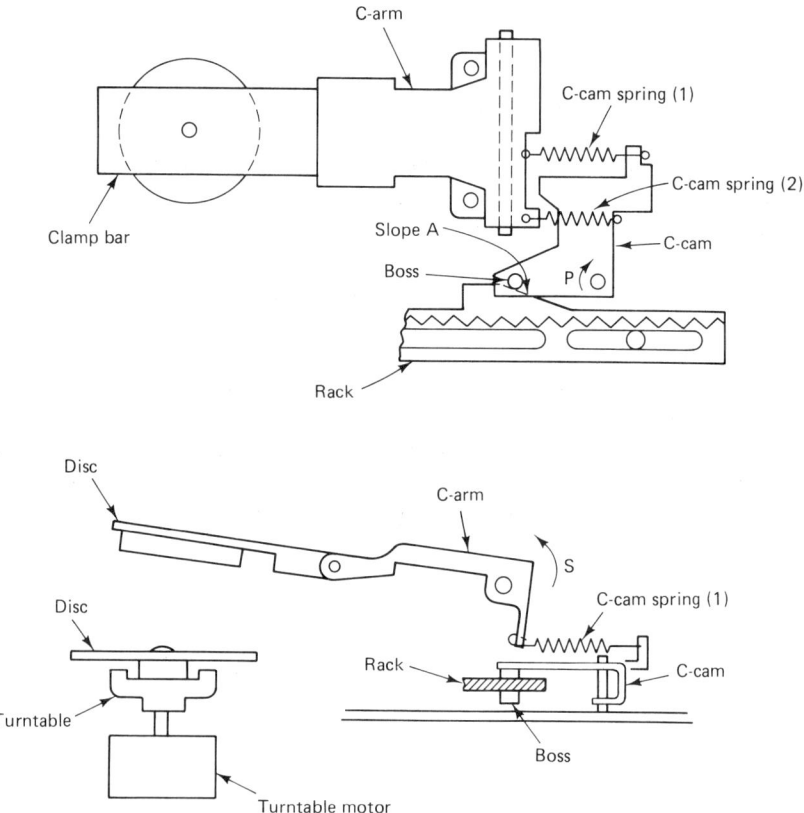

FIGURE 6-29 Details of disc clamping.

6-2.3 Gaining Access to the Components

This section describes the basic procedures to open the player for service. Keep in mind that these procedures are "typical" for horizontal players. Always follow any disassembly procedures found in the service literature.

Figure 6-30 shows the procedure for taking off the cover. Slide off the back cover after disengaging the screws (1).

Figure 6-31 shows the procedure for removing the escutcheon plate. After removing the cover, disengage screws (2) and (3), and wire-holder fixing screw (4). Pull the escutcheon plate to the front.

Figure 6-32 shows the procedure for removing the unit mechanism. After removing the escutcheon plate, disengage screws (5) and (6). Slide the unit mechanism backward (in the direction of the arrow), and disconnect the unit lead wires from the unit mechanism.

Figures 6-33 through 6-36 show the procedures for removing the various printed wiring boards (PWBs), and the power transformer. After removing

6-2 Horizontal Front-load Mechanical Section (Single-load Motor)

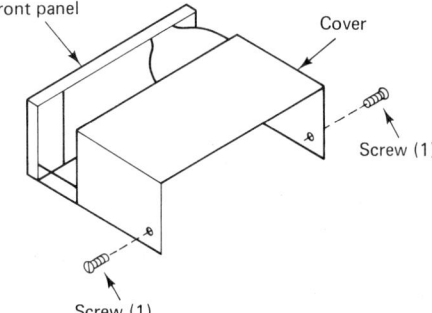

FIGURE 6-30 Procedure for removing the cover of a typical front-load CD player with horizontal tray.

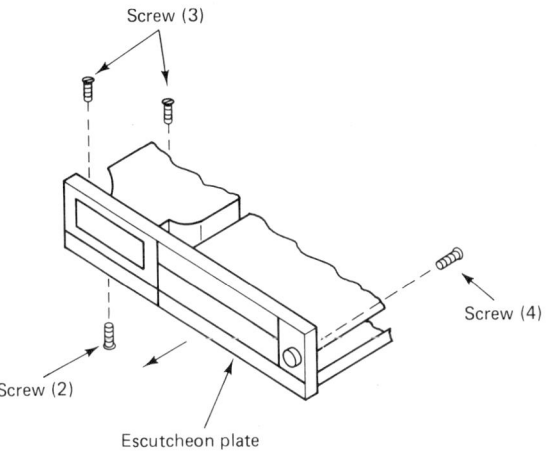

FIGURE 6-31 Procedure for removing the escutcheon plate of a typical front-load CD player with horizontal tray.

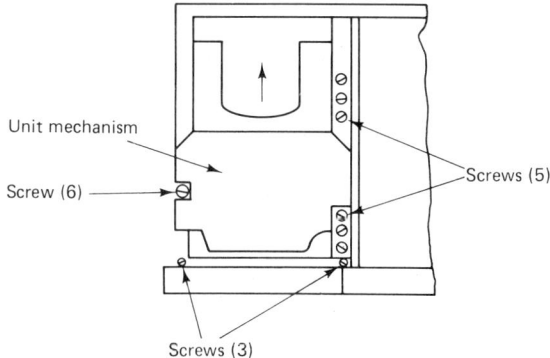

FIGURE 6-32 Procedure for removing the unit mechanism of a typical front-load CD player with horizontal tray.

190 Mechanical Operation, Adjustment, and Replacement

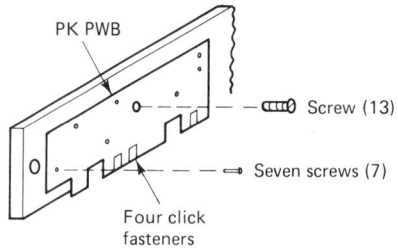

FIGURE 6-33 Procedure for removing PK PWB from typical front-load CD player with horizontal tray.

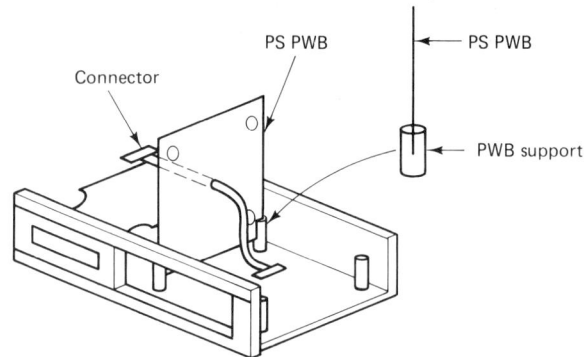

FIGURE 6-34 Procedure for removing PS PWB from typical front-load CD player with horizontal tray.

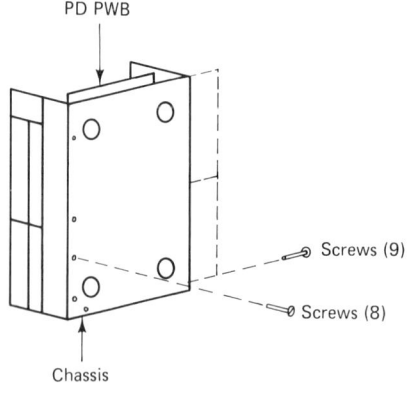

FIGURE 6-35 Procedure for removing PD PWB from typical front-load CD player with horizontal tray.

6-2 Horizontal Front-load Mechanical Section (Single-load Motor) 191

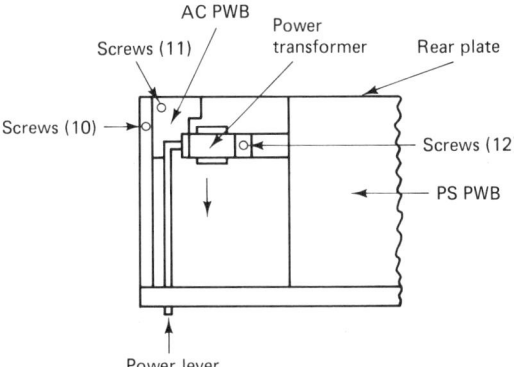

FIGURE 6-36 Procedures for removing AC PWB and power transformer from typical front-load CD player with horizontal tray.

the escutcheon plate, disengage screws (7), and then take off lower click fasteners to remove the PK PWB. Hold the upper end of the plastic PWB support (Fig. 6-34) at both sides, and remove the support from the PS PWB. It is convenient if the removed PS PWB is inserted into the slit of the support and kept there during repair. Disengage the screws that hold the chassis in the PWB support. Stand the player with the unit mechanism down (Fig. 6-35). Disengage screws (8) and (9) and remove the chassis. After removing the unit mechanism, pull the lever (Fig. 6-36) in the direction of the arrow to remove the lever. Disengage screws (10) and (11) and remove the AC PWB in the direction of the rear plate. After removing both the unit mechanism and the AC PWB, disengage screws (12) and remove the power transformer.

Figure 6-37 shows the procedure for removing the output volume control and headphone jack. After removing the escutcheon plate, lift the lower sub-

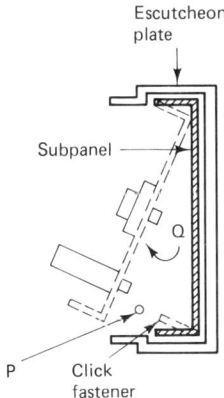

FIGURE 6-37 Procedure for removing the output volume control and headphone jack of typical front-load CD player with horizontal tray.

192 Mechanical Operation, Adjustment, and Replacement

panel click fasteners in the direction of the P-arrow. Rotate the subpanel in the direction of the Q-arrow, engaging the upper part, and remove the subpanel. Then remove the output volume control and headphone jack attached to the subpanel.

After removing the escutcheon plate, take off the PK PWB and disengage screw (13) (Fig. 6-33). The control assembly can then be removed.

6-2.4 Changing the Pickup Drive Belt

Figure 6-38 shows the basic procedures required to change the pickup assembly drive belt. Disengage screws (14) and remove the unit base cover. Disconnect the LED connector. Turn the power on. Press the disc OPEN/CLOSE switch to open the disc tray. Use tweezers to remove the old belt and to install a new belt. To mount the new belt, first install the belt on the pulley, and then on the motor shaft, using tweezers. Be careful not to touch the objective lens during this process.

6-2.5 Adjusting the Loading Mechanism

Figures 6-39 through 6-43 show the procedures for adjusting the loading mechanism, including the open/close limit switches and the laser safety interlock switches.

Adjusting the tray closing position. Close the tray as shown in Fig. 6-39. Turn the *right adjusting screw* so that the screw just contacts the tray. Then turn the right adjusting screw another half-turn (about 0.25 mm). Repeat the

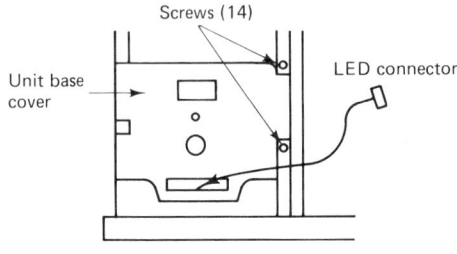

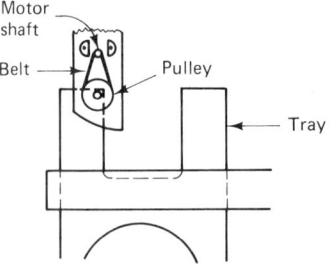

FIGURE 6-38 Procedures required to change the pickup assembly drive belt of typical front-load CD player with horizontal tray.

6-2 Horizontal Front-load Mechanical Section (Single-load Motor) 193

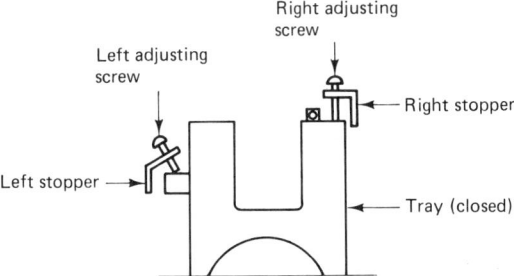

FIGURE 6-39 Adjusting the tray closing position of typical front-load CD player with horizontal tray.

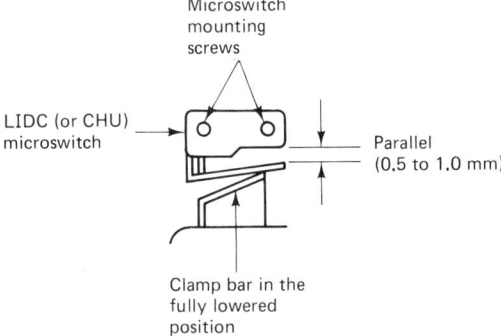

FIGURE 6-40 Adjusting the tray-closed microswitch position of typical front-load CD player with horizontal tray.

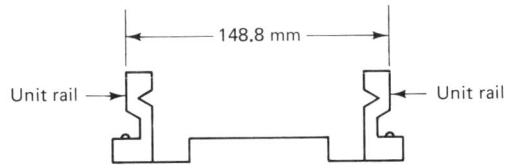

FIGURE 6-41 External dimensions for unit rails.

194 Mechanical Operation, Adjustment, and Replacement

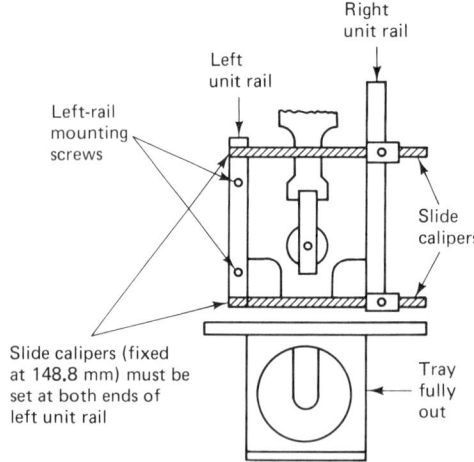

FIGURE 6-42 Adjusting tray-mounting unit rails of typical front-load CD player with horizontal tray.

same procedure for the left adjusting screw. Apply a sealer (such as Nejilock) to the adjusting screws to prevent them from loosening.

Adjusting the tray-closed microswitch position. Adjust the LIDC microswitch (also called the chuck or CHU switch in some literature) so that the switch is actuated when the clamp bar is fully lowered, using the dimensions in Fig. 6-40 as a guide. Tighten the microswitch mounting screws in this position.

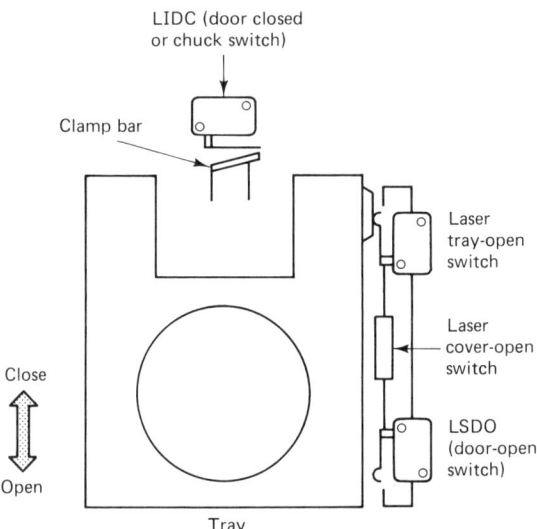

FIGURE 6-43 Relationship of laser-interlock switches and loading-mechanism limit switches to tray and clamp bar.

Adjusting the tray mounting unit rails. The tray mounting unit rails must be perfectly parallel, as shown in Figs. 6-41 and 6-42. Remove the player cover and unit base cover. Pull out the tray. Loosen (but do not remove) the left rail mounting screws. Fix slide calipers at 148.8 mm (or whatever dimension is specified in the service literature). Secure the calipers on the rails as shown, and check that the rails are parallel. Repeat this two or three times for best accuracy. Tighten the mounting screws in this position. Now move the tray back and forth. The tray must not bind at any point from fully open to fully closed. Equally important, there must be no chattering or vibration when the tray is moved.

Adjusting the loading mechanism switches. Figure 6-43 shows the relationship of the laser interlock switches and the loading mechanism limit switches to the tray and clamp bar. As shown in Fig. 6-40, the LIDC (door closed or chuck) switch is actuated (closed) when the clamp bar is down. The LSDO (door open) switch is actuated (closed) by the tray when the tray is open. The laser tray-open switch is closed only when the tray is fully in, and opens when the tray is in any other position. The laser cover-open switch is closed only when the player cover is in place, and opens when the cover is removed. As long as these conditions are met, the actual mounting dimensions for the switches are not critical (with a possible exception of the LIDC dimensions, Fig. 6-40). Make certain to tighten the switch mounting screws once you are certain that the switches actuate properly. (This same condition is true for the LMSI pickup inner-limit switch shown in Fig. 6-23.)

6-2.6 Further Disassembly of the Unit Mechanism

We do not go into further disassembly of the unit mechanism here. Typically, you can remove and reinstall the tray mechanism, disc clamp and springs, turntable motor coil assembly (and possibly the turntable motor and turntable assembly), pickup assembly, pickup motor, and loading motor. Figure 6-23 shows the relationship of these components in a typical horizontal front-load player. However, the procedures required for disassembly and reassembly are an area where one CD player can differ greatly from another player. You *must* follow the procedures and study the exploded-view illustrations found in the literature for the particular player you are servicing. The procedures we have covered thus far in this section can serve as a guide to understanding the service literature.

6-3 HORIZONTAL FRONT-LOAD MECHANICAL SECTION (TWO MOTORS)

Some horizontal front-load players have a separate motor to operate the disc clamp (or chucking arm, as it may be called). Figure 6-44 shows such an arrangement. Figure 6-45 illustrates the associated wiring. Before we get into

196 Mechanical Operation, Adjustment, and Replacement

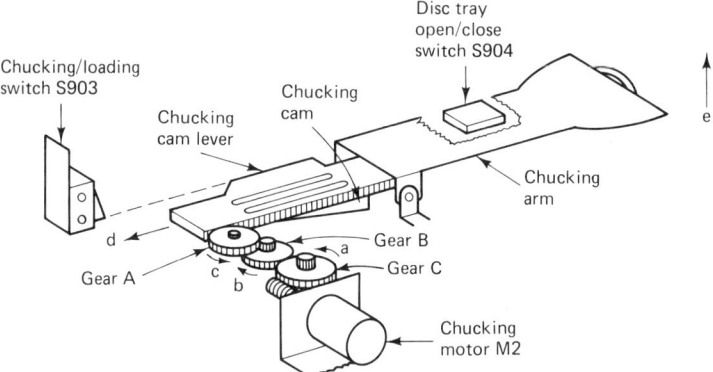

FIGURE 6-44 Chucking mechanism of typical front-load CD player with separate chucking motor.

chucking arm operation, let us consider the sequence of the loading process.

As shown in Fig. 6-45, the loading motor M1 and chucking motor M2 are driven with the amplifier IC304 output signals (at pin 16 of IC304). The load-out and load-in signals are taken from pins 19 and 20 of system microprocessor IC102. Switches are used to connect M1 and M2, or to make the motors ready for operation, or to indicate the status of the mechanical components.

6-3.1 Tray-open Sequence

The following sequence of operation occurs from the "disc tray closed" state to the "disc tray open" state.

When the OPEN/CLOSE switch S903 is operated, the output at pin 19 of IC102 goes high (about +3.2 V). Due to the inversion at pin 12 of IC304, the amplified output at pin 16 of IC304 goes low (about -9 V).

The chucking motor M2 is supplied power through the chucking/loading switch S905 (which is in the chucking position when the tray is fully in), and the disc tray open/close switch S904 (which is closed when the tray is fully in). The chucking motor M2 starts to rotate, and the chucking arm moves up to unclamp the disc (Sec. 6-3.3).

When the disc is unclamped (chucking is released), S905 switches to the loading position. This removes power from the chucking motor M2 and applies power to the loading motor M1, causing the disc tray to start moving out of the player. When the tray has moved about 3 mm, S904 opens, preventing power from being applied to the chucking motor M2.

When the tray is fully open or extended, disc tray position switch S907 is closed. The input at pin 40 of IC102 is grounded (zero volts). The output

6-3 Horizontal Front-load Mechanical Section (Two Motors) 197

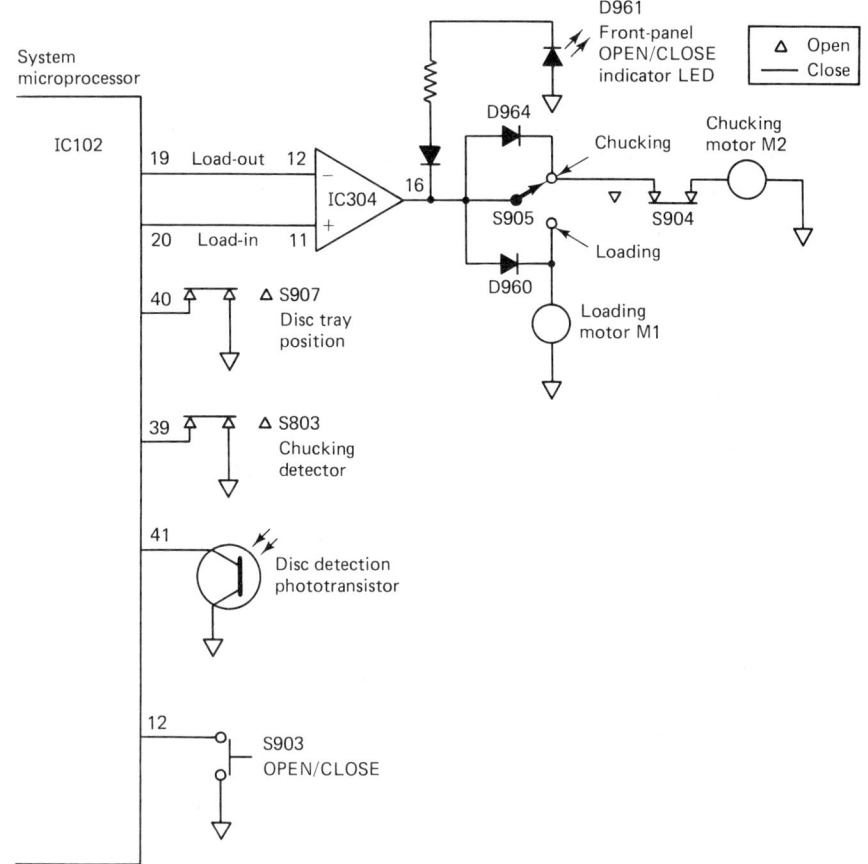

FIGURE 6-45 Wiring for mechanical section of typical front-load CD player with separate chucking motor.

from pin 19 of IC102 is removed (zero volts) and power is removed from loading motor M1. This completes the unloading sequence.

6-3.2 Tray-close Sequence

The following sequence of operation occurs from the "disc tray open" state to the "disc tray closed" state.

When OPEN/CLOSE switch S903 is operated, the output at pin 20 of IC102 goes high. Because there is no inversion at pin 11 of IC304, the output at pin 16 of IC304 goes high (about +10 V).

The loading motor M1 is supplied power through S905 (now in the loading position), and the disc tray is closed (moves within the player).

When the disc tray has reached the fully-in position, S904 is closed, connecting M2 to power through D964. Chucking motor M2 moves the chucking arm down over the disc. A short time after chucking is complete, S905 switches to the chucking position, shunting D964.

Power to loading motor M1 is maintained throughout the chucking process through D960. This insures that the disc tray does not move until locked (refer to Sec. 6-3.4).

When the chucking arm reaches the final position (disc fully clamped on the turntable), chucking detector switch S803 is closed. The input at pin 39 of IC102 is grounded (zero volts). The output from pin 20 of IC102 is removed (zero volts) and power (from pin 16 of IC304) is removed from both motors. This completes the loading sequence.

6-3.3 Chucking Arm Operation

Figure 6-44 shows the chucking mechanism at the moment when chucking is complete. The following sequence of operation takes place from the "chucking complete" state to the "release of chucking" state.

Chucking motor M1 rotates, and gears A, B, and C rotate in directions a, b, and c.

The chucking cam lever and the chucking cam move in direction d.

The chucking cam pushes the chucking arm in direction e. The chucking function is then released (disc unclamped).

When the chucking cam lever reaches the final position, S905 switches over to the loading position, and the tray moves out.

6-3.4 Disc Tray Fixing

During the initial phase of the chucking operation, the disc tray is fixed or held in position. This is shown in Fig. 6-46. The sequence is as follows.

At the beginning of the chucking operation, the chucking cam lever moves in direction K. The lock arm is pushed in direction L by the chucking cam lever, and the lock arm engages with the lock cam. The disc tray is then locked in the closed position.

6-3.5 Disc Detector

As shown in Fig. 6-45, a disc-detection phototransistor is connected to pin 41 of IC102. As discussed in Sec. 4-1.4 (and shown in Fig. 4-2) the purpose of the disc detector is to tell the system microprocessor that a disc is in place or not in place.

If a disc is in place, the phototransistor is covered, and the input to pin 41 of IC102 is not grounded (high). If a disc is not in place, surrounding light is applied to the phototransistor, which conducts and grounds pin 41 (pro-

6-3 Horizontal Front-load Mechanical Section (Two Motors)   199

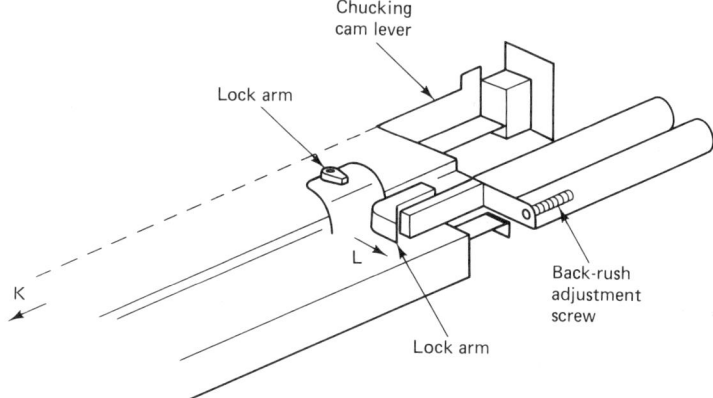

FIGURE 6-46 Disc tray-fixing mechanism.

ducing a low at pin 41). These high and low signals at pin 41 tell IC102 the status of the disc.

In many players with a disc detector, the turntable will not operate, and the normal play function cannot be selected, without a disc in place. Keep this point in mind when troubleshooting a "player will not play" symptom. Make sure that there is a disc in place and that light is not leaking to the disc-detector phototransistor (or that the phototransistor is not malfunctioning). Also remember that most players do not have a disc-detector system.

7

TROUBLESHOOTING and ADJUSTMENT

This chapter describes a series of troubleshooting and adjustment procedures for a cross section of CD players. As discussed in the Preface, it is not practical to provide a specific troubleshooting procedure for every CD player. Instead, we describe a universal troubleshooting approach, using specific examples of CD players. These examples just happen to be some of those players discussed in Chapters 1 through 6. In this way, you can relate the theory (Chapters 1 and 5) to the troubleshooting procedures in this chapter; then you can relate both to the specific CD player you are servicing.

Because adjustments are closely related to troubleshooting, we also describe typical adjustment procedures for CD players. Again, the players covered are some of those described in Chapters 1 and 5, using the test equipment and tools described in Chapter 4. When servicing other players, *you must follow* the manufacturer's troubleshooting/adjustment instructions exactly. Each type of player has its own electrical and mechanical test/adjustment points and procedures, which may or may not be different from procedures for other players.

Using the adjustment procedure examples, you should be able to relate the procedures to a similar set of adjustment points on most CD players. Where it is not obvious, we also describe the purpose of the adjustment procedure. The waveforms or signals measured at various test points during adjustment are also included here. By studying the wave forms and signals, you should be able to identify typical signals found in most CD players, even though the signals may appear at different points for your particular player.

It is assumed that you are already familiar with the basics of electronic troubleshooting, including solid-state troubleshooting. If not, and you plan to service CD players, you are in terrible trouble. Your attention is directed to the author's best-selling *Handbook of Practical Solid-State Troubleshooting* (Englewood Cliffs, N.J.: Prentice-Hall, Inc., 1971), the *Handbook of Basic Electronic Troubleshooting* (Englewood Cliffs, N.J.: Prentice-Hall, Inc., 1976), and the *Handbook of Advanced Troubleshooting* (Englewood Cliffs, N.J.: Prentice-Hall, Inc., 1983).

7-1 THE BASIC TROUBLESHOOTING FUNCTIONS

Troubleshooting can be considered as a step-by-step logical approach to locate and correct any fault in the operation of equipment. In the case of a CD player, seven basic functions are required.

First, you must study the player using service literature, user instructions, schematic diagrams, and so on, to find out how each circuit works when operating normally. In this way, you will know in detail how a given player should work. This is why the theory of operation for typical players is included in Chapter 5. Of course, you must study the service literature for the particular player you are servicing. The functions and features of all CD players are similar, *but not identical,* to those of all other players. If you do not take the time to learn what is normal, you will never be able to distinguish what is abnormal. For example, some players simply produce better sound than other players, even when operating normally. (Frequency response, dynamic range, and signal-to-noise ratio are greater for one player.) You can waste hours of precious time (money) trying to make the inferior player perform like the quality instrument if you do not know what is "normal" operation. This is especially important when working in audio equipment, where all customers claim to have a "golden ear."

Second, you must know the function of, and how to manipulate, *all* player controls. This is why the operating procedures for typical CD players are included in Chapter 3. Again, you must learn the operating controls for the player being serviced. It is also assumed that you know how to operate the controls of the stereo system used to amplify and reproduce the CD player output. An improperly adjusted stereo system can make a perfectly good player appear to be bad. (For example, if the graphic equalization controls are set to some weird combination, any CD player can sound equally weird.) One suggestion for evaluation of a CD player *in the shop* is to have at least one stereo system of known quality. All players passing through the shop can be compared against the same standard. In any event, it is difficult, if not impossible, to check out a player without knowing how to set the controls. Besides, it makes a bad impression on the customer if you cannot find the disc tray, especially on the second service call.

Third, you must know how to interpret service literature and how to use test equipment. Along with good test equipment that you know how to use, well-written service literature is your best friend. In general, CD player service literature is good as far as procedures and drawings are concerned. Unfortunately, CD player literature is often weak when it comes to descriptions of how circuits operate (theory of operation). The "how it works" portion of most player literature is often sketchy, or simply omitted, on the assumption that you and everyone else know CD player theory as well as circuit functions.

Fourth, you must be able to apply a systematic, logical procedure to locate troubles. Of course, a "logic procedure" for one type of player is quite illogical for another. For example, it is quite illogical to check the loading-circuit microswitches for a top-load player (since such switches generally do not exist on top-load models). Likewise, many vertical-door players do not have laser safety interlock switches, and many players of all types do not have disc-detection circuits. However, all front-load players with horizontal trays have loading-circuit microswitches as well as laser safety interlocks. For this reason, we discuss logic troubleshooting approaches for various types of players, in addition to basic troubleshooting procedures.

Fifth, you must be able to analyze logically the information of an *improperly operating player.* For that reason, much of the troubleshooting information in this chapter is based on *trouble symptoms* and their relation to a particular circuit or group of circuits in the player, as discussed in Sec. 7-2. The information to be analyzed may be in the form of performance, (such as failure of the disc to load normally) or may be indications taken from test equipment (such as waveforms or signals monitored with an oscilloscope). Either way, it is *your analysis* of the information that makes for logical, efficient troubleshooting.

Sixth, you must be able to perform complete checkout procedures on a player that has been repaired. Such checkout may be only simple operation, such as selecting each mode of operation in turn. At the other extreme, the checkout can involve complete adjustment of the player, both electrical and mechanical. This brings up a problem. Although adjustment of controls (both internal and front-panel) can affect circuit operation, such adjustment can also lead to false conclusions during troubleshooting. There are two extremes taken by some technicians during adjustment.

On one hand, the technician may launch into a complete alignment procedure once the trouble is isolated to a circuit. No control, no matter how inaccessible, is left untouched. The technician reasons that it is easier to make adjustments than to replace parts. While such a procedure eliminates improper adjustment as a possible fault, the procedure can also create more problems than are repaired. Indiscriminate adjustment is the technician's version of "operator trouble."

At the other extreme, a technician may replace part after part where a simple screwdriver adjustment will repair the problem. This usually means that the technician simply does not know how to perform the adjustment procedure or does not know what the control does in the circuit.

To take the middle ground, do not make any internal adjustments during the troubleshooting procedure until trouble has been isolated to a circuit, and then only when the trouble symptom or test results indicate possible maladjustment. This middle-ground approach is taken throughout this chapter.

In any event, some checkout is required after any troubleshooting. One reason is that there may be more than one problem. For example, an aging part may cause high current to flow through a resistor, resulting in burnout of the resister. Logical troubleshooting may lead you quickly to the burned-out resistor, and replacement of the resistor restores operation. However, only a thorough checkout can reveal the original high-current condition that caused the burnout. Another reason for after-service checkout is that the repair may have produced a condition that requires readjustment (such as after replacement of the pickup assembly or turntable motor).

Seventh, you must be able to use the proper tools to repair the trouble. As discussed in Chapter 4, CD player service requires all the common hand tools and test equipment found in audio/stereo service, plus some special tools that are unique to the particular player. As a minimum, you must have (and be able to use) various metric tools, and you must have an assortment of test discs (at least some known-good discs). These items are generally not familiar to the average TV service technician (unless that technician also happens to service VCRs, videodisc players, tape recorders, stereo decks, etc.).

In summary, before starting any troubleshooting job, ask yourself these questions: Have I studied all available service literature to find out how the player works? Can I operate the player properly? Do I really understand the service literature, and can I use all required test equipment and tools properly? Using the service literature and/or previous experience on similar players, can I plan out a logical troubleshooting procedure? Can I analyze logically the results of operating checks, as well as checkout procedures involving test equipment? Using the service literature and/or experience, can I perform complete checkout procedures on the player, including electrical/mechanical adjustment, and so on, if necessary? Once I have found the trouble, can I use common hand tools to make the repairs? If the answer is no to any of these questions, you simply are not ready to start troubleshooting any CD player. Start studying!

7-2 THE TROUBLESHOOTING APPROACH

The remainder of this chapter is devoted to adjustment/troubleshooting approaches for typical CD players. *Note that two sets of adjustment/troubleshooting procedures are included,* one set for early-model players and another set for late-model players. The early-model players often use more discrete components in many circuits, whereas late-model players tend to combine many circuit functions in a single IC (particularly in the various servo circuits).

While the basic circuit functions are essentially the same for all CD players, the adjustment procedures and troubleshooting approaches are somewhat different for early- and late-model units. For example, early-model players usually require several (at least two or three each) adjustments in the focus, tracking, turntable, and pickup servo circuits, but do not require adjustment of the sample/hold (S/H) circuits. On the other hand, the S/H circuits of most late-model players can be adjusted, but the various servos have only one adjustment control for each circuit.

The troubleshooting approach is based on *trouble symptoms*. A series of trouble symptoms is listed in the appropriate sections, ahead of the related troubleshooting sections. These symptoms can apply to any CD player, but are related specifically (in most cases) to the players described in Chapters 5 and 6. Each trouble symptom is referred to one or more troubleshooting procedure (by section number) that applies to the circuit groups of the players discussed in Chapter 5.

In some cases, the troubleshooting procedure requires adjustments, both electrical and mechanical. For that reason, the electrical adjustments are given ahead of the related troubleshooting procedures. (Mechanical adjustments, including the switches used in mechanical operation, are discussed in Chapter 6.) The adjustment procedures are then referred to in the troubleshooting procedure as necessary.

7-3 ELECTRICAL ADJUSTMENT PROCEDURES FOR EARLY-MODEL PLAYERS

The following paragraphs describe complete adjustment procedures for a CD player such as described in Sec. 5-9. Each procedure is accompanied by diagrams that show the electrical locations for all adjustment controls and measurement points (test points, or TP), as well as the waveforms or signals that should appear at the test points.

Keep in mind that the procedures described here are the only procedures recommended by the manufacturer for that particular model of CD player. Other manufacturers may recommend more or less adjustment. It is your job to use the correct procedures for each player you are servicing.

Also remember that some disassembly and reassembly may be required to reach test and/or adjustment points. We do not include any disassembly/reassembly here for two reasons. First, such procedures are unique and can apply to only one model of player. More important, disassembly and reassembly (both electrical and mechanical) are areas where CD player service literature is generally well written and illustrated. Just make sure that you observe all the notes, cautions, and warnings found in the disassembly/reassembly sec-

7-3 Electrical Adjustment Procedures for Early-model Players

tions of the player service literature. The procedures for removal of covers and gaining access to parts for some CD players are discussed in Chapter 6.

7-3.1 Test Equipment Required

The only test equipment required for complete electrical adjustment of the player described in Sec. 5-9 is a 10-MHz dual-trace oscilloscope, a digital voltmeter, and an audio generator with variable output. However, you should have a test disc (if specified in the service literature) and/or a known-good disc for test. Also, the author recommends a good stereo amplifier/speaker system to monitor the player.

7-3.2 Presetting Adjustment Controls

Before performing any adjustments, preset the adjustment controls to the mid- or medium position, and set the antishock switch (if any) to off. A possible exception to this is the laser diode output adjustment control. Next we will tell you why.

7-3.3 Laser Diode Output Adjustment

Figure 7-1 is the laser diode output adjustment diagram. Normally, the laser-diode output should not be adjusted unless the pickup has been replaced or troubleshooting indicates that the laser-diode output is not correct (possibly low). If the pickup is replaced, or you must adjust the laser-diode output, preset the control (R049 in Fig. 7-1) to zero, and then increase the setting as required. (However, some service literature recommends that the laser-diode output control be preset to the midpoint.)

Checking the laser-diode drive current. Keep in mind that laser diodes can be damaged by current surges. (This is true of any semiconductor device, but more so of laser diodes.) Also, the current threshold level is slightly different for each laser. Typically, the laser diodes used in CD players have drive currents in the 40- to 70-mA range, although some can operate satisfactorily at 100 mA. Generally, 150-mA drive current is sufficient to damage (if not totally destroy) any CD laser diode. As laser diodes age, they may require more drive current to produce the required amount of light. Usually the service literature spells out the "safe" limits of laser drive current.

The simplest way to check laser-diode drive current is to measure the voltage across a resistor in series with the diode, such as R046 in Fig. 7-1, and then calculate the current. For example, if the recommended laser-diode current is 40 to 70 mA, and the series resistance is 22 ohms, the voltage should be between 0.88 and 1.54 V (measured with a digital voltmeter). This check

206 Troubleshooting and Adjustment

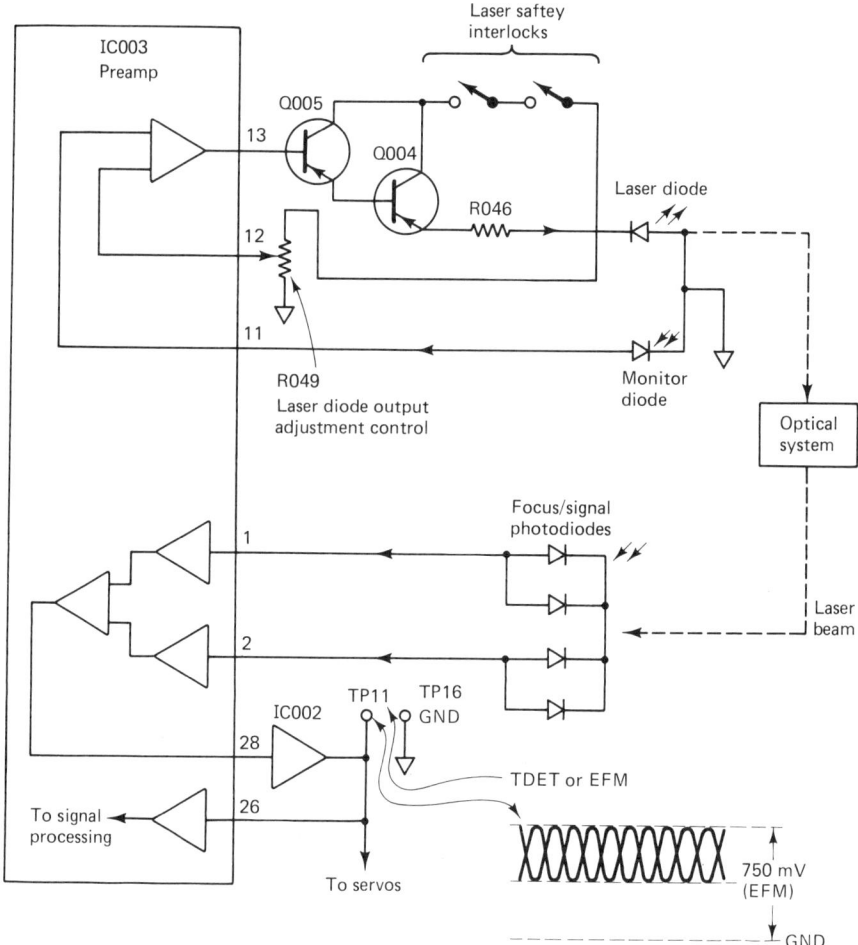

FIGURE 7-1 Laser-diode output adjustment diagram (early-model).

can be done before you adjust the laser diode output, and *should be done* after any adjustment of the laser.

Monitoring the laser output with a light meter. Some service literature recommends that you monitor the output of the laser diode with a light meter. However, this is generally not necessary. It is far more practical (and much easier) to adjust the laser-diode output until you get an EFM signal of correct amplitude, as we discuss next.

After the controls are present, proceed as follows:

1. Connect the oscilloscope between TP11 (TDET) and TP16 (GND), as shown in Fig. 7-1. With this connection, you are monitoring the

7-3 Electrical Adjustment Procedures for Early-model Players 207

EFM signal (after the photodector output has been preamplified by IC003). The EFM signal (at this point) is returned to IC003 for further processing, and is also used by the tracking, focus, and pickup motor servos.

2. Load a disc in the player and select the PLAY mode. The EFM signal should appear on the oscilloscope and produce a waveform similar to that of Fig. 7-1.

3. Adjust R049 until the level of the EFM signal is 750 mV. Typically, the EFM signal (at this point) is in the range of 550 to 950 mV. Always check the service literature for the correct EFM signal amplitude.

Note that R049 sets the drive current to the laser diode through Q005, Q004, and circuits within IC003. If it is necessary to increase the drive current (as measured across R046) beyond the safe limits to get the proper EFM signal at TP11, then IC003, Q004, and Q005 (or the laser diode itself) may be faulty.

7-3.4 Tracking Servo Offset Adjustment

Figure 7-2 is the tracking servo offset adjustment diagram.
After the controls are preset, proceed as follows:

1. Connect the oscilloscope between TP11 (TDET) and ground as shown in Fig. 7-2. With this connection, you are still monitoring the EFM signal, as in Sec. 7-3.3. However, you are now adjusting offset of the tracking-error signal (TER), which is applied to the tracking actuator coil in the optical pickup. In effect, you are adjusting the optical pickup (through the servo and tracking actuator coil) so that the laser beam is properly centered on the tracks. Note that R034 sets the offset of the two tracking diodes, but not the four remaining focus/signal diodes.

2. Load a disc in the player and select the PLAY mode. The EFM signal should appear on the oscilloscope and produce a waveform similar to that of Fig. 7-2.

3. Adjust R034 until the EFM signal is at maximum amplitude (indicating that the optical pickup is centered on the tracks).

7-3.5 Focus Servo Offset Adjustment

Figure 7-3 is the focus servo offset adjustment diagram.
After the controls are preset, proceed as follows:

1. Connect the oscilloscope between TP11 (TDET) and ground as shown in Fig. 7-3. With this connection, you are again monitoring the EFM

208 Troubleshooting and Adjustment

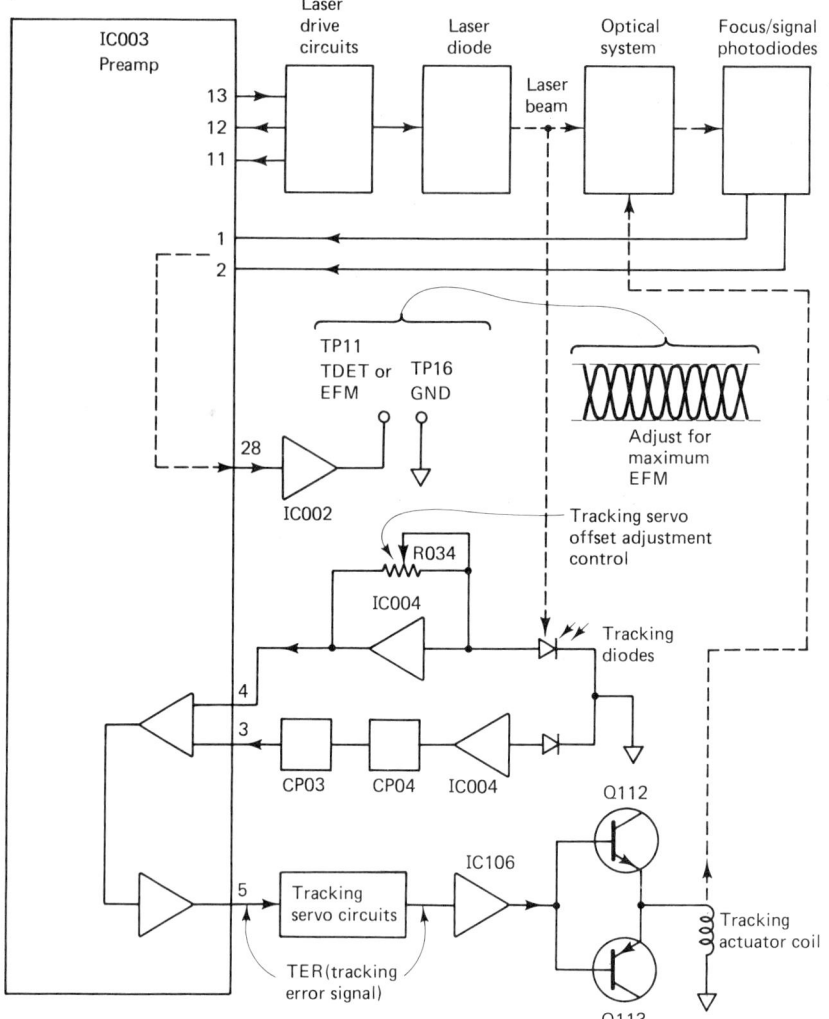

FIGURE 7-2 Tracking servo offset adjustment diagram (early-model).

signal, (as in Sec. 7-3.3). However, you are now adjusting offset of the focus error signal (FER), which is applied to the focus actuator coil in the optical pickup. In effect, you are adjusting the optical pickup (through the servo and focus actuator coil) so that the laser beam is properly focused on the tracks. Note that R128 sets the offset of the four focus/signal diodes, but not the two remaining tracking diodes.

7-3 Electrical Adjustment Procedures for Early-model Players 209

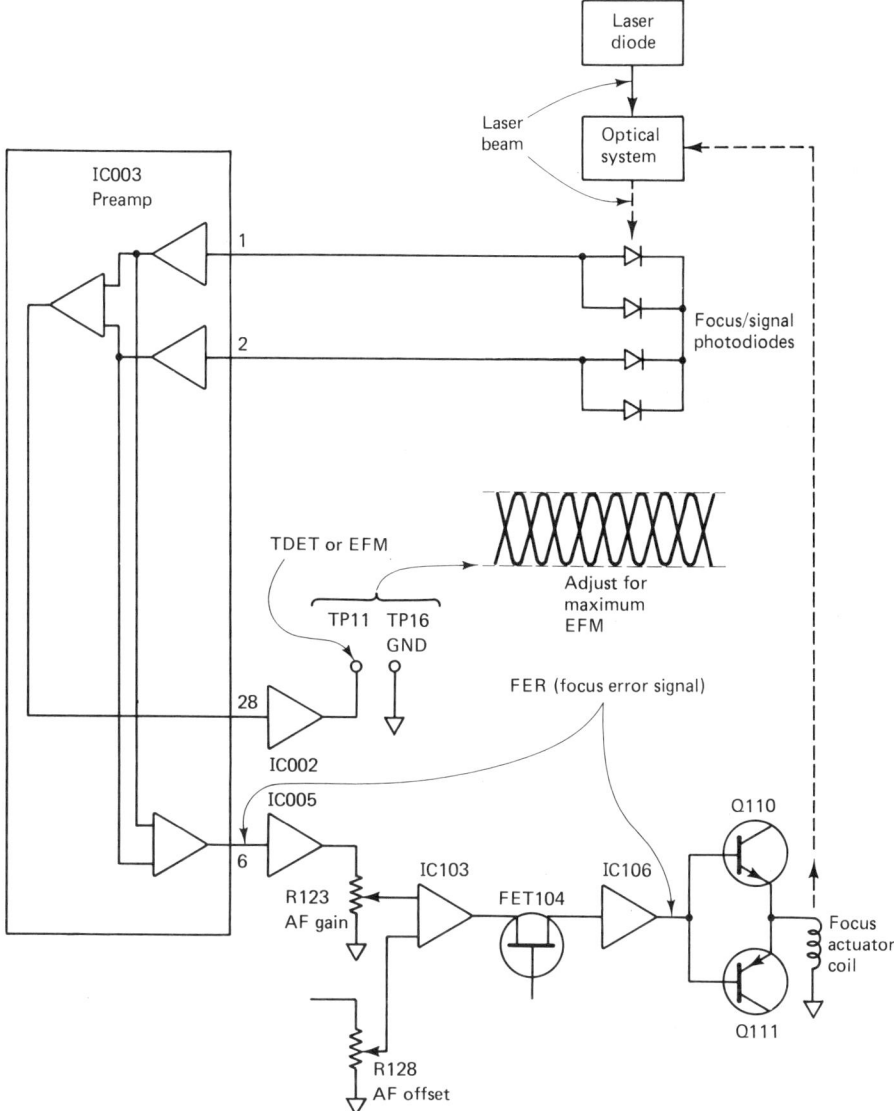

FIGURE 7-3 Focus servo offset adjustment diagram (early-model).

2. Load a disc in the player and select the PLAY mode. The EFM signal should appear on the oscilloscope and produce a waveform similar to that of Fig. 7-3.
3. Adjust R128 until the EFM signal is at maximum amplitude (indicating that the optical pickup is focused on the tracks).

7-3.6 Focus Servo Gain Adjustment

Figure 7-4 is the focus servo gain adjustment diagram.
After the controls are preset, proceed as follows:

1. Connect the oscilloscope and audio signal generator to TP4 (AF−) and TP6 (AF+), as shown in Fig. 7-4. With this connection, you are monitoring the focus error signal (FER) from IC003. The FER signal (at this point) is applied to the focus actuator coil in the optical pickup. In effect, you are setting the gain of the focus servo loop.

Note that the phase-shift networks (capacitors and resistors) shown in Fig. 7-4 are not required on all players. Instead, the adjustment

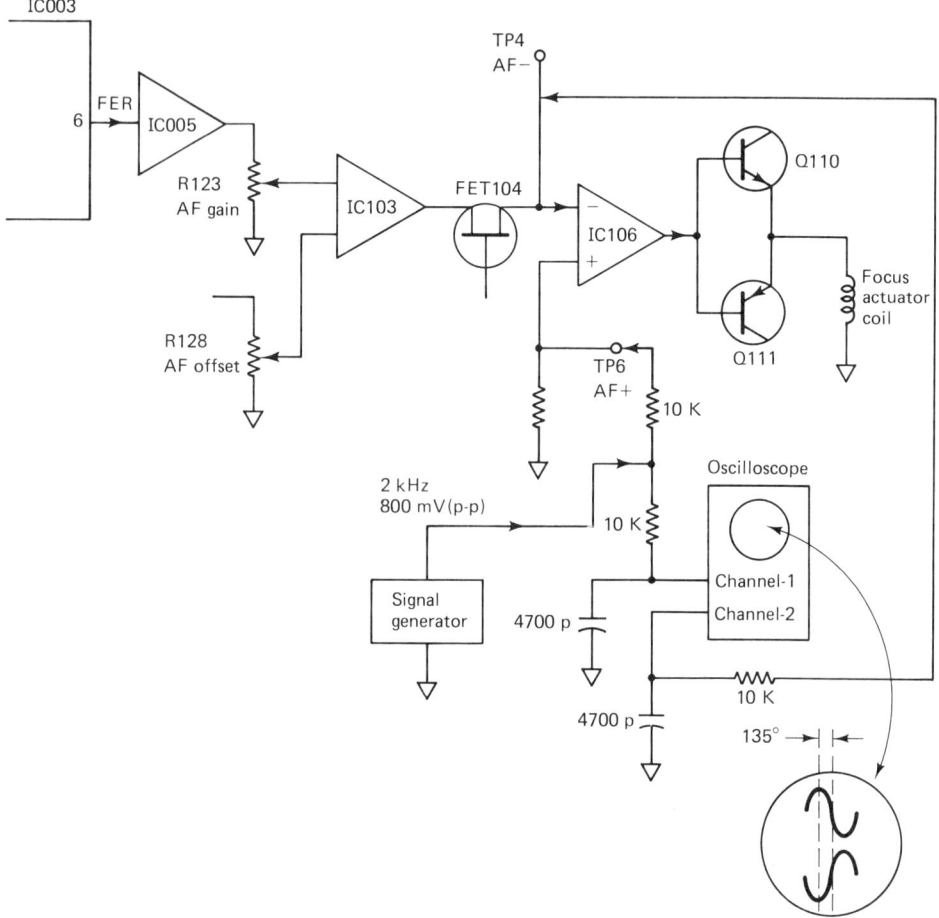

FIGURE 7-4 Focus servo gain adjustment diagram (early-model).

7-3 Electrical Adjustment Procedures for Early-model Players 211

instructions found in the service literature for such players describe connections between the AF− and AF+ test points and other nearby components on the printed wiring board. The networks are shown here to help you understand the purpose of the adjustment. Always check the service literature for proper test connections.

2. Set the frequency of the signal generator to 2 kHz. Adjust the signal generator output to 800 mV(p-p).
3. Load a disc in the player and select the PLAY mode. The two FER signals should appear on the dual-trace oscilloscope and produce two waveforms (channel-1 and channel-2) similar to that of Fig. 7-4.
4. Adjust R123 so that the phase between the channel-1 and channel-2 FER signals is 135°, as shown in Fig. 7-4. This indicates that there is sufficient gain in the focus servo loop.

7-3.7 *Tracking Servo Gain Adjustment*

Figure 7-5 is the tracking servo gain adjustment diagram.
After the controls are preset, proceed as follows:

1. Connect the oscilloscope and audio signal generator to TP5 (TR−) and TP7 (TR+) as shown in Fig. 7-5. With this connection, you are monitoring the tracking error signal (TER) from IC003. The TER signal (at this point) is applied to the tracking actuator coil in the optical pickup. In effect, you are setting the gain of the tracking servo loop.

   Note that the phase-shift networks (capacitors and resistors) shown in Fig. 7-5 are not required on all players. Instead, the adjustment instructions found in the service literature for such players describe connections between the TR− and TR+ test points and other nearby components on the printed wiring board. The networks are shown here to help you understand the purpose of the adjustment. Always check the service literature for proper test connections.

2. Set the frequency of the signal generator to 1.8 kHz. Adjust the signal generator output to 400 mV (p-p).
3. Load a disc in the player and select the PLAY mode. The TER signals should appear on the dual-trace oscilloscope and produce a circular pattern similar to that shown in Fig. 7-5. (This oscilloscope pattern is called a *resurge graph* in some literature).
4. Turn on the antishock switch.
5. Adjust R119 so that the pattern is circular, as shown in Fig. 7-5.
6. Turn off the antishock switch, and recheck the circular pattern.

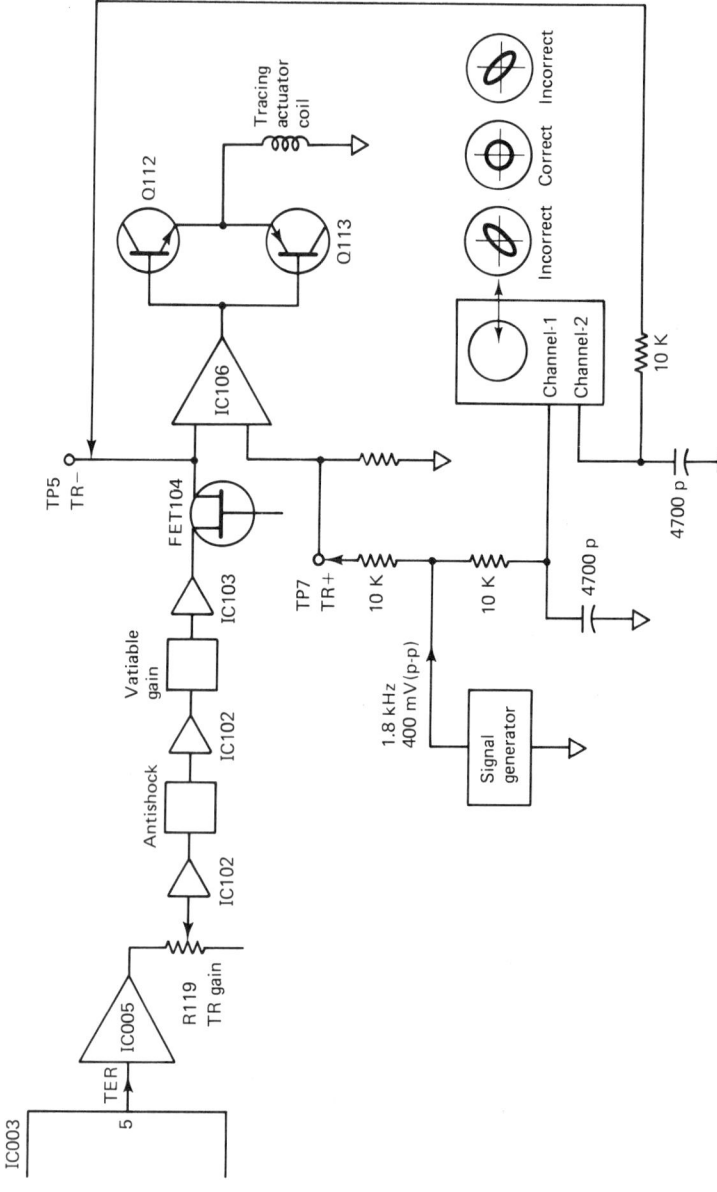

FIGURE 7-5 Tracking servo gain adjustment diagram (early-model).

Note that on players without antishock circuits, this adjustment is performed by turning the power off and on and then selecting PLAY. The waveform should remain circular. However, there may be a slight delay or surge (where the waveform is elliptical) before the pattern returns to a circle (after power is turned on). If the delay is prolonged, or if the pattern remains elliptical, continue adjustment of R119 until you get the circular pattern. This indicates that there is sufficient gain in the tracking servo loop.

7-3.8 Disc Motor Hall Gain Adjustment

Figure 7-6 is the disc (turntable) motor Hall gain adjustment diagram.
After the controls are preset, proceed as follows:

1. Connect the oscilloscope between TP9 (DMCA) and ground, as shown in Fig. 7-6. Note the amplitude of the DMCA signal. With this connection, you are monitoring the drive signals applied to the disc motor coil A.
2. Connect the oscilloscope between TP10 (DMCB) and ground, as shown in Fig. 7-6. With this connection, you are monitoring the drive signals applied to the disc motor coil B.
3. Adjust R256 until the DMCB signal is the same amplitude as the DMCA signal. In effect, you are setting the gain of the disc motor coil B drive so that both motor coils A and B receive signals of equal amplitude. Typically, the DMCA and DMCB signals (at this point) are about 2 V (p-p).

7-3.9 Disc Motor Offset Adjustment

Figure 7-7 is the disc (turntable) motor Hall offset adjustment diagram.
After the controls are preset, proceed as follows:

1. Connect capacitor C1 and resistor R1 to the oscilloscope, as shown in Fig. 7-7.
2. Connect the oscilloscope between TP9 (DMCA) and ground, as shown in Fig. 7-7. With this connection, you are monitoring the drive signals applied to the disc motor coil A (through an integrating network).
3. Adjust R232 until the integrated DMCA voltage is zero.
4. Connect the oscilloscope between TP10 (DMCB) and ground as shown in Fig. 7-7. With this connection, you are monitoring the drive signals applied to the disc motor coil B (through an integrating network).
5. Adjust R237 until the integrated DMCB voltage is zero.

214 Troubleshooting and Adjustment

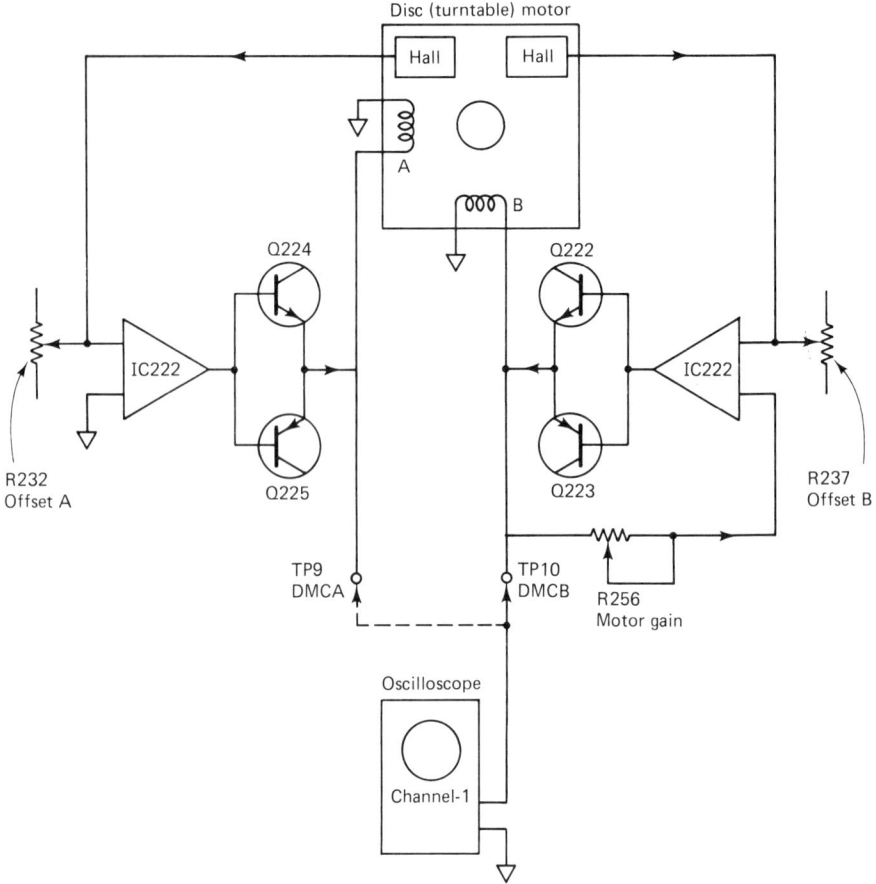

FIGURE 7-6 Disc (turntable) motor Hall gain adjustment diagram (early-model).

6. Recheck the DMCA voltage (Step 3) and readjust R232 if necessary to reduce the voltage to zero. Then recheck the DMCB voltage (Step 5) and adjust R237 if necessary. It may be necessary to work between R232 and R237 to bring both the integrated DMCA and DMCB voltages to zero.

7-4 INTRODUCTION TO EARLY-MODEL CD PLAYER TROUBLESHOOTING

Figure 7-8 is a trouble symptom chart for CD players such as described in Sec. 5-9. The chart provides a list of various symptoms common to most early-model front-load players (both vertical-door and horizontal-tray). After se-

7-4 Introduction to Early-model CD Player Troubleshooting 215

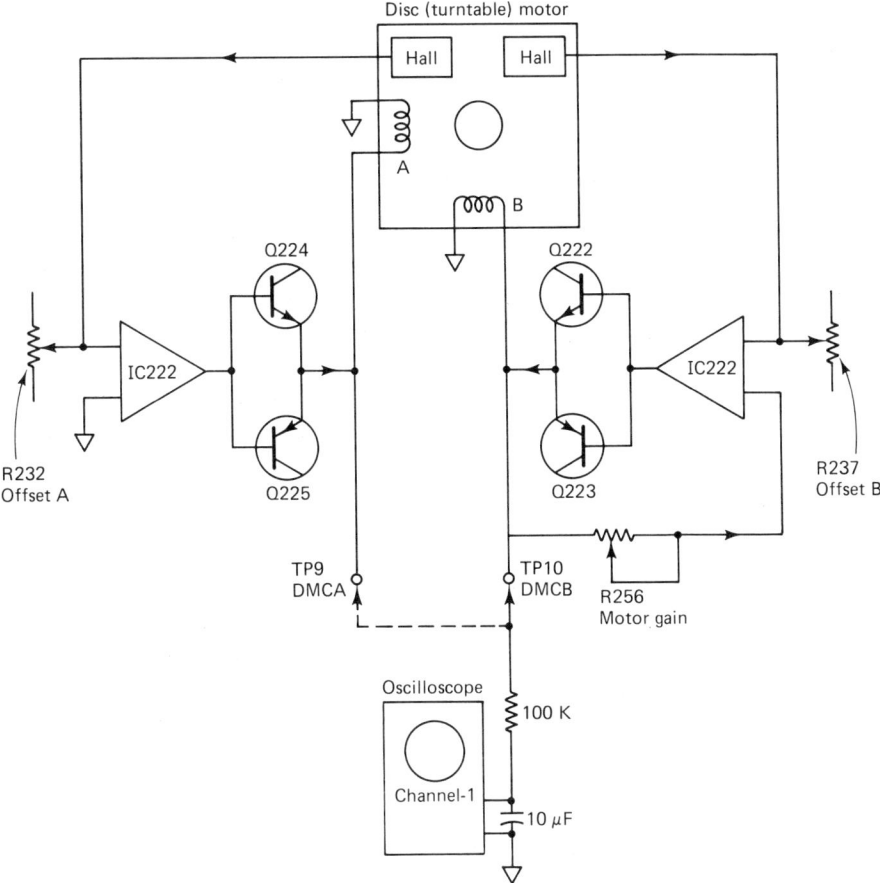

FIGURE 7-7 Disc (turntable) motor Hall offset adjustment diagram (early-model).

lecting the symptom which matches that of the CD player being serviced, follow the steps in the troubleshooting procedures (indicated by section number in the right-hand column). These procedures help isolate the problem to a defective module or component. Listed in each troubleshooting procedure are the electrical and mechanical adjustments (if any) associated with the related module or circuit. The electrical adjustments are described in Sec. 7-3. Mechanical adjustments are discussed in Chapter 6. Always check the adjustments, if practical, before proceeding with service or troubleshooting.

7-4.1 Preliminary Checks

It is always good practice to make a few basic preliminary checks before going on with troubleshooting. Check the following before you tear into the player with soldering tool and pickax.

SYMPTOM	TROUBLESHOOTING PROCEDURE SECTION NO.
Door or tray does not open or close properly	7-5
Laser diode problems	7-6
Pickup does not move to inner limit when power is applied	7-7
Pickup does not change speed during search	7-8
Pickup does not focus properly	7-9
Pickup does not track properly	7-10
Disc motor (turntable) does not rotate properly	7-11
Signal-processing problems (excessive dropout)	7-12
Audio circuit problems	7-13
Programming and operating problems	7-14

FIGURE 7-8 Early-model CD player troubleshooting chart.

The *transit or shipping screw* must be removed or loosened before the player can operate normally.

If practical, check that the user or customer stereo system is operating normally *before* you do any extensive service on the CD player. Of course, this is not too practical if the customer drops the player on your bench with comments like "it doesn't work" or "it sounds terrible on my system."

Always inspect the modules and plug-in PWBs for *bad solder connections* and *broken copper bands* or for *loose or unseated boards*. Use a pencil eraser to clean the module and board contacts, if bad contacts are suspected.

Cleaning the *objective lens* (Sec. 4-4) should become a routine part of servicing any CD player. A dirty objective lens can cause a variety of symptoms (intermittent or poor focus, skipping across the disc, erratic play, and excessive dropouts, to name a few).

These same symptoms can also be caused by a *defective disc*. This can be verified if the problem occurs only at one particular area on the disc, or if the player operates normally with other discs. Compact discs are subject to dents, pinholes, cracks, bubble, eccentricity, scratches, and fingerprints. Only fingerprints can be cured by cleaning, as discussed in Chapter 4.

Prior to replacing the pickup assembly (also called the *slide assembly* or *sled* in some troubleshooting literature) or making any adjustments that affect the pickup, always check for any mechanical problems that can affect player operation. Look for misadjusted pickup rails or guides, or anything that could inhibit pickup movement. The pickup must move smoothly beneath or behind the disc. There must be no binding at any point (indicating that the pickup rails or guides are adjusted too tightly). However, if a mechanical "ratcheting" or "chattering" sound is heard, it is possible that the pickup rails or guides are adjusted too loosely. Refer to Chapter 6 for all mechanical adjustments.

It is assumed that if you have such obvious symptoms as "none of the front-panel LEDs light when the POWER switch is pressed," you will check the fuses (right after you have checked that the power cord is plugged in). It is also assumed that you will check the various power-supply voltages if entire sections (or functions) appear to be inoperative. If any or all of the power-supply outputs are absent or abnormal, check the corresponding filter circuits, IC voltage regulators, diodes, and transformer. This means you must locate the power-supply circuits on the schematic and/or block diagram and measure the voltages. If you cannot do either of these, do not bother to read the rest of this chapter!

It is also assumed that if a particular player function can be selected, but the corresponding front-panel display (typically a fluorescent display) does not light, that the fault is most likely in the display itself or in the fluorescent display driver. Again, it is a relatively simple matter of checking that the driver receives the corresponding signal from the front-panel switch (which is also applying the signal to the system microprocessor) and that the driver applies the corresponding signal to the display. Again, if you do not think you can do this, you may have trouble with CD player troubleshooting!

7-5 DOOR OR TRAY DOES NOT OPEN OR CLOSE PROPERLY

Figure 7-9 is the troubleshooting diagram. Note that this diagram applies (typically) to front-load players with either vertical door or horizontal tray (but with only one loading motor, the most popular models).

If the door will not open or close, first check that the system microprocessor IC601 is receiving a signal (at pin 17) from the front-panel OPEN/CLOSE switch S619. If not, suspect S619 and/or the wiring between S619 and IC601. Next, check that the LIDM loading motor receives a signal from the emitters of Q116 and/or Q117 when S619 is pressed. If so, suspect the motor. If not, you have a problem between IC601 and the motor.

Next check that there is a signal at the bases of Q117 and Q116, and/or at the output of IC110 (whichever is most convenient) each time S619 is pressed. There should be a signal each time, and the signal should be inverted each time. If neither signal is present, suspect IC110. If only one signal is present, and the output of IC110 does not invert each time S619 is pressed, suspect IC601. Check for an OPEN signal at IC601-30 and a CLOSE signal at IC601-31 as S619 is pressed. If the signals are not present at pins 30 and 31, in turn, suspect IC601. If the signals are present at pins 30 and 31 of IC601, but the signals do not invert at the emitters of Q116/Q117, suspect IC110. If

218 Troubleshooting and Adjustment

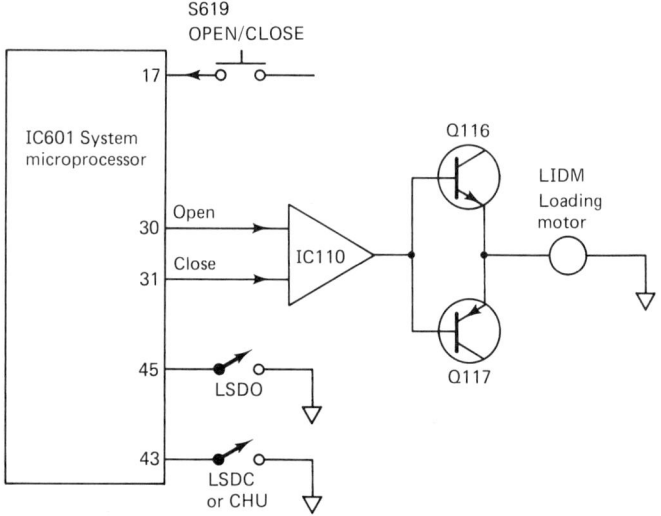

FIGURE 7-9 Tray or door troubleshooting diagram (early-model).

inverted signals are present at the bases of Q116/Q117, but the door does not open (or close) suspect Q116 and/or Q117.

If the door opens, but not fully, check when the LSDO door-open microswitch actuates, as indicated by a change in the signal at pin 45 of IC601. If necessary, adjust the LSDO switch as described in Chapter 6. Also look for any mechanical condition that might prevent the door from opening fully, using the descriptions of mechanical operation in Chapter 6 as a guide (binding gears, jammed crossed rollers, improperly adjusted guide rails, etc.).

If the door opens fully, but the loading motor does not stop, the problem is almost always one of an improperly adjusted LSDO switch. However, it is possible for the LSDO switch to actuate properly and produce a signal at IC601-45, but the motor does not stop. IC601 is at fault in that case.

If the door closes, but not fully, check when the LIDC (or CHU) microswitch actuates, as indicated by a change in the signal at pin 43 of IC601. If necessary, adjust the LIDC switch as described in Chapter 6. Also look for any mechanical condition that might prevent the door from closing. (Look for foreign objects in the door hinges or tray, and for wiring that has worked its way out of place.)

If the door closes fully, but the loading motor does not stop, the problem is probably an improperly adjusted LIDC switch, but could be IC601. Look for a change at IC601-43, which should occur when the vertical door is fully closed, or when the tray is fully in, and the clump or chuck is fully down on the disc.

7-6 LASER-DIODE PROBLEMS

Operation of the CD player is dependent on the laser diode producing a laser beam of correct level. For example, if the laser beam is absent, there is no EFM signal. If the beam is weak, the EFM signal is weak. Likewise, if the monitor diode does not monitor the laser-diode output properly, the laser beam can change to an incorrect level without being sensed by the laser-drive circuits. Any of these conditions can produce a variety of symptoms. So if you suspect that the laser circuits are malfunctioning, of you have symptoms with no apparent cause, start by adjusting the laser circuits as described in Sec. 7-3.3. This will probably reveal any obvious problems in the laser circuits. If not, proceed with the following, using the troubleshooting diagram of Fig. 7-10.

If there is no drive current to the laser diode (as measured across R046), check for a drive signal at pin 13 of IC003. If present, but there is no drive to the laser, suspect R046, Q004, and Q005, or possibly the laser diode itself. (Keep in mind that you must override the laser safety interlocks, *both* tray

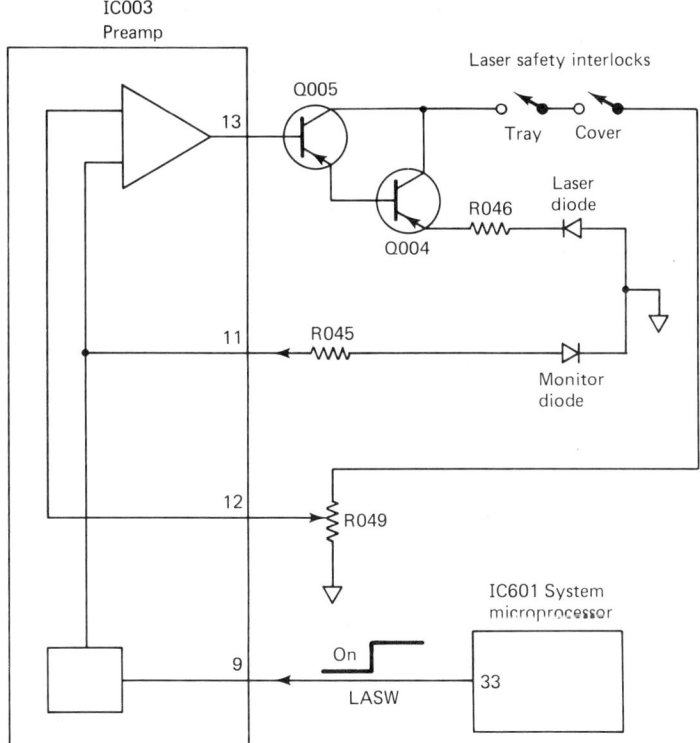

FIGURE 7-10 Laser-diode troubleshooting diagram (early-model).

and cover, for Q004 and Q005 to operate.) If there is no drive signal at IC003-13, check for an LASW drive signal from IC601 to IC003-9. If the LASW is absent, suspect IC601. If the LASW is present, check the voltages at pins 11 and 12 of IC003. If the voltage at IC003-11 is absent, or drastically different from that of pin 12, suspect the monitor diode or R045.

7-7 PICKUP DOES NOT MOVE TO INNER LIMIT WHEN POWER IS APPLIED

Figure 7-11 is the troubleshooting diagram. When power is first applied, the pickup moves to the inner limit (start of disc) whether a disc is installed or not. The system microprocessor applies a temporary SLR (slide or pickup motor reverse) signal to the pickup servo. In the player of Fig. 7-11, the temporary SLR signal is generated by a reset circuit C603-R610, which charges and discharges into pin 21 of IC601 through IC602. This produces a temporary

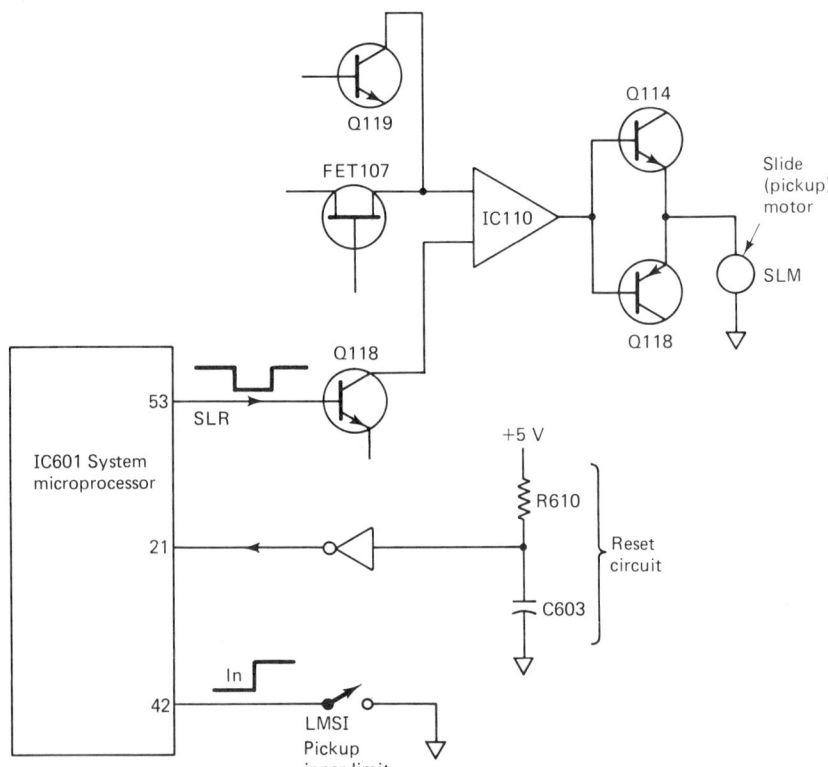

FIGURE 7-11 Slide (pickup) motor inner-limit troubleshooting diagram (early-model).

SLR at IC601-53, causing the pickup to move until the inner-limit LMSI switch is actuated.

If the pickup does not move when power is first applied (you may not be able to see the pickup, but you should hear the motor), check for an SLR signal at IC601-53. If absent, suspect IC601, R610, C603, and IC602. If the SLR is present, but the motor does not run, suspect Q118, IC110, Q114, Q115, and the motor. Also check for motor-drive voltage at the emitters of Q114/Q115. If the drive to the SLM motor is present, but the motor does not run, suspect the motor. If the motor runs, but the pickup does not move, look for mechanical problems (jammed gears, binding rollers, improperly adjusted rails, etc.).

If the pickup moves, but does not stop at the inner limit, check when the LMSI inner-limit microswitch actuates, as indicated by a change in the signal at pin 42 of IC601. If necessary, adjust the LMSI switch as described in Chapter 6. Also check for any mechanical condition that might prevent the pickup from moving to the inner (and outer) limits.

If the pickup reaches the inner limit, but the motor does not stop, the problem is almost always an improperly adjusted LMSI switch. However, it is possible for the LMSI switch to actuate properly and produce a signal at IC601-42, but the motor does not stop. IC601 is at fault in that case.

7-8 PICKUP DOES NOT CHANGE SPEED DURING SEARCH

Figure 7-12 is the troubleshooting diagram. When fast forward (FF) or fast reverse (FR) is selected at the front panel, or during program search, system microprocessor IC601 produces search-reverse (SLR) and search-forward (SLF) pulses, which are applied to the pickup motor SLM through Q118, Q119, IC110, Q114, and Q115. This produces increased current to the pickup motor SLM, and thus increases speed.

In the player of Fig. 7-12, FR is selected when S614 closes and applies the corresponding signal to pin 19 of IC601. S615 closes when FF is pressed, applying a signal to IC601-18.

If the pickup does not move faster (than during normal PLAY mode) when either FF or FR are pressed, check for the corresponding SLR or SLF pulses at IC601. If absent, suspect IC601. If SLR is present, but the pickup does not change speed, suspect Q118. If SLF is present, but there is no change in the pickup motor speed, suspect Q119.

7-9 PICKUP DOES NOT FOCUS PROPERLY

Figure 7-13 is the troubleshooting diagram. When play first begins, the focus servo receives a focus up-down (FUD) signal from IC601 through integrator R166/C115 and R165. These FUD pulses move the focus actuator up and down

222 Troubleshooting and Adjustment

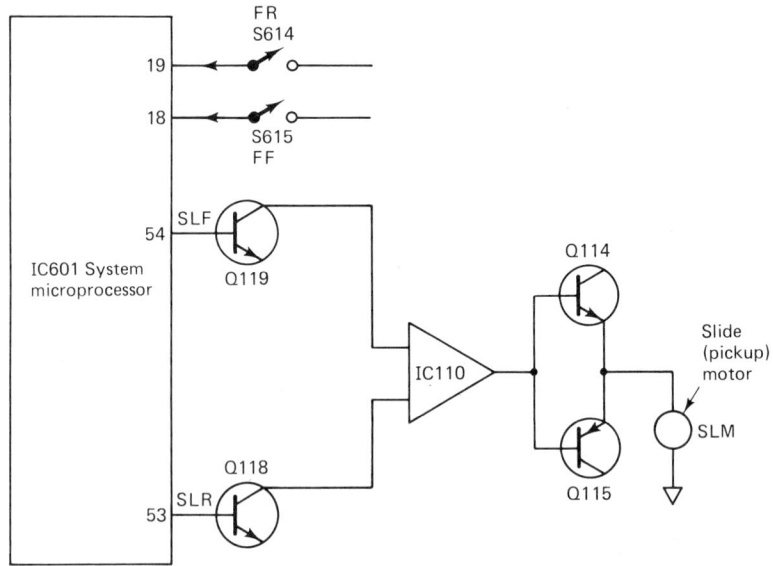

FIGURE 7-12 FF and FR speed-change troubleshooting diagram (early-model).

two or three times as necessary to focus the beam on the disc track. Once focus is obtained, a focus-ok (FOK) signal is generated by IC003 and applied to IC601 through D102. If an FOK signal is not received after two or three tries (one or two tries on some players), IC601 shuts the system down and play stops (turntable stops and the pickup moves to the inner limit). On most players, this also occurs if there is no disc in place, so the FOK function serves as a disc detector.

If focus is obtained, the focus-error (FER) signal is applied to the focus actuator through the focus servo, as shown in Fig. 7-13. The FER signal keeps the pickup focused on the disc tracks throughout play. On most players, when the pickup reaches the outer limit of the disc where there are no tracks, focus is lost, the FOK signal is removed, and IC601 shuts down the system.

If you suspect problems in the automatic focus (AF) system, install a disc, select PLAY, and check that the pickup moves up and down two or three times and then settles down. If not, first check that the laser is on as described in Sec. 7-6. If the laser is on but there is no focus, try adjusting the focus servo as described in Secs. 7-3.5 and 7-3.6. Then make a quick check of the lens actuator as described in Sec. 6-1.1. If the actuator coil appears to be good, and the problem cannot be corrected by adjustment, check the focus servo as follows.

Focus actuator does not move up and down. If the FUD pulses are not present just after PLAY is selected, suspect IC601. Check for pulses at the

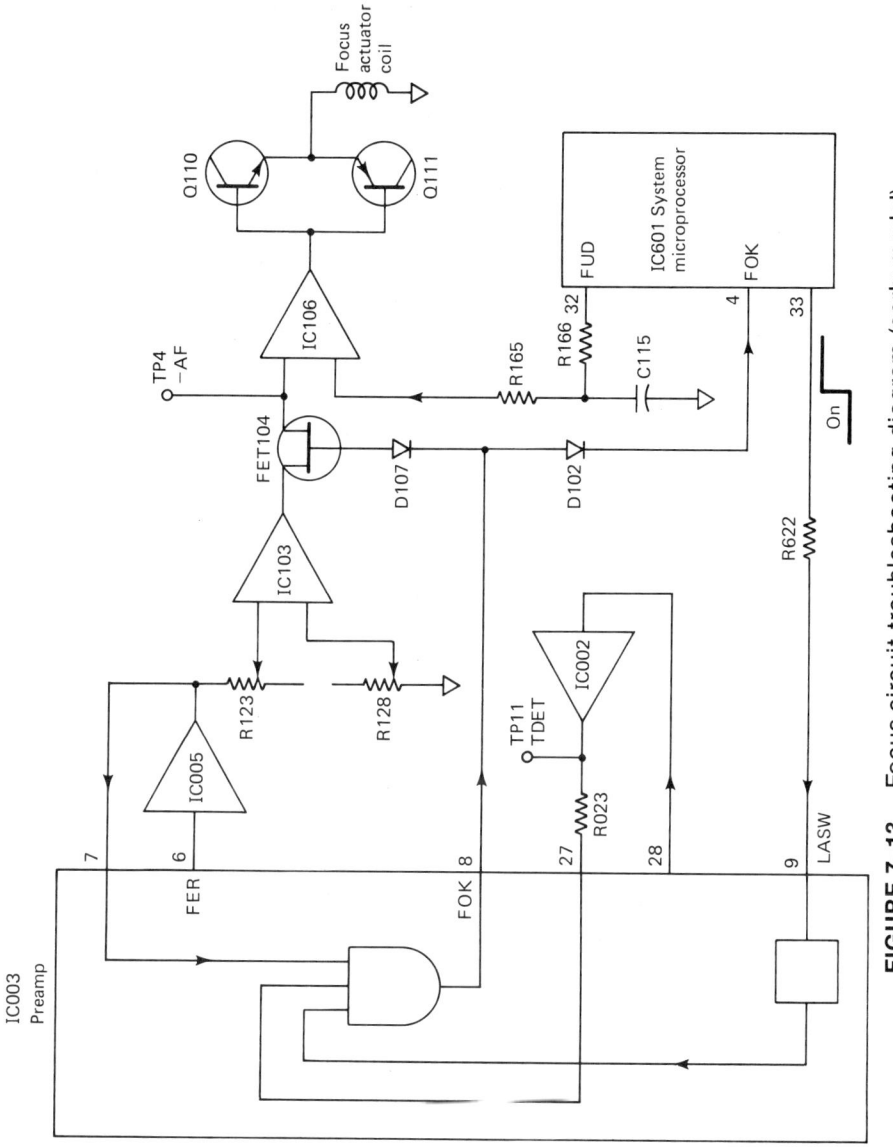

FIGURE 7-13 Focus-circuit troubleshooting diagram (early-model).

224 Troubleshooting and Adjustment

emitters of Q110/Q111 or at the focus actuator coil, whichever is most convenient. If FUD pulses are absent at the coil, but present at IC601-32, suspect C115, R166, R165, IC106, Q110, and Q111.

Focus actuator moves, but no focus is obtained. Check for the FOK signals at pin 4 of IC601 and pin 8 of IC003. (If the FOK signals are not present, IC601 should shut the system down.) If the FOK signals are absent at IC003-8, suspect IC003, or possibly the four pickup signal/focus photodiodes. Also note that the FOK signal is not generated unless there is an LASW signal applied to pin 9 of IC003 from IC601 (through R622).

Next check for FER signals at IC003-6 and IC003-7. If FER signals are present at pin 6 but not pin 7, suspect IC005. If FER signals are absent at IC003-6, suspect IC003, or possibly the pickup signal/focus photodiodes.

If you suspect the signal/focus photodiodes, monitor the EFM signal at TP11 (TDET). If the EFM signal is good, it is reasonable to assume that all four focus/signal photodiodes are good.

Trace the FER signal from ICOO3-6 to the focus-actuator coil. Test point TP4, which is the output of analog switch FET104, is a good place to start in the circuit of Fig. 7-13. Then check the FER signal at the emitters of Q110/Q111.

If FER is present at TP4, but not at the focus-actuator coil, suspect IC106, Q110, and Q111. If the FER signal is absent at TP4, suspect FET104, IC103, R123, and R128.

Also note that switch FET104 must be turned on by FOK signals applied through D107. The positive FOK signal reverse-biases D107, turning FET104 on. If FOK is absent, D107 is forward-biased, and FER signals cannot pass through FET104.

7-10 PICKUP DOES NOT TRACK PROPERLY

Figure 7-14 is the troubleshooting diagram. In most players, it is often difficult to separate tracking and focus servo problems. For example, unless there is an FOK signal applied to FET102 through D150, the tracking-error (TER) signal does not pass to the tracking actuator. Both the focus and tracking servos use the laser beam as a source of error signal, although different photodiodes are used. To further complicate the problem, the TER signal is also used by the pickup motor SLM as a fine speed control. If TER is lost, both the radial tracking coil and the pickup motor have no control signals. Either condition can produce symptoms of improper tracking.

As if that were not enough, in some players the TER signal is passed through antishock and variable-gain circuits and through error-detection circuits, which can interrupt the TER signals when errors are detected (in the disc or because of improper tracking). Failure in any of these circuits can cut

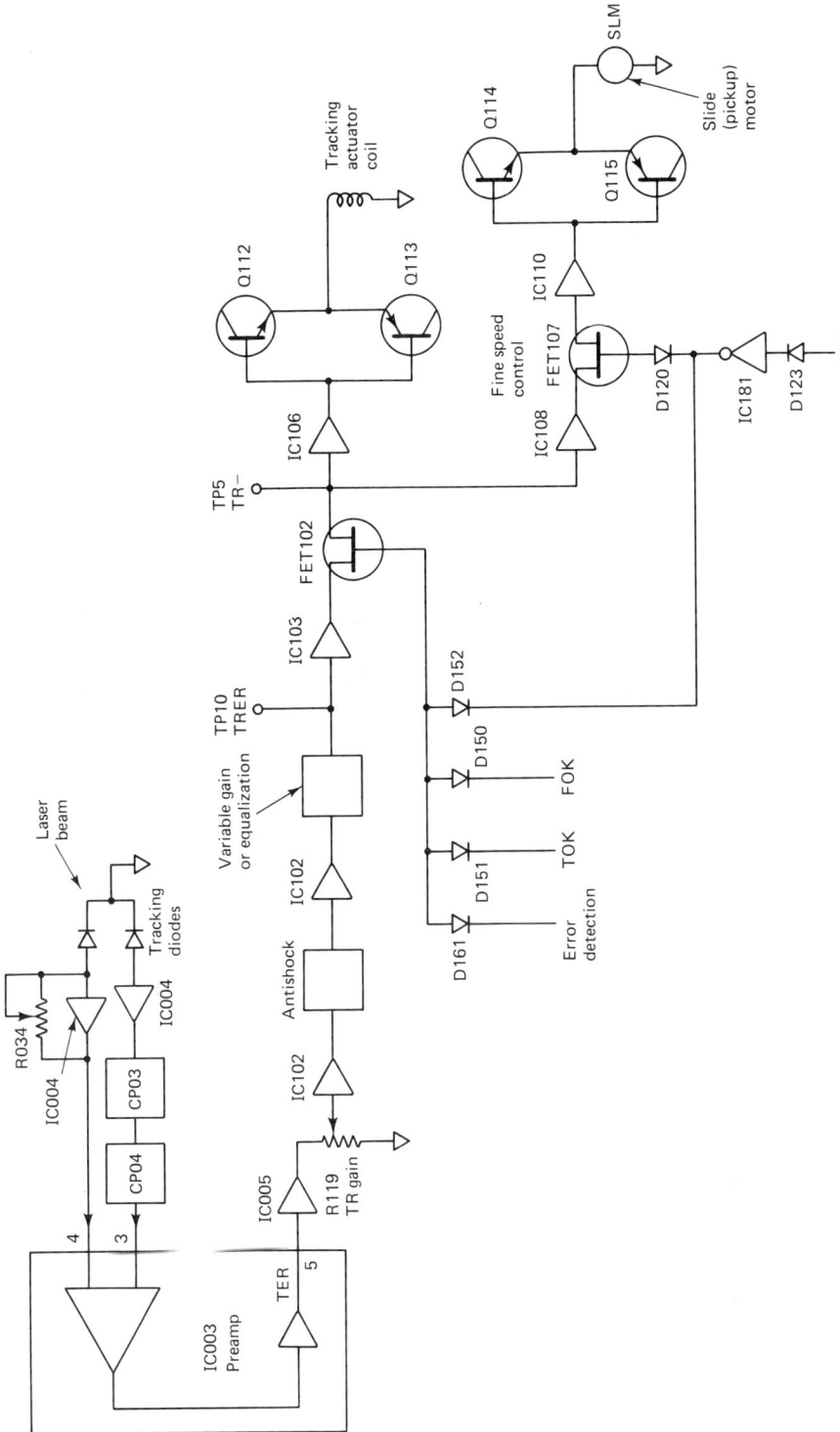

FIGURE 7-14 Radial-tracking-circuit troubleshooting diagram (early-model).

226 Troubleshooting and Adjustment

off or alter the TER signal, making it appear that either radial tracking or pickup motor servos are at fault (when actually the servos are good). Finally, in most players, when a jump condition is selected at the front panel (say from one program to another), the normal TER signal is interrupted and replaced by jump signals. Fortunately, a failure in the jump circuits is usually easy to locate.

So before you tear into the pickup tracking and motor servos, make the following checks. First try to correct any tracking problems with adjustment, as described in Secs. 7-3.4 and 7-3.7. Next, make a quick check of the tracking actuator coil, as described in Sec. 6-1.1. Finally, see if the pickup moves to the inner limit when power is first applied, as described in Sec. 7-7. (This confirms that the pickup motor, IC110, Q114, and Q115 are good.) If the pickup motor is operating and the tracking coil appears to be good, but tracking problems cannot be resolved by adjustment, check the tracking and pickup servos as follows.

Check the TER signal from its source to both the tracking-actuator coil and pickup motor. TP5 (the output of FET102) is a good place to start in the circuit of Fig. 7-14. Then check the TER signal at the emitters of Q112/Q113 (tracking actuator) and Q114/Q115 (pickup motor). If the TER is present at TP5 but not at the tracking-actuator coil, suspect IC106, Q112, and Q113. If TER is present at TP5 but not at the pickup motor, suspect IC108, FET107, IC110, Q114, and Q115.

If the TER signal is absent at TP5, check for a signal at TP10 (TRER). If the signal is present at TP10 but not at TP5, suspect IC103 and FET102.

Also note that switch FET102 must be turned on by FOK signals applied through D150, TSW signals through D152 (actually $\overline{TSW}$ signals since the TSW is inverted by IC181), TOK signals through D151, and error-detection signals through D161. If any of the four diodes (D150, D151, D152, D161) are not reverse-biased, FET102 remains cut off, and the TER signals do not pass.

If the TER signal is absent at TP10, check for TER signals at pin 5 of IC003. If TER is absent at IC003-5, suspect CP03, CP04, IC004, R034, and the two radial tracking diodes.

If the TER signal is present at IC003-5 but absent at TP10, suspect IC005, R119, IC102, the antishock circuits, and the variable gain or equalization circuits.

7-11 DISC MOTOR (TURNTABLE) DOES NOT ROTATE PROPERLY

Figure 7-15 is the troubleshooting diagram. It is not difficult to tell if the disc motor fails to rotate. Likewise, the cause of such a total failure is generally simple to locate. For example, you can check at TP9 (DMCA) and TP10

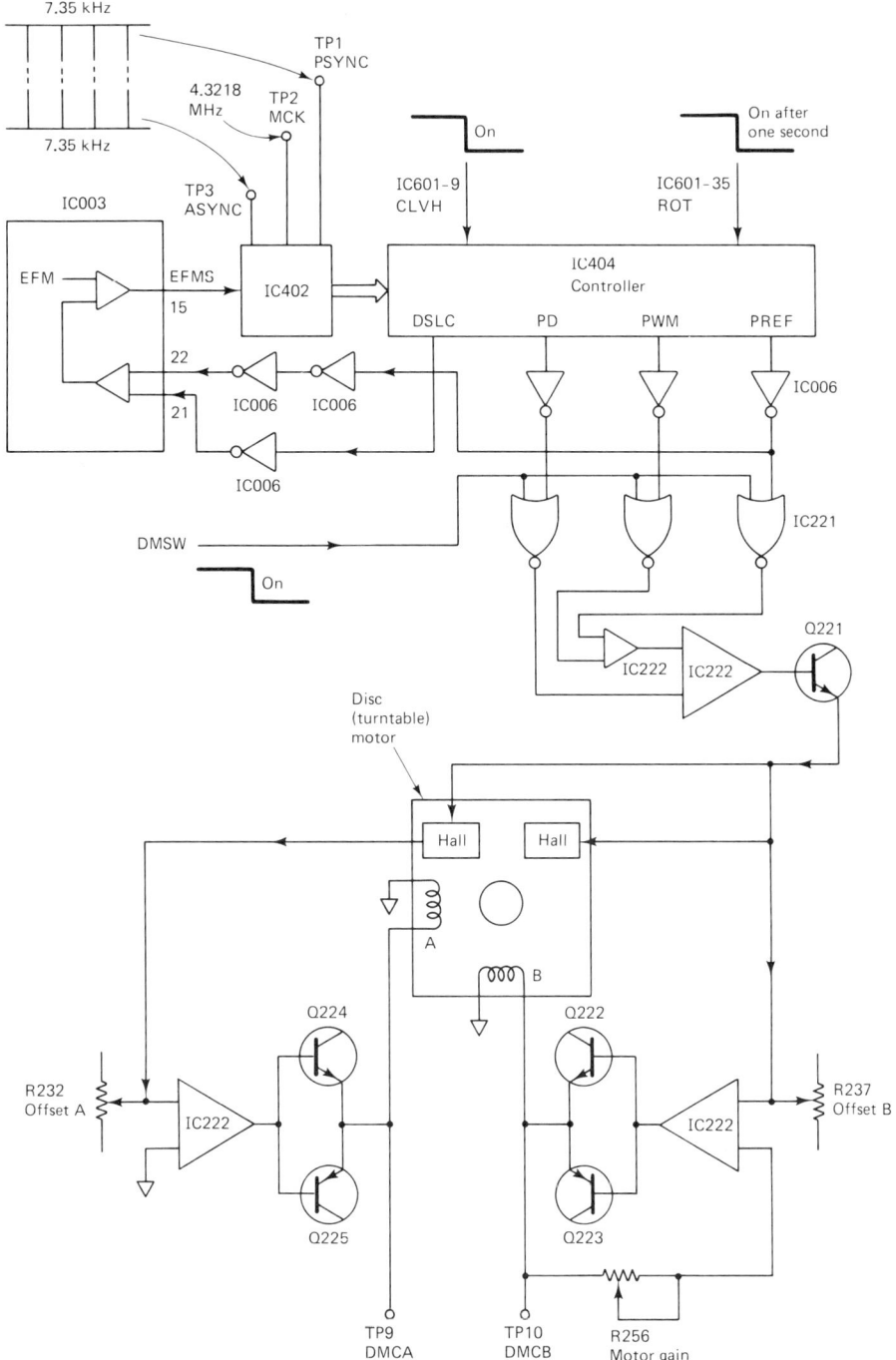

FIGURE 7-15 Disc (turntable) motor troubleshooting diagram (early-model).

228 Troubleshooting and Adjustment

(DMCB) for drive signals to the motor windings. If the drive signals are present but the motor does not turn, suspect the motor. If either of the drive signals is not present, trace from the Hall elements to the motor windings and from the controller IC404 to the Hall elements.

Keep one point in mind before you decide there is a problem in the disc motor control circuits. The DMSW, CLVH, and ROT signals come from the system microprocessor IC601. In most players, if the microprocessor does not receive an FOK (and possibly a TOK) signal from the focus and tracking circuits, the DMSW, CLVH, and ROT signals are set to prevent controller IC404 from passing the PREF, PWM, and PD signals to the disc motor control circuits. Typically, both DMSW and CLVH are made low to turn on the disc motor. ROT goes low about one second after PLAY is selected. If DMSW, CLVH, and ROT all remain high after PLAY is selected, check for FOK and TOK signals to IC601. Of course, if only one of the three signals remains abnormal, IC601 is most likely at fault.

Unfortunately, the problem is not quite that simple if the motor rotates, but you are not sure of the correct speed. (Particularly when you consider that the motor speed is constantly changing.) You must rely on waveform measurements and adjustments. So the first logical step in disc motor circuit troubleshooting is to perform the adjustments as described in Secs. 7-3.8 and 7-3.9. If you do not get the DMCA and DMCB signals called for in the adjustment procedures, trace back to the Hall elements and controller.

If you get the DMCA and DMCB drive signals, and the motor is turning (indicating that DMSW, ROT, and CLVH from IC601 are good), but you are unable to set the gain and offset as described in the adjustment procedures, check all the waveforms associated with disc motor control, as follows:

Check the PWM, PREF, and PD waveforms from IC404. If any of these are absent or abnormal, suspect IC404. Trace the PWM, PREF, and PD signals through to the disc motor. If the signals do not reach the disc motor, suspect IC006, IC221, IC222, and Q221.

Also note that PREF is applied to IC003, along with the DSLC signal from IC404, to form the EFMS signal, which is returned to IC404 (through IC402). If the EFMS signal is absent, IC404 does not produce the PREF, PWM, and PD signals. Of course, if the EFMS signal is not applied to IC402, several other problems occur. We discuss EFMS further in Sec. 7-12.

One way to check if the EFMS signal is being processed properly is to compare the signals at TP1 (PSYNC) and TP3 (ASYNC), using a dual-trace oscilloscope. As shown in Fig. 7-15, both signals should be synchronized. If not, or if either signal is missing, suspect IC402.

As you can see, the disc motor control circuits are closely interrelated with the signal-processing circuits. A failure in signal processing can also cause the disc motor control circuits to appear defective. So if you are unable to locate a problem in the disc motor control circuits, try checking the signal-processing circuits, which we just happen to discuss next.

7-12 SIGNAL-PROCESSING CIRCUIT PROBLEMS

Figure 7-16 is the troubleshooting diagram. Failure of the signal-processing circuits can cause a variety of failure symptoms. For example, as discussed, if the DMSW, ROT, and CLVH signals are absent or abnormal, the disc motor does not operate properly. Also, since the main function of signal processing is to convert digital information (taken from the disc) into audio information, any failure in signal processing can also cause the audio section to appear defective. To make the troubleshooting process more difficult, the signal-processing circuits are under direct control of the system microprocessor (and feed signals to the microprocessor). A failure in the system microprocessor can make the signal-processing circuits appear defective.

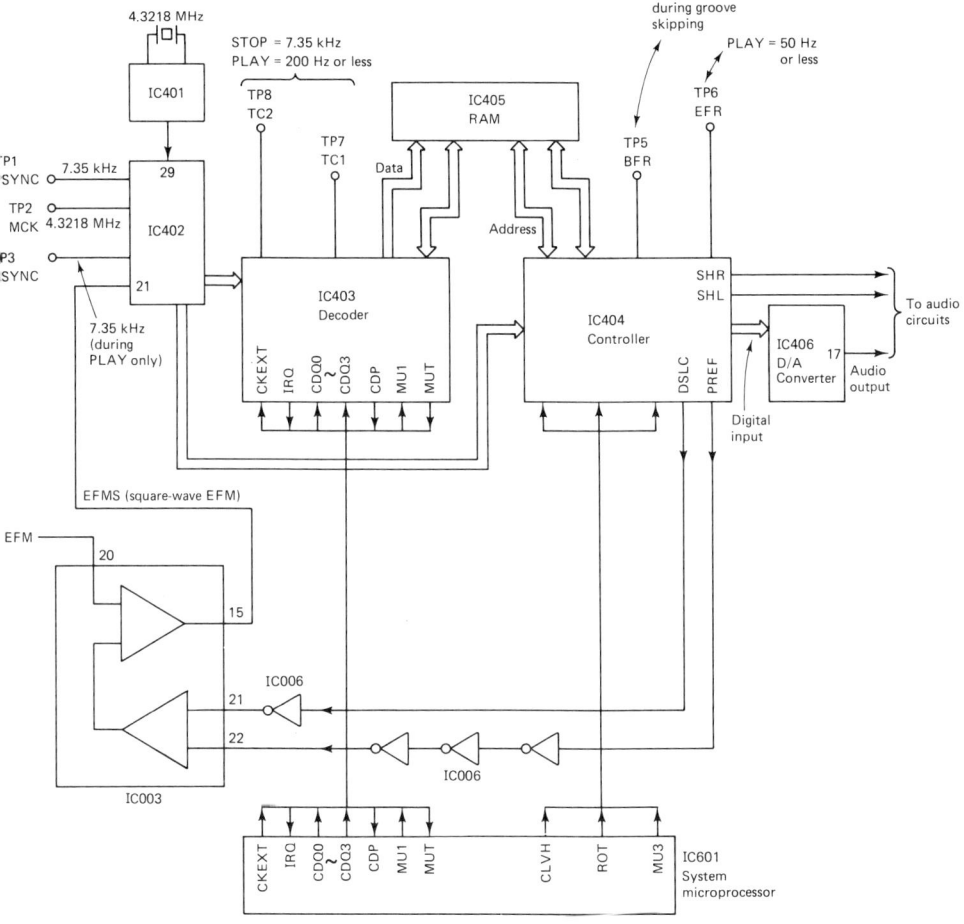

FIGURE 7-16 Signal-processing circuit troubleshooting diagram (early-model).

230 Troubleshooting and Adjustment

There is no sure way to tell if the problem is in signal processing or audio. However, here are two tips to study before you begin checking all the signal-processing circuit waveforms.

First, check the output at pin 17 of D/A converter IC406 for audio signals. You should get a mixture of both left- and right-channel audio signals at IC406-17. The level of the audio will probably be very low. However, if there is no audio at this point, suspect the signal-processing circuits. If there is measurable audio at IC406-17, the problem is likely in the audio circuits. Refer to Sec. 7-13.

Second, if there are excessive audio dropouts (with a known-good disc), and the front-panel indications are not normal (such as the time code not moving), the problem is likely in the signal-processing circuits. Check all the waveforms to and from the signal-processing circuits shown in the service literature. Pay particular attention to the following:

Check for a 4.3218-MHz signal at TP2 (MCK) of IC402. If missing, suspect the crystal IC401 and IC402.

Check TP1 (PSYNC) and TP3 (ASYNC) for 7.35-kHz signals. The ASYNC should *be present only during* PLAY, but PSYNC should be available in both STOP and PLAY.

Make certain that PREF and DSLC signals are applied to IC003 and then returned to IC402 as *square-wave* EFMS signals, as described in Sec. 7-11. If EFMS is missing, check for *high-frequency* EFM signals at pin 20 of IC003.

Check all the waveforms between IC601 and IC403 shown in Fig. 7-16 (including CKEXT, IRQ, CDQ0 through CDQ3, CDP, MU1, and MUT). It is not practical to analyze these waveforms. However, if you can measure a data stream on each line with an oscilloscope, it is reasonable to assume that the signal is correct. If one or more of these signals is missing, suspect IC601 or IC403, or both. Remember that a signal from IC601 can depend on a signal from IC403, and vice versa. So it may be necessary to replace both ICs to find the problem.

Before you pull IC403, check TP7 (TC1) and TP8 (TC2). Both of these test points (which indicate the accuracy of the C1- and C2-decoding processes within IC403) should produce a 7.35-kHz signal during STOP, but then drop to 200 Hz or less when PLAY is selected. If not, suspect IC403.

Check all the waveforms between IC601 and IC404 shown in Fig. 7-16 (including CLVH, ROT, and MU3). Again, do not try to analyze the waveforms (except on a present or absent basis). If any waveform is missing, suspect IC601. However, keep in mind that IC601 may not produce the signals unless other signals (such as FOK and TOK) are applied to IC601, as discussed in Sec. 7-11.

Before you pull IC404, check TP5 (BFR) and TP6 (EFR), which indicate the accuracy of the synchronizing and detection functions within IC404). In the PLAY mode, BFR should always be zero, except during groove skipping.

In PLAY, EFR may produce a signal, but at a frequency below 50 Hz. The EFR and BFR signals are undefined during STOP.

7-13 AUDIO CIRCUIT PROBLEMS

Figure 7–17 is the troubleshooting diagram. As discussed in Sec. 7-12, the first check of the audio circuits is to monitor the output of the D/A converter IC406-17. Next, check the sample-and-hold SHR and SHL signals from IC404.

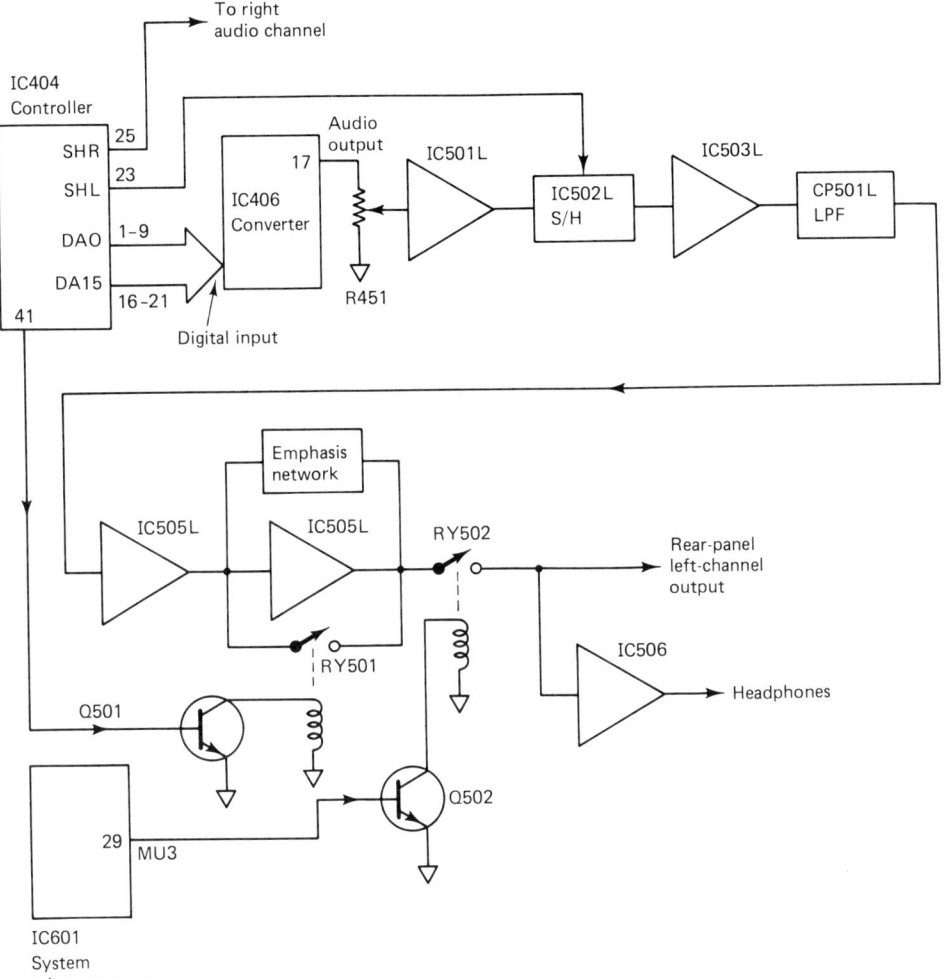

FIGURE 7–17 Audio-circuit troubleshooting diagram (early-model).

232 Troubleshooting and Adjustment

If the SHR and SHL signals are present, and there is audio at IC406-17, but there are audio problems, trace the audio signal from the D/A converter IC406 to the headphones and/or rear-panel stereo output jacks.

Also look for any muting or emphasis signals from the system-control microprocessor IC601 and/or controller. For example, if the MU3 signal from IC601 is low, Q502 does not conduct and audio-control relay R501 remains open. This prevents audio from passing to the output jacks and headphones. Note that in some players, a mute signal is also applied to the signal-control circuits to prevent digital information from passing to the D/A converter. This results in no audio output from the D/A converter.

Note that the emphasis network (discussed in Sec. 5-9) is controlled by RY501 and Q501, which receive a control signal from IC404-41. If the disc is recorded with (or without) emphasis, this is sensed by the signal-processing circuits, and the emphasis network is cut in (or out) as required.

7-14 PROGRAMMING AND OPERATING PROBLEMS

We do not describe troubleshooting to locate programming or operating problems. Such problems almost always are the fault of the system microprocessor or possibly the front-panel wiring. For example, if you press the PROGRAM, REPEAT, CALL, PAUSE, STOP, PLAY, FF, FR, or any other front-panel control, and the player does not respond properly, check that the system microprocessor receives the command signal from the front-panel button or switch. If not, check the corresponding switch and wiring. If the command is received, suspect the system microprocessor.

Some players have two system microprocessors. One microprocessor receives front-panel commands. The other microprocessor applies commands and instructions to the player circuits. However, the present trend is to combine all functions into one system microprocessor (typically a 64-pin LSI). This is true of the late-model players, which we discuss next.

Also, as discussed in Sec. 7-4, if a programing or operating function can be selected, but you do not get the corresponding front-panel indication (fluorescent display or LED), check the circuits to the display (including any driver ICs).

7-15 ELECTRICAL ADJUSTMENT PROCEDURES FOR LATE-MODEL PLAYERS

All the notes described in Sec. 7-3 for early-model players also apply to late-model players. However, the procedures are somewhat different.

7-15 Electrical Adjustment Procedures for Late-Model Players

7-15.1 Test Equipment Required

As in the case of early-model units, you can perform all the electrical adjustments for late-model players with a 10-MHz dual-trace oscilloscope, a digital voltmeter, and an audio generator with variable output. A known-good disc and a good stereo amplifier/speaker system are also most helpful.

7-15.2 Presetting Adjustment Controls

Before performing any adjustments, preset all adjustment controls to the center position, except for the laser-diode output adjustment control (which should be set to minimum).

7-15.3 Laser-Diode Output Adjustment

Figure 7–18 is the laser-diode output adjustment diagram. Again, the laser-diode output should not be adjusted unless the pickup has been replaced or troubleshooting indicates that the diode output is not correct (possibly low). If the pickup is replaced, or you must adjust the laser-diode output, preset the R629 to minimum or zero and then increase the setting as required. Note that in the circuit of Fig. 7–18, the chuck or CHU switch SW03 must be in the closed (tray-in) position before power is applied to drive transistor Q601 and the laser diode. This eliminates the need for separate laser safety interlock switches. However, during adjustment and troubleshooting, you must manually set SW03 to the closed position before the laser diode can receive power.

Observe all the notes described in Sec. 7-3.3 concerning laser-diode adjustment, such as checking laser drive current and monitoring laser output.

After the controls are preset, proceed as follows:

1. Connect the oscilloscope between TP13 (TDET) and TP16 (GND), as shown in Fig. 7–18. With this connection, you are monitoring the EFM signal (after the photodetector output has been preamplified by IC601). The EFM signal (at this point) is returned to IC601 for further processing, and is also used by the tracking, focus and pickup motor servos as well as the signal-processing circuits.

2. Load a disc in the player and select the PLAY mode. The EFM signal should appear on the oscilloscope and produce a waveform similar to that of Fig. 7–18.

3. Adjust R629 until the level of the EFM signal is 700 mV (or as specified in the service literature, typically between 550 and 950 mV).

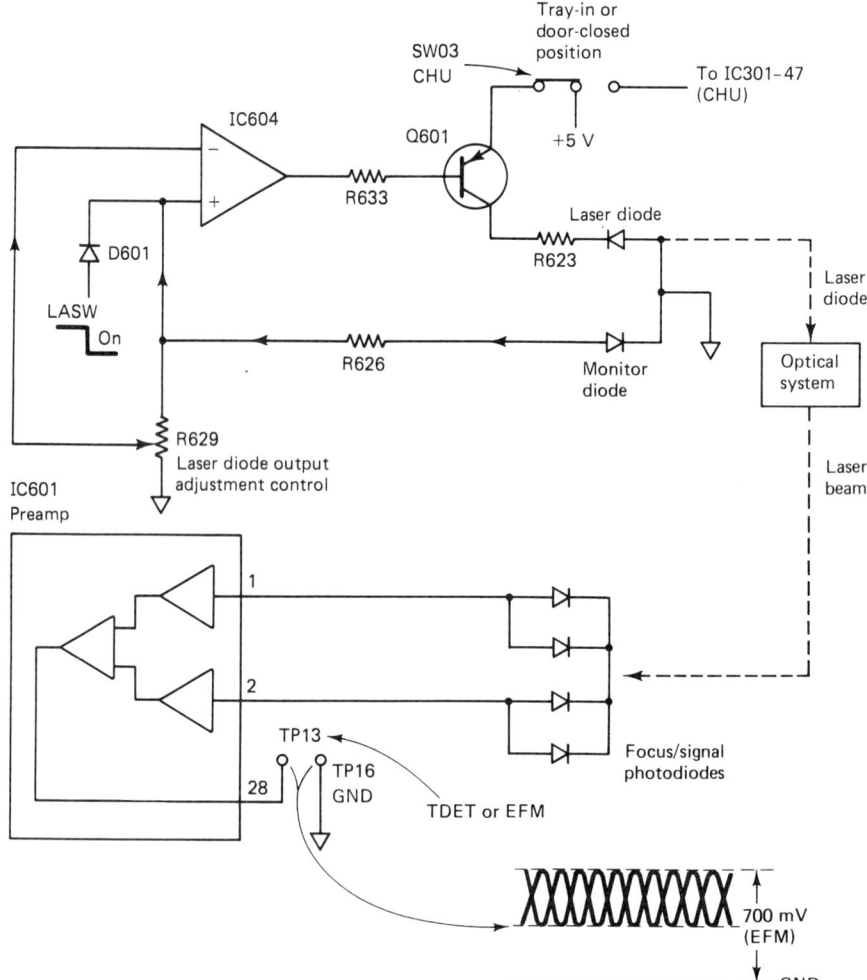

FIGURE 7-18 Laser-diode output adjustment diagram (late-model).

7-15.4 Slide (Pickup) Motor Offset Adjustment

Figure 7-19 is the slide or pickup motor offset adjustment diagram. This adjustment (which is generally not available on early-model players) determines where the pickup accesses the beginning of the disc. If this adjustment is not correct, the program information at the beginning of the disc (sometimes called the *disc directory*) may not be read properly. Keep in mind that this adjustment controls the pickup motor servo and is not to be confused with the inner-limit microswitch adjustment described in Chapter 6 and Sec. 7-19.

7-15 *Electrical Adjustment Procedures for Late-model Players* 235

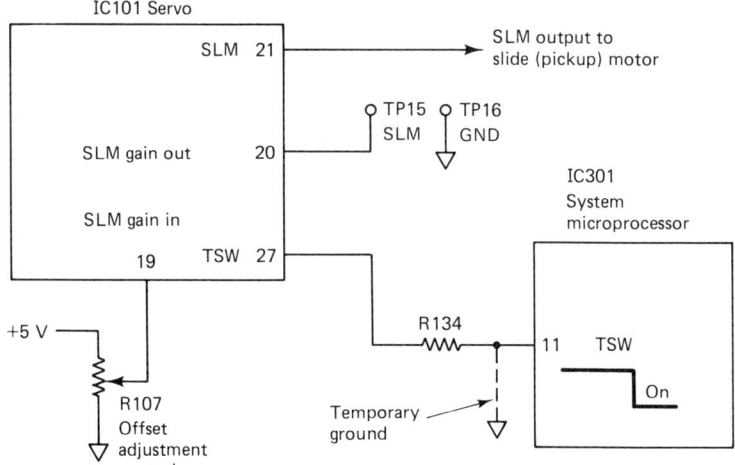

FIGURE 7-19 Slide (pickup) motor offset adjustment diagram (late-model).

Of course, the two adjustments are interrelated. For example, if you set the microswitch so that the pickup motor cannot reach the inner limit of the disc, the servo cannot be adjusted to access the full disc directory. However, if the pickup inner-limit microswitch is properly set, you should have no trouble in setting the pickup servo offset.

After the controls are preset, proceed as follows:

1. Connect the d-c voltmeter between TP15 (SLM) and TP16 (GND), as shown in Fig. 7-19. With this connection, you are monitoring the motor-gain output from IC101.
2. Load a disc in the player and select the PLAY mode.
3. While the disc is playing, connect a jumper between ground and the junction of R134 and IC301-11, as shown in Fig. 7-19. This simulates a low TSW signal at the system microprocessor IC301. If the TSW line goes high, IC301 shuts the system down.
4. Set the player to STOP.
5. After about 10 seconds, measure the d-c level at TP15, and adjust R107 so that the reading at TP15 is 0 V ± 50 mV. Adjust R107 in small increments and wait for the voltage level to stabilize before continuing to adjust.

Make certain to remove the jumper once adjustment is complete.

7-15.5 Tracking Servo Offset Adjustment

Figure 7–20 is the tracking servo offset adjustment diagram.
After the controls are preset, proceed as follows:

1. Connect the oscilloscope between TP13 (TDET) and ground, as shown in Fig. 7–20. With this connection, you are monitoring the EFM signal, as in Sec. 7-15.3. However, you are adjusting the offset of the tracking-error signal (TER), which is applied to the tracking-actuator coil in the optical pickup. In effect, you are adjusting the optical pickup (through the servo and tracking-actuator coil) so that the laser beam is properly centered on the tracks. Note that R603 sets

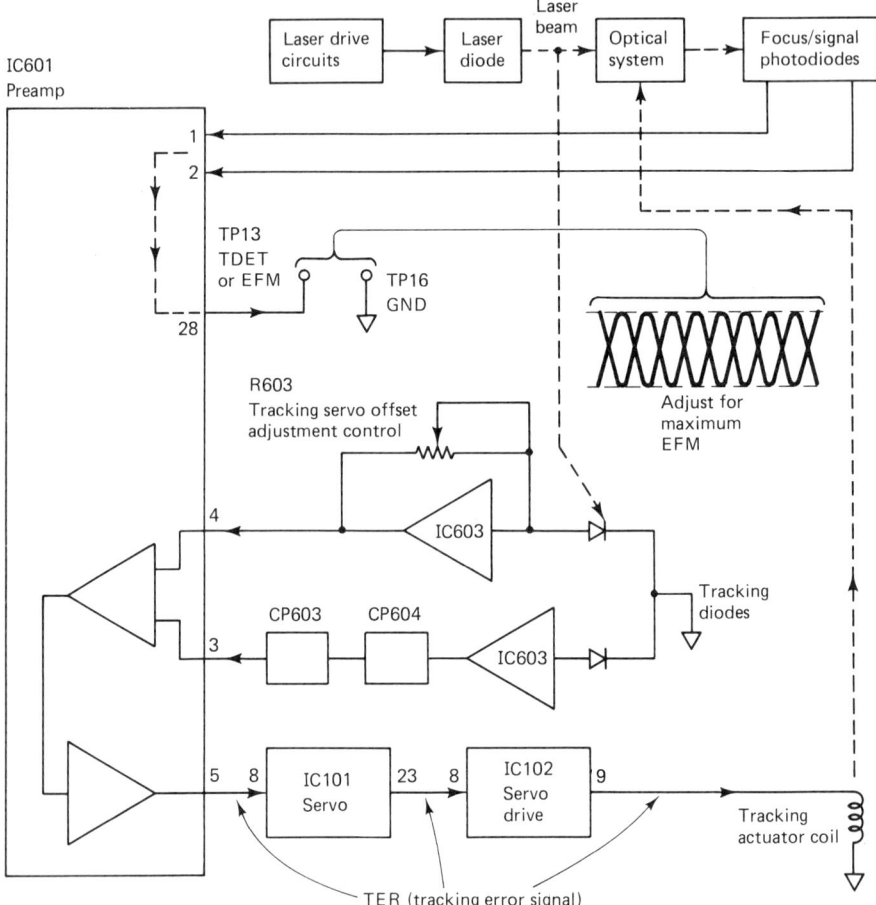

FIGURE 7–20 Tracking servo offset adjustment diagram (late-model).

7-15 Electrical Adjustment Procedures for Late-model Players

the offset of the two tracking diodes, but not the four remaining focus/signal diodes.

2. Load a disc in the player and select the PLAY mode. The EFM signal should appear on the oscilloscope and produce a waveform similar to that of Fig. 7-20.
3. Adjust R603 until the EFM signal is at maximum amplitude (indicating that the optical pickup is centered on the tracks).

On some players, the display may become erratic and the audio will mute after making this adjustment. If so, set the player to STOP and then go back to PLAY. This should eliminate the erratic display.

7-15.6 Focus Servo Offset Adjustment

Figure 7-21 is the focus servo offset adjustment diagram.
After the controls are preset, proceed as follows:

1. Connect the oscilloscope between TP13 (TDET) and ground, as shown in Fig. 7-21. With this connection, you are again monitoring the EFM signal, as in Sec. 7-15.3. However, you are now adjusting offset of the focus-error signal (FER), which is applied to the focus actuator coil in the optical pickup. In effect, you are adjusting the optical pickup (through the servo and focus-actuator coil) so the laser beam is properly focused on the tracks. Note that R116 set the offset of the four focus/signal diodes, but not the two remaining tracking diodes.
2. Load a disc in the player and select the PLAY mode. The EFM signal should appear in the oscilloscope and produce a waveform similar to that of Fig. 7-21.

Adjust R116 until the EFM signal is at maximum amplitude (indicating that the optical pickup is focused on the tracks).
Again, if the display becomes erratic after this adjustment, stop and restart the player.

7-15.7 Disc Motor Hall Gain Balance

Figure 7-22 is the disc motor Hall gain balance adjustment diagram.
After the controls are preset, proceed as follows:

1. Connect channel-1 of the oscilloscope to TP18 (DMCA), channel-2 to TP17 (DMCB), and the oscilloscope common to TP16 (GND), as shown in Fig. 7-22. With this connection, you are monitoring the

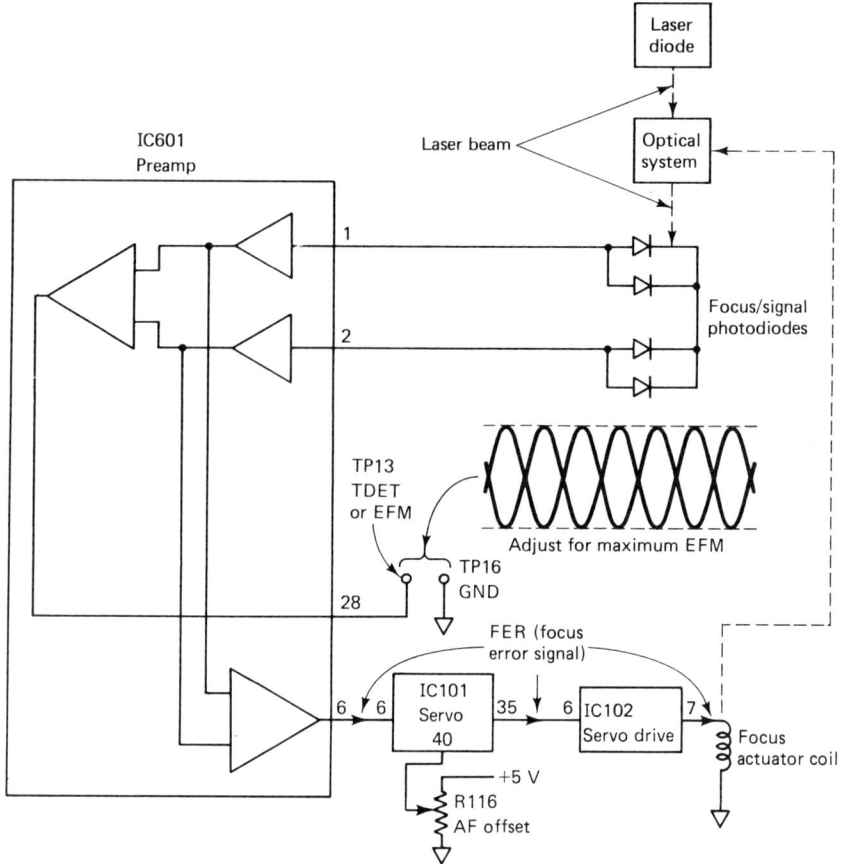

FIGURE 7-21 Focus servo offset adjustment diagram (late-model).

drive signals to both coils (A and B) of the disc motor from the disc motor drive IC201.

2. Load a disc in the player and select the PLAY mode.
3. Adjust R201 so that the output levels at TP18 (DMCA) and TP17 (DMCB) are equal. Typically, the DMCA and DMCB signals (at this point) are about 2 V (p-p).

7-15.8 Sample-and-hold Offset Adjustment for TER

Figure 7-23 is the sample-and-hold offset adjustment diagram. Note that most early-model players do not have a similar circuit and adjustment. Also note that this adjustment is not to be confused with the sample-and-hold circuits (found in the audio circuits after the D/A converter) that synchronize the left-

7-15 Electrical Adjustment Procedures for Late-model Players 239

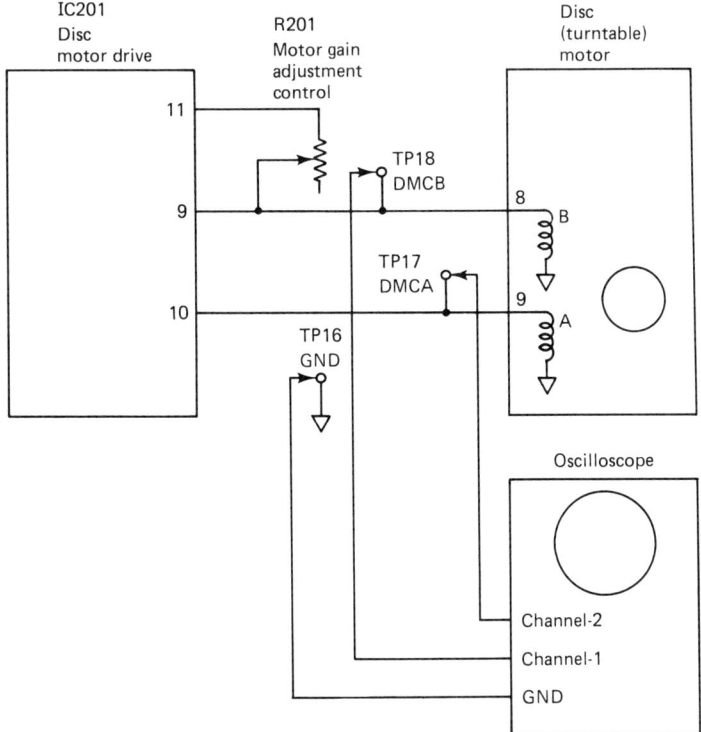

FIGURE 7-22 Disc motor Hall gain balance adjustment diagram (late-model).

and right-channel stereo channels. The sample-and-hold circuits shown in Fig. 7-23 are located in the pickup servo IC101; they control the tracking-error or TER signals applied to the tracking-actuator coil through the servo.

During this test, you play a disc with a *simulated defect* and adjust the TER signals to produce the best response (minimum audio dropout). As shown in Fig. 7-23, the defect is simulated by placing a black (nonreflective) tape on the mirror side of the disc. (It is usually easier to work with the straight tape rather than the wedge, but that is a matter of opinion.) You then monitor the EFM signal and adjust the TER circuits so that audio dropout (immediately after the defect is simulated by the tape) is minimum. It is hoped that the dropout can be eliminated completely.

You can also make this adjustment by ear. The simulated defect produces a chattering or ticking sound in the headphones or loudspeakers. You adjust for a minimum of such sounds. However, it is generally more accurate to monitor the EFM signal with an oscilloscope at the TDET test point, as shown. (Or you can monitor both ways simultaneously.) If you monitor by ear, make

240 Troubleshooting and Adjustment

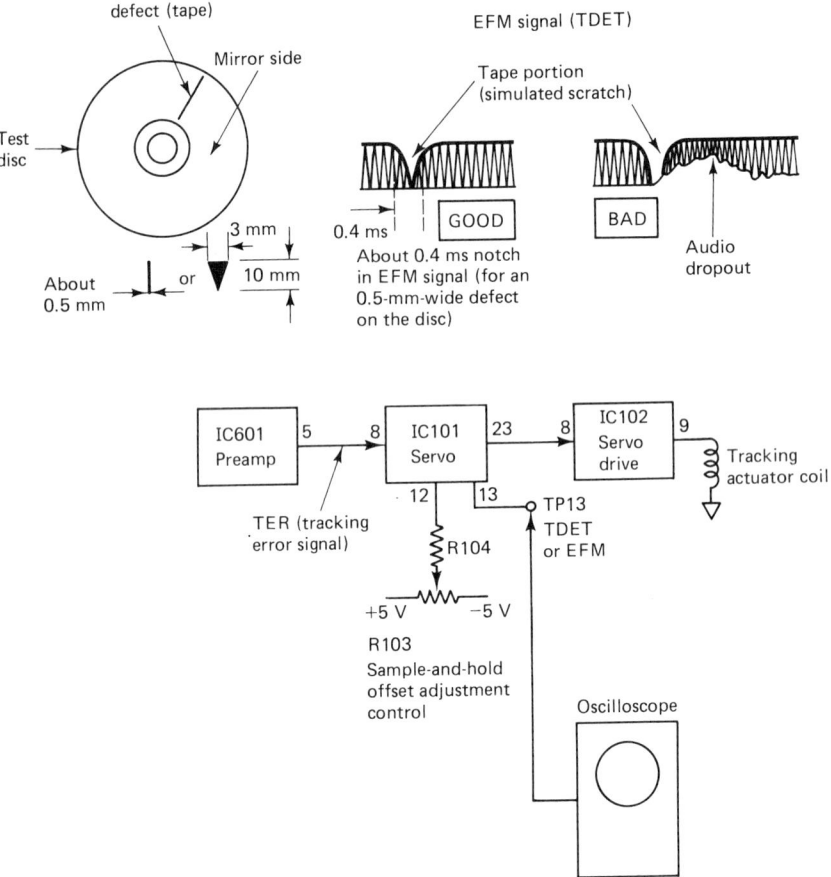

FIGURE 7-23 Sample-and-hold offset adjustment (TER) diagram (late-model).

certain not to turn the volume up too far. The simulated defect can make considerable noise!

After the controls are preset, proceed as follows:

1. Connect the oscilloscope to TP13 (TEDT) and ground, as shown in Fig. 7-23, to monitor the EFM signal.
2. Load a disc in the player and select the PLAY mode.
3. Adjust R103 for minimum audio dropout shown on the EFM display, or for minimum chattering on the headphones/loudspeakers, or both.

Note that with such a defect, a portion of the EFM display will be cut out (typically a notch or wedge, starting from the top of the display, as shown), no matter how you set R103. However, you should be able to eliminate all (or most) of the audio dropout (as indicated by a cutout at the bottom of the EFM display). If there is considerable audio dropout at all settings of R103, the pickup servo IC101 may be defective.

7-16 INTRODUCTION TO LATE-MODEL CD PLAYER TROUBLESHOOTING

Figure 7-24 is a trouble symptom chart for late-model CD players. Note that the symptoms given are essentially the same as for early-model players (Fig. 7-8). This is because all CD players perform essentially the same functions (although late-model players may have additional features of programming, front-panel display, etc.). However, the circuits found in late-model players are often substantially different from those of the early-models. As discussed, the basic difference is that late-model players combine many of the discrete component circuits into a few ICs.

After selecting the symptom in Fig. 7-24 which matches that of the CD player being serviced, follow the steps in the troubleshooting procedures (indicated by section number in the right-hand column). These procedures help isolate the problem to a defective module or component. Listed in each troubleshooting procedure are the electrical and mechanical adjustments (if any) associated with the related module or circuit. The electrical adjustments are described in Sec. 7-15. Mechanical adjustments are discussed in Chapter 6. Always check the adjustments, if practical, before proceeding with service or troubleshooting.

SYMPTOM	TROUBLESHOOTING PROCEDURE SECTION NO.
Tray does not open or close properly	7-17
Laser diode problems	7-18
Pickup does not move to inner limit when power is applied; disc directory not read properly	7-19
Pickup does not focus properly	7-20
Pickup does not track properly	7-21
Disc motor (turntable) does not rotate properly	7-22
Signal processing circuit problems	7-23
Audio circuit problems	7-24
Programming and operating problems	7-25

FIGURE 7-24 Late-model CD player troubleshooting chart.

7-16.1 Preliminary Checks

All the preliminary checks described in Sec. 7-4.1 apply to late-model CD players.

7-17 TRAY DOES NOT OPEN OR CLOSE PROPERLY (LATE-MODEL)

Figure 7-25 is the troubleshooting diagram. Note that this diagram applies (typically) to front-load players with horizontal disc tray and one loading motor.

If the tray will not open or close, first check that the system microprocessor IC301 is receiving a signal from the front-load OPEN/CLOSE switch S318. If not, suspect S318 and/or the wiring between S318 and IC301. Next, check that the loading motor receives a signal from pin 12 of IC102 when S318 is pressed. If so, suspect the motor. If not, you have a problem between IC301 and the motor (through IC102).

Next, check that there are signals at pins 10 and 11 of IC102 each time S318 is pressed. The signals should invert each time S318 is pressed (pin 10

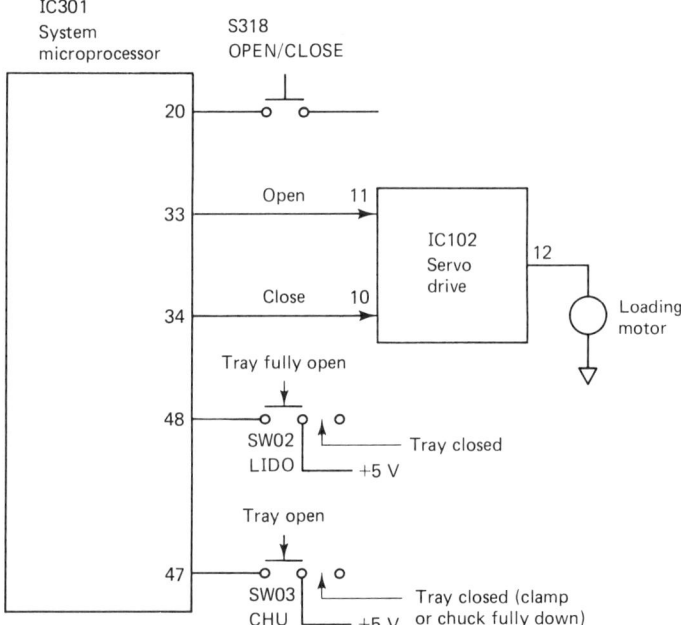

FIGURE 7-25 Tray open/close troubleshooting diagram (late-model).

high and 11 low, then vice versa). Check for corresponding inverted signals at pins 33 (open) and 34 (close) of IC301. If the signals are absent or do not invert when S318 is pressed, suspect IC301.

If the tray opens, but not fully, check when LIDO switch SW02 actuates, as indicated by a change (low to high) in the signal at pin 48 of IC301. If necessary, adjust SW02 (tray open or door open) as described in Chapter 6. Also look for any mechanical condition that might prevent the tray from opening fully, using the descriptions of mechanical operation in Chapter 6 as a guide (binding gears, jammed cross rollers, improperly adjusted guide rails, etc.).

If the tray opens fully, but the loading motor does not stop, the problem is almost always one of an improperly adjusted SW02. However, it is possible for the switch to actuate properly and produce a signal at IC301-48, but the motor does not stop. IC301 is at fault in that case.

If the tray closes, but not fully, and the clamp or chuck does not hold the disc in place on the turntable, check when CHU switch SW03 actuates, as indicated by a change (from high to low) in the signal at pin 47 of IC301. If necessary, adjust SW03, as described in Chapter 6. Also look for any mechanical condition that might prevent the door from closing. (Look for foreign objects in the clamp or chuck hinges and tray, and for wiring that has worked its way out of place.)

If the tray closes, and the clamp or chuck goes fully down, but the loading motor does not stop, the problem is likely an improperly adjusted SW03, but could be IC301. Look for a change (from high to low) at IC301-47, which should occur when the tray is fully in and the clamp or chuck is fully down on the disc.

7-18 LASER-DIODE PROBLEMS (LATE-MODEL)

Operation of any CD player (late- or early-model) depends on the laser diode producing a laser beam of correct level. Simply, if the laser beam is absent, there is no EFM signal; if the beam is weak, the EFM signal is weak. Likewise, if the monitor diode does not monitor the laser-diode output properly, the laser beam can change to an incorrect level (high or low), without being sensed by the laser-drive circuits. Any of these conditions can produce improper tracking which, in turn, can produce an even weaker EFM.

So, if you have symptoms with no apparent cause (improper tracking that cannot be corrected by adjustment; excessive audio dropout with a known-good disc, etc.), suspect the laser circuits. Start by adjusting the laser circuits as described in Sec. 7-15.3. This will reveal any obvious problems in the laser circuits and indicate if the EFM signal is satisfactory. If not, proceed with the following, using the troubleshooting diagram of Fig. 7–26.

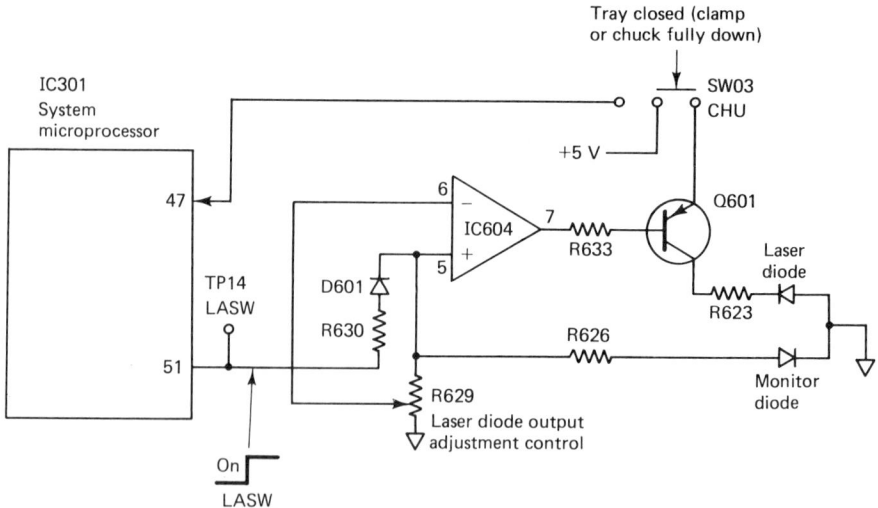

FIGURE 7-26 Laser-diode troubleshooting diagram (late-model).

If the laser diode appears to be inoperative, check if Q601 is receiving +5V through CHU switch SW03. If not, suspect SW03 or adjustment of SW03 (Sec. 7-17). Note that when CHU switch SW03 is in the open position, +5 V is applied to pin 47 of IC301 to indicate that the tray is open and/or the clamp or chuck is not fully down. This disables a number of IC301 system-control functions (including LASW). When the clamp or chuck is fully down, SW03 moves to the close position, and the laser diode receives power through Q601.

If power is applied to the laser and Q601 through SW03, look for an LASW signal (low) at pin 51 of IC301 and/or TP14 (LASW). If LASW is absent (high), suspect IC301. If present, check for a signal at pin 5 of IC604. If abnormal, suspect D601. Also look for a signal at pin 6 of IC604 from the monitor diode (through R629). If abnormal, suspect the monitor diode and/or R629.

If signals are present at both pins 5 and 6 of IC604, look for drive signals at pin 7 of IC604 and the base of Q601. If absent, suspect IC604. If present, suspect Q601.

7-19 PICKUP DOES NOT MOVE TO INNER LIMIT WHEN POWER IS APPLIED; DISC DIRECTORY DOES NOT READ PROPERLY (LATE-MODEL)

Figure 7-27 is the troubleshooting diagram. When power is first applied, the pickup moves to the inner limit (start of disc). The system microprocessor applies a temporary SLR (slide or pickup motor reverse) signal to the pickup

7-19 Pickup and Disc Directory Problems (Late-model) 245

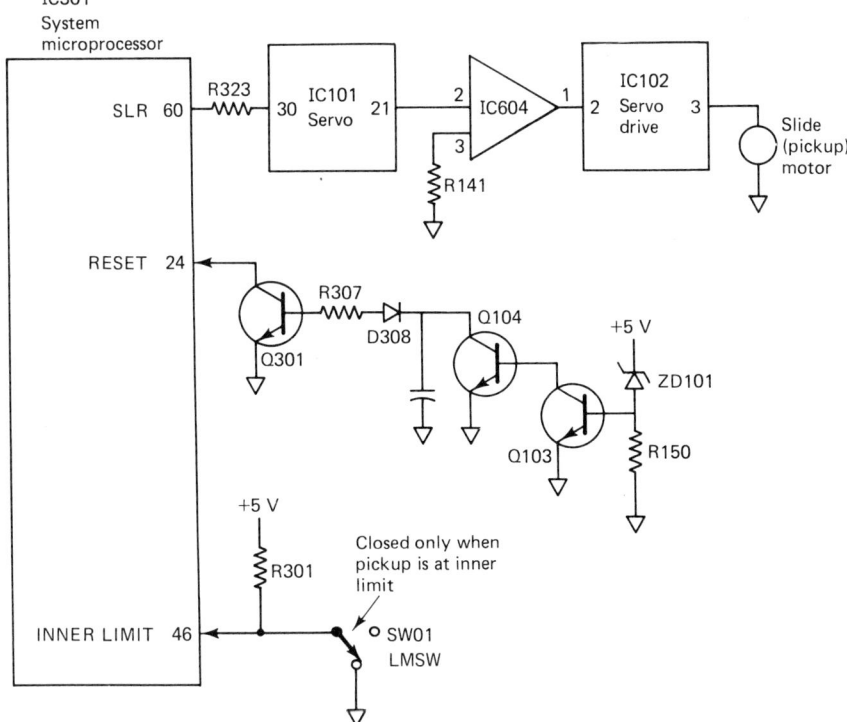

FIGURE 7-27 Slide (pickup) motor inner-limit troubleshooting diagram (late-model).

servo. In the player of Fig. 7-27, the temporary SLR signal is generated by a reset circuit (consisting of Q103, Q104, and Q301), which applies a reset signal at pin 24 of IC301. This produces a temporary SLR at IC301-60 which is applied to the pickup motor through IC101, IC604, and IC102. The SLR signal causes the pickup to move inward until the inner-limit LMSW switch SW01 is actuated.

The pickup should stop at a point where the disc directory or program information can be read in full. However, the point at which the pickup accesses the disc is determined by the slide (pickup) motor offset adjustment, described in Sec. 7-15.4. So, if the pickup appears to move to the inner limit when power is applied, but the disc directory is not read properly (say that the total playing time, or number of programs on the disc, is not given on the front-panel display), try correcting the problem by adjustment of the motor offset (before tearing into the motor servo circuits). Of course, if the pickup motor does not run, runs but does not move far enough in (obviously), or continues to run when the inner limit is reached, then proceed as follows:

If the pickup does not move when power is first applied (you may not

246 *Troubleshooting and Adjustment*

be able to see the pickup, but you should hear the motor), check for an SLR signal at IC301-60. If absent, suspect IC301, or Q301 and the associated parts of the reset circuit. If the SLR is present but the motor does not run, suspect IC101, IC604, IC102, and the motor itself. Also check for motor drive voltage at the output of IC102 and at the motor. If drive to the motor is present but the motor does not run, suspect the motor. If the motor runs but the pickup does not move, look for mechanical problems (jammed gears, binding rollers, improperly adjusted rails, etc.).

If the pickup moves, but does not reach the inner limit, check when the inner-limit LMSW switch SW01 actuates, as indicated by a change (high to low) in the signal at pin 46 of IC301. If necessary, adjust the LMSW switch, as described in Chapter 6. Also check for any mechanical condition that might prevent the pickup from moving to the inner (and outer) limits. Before adjusting the LMSW switch, check adjustment of the servo offset, as described in Sec. 7-15.4. If the offset can be adjusted so that the pickup accesses the disc properly (the disc directory can be read in full), the LMSW switch is probably adjusted correctly. Generally, the LMSW switch does not go out of adjustment unless there has been tampering or parts have been replaced (such as a new pickup or limit switch).

If the pickup reaches the inner limit but the motor does not stop, the problem is almost always one of an improperly adjusted LMSW switch. However, it is possible for the LMSW switch to actuate properly and produce a signal (low) at IC301-46, but the motor does not stop. IC301 is at fault in that case.

7-20 PICKUP DOES NOT FOCUS PROPERLY (LATE-MODEL)

Figure 7–28 is the troubleshooting diagram. When play first begins, the focus-actuator coil receives a focus up-down (FUD) signal from IC301 through IC101 and IC102. These FUD pulses move the focus actuator up and down two or three times as necessary to focus the beam on the disc track. Once focus is obtained, a focus-ok (FOK) signal is generated by IC601 and applied to both IC301 and IC101. If an FOK signal is not received after two or three tries, IC301 shuts the system down and play stops (turntable stops and the pickup moves to the inner limit). On most players, this also occurs if there is no disc in place, so the FOK function serves as a disc detector.

If focus is obtained, the focus-error (FER) signal from IC601 is applied to the focus actuator through IC101 and IC102. The FER signal keeps the pickup focused on the disc tracks throughout play. On most players, when the pickup reaches the outer limit of the disc, where there are no tracks, focus is lost, the FOK signal is removed, and IC301 shuts down the system.

If you suspect problems in the automatic focus (AF) system, install a

7-20 Pickup Does Not Focus Properly (Late-model)

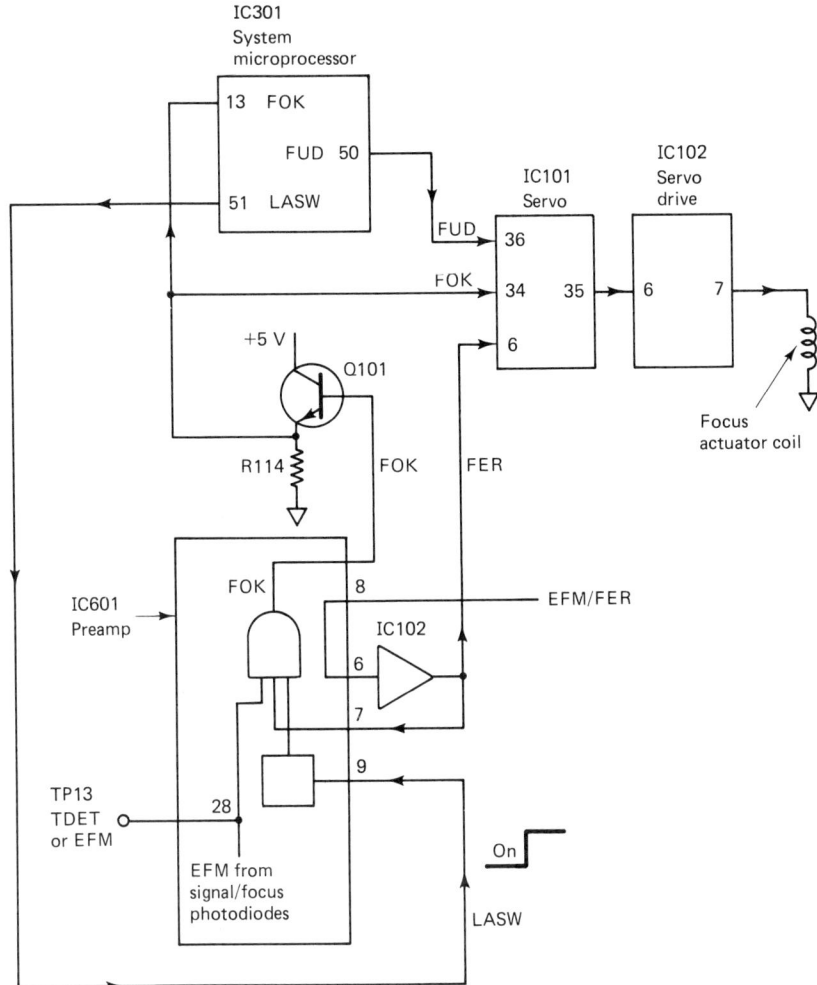

FIGURE 7-28 Focus circuit troubleshooting diagram (late-model).

disc, select PLAY, and check that the pickup moves up and down two or three times and then settles down. If not, first check that the laser is on, as described in Sec. 7-18. If the laser is on but there is no focus, try adjusting the focus servo as described in Sec. 7-15.6. Then make a quick check of the lens actuator, as described in Sec. 6-1.1. If the actuator coil appears to be good and the problems cannot be corrected by adjustment, check the focus servo as follows.

Focus actuator does not move up and down. If the FUD pulses are not present just after PLAY is selected, suspect IC301. Check for pulses at pin 50 of IC301, pins 35 and 36 of IC101, pins 6 and 7 of IC102, and at the focus coil.

Focus actuator moves, but no focus is obtained. Check for FOK signals at pin 34 of IC101, pin 13 of IC301, and pin 8 of IC601. (If the FOK signals are not present, IC301 should shut the system down.) If the FOK signals are absent at IC601-8, suspect IC601, or possibly the four pickup signal/focus photodiodes. If FOK signals are absent at IC101-34, suspect Q101. Also note that the FOK signal is not generated unless there is an LASW signal applied to pin 9 of IC601.

Next check for FER signals at IC601-6 and IC601-7. If FER signals are present at pin 6, but not at pin 7, suspect IC102. If FER signals are absent at IC601-6, suspect IC601, or possibly the pickup signal/focus photodiodes.

If you suspect the signal/focus photodiodes, monitor the EFM signal at TP13 (TDET). If the EFM signal is good, it is reasonable to assume that all four focus/signal photodiodes are good.

7-21 PICKUP DOES NOT TRACK PROPERLY (LATE-MODEL)

Figure 7–29 is the troubleshooting diagram. In most late-model players, it is often difficult to separate tracking and focus servo problems. For example, unless there is an FOK signal applied to IC101 through Q101, the tracking-error (TER) signal does not pass to the tracking actuator. Both the focus and tracking servos use the laser beam as a source of error signal, although different photodiodes are used. To further complicate the problem, the TER signal is also used by the pickup motor as a fine speed control. (In most late-model players, this is done in IC101.) If TER is lost, both the radial tracking coil and the pickup motor have no control signals. Either condition can produce symptoms of improper tracking.

In some players, the TER signal is passed through variable-gain circuits and through error-detection circuits which can interrupt the TER signals when errors are detected (in the disc or because of improper tracking). Failure in any of these circuits can cut off or alter the TER signal, making it appear that either radial tracking or pickup motor servos are at fault (when actually the servos are good).

First try to correct any tracking problems with adjustment, as described in Sec. 7-15.5 and 7-15.8. Next, make a quick check of the tracking actuator coil, as described in Sec. 6-1.1. Finally, see if the pickup moves to the inner limit when power is first applied, as described in Sec. 7-19. (This confirms that the pickup motor, reset circuit, and the basic servo circuits of IC101 and IC102 are good.) If the pickup motor is operating, and the tracking coil appears to

7-21 Pickup Does Not Track Properly (Late-model) 249

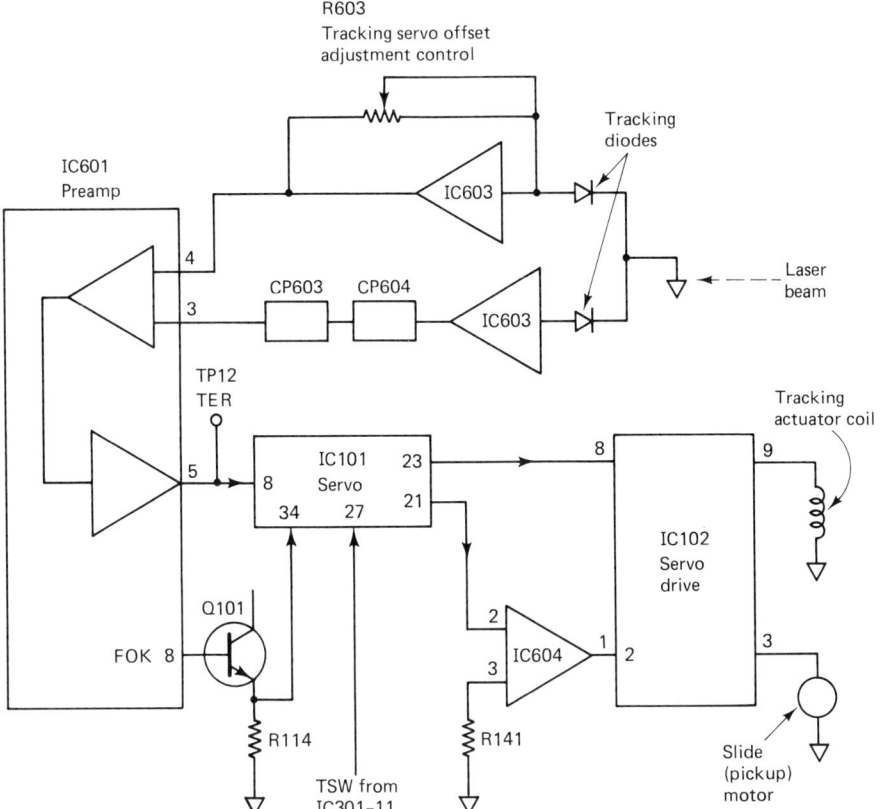

FIGURE 7-29 Tracking circuit troubleshooting diagram (late-model).

be good, but tracking problems cannot be resolved by adjustment, check the tracking and pickup servos as follows:

Check the TER signal from its source to the tracking actuator coil (and to the pickup motor, in most players). TP12 (TER) is a good place to start in the circuit of Fig. 7-29. Then check at the tracking-actuator coil. If the TER is present at TP12, but not at the coil, suspect IC101 and IC102. Look for a TER signal at pin 23 of IC101. If present, the problem is likely in IC102. If absent, the problem is localized to IC101.

Check for TER signals at the slide or pickup motor. If present at the tracking coil but not at the motor, suspect IC102 and IC604. Also check for TER signals at pin 21 of IC101. Also note that the TER is not applied to the pickup motor in all players.

However, before you pull IC101, keep in mind that IC101 must receive

250 Troubleshooting and Adjustment

a number of signals before the TER signals can pass. For example, TC101 must be turned on by FOK and TSW signals. Also, the TER signals are analyzed by error-detection circuits within IC101. (These error-detection functions include MDET/MEDET or mirror detection and PDET/PEDET or pit detection. Descriptions of similar circuits, using discrete components, are given in Sec. 5-9.6.) If any of these signals or voltages are absent or abnormal, IC101 remains cut off, and the TER signals do not pass. So always check the signals and voltages at the pins of IC101 (using the service literature values) before you decide IC101 is defective.

If the TER signal is absent at TP12, check for TER signals at pin 5 of IC601. If the TER is absent at IC601-5, suspect IC601, IC603, CP603, CP604, R603, and the two radial tracking diodes.

7-22 DISC MOTOR (TURNTABLE) DOES NOT ROTATE PROPERLY (LATE-MODEL)

Figure 7-30 is the troubleshooting diagram. It is not difficult to tell if the disc motor fails to rotate. Likewise, the cause of such a total failure is generally simple to locate. For example, you can check at TP17 (DMCA) and TP18 (DMCB) for drive signals to the motor windings. If the drive signals are present but the motor does not turn, suspect the motor. If either of the drive signals is not present, trace from the disc motor to IC201, and from IC402 to IC201.

Before you decide there is a problem in the disc motor-control circuits, remember that DMSW, CLVH, and ROT signals must come from the system microprocessor IC301. In most players, if IC301 does not receive an FOK (and possibly a TOK) signal from the focus and tracking circuits, the DMSW, CLVH, and ROT signals are set to prevent controller IC402 and disc motor drive IC201 from passing the PREF, PWM, and PD signals to the motor-control circuits. Typically, both DMSW and CLVH are made low to turn on the disc motor when PLAY is selected. ROT goes low about one second after PLAY is selected. If DMSW, CLVH, and ROT all remain high after PLAY is selected, check for FOK and TOK signals to IC301. Of course, if only one of the three signals remains abnormal, IC301 is most likely at fault.

The problem is not quite that simple if the motor rotates, but you are not sure of the correct speed. (Particularly when you consider that the motor speed is constantly changing.) You must rely on waveform measurements and adjustments. So the first logical step in disc motor circuit troubleshooting is to perform the adjustments as described in Sec. 7-15.7. If you do not get the DMCA and DMCB signals called for in the adjustment procedures, trace back to IC201 and IC402.

If you get the DMCA and DMCB drive signals, and the motor is turning (indicating that the DMSW, ROT, and CLVH from IC301 are good), but you

7-22 Disc Motor (Turntable) Does Not Rotate Properly (Late-model)

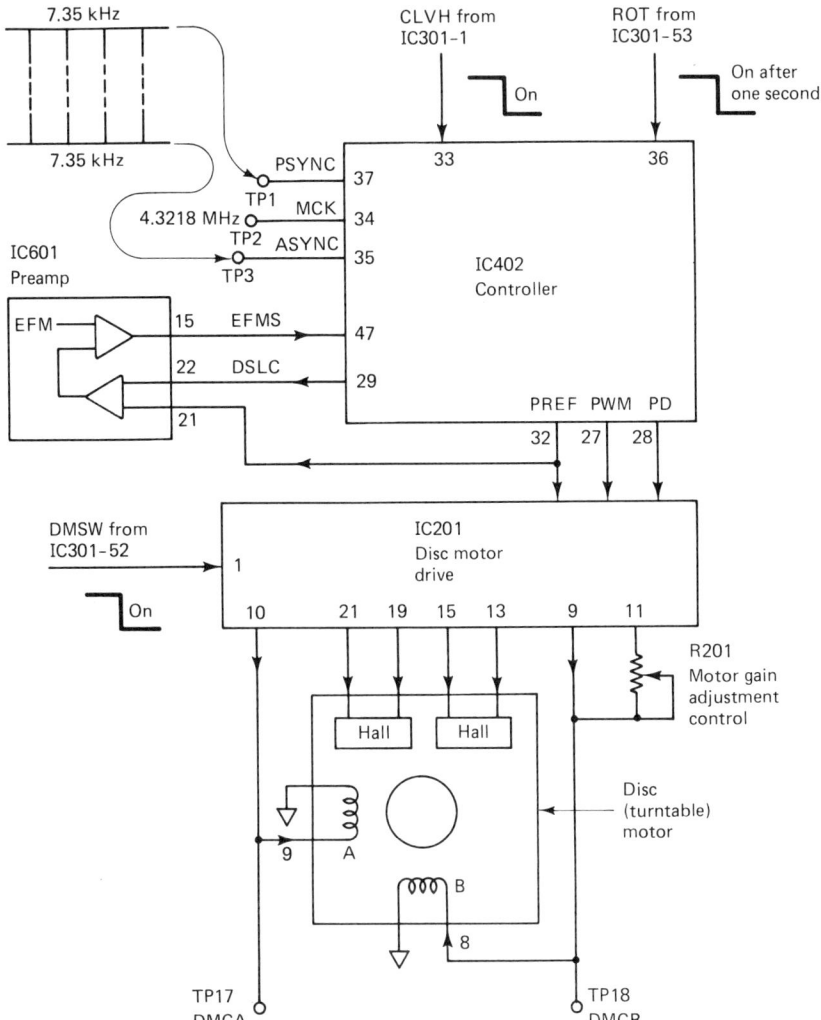

FIGURE 7-30 Disc (turntable) motor troubleshooting diagram (late-model).

are unable to set the output levels as described, check all the waveforms associated with the disc motor control as follows:

Check the PWM, PREF, and PD waveforms from IC402. If any of these are absent or abnormal, suspect IC402. Next, trace the signals between IC201 and the disc motor. If any of these signals are absent or abnormal, suspect IC201. If all signals appear to be normal (check the service literature for waveforms and amplitude), suspect the disc motor (probably the Hall elements, but possibly the windings).

252 Troubleshooting and Adjustment

Also note that PREF is applied to IC601, along with the DSLC signal from IC402, to form the EFMS signal that is returned to IC402. If the EFMS signal is absent, IC402 does not produce PREF, PWM, and PD signals. Of course, if the EFMS signal is not applied to IC402, several other problems occur. We discuss EFMS further in Sec. 7-23.

One way to check if the EFMS signal is being processed properly is to compare the signal at TP1 (PSYNC) and TP3 (ASYNC), using a dual-trace oscilloscope. As shown in Fig. 7-30, both signals should be synchronized. If not, or if either signal is missing, suspect IC402.

As you can see, the disc motor-control circuits are closely interrelated with the signal-processing circuits. A failure in signal processing can also cause the disc motor-control circuits to appear defective. So if you are unable to locate a problem in the disc motor-control circuits, try checking the signal-processing circuits.

7-23 SIGNAL-PROCESSING CIRCUIT PROBLEMS (LATE-MODEL)

Figure 7-31 is the troubleshooting diagram. Failure of the signal-processing circuits can cause a variety of failure symptoms in the audio circuits and disc motor-control circuits. Likewise, a failure in system control can produce corresponding failures in signal processing. As discussed in Sec. 7-12, there is no sure way to tell if the problem is in signal processing, system control, disc motor, or audio.

As a first step, check the output at pin 17 of D/A converter IC403 for audio signals. You should get a mixture of both left- and right-channel audio signals at IC403-17. The level of the audio is typically low. However, if there is no audio at this point, suspect the signal-processing circuits. If there is measurable audio at IC403-17, the problem is likely in the audio circuits. Refer to Sec. 7-24.

Second, if there are excessive audio dropouts (with a known-good disc), and the front-panel indications are not normal (such as the time code not changing), the problem is likely in the signal-processing circuits. Check all the waveforms to and from the signal-processing circuits shown in the service literature. Pay particular attention to the following:

Check for a 4.3218-MHz signal at TP2 (MCK) of IC402. If missing, suspect the crystal IC401 and IC402.

Check TP1 (PSYNC) and TP (ASYNC) for 7.35-kHz signals. The ASYNC should be present only during PLAY, but PSYNC should be available in both STOP and PLAY.

Make certain that PREF and DSLC signals are supplied to IC601 and then returned to IC402 as square-wave EFMS signals. If EFMS is missing, check for high-frequency EFM signals at pin 20 of IC601.

7-23 Signal-Processing Circuit Problems (Late-model) 253

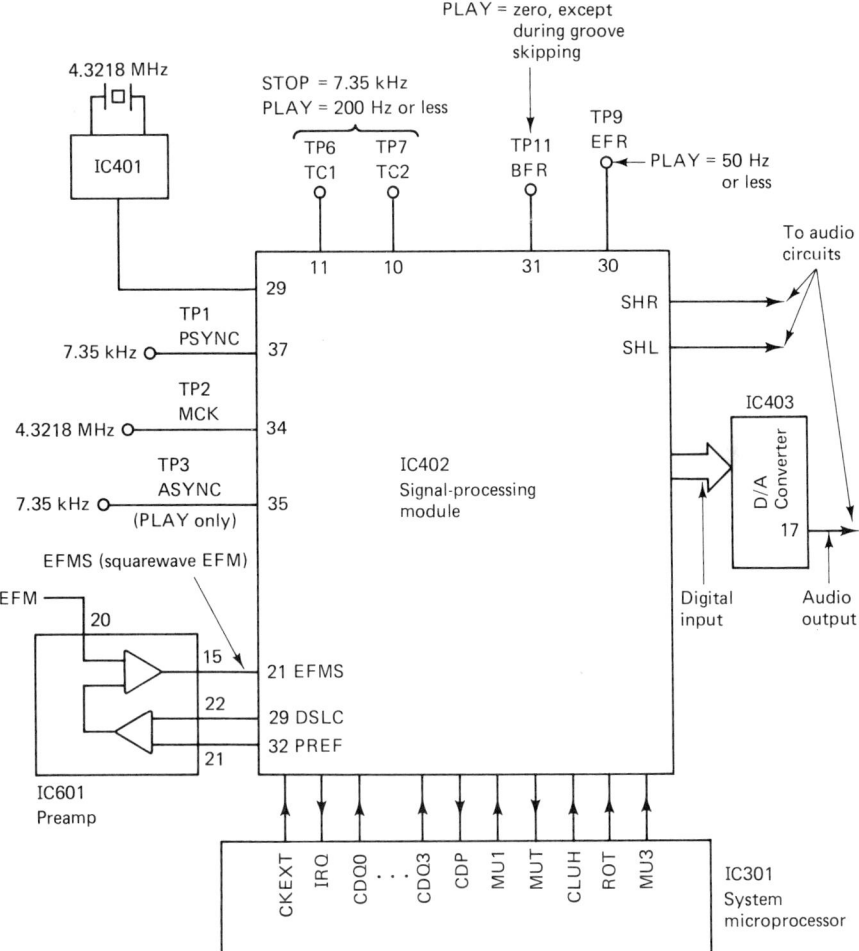

FIGURE 7-31 Signal-processing circuit troubleshooting diagram (late-model).

Check all the waveforms between IC301 and IC402 shown in Fig. 7-31. It is not practical to analyze these waveforms. However, if you can measure a data stream on each line with an oscilloscope, it is reasonable to assume that the signal is correct. If one or more of these signals is missing, suspect IC301 or IC402, or both. Remember that a signal from IC301 can depend on a signal from IC402, and vice versa. So it may be necessary to replace both ICs to find the problem. Also remember that IC301 may not produce the signals unless other signals (such as FOK and TOK) are applied to IC301.

Before you pull IC402, check TP6 (TC1) and TP7 (TC2). Both of these test points (which indicate the accuracy of the C1- and C2-decoding processes within IC402) should produce a 7.35-kHz signal during STOP, but then drop to 200 Hz or less when PLAY is selected. If not, suspect IC402. Next, check TP11 (BFR) and TP9 (EFR), which indicate the accuracy of the synchronizing and detection functions within IC402. In PLAY, BFR should always be zero, except during groove skipping. In PLAY, EFR may produce a signal, but at a frequency below 50 Hz. The EFR and BFR signals are undefined during STOP.

7-24 AUDIO CIRCUIT PROBLEMS (LATE-MODEL)

Troubleshooting for the audio circuits of late-model players is essentially the same as for early-model units described in Sec. 7-13. For that reason, we do not repeat the procedures here.

7-25 PROGRAMMING AND OPERATING PROBLEMS (LATE-MODEL)

As discussed in Sec. 7-14, programming and operating problems are almost always the fault of the system microprocessor or front-panel wiring and switches. One possible difference between early- and late-model system-control microprocessors is that late-model processors may have clock circuits separate from the system clock used by the signal-processing circuits (such as IC401, shown in Fig. 7-31). Such a configuration is shown in Fig. 7-32. The system-control microprocessor IC301 has an 800-kHz crystal connected at pins 28 and 29. Always look for any clock circuits and check for signals of the corresponding frequency. If the clock for IC301 is absent or abnormal, IC301 cannot perform any of the system-control functions properly, resulting in total failure of virtually all other circuits.

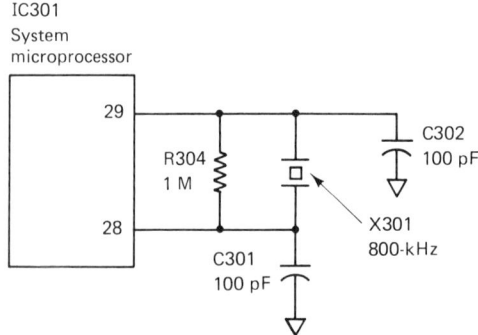

FIGURE 7-32 Separate clock circuit for system-control microprocessor.

INDEX

A

Acuator, 2
A/D conversion, 19, 28
Antishock, 150
Astigmatism, 16
Audio circuits, 145
  troubleshooting, 231, 254
Automatic focus, 16

B

Beams, laser, 14
Belt replacement, 172, 192
Binary format, 10
Binary-coded waveform, 28
Bit sync, 141

C

Channel modulation, 31, 34
CIRC, 30

Clamping, disc, 183, 192
Cleaning discs, 84
CLV, 18, 20
Cover interlock, 157

D

D/A conversion, 18-19, 41, 126, 145
Data decoding, 126
Data processing, 17
Data strobe, 17, 140
Decoding, 37, 113, 142
Demodulation, 120
Demultiplexer, 40
Detection, disc information, 139
Diffraction grating, 14
Digital filter, 40, 126
Digital sound, 19
Disc cleaning, 84
Disc detector, 198
Disc directory, 25
  troubleshooting, 244
Disc drive, 158

Disc handling, 59
Disc loading/unloading, 183, 192
Disc scanning, 23
Disc test, 82
Distortion meter, 82
Door troubleshooting, 217
Drive motor, 2, 7

E

EFM, 32, 34, 37, 126, 138
Encoding, 26
Error correction, 21, 30, 118, 141, 146
Eye pattern, 138

F

Flats, 3, 10, 13, 36
Focus, 13, 16, 47, 99, 131,
  adjustments, 207, 210, 237
  coil checks, 167
  error, 96
  troubleshooting, 222, 246
Frames, 31, 35
  sync, 141
Front-load, 22

G

Guard diode, 44

H

Hall effect, 158
  adjustments, 213, 237
Harmonic distortion, 21
HF (high frequency) amplifier, 99
  signal, 138

I

Index numbers, 23
Installation, 57
Interleaving, 17, 33, 39
Interlocks, 157, 182
Intermodulation distortion, 21, 27

J

Jump circuits, 151

L

Laser, 3, 8
  adjusting, 77, 205, 233
  control, 93
  monitor, 157
  power supply, 18
  safety, 77, 166, 182
  troubleshooting, 219, 243
Leakage current, 53
Lid switch, 130
Loading, disc, 183, 192
  motor, 7, 22
LP records, 3

M

Memory stop, 23
Microcomputer, 23
Microprocessor, 23
Microswitches, 178
  adjustment, 194
Monitor diode, 43, 94, 157
Motor replacement, 176
Multiplexer, 30
Multiposition errors, 39
Music sensor, 71
Mute, 130

O

Objective lens, 2, 47
Optics, 94, 183
   handling, 80
   pickup, 2, 13, 42, 165
   troubleshooting, 220, 244, 248

P

Parity bits, 21, 33, 142
Pause, 71, 130
   bits, 37
PCM, 1, 10
Photodiodes, 94
Pickup, 2, 8, 13
   adjustment, 234
   motor, 154
   motor replacement, 176
   replacement, 178
   troubleshooting, 220, 224, 244, 248
Pits, 3, 10, 13, 36
Power supply, 90
Power-line connections, 58
Preamp, 17
Prism, 43, 45
Programming, 23, 71

Q

Quantization, 20, 28

R

Radial error, 48, 96, 98
Radial servo, 104
Radial tracking, 14, 135
   adjustments, 207, 211, 236
Random-memory programming, 23

Remote control, 69
Repeat play, 24, 71
RF signal, 138
Rotating arm, 2, 43

S

Safety, 73, 80, 166
Sampling, 10, 28
Self-program search, 23
S/H (sample/hold), 18, 27
   adjustments, 238
Shipping screw, 55
Signal control, 140
Signal processing, 17
   troubleshooting, 229, 252
Sled, 2
Slide adjustments, 234
Slide motor, 154
Slide-type optics, 2, 48
Stereo amplifier, 41, 82
Subcoding, 31, 37, 126
Symbol sync, 141
Sync, symbol and frame, 35
Sync signals, 17
System control, 18

T

Tangential tracking, 18
Test disc, 82
Test equipment, 81
Tools, 82
Top-load, 22
Track detector, 116
Track numbers, 24
Tracking, 13
Tracking coil checks, 167
Tracks, disc, 9
Transit screw, 55, 167
Tray interlock, 157
Tray troubleshooting, 217, 242

Turntable, 102, 158, 165, 180
   adjustment, 213, 237
   motor replacement, 176
   troubleshooting, 226, 250

U

Unitorque motor, 158
Unloading, disc, 183, 192

V

Volume control setting, 60

W

Wow and flutter, 21